WORLDS
IN A
MUSEUM

WORLDS
IN A
MUSEUM

Exploring Contemporary Museology

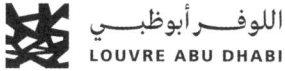

LOUVRE ABU DHABI

Ecole du Louvre
Palais du Louvre

LEUVEN UNIVERSITY PRESS

This book was published following the symposium Worlds in a Museum/ Des mondes en musées / في رحاب المتحف *held 10-11 November 2018 at Louvre Abu Dhabi on the occasion of its first anniversary and jointly organised by Louvre Abu Dhabi and École du Louvre.*

Louvre Abu Dhabi
Publications
Laurent Germeau, Publications Manager
Amanda Nicole Smith, Project Manager
Mohamed Zaggar, Senior Editor
Brian Kerrigan, Senior Visual and Images Officer

Scientific, Curatorial and Collection Management
Souraya Noujaim, Scientific, Curatorial and Collections Management Director
Guilhem André, Chief Curator – Asian and Medieval Arts
Rose-Marie Mousseaux, Chief Curator – Early Modern Period

École de Louvre
Publications
Françoise Blanc, Head of Publications and Symposiums (Responsable des Éditions et colloques)

Published by Leuven University Press, Louvre Abu Dhabi and École du Louvre, 2020
© Department of Culture and Tourism – Abu Dhabi, 2020
Louvre Abu Dhabi, Saadiyat Cultural District, Abu Dhabi, United Arab Emirates

© 2020 by Leuven University Press / Presses Universitaires de Louvain / Universitaire Pers Leuven
Minderbroedersstraat 4, B-3000 Leuven (Belgium).

ISBN 978 94 6270 233 2
e-ISBN 978 94 6166 332 0
D / 2020/ 1869 / 59
NUR: 657

Project management: Amanda Nicole Smith
Arabic translation: Bahia Zemni
English translation: Timothy Stroud
English editing: Simon Ferdinand
French editing: Françoise Blanc
Arabic editing: Mohamed Zaggar
Typesetting: Crius Group
Cover design: Bart van den Tooren
Cover illustration: Detail of a pair of namban six-fold screens: Portuguese Arriving in Japan for Trade, Japan, c. 1625, Ink, colours, gold and gold leaf on paper, 171 x 376.6 cm, Louvre Abu Dhabi, inv. LAD 2015.018.001 © Department of Culture and Tourism – Abu Dhabi/ Photo: Thierry Ollivier

www.lup.be | www.louvreabudhabi.ae | www.ecoledulouvre.fr

Table of Contents

PART I
Museums and Globalisation

PART 4
Centre and Periphery

New Identities of Museums in a Globalised World

In November 2018, just twelve months after its opening to the public, Louvre Abu Dhabi hosted *Worlds in a Museum* in collaboration with the École du Louvre. A two-day event, the symposium brought together an international assemblage of museum leaders, curators and academics to discuss the potential purposes and new identities of museums in an increasingly globalised and interconnected world.

The symposium was also a way of marking Louvre Abu Dhabi's first anniversary, not with fanfare and celebrations, but with serious questions, spirited discussion and informed debate. At stake was the question of how museums might become more welcoming places of encounter and discovery in the 21st century, accessible to audiences of all backgrounds and ages, while delivering a more inclusive, diverse and comprehensive understanding of the past.

These were the very same issues that had informed the decade-long process of realising Louvre Abu Dhabi, a journey that began with the signing, in March 2007, of an unprecedented agreement between the governments of Abu Dhabi and France. The aim then was not just to establish the first universal museum in the Arab world, but to use the knowledge and expertise of 16 of France's most illustrious national museums to help create a fundamentally different type of institution, one whose unique curatorial perspective is informed by changing values and the museum's location at one of the great crossroads of humanity.

The result is a particularly polyphonic museum that looks toward a future in which long-established hierarchies have been replaced by newer, more inclusive ways of seeing while simultaneously drawing on a deeply rooted intellectual inheritance that extends back to the establishment of the great Enlightenment institutions of the 18th and 19th centuries.

This duality is most obviously expressed in Louvre Abu Dhabi's name, which not only speaks of the museum's essential hybridity but of reconfigured relationships between the global and the local, the East and the West and between established centres of knowledge production and territories that were once considered a part of the periphery.

Two years on from the symposium, Louvre Abu Dhabi is still very much a new museum but it is already making an invaluable contribution towards some of the issues and questions discussed during *Worlds in a Museum,* not least in the ways in which it has succeeded in attracting an audience that is as diverse as the objects in our collections.

Nowhere is this process of reconfiguration more eloquently expressed than in the museum's unique approach to the exhibiting and exploring the past, a mode of presentation that eschews museological orthodoxies by bringing objects from different cultures together in dialogue.

The result is a profoundly different way of understanding history and our place within it, one that addresses the great thematic issues that have preoccupied humanity since the dawn of history. Where did we come from and why are we here? What is our place in the world and what happens when we die? How should we relate to the natural world and learn from each other to live in harmony and prosperity?

Driven by a desire to be universal rather than encyclopaedic, Louvre Abu Dhabi's displays are not only more geographically balanced but less dense and exquisitely arranged. This makes them more accessible to the general public, especially when it comes to making comparisons between cultures and epochs from the multiple perspectives of family, faith and power, technology, gender, identity and daily life.

Francis Bacon stated, a full 400 years before our symposium was held, that "if we are to achieve things never before accomplished, we must employ methods never before attempted." This rings true for our unique foundation bringing the best of France and the United Arab Emirates together in an unparalleled cultural offering and in our innovative ways of displaying works. As such, we sincerely hope that Louvre Abu Dhabi's efforts represent a new and dynamic model of a museum that promotes curiosity, equality and mutual respect by encouraging global citizens to see themselves and each other in a subtly different light.

Manuel Rabaté
Director, Louvre Abu Dhabi

"It Always Seems Impossible Until It Is Done"

"It always seems impossible until it is done." These words spoken by Nelson Mandela, who was born a full century before the *Worlds in a Museum* symposium took place, will always resonate with those of us who worked to turn Abu Dhabi's vision into a reality. As we celebrate The Year of Zayed in 2018, also marking 100 years since the birth of the founder of the United Arab Emirates Sheihk Zayed bin Sultan Al Nahyan, the unprecedented ambitions of these two visionary leaders to achieve the unimaginable is evident now more than ever.

Louvre Abu Dhabi may have been a decade in the planning, construction and preparation, but that is fitting, perhaps, for what is both an institution that will serve and inspire so many future generations and a curatorial and architectural achievement that will surely be studied and celebrated for many years to come.

A global symbol of intercultural cooperation and the UAE's unparalleled ambition, Louvre Abu Dhabi was born of an unprecedented agreement between the governments of Abu Dhabi and France. But it is also the product of the profound collaboration we continue to enjoy with our French partner institutions and with museums throughout the UAE, the region and beyond whose ongoing support has allowed Louvre Abu Dhabi to develop a truly universal perspective on the history of humanity.

At the time of the symposium, it gave me great pleasure to announce that the museum had welcomed more than a million visitors in the twelve months since its opening, a figure that exceeded all of our expectations. What is even more gratifying, however, are the scenes that I have witnessed during my own visits to Louvre Abu Dhabi, everyday moments that represent an even more profound sense of success.

Once I stopped in museum to watch an Emirati guide as they discussed the similarities between ancient Egypt, Rome and Mesopotamia with an international group of visitors; on another occasion I listened as a member of the museum's education team explored the idea of the universal with an attentive group of local schoolgirls.

To me these examples speak to the very core of our ambitions and to Louvre Abu Dhabi's *raison d'être*: to help build future generations of informed and cultured global citizens with an awareness, not just of history, but of their own place and standing in the world. Achieving this will be our true measure of success, not just for Louvre Abu Dhabi and the forthcoming Zayed National Museum and Guggenheim Abu Dhabi, institutions that will underpin the Saadiyat Island Cultural District, but of our whole cultural strategy.

As well as marking our first anniversary, 2018 was an important year in several other respects that also relate directly to the themes that were discussed during *Worlds in a Museum*. Two weeks before the symposium, the Department of Culture and Tourism – Abu Dhabi unveiled its plans for the conservation and redevelopment of the UAE's oldest archaeological and ethnographic museum, which is located in the ancient oasis town of Al Ain, a UNESCO World Heritage Site.

The Al Ain Museum was the vision of Sheikh Zayed bin Sultan al Nahyan, the UAE's first president and founding father, who planned and opened the institution in 1971 even as he was preparing for the process of independence and federation that would eventually create the United Arab Emirates.

Sheikh Zayed not only understood the importance of museums and the need to protect and cherish our heritage, but he also appreciated the role that they play in building the future, through education, culture and inspiration and the development of an informed and sophisticated citizenry, which is and will always be our nation's most precious resource.

Mohamed Al Mubarak
Chairman, Department of Culture and Tourism – Abu Dhabi

A Universal Curriculum:
École du Louvre and the Global Classroom

With the opening of new museums in Lens and Abu Dhabi, the Musée du Louvre has reached out to engage with diverse new audiences beyond Paris. In this expansion, it has worked with a range of institutions—some new collaborators, others longstanding partners. Among the constellation of institutions associated with the Louvre is the École du Louvre, a centre of learning in art history, archaeology, and anthropology of which I am Director. In 2018, we had the honour of collaborating with teams at Louvre Abu Dhabi and Agence France-Muséums on a conference celebrating the first anniversary of Louvre Abu Dhabi. In contributing to this volume, which marks that anniversary, I would like to take the opportunity to provide an overview of the École du Louvre, surveying its history, indicating some of its distinct intellectual concerns, and highlighting some exciting new developments.

Founded in 1882, during the Third Republic, the École du Louvre is a venerable old lady in comparison with the young and dynamic Louvre Abu Dhabi. At the time of its creation, it had two objectives: on one hand, to organise a school of archaeology and art history that taught in direct contact with the works in the Musée du Louvre, in order to train students to become curators and related professionals. On the other hand, it sought to help develop the knowledge of a broad public that was to form the initial core of enlightened museumgoers during the late nineteenth century. The initial activities of the École du Louvre, therefore, were to train those who were to take responsibility for the museum's collections and educate those members of the public who would benefit from those collections as museum visitors. To accomplish the latter, it allowed people to sit in on academic courses for free as auditors.

Today, the École du Louvre is a modern school teaching nearly 2,000 students and providing cultural knowledge to approximately 16,000 auditors. These auditors may choose among a range of courses, not just in Paris but also in some twenty partner cities around France, which are held during the day or evening, whether for an entire year, a few weeks, or a single intensive week in summer. A distinctive feature of the École du Louvre is that the teachers are mostly museum professionals, who wish to transmit the vision of national heritage and the practice of art history that they have developed through work-ing in daily contact with art and historical artefacts. The results are innovative teaching methods, even if the rhythm of study is similar to that of a university. What is unique to the school's teaching programme—and here we are drawing close to some of the topics broached in this volume—is the goal of universality. For the first three years, students at the École du Louvre follow what we call a 'general art history course'. This lays the foundations for a universal history of art, which extends from the first instances of art produced during the prehistoric period to the very latest in contemporary art, leaving no region of the planet unexamined. This overview is supplemented by supervised work carried out in front of the works themselves, in the museums and at the monuments of Paris and the surrounding area. Students at the École du Louvre are nomads: with a pack on their back, they travel to a different museum each day. Although of course they have a certain predilection for the Louvre museum—our very close neighbour, since the École is situated inside the palace—all the museums in the French capital and its hinterland are involved in the programme.

Another central discipline at the École du Louvre is museology. Students come from all around the world to study museology at the school. The field of museology is in con-stant evolution. This is particularly apparent today, not least because Louvre Abu Dhabi has challenged us to change the ways in which we look at things and tackle questions relating to the presentation of works, museographic devices, and how museums address publics that come from such a diverse range of backgrounds. I would also like to men-tion that the École du Louvre offers six Master's courses, twenty partnerships with other countries, and has a dynamic research department with numerous students pursuing their PhDs.

The École du Louvre of tomorrow intends quite simply to maintain its originality, while also strengthening its methods. Education and research carried out at the École du Louvre both begin and end with works of art. Our art history is history in a material form. Although of course we take artworks' historical context and critical reception into account, our work always centres on the works themselves. We do not claim that ours is the best art history in France, but we practise it in unique fashion and value our meth-ods, different as they are to those of a university. We are a school that emphasises percep-tion and awareness. This is not to suggest, though, that emphasising works' material and technical history or evolution over time (physical alterations, changes of location and ownership) prevents us from recognising the value of interpretation.

Another of our goals is to develop and exploit the research carried out in French museums and institutions, and train young researchers with expertise in the issues faced by museums. In the autumn of 2021, the École du Louvre will open its own research centre, which will allow our researchers to collaborate with those of our partner universities. Under the direction of senior researchers permanently tied to the École du Louvre, they will explore new perspectives and tackle new questions. For example, they will compare issues related to the digital world with collections of works that have as of yet been little studied. Charting important new directions, this new centre will also engage with some of the topics at stake in this volume, such as debates around cultural appropriation and globalisation.

We are planning to develop international programmes too. It is of fundamental importance to open the school up to the outside world, thereby taking a further step towards universality. This is one of the reasons that I am so pleased about our partnerships with new museums such as Louvre Abu Dhabi. I would also like to emphasise how important it is to us that we continue our policy of inclusion. We do our utmost to ensure the success of all the students at the school. This goes above all for those who come from less favoured social and cultural backgrounds, some of whom may feel a little inhibited in their desire to enter the heritage professions. It is essential that they be given all the tools for achieving not just academic success but also social ease, so that they too can be players in the cultural world of tomorrow.

Given that this essay was prompted by Louvre Abu Dhabi's first anniversary, I would like to conclude by reflecting on what connects the École du Louvre with Louvre Abu Dhabi. Both have the same intellectual and perceptive outlook in that they are both invested in universality. In putting all eras, cultures, and civilisations in dialogue with one another, Louvre Abu Dhabi encourages its visitors to assimilate the concept of the universal. Visitors to the galleries feel this relationship physically and enter into its intellectual perspective as they move among artefacts. As such, Louvre Abu Dhabi offers a visible experience of universality. Something of that experience is captured, I hope, in this volume. Its very title, *Worlds in a Museum*, signals a wish to both situate Louvre Abu Dhabi in the context of the museums of the world and raise the issue of how museum curators can do justice to the breadth and the variety of all world cultures and artistic traditions. It is in this common concern with universality that the École du Louvre and Louvre Abu Dhabi are fundamentally linked.

Claire Barbillon

A World in Dialogue:
Introducing Louvre Abu Dhabi

Louvre Abu Dhabi opened on 8 November 2017. Since then, the institution has been forging its distinct voice within the global museum community. This volume is the product of the symposium *Worlds in a Museum* that was held in November 2018 to celebrate the first year anniversary of the opening of Louvre Abu Dhabi. The symposium and its proceedings mark a decisive stage in the evolution of the museum. This brief essay introduces Louvre Abu Dhabi's mission and activities, ambition and challenges from the perspective of its first Scientific, Curatorial, and Collections Management Director.

Today, the word 'museum' covers a wide range of creative entities. Its principles of conservation and knowledge date back to the Museum of Alexandria. The term is also identified with the Greek word *Museion*, "the Temple of the Muses", one of the centres of ancient learning. Those principles have perpetuated throughout the centuries, with treasures and collections accumulating in palaces, holy places and private collections. Over time, such collections have been made increasingly accessible to ever-broader swathes of society. The quintessential Enlightenment idea of universal culture has opened up collective heritage to all nations. Progressively, we have seen the development of the contemporary idea of museums as a repository of knowledge, an institution entrusted with the preservation of humanity's heritage.

Louvre Abu Dhabi is taking the world of museums a step further. The museum's artefacts and exhibits relate to areas and civilisations around the world, from prehistory, through modernity, to the contemporary era. Our displays present a cross-disciplinary view of the history of art, organised according to artistic, social, and cultural themes that span the history of humankind. This intentional and distinctive curatorial approach is a direct response to the challenges of globalisation. Indeed, I would suggest that the emergence of a globalised world, in which the boundaries of artistic forms and cultural traditions are blurred, demands a comprehensive reassessment of the status of the artwork and Western narratives of art history. Our chrono-thematic approach draws attention to the similarities as well as the specificities of the many forms of artistic expression of humanity, beyond any geographical limitations. This approach is reflected in the museography that conveys the ideals of a universal museum and cultural dialogue. Universality is the foundation of our museum and not just a rhetorical gesture. Accordingly, Louvre Abu Dhabi instigates a dialogue among artworks that reveals formal coherences and codes and highlights common values, forms and symbols. Bringing together multifaceted perspectives on the evolution of humanity, Louvre Abu Dhabi tells the story of key historical shifts and explores some of the foundational phenomena of civilisations.

We offer a space for exchange and experimentation. The programming of our temporary exhibitions affirms the museum's interest in cross-cultural transfer and innovative approaches to research. Globalisation and migration may have become the key words of our age, but the phenomena they embrace are not as recent as they seem. At each stage of history, globalisation drew a complex map of commercial, artistic, intellectual, and scientific movements and exchanges. So far, the temporary exhibitions of Louvre Abu Dhabi have invited audiences to decode the meaning of art and cultural encounters in a world of constant transcultural dialogue. The narratives of those exhibitions have taken the audience on a journey through the caravan routes and the high seas passing through the great masters of classical paintings, demonstrating that humanity's scientific discoveries do not undermine but rather stimulate aesthetic expression.

Our seasonal programming aims to reaffirm the universal identity of Louvre Abu Dhabi, to develop ties between the permanent galleries and temporary exhibitions, to broaden the narrative of the permanent galleries and enrich it with other perspectives, and to attract new audiences as well as cultivate and retain existing ones. This programming takes into account the cultural contexts of the United Arab Emirates and Abu Dhabi, integrating artworks from the region into a wider, universal narrative.

Moreover, in exploring great moments in the history of art and societies, we open eyes, broaden horizons through the visual arts and establish Louvre Abu Dhabi as a leading player in culture and research. The museum's universal scope is grounded in historical and anthropological interpretations of art and material culture. Recent interest in mobility, transculturality, and global perspectives in research of art history has brought new approaches to historical artefacts. Those developments have led to an increased blurring of the boundaries that once separated the various disciplines of art history. In drawing on those dynamic and hybrid intellectual trends, Louvre Abu Dhabi aims to define a new perspective of global art history, as seen from this particular part of the world.

Altogether, Louvre Abu Dhabi is a museum for everyone, a museum pervaded with a shared sense of human history. During its first year of opening, we hosted over one million of visitors, a major achievement for a young institution. Beyond the figures and indicators, many departments in the museum face the same questions: how to improve the visitor's perception and reception of the museum, how do we best appropriate the different venues of the building, the content of the narrative and optimise our outreach.

These interrogations around how to improve and advance, combined with our core mission, have led us to plan the next phases in Louvre Abu Dhabi's evolution. As such, we are developing a policy to foster academic research in five main fields that are crucial to the museum's success in the long-term. These entails collections, connected and global art history, preventive conservation, museum studies and translation. These pillars of research, involving academic collaborations with the humanities, social and analytical sciences, anthropology, archaeology and, of course, art history will see the creation of a new pole of Museum Studies. The specificities of the museum's curatorial approach, the unique preventative conservation measures, and the challenges of being an entirely trilingual museum are just a few of the elements that nourish these forthcoming research projects.

As we move into Louvre Abu Dhabi's next chapter, we are excited to question the very notion of the masterpiece, pen publications of new thought, and blur the parameters of pre-defined canons and categories of art history. The invaluable discussions that took place during the *Worlds in a Museum* symposium contribute wholeheartedly to our progressive thought process. As an institution, we will continue to analyse, expand upon and question the role of the museum in an ever more globalised world with the aim of generating new perspectives for future generations.

Souraya Noujaim

PART 1

MUSEUMS

AND

GLOBALISATION

Introduction

L'Imagination au Pouvoir! Challenges and Perspectives for Universal Museums in the Twenty-First Century

Noëmi Daucé

"The narratives of the world are numberless". Roland Barthes began his introduction to *The Structural Analysis of Narrative* with this assertion in 1966[1], in considering all supports of transmission of these narratives, whether they be shared orally or written down, translated in frozen figurations or illustrated in live motion. This desire to form a consistent and relevant frame to understand and embrace the world, acknowledging the multiplicity of angles and perspectives, is undoubtedly applicable to the world of the museums, especially to museums of global cultures in the early twenty-first century. Jean Luc Martinez, Hartwig Fischer and James Cuno explore the very notion of universal museums, considering the specific background of the institutions they respectively preside over. They highlight the variety of their unique collections, their strengths and weaknesses but also tackle the implicit tensions born out the intricate history of their constitutions. Part of their contributions are also dedicated to the range of innovative strategies employed to reach global audiences with diverse individual and collective expectations.

New approaches to museum narratives encourage curators to explore the spaces between existing collections, offering new insights into overlooked historical recesses. As such, they open windows onto a variety of ancient and modern worlds, and create meeting places at which the strange and the wonderful, the exotic and the familiar, come together. In this light, museums would seem to do more than simply inculcate knowledge and stimulate the imagination. Indeed, following Edward Said, James Cuno suggests that they host uprooted heritages and preserve otherwise excluded forms of cultural difference.

Martinez and Fischer preside over the Louvre and British Museum respectively. Whether they come from just down the street or distant continents, visitors flock to these significant cultural hubs to appreciate and respond to works of art, which also stem from cultures around the world.

Among the major challenges facing institutions such as these are the tasks of ensuring that their encyclopedic collections are accessible, the knowledge that they contain is transmissible, and visitor's varied experiences both complement one another and give rise to productive tensions.

In line with the unprecedented development of mobility on a global scale during the past decades, museums have displayed their collection far beyond their traditional boundaries to reach new audiences. The beginning of the 21ˢᵗ century has seen an unparalleled increase in international partnerships and travelling exhibitions, developing more inclusive and multipolar narratives. As an illustration, Cuno and Fischer refer to the exhibition *India and the World* that was inaugurated in November 2017, at the same time that Louvre Abu Dhabi opened its doors, a remarkable opportunity to refresh the narrative of the world's cultures, to circulate collections and reach out to visitors in Mumbai and New Delhi. Accordingly, Martinez's reference to the Louvre Lens, which opened in 2012, highlights the innovative approach revealing continuities rather than division in the long perspective of global art history. The integration of the museum in a distinctive regional context was another challenge: local anchorage was addressed through a programme of custom-sized special exhibitions which payed tribute to the deep history of this industrial basin and its strategical location, in relation to Northern Europe, the United Kingdom, Belgium and the Netherlands.

Finally, the three authors argue for the importance of global perspective and universal museums, whose relevance in a globalised society seems increasingly accurate, bringing to light the richness and diversity of world cultures and, quoting James Cuno, "a shared sense of human history". With an innovative narrative inherited from the last decades of experimentation in the field of museology, but also rooted in the prime definition of a museum as a place of wonder, Louvre Abu Dhabi takes on the challenges of the twenty first century, offering visitors a renewed vision of the global *theatrum mundi*.

Notes

1   R. Barthes, 1966. "Introduction à l'analyse structurelle des récits", in Communications, 8, *Recherches sémiologiques : l'analyse structurale du récit*, p. 1.

Global History and the Art Museum

James Cuno

As a way of thinking through this volume's central themes of museums and globalisation, I recently reread Patrick Geary's *The Myth of Nations: The Medieval Origins of Europe* and Sebastian Conrad's *What is Global History?* In light of the rise of populist ethnonationalism across so much of the western world, these two books have taken on urgent new resonances, which have implications for contemporary curatorial practice.

The first book explores the complex histories of European identity and the roles that historians have played in laying the intellectual foundations of modern nationalities. Geary begins with a string of challenging statements. Modern history, he proposes, was born in the nineteenth century. Conceived and developed as an ideological instrument of European nationalism, the history of Europe's nations has been astonishingly effective. In establishing national narratives and myths, however, modern history has turned our understanding of the past into a toxic waste dump, filled with the poison of ethnic nationalism. This poison has seeped deep into popular consciousness. Cleaning up this waste, he suggests, represents perhaps the most daunting challenge facing historians today.

Attempts to purge our sense of the past of all-too modern forms of nationalist compartmentalisation and homogenisation have to cut against deeply ingrained historical narratives. Geary traces the processes through which modern nationalism developed and disseminated through European cultures. Often, the germ of nationalism first takes hold in scholarship: a small coterie of 'awakened' individuals study the language, culture, and history of a given people, who are seen as the ancient forerunners or vernacular pulse of a nascent nation. These ideas are then taken up and transmitted by groups of 'patriots', leading to the mass embrace of a modern national movement.

In showing how these successive stages played out in Germany, which offers an especially pronounced instance of modern nation building, Geary cites the philosopher Johann Gottlieb Fichte. In his 'Fourth Address to the German Nation' (1808), Fichte declared that Germans alone among 'neo-Europeans' remained in the original place inhabited by 'their ancestral stock'.[1] Unlike other national peoples, he expands, Germans alone retained their original language, which Fichte claims derives entirely from indigenous precedents. The following year, Freiherr von Stein, the Prussian Minister of State, founded the Gesellschaft für ältere deutsche Geschichtskunde ('Society for Older German Historical Knowledge', 1809), which was dedicated to the publication of the *Monumenta Germaniae Historica*, a compendium of texts laying the foundations of German identity. Attempts to ground German nationalism in the distant past were gathering momentum. This only increased as Gustaf Kossinna, who was appointed professor of German archaeology at the University of Berlin in 1902, developed what today we would call ethnoarchaeology. According to 'Kossinna's law', culturally coherent sets of archeological artefacts can be 'scientifically' connected to linguistic groups. In their implications, Kossinna's theories encouraged a wave of irredentist rhetoric and practice in the twentieth century. Modern states such as Germany laid claim to regions of neighbouring countries on the grounds that they were part of the invading nation's original homelands.

The example of Germany, then, demonstrates how the historical study of national peoples has been deeply entangled in the cultural, political, and ultimately military articulation of modern nationalism. Geary's book is an argument against such misuse of history for ethnonationalist purposes and a warning to his professional peers: 'We historians', he writes,

> are necessarily to blame for the creation of enduring myths about peoples, myths that are both tenacious and dangerous. By constructing a continuous, linear story of the peoples of Europe, we validate the attempts of military commanders and political leaders to claims that they did indeed incorporate ancient traditions of peoples.[2]

Sebastian Conrad picks up where Geary leaves off. His argument emphasises how 'the genesis of the social sciences and humanities was tied to the nation-state' too.[3] Conrad continues:

> In their themes and questions, and even in their societal function, fields like history, sociology, and philology remained tied to a country's own society. Beyond that, the 'methodological nationalism' of the academic disciplines meant that, theoretically, the nation-state was presupposed as the fundamental unit of investigation, a territorial entity that served as a 'container' for a society. The commitment to territorially bounded containers was more pronounced in the field of history than in some of its neighboring disciplines. Knowledge of the world was thereby discursively and

institutionally pre-structured in such a way as to obscure the role of exchange relationships. History, in most quarters, was limited to national history.[4]

In seeking to foster and consolidate (but also critically parse) alternatives to the national paradigm in historical practice, Conrad identifies three varieties of global history. First is the history of everything: 'From such an omnivorous perspective, everything that ever happened on the earth is a legitimate ingredient of global history'.[5] Second is the historical study of exchange and connections: 'The common thread connecting these kind of studies is the general insight that no society, nation, or civilization exists in isolation'.[6] Third is the comparison of individual nations or institutions undergoing either similar domestic challenges or common global transformations.

For Conrad global history is concerned with processes of mobility and exchange, which both transcend borders and boundaries. Attending to forms of transregional travel and transaction across history, he proposes, the historian might overcome fragmentation and 'arrive at a more comprehensive understanding of the interactions and connections that have made the modern world'.[7] As such, global history offers an indispensable counterargument to nationalist historical projects. What is more, this view and practice of history is in keeping with the world as we currently experience it, a world of entanglements and networks, of spreading and overlapping economic, political, and cultural developments.

In my practice as a curator and art historian, I have argued for the importance of a global perspective in the work of art museums. My book *Museums Matter* argued that art museums, in presenting representative examples of the world's artistic legacy, encourage a broad understanding of difference in the world and a shared sense of human history. In *Who Owns Antiquity?* I argued that encyclopaedic museums counter the ethnonationalist narratives through which modern nation states assert their continuity with the remains of past cultures found within their sovereign borders.

As a first example, consider an ivory casket in the Art Institute of Chicago's collection (fig. 1). Likely made in Sicily early in the thirteenth century, the casket is covered with thin plaques made of African ivory. The ivory was acquired through trade with Muslim merchants along the Swahili coast, perhaps in exchange for silk or cotton obtained in trade across the Indian Ocean. In Sicily, the plaques were cut, decorated with Arab-inspired arabesques, gazelles, peacocks, and made into a box to hold jewellery or other domestic valuables. Later, a Christian owner used it as a reliquary. For another example, consider a fourteenth-century German monstrance, which was once part of an ecclesiastical treasury (fig. 2). Made of gilt silver, it takes the shape of a medieval

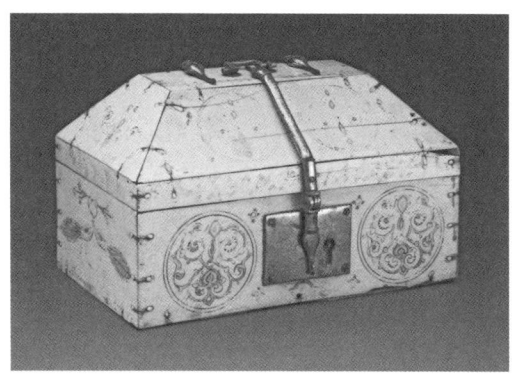

Figure 1. Casket, 1200/25. Sicily. Ivory, brass,
tempera, and gold leaf, 3 7/8 × 6 ¼ × 3 ¼ in.
(Plate 1, p. 226).
The Art Institute of Chicago, Samuel P. Avery
Endowment, 1926.389. Photograph by Robert
Hashimoto.

Figure 2. Monstrance with Tooth of St. John the Baptist,
1375/1400. Germany. Lower Saxony, Brunswick. Gilt silver
(17 ⅞ × 5 ¼ in.). Rock crystal, 900/1000. Egypt, Fatimid
Dynasty. (Plate 2, p. 227)
The Art Institute of Chicago, Gift of Mrs. Chauncey McCormick,
1962.91 side 1. Photograph by Robert Hashimoto.

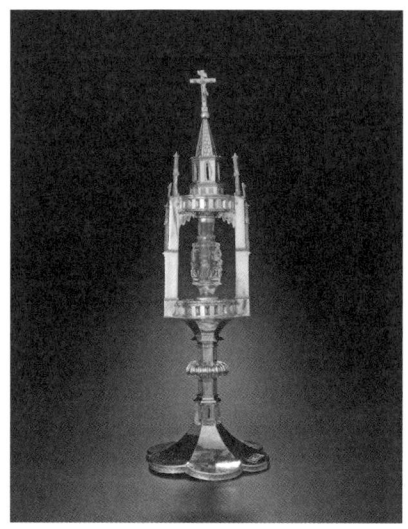

church building and is surmounted by a deli-
cate crucifix. At the centre of the monstrance
is a translucent rock-crystal bottle containing
a tooth. According to an inscription on a piece
of paper in the relic's linen wrapping, the tooth
belonged to Saint John the Baptist. The bottle
itself was made in Fatimid Egypt. Late in the
eleventh century, the palace of the Fatimid ruler, the caliph al-Mustansir, was looted.
Much of its treasury—tens of thousands of objects in gold, silver, precious stone, or
rock crystal—was either removed or melted down. Many items made their way first to
the Byzantine court in Constantinople and then on to Europe after the sacking of the
Byzantine court in 1204 as part of the Fourth Crusade.

Through a simple examination of just these two objects, a global history of the
Mediterranean can be told: a history of trade; exchange; hybridity of form and iconography; use and reuse; conflicting beliefs; and political power. All of which attests to the
central fact of museum collections: namely, that the aesthetic objects they contain have

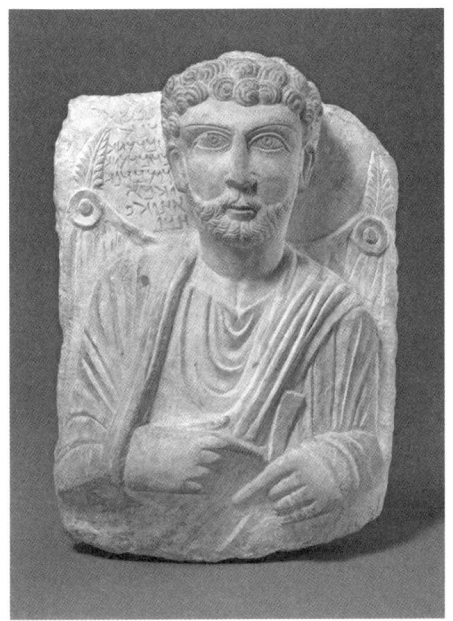 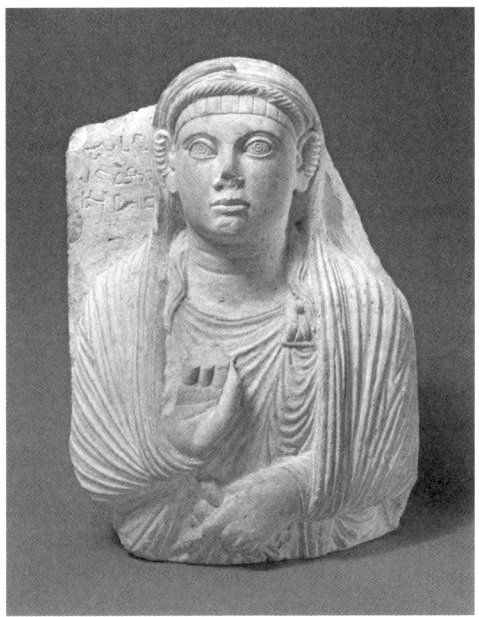

Figure 3. Left: Gravestone with Bust of a Man. Palmyra (Syria), 2nd century A.D. Limestone, H. 20 in.
(50.8 cm). Right: Gravestone with Bust of a Woman. Palmyra (Syria), 2nd century A.D. Limestone, H. 20 in.
(50.8 cm). (Plate 3, p. 228)

Both images from *The Year One, Art of the Ancient World East and West*, The Metropolitan Museum of Art, Yale University
Press © 2000 by The Metropolitan Museum of Art.

been imprinted with the historical circumstances of their making. This is also true of
special exhibitions. Consider just three, two organised by the Metropolitan Museum of
Art—*The Year One: Art of the Ancient World East and West* and *Lost Kingdoms: Hindu-
Buddhist Sculpture of Early Southeast Asia*—and a third, *India and the World*, a collab-
oration between the British Museum, Chhatrapati Shivaji Maharaj Vastu Sangrahalaya,
Mumbai, and the National Museum, Delhi.

The Year One brought together 141 works of art made by people living along routes
of contact from the Atlantic Ocean, across the Mediterranean Sea and Asia, to the
Pacific. These included busts of a man and woman (fig. 3) made in the second century CE in or near Palmyra. This ancient oasis settlement lies on the trade routes running across northern Syrian desert, which connected the Roman Empire with Parthian
(ancient Iranian) territory east of the Euphrates, India, the head of the Persian Gulf,
and the Silk Road to China. These transregional contacts are manifest in the figurative

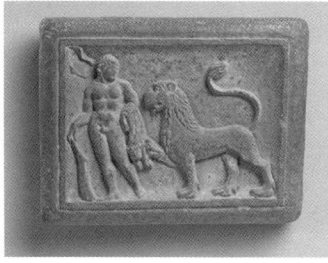 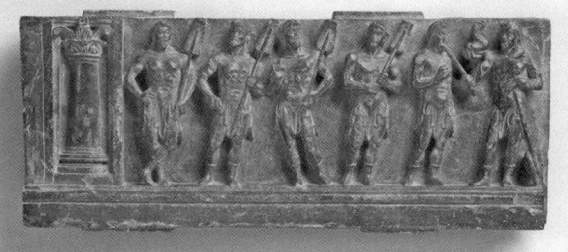

Figure 4. Left: Weight Depicting Herakles and the Memean Lion. Pakistan (ancient region of Gandharda), 1st century B.C. Schist, 10 ¼ × 13 ¾ in. (26 × 34.9 cm); Right: Stair Riser with Marine Deities. Pakistan (ancient region of Gandhara), 1st century A.D. Schist, 6 ⅝ × 17 in. (16.9 × 43.2 cm). (Plate 4, p. 229)
Both images from *The Year One, Art of the Ancient World East and West*, The Metropolitan Museum of Art, Yale University Press © 2000 by The Metropolitan Museum of Art.

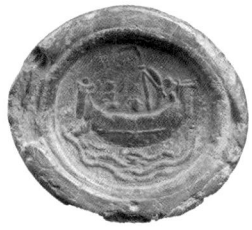

Figure 5. Impression from a Seal Depicting a Ship at Sea, 4th-5th century CE. India, probably Bengal or Andhra Pradesh. Clay. H. 1 ¾ in. (4.5 cm); W. 2 in. (5 cm). Lent by National Museum, Bangkok, Thailand (2309). (Plate 5, p. 229)
Art Resource, NY (ART586839) © The Metropolitan Museum of Art.

style of the two busts, which reflect both Greco-Roman and Parthian elements: the pose of the hand emerging from deep folds in the drapery recalls similar elements of Greek sculpture, while the frontal posture and spiraling pattern of their hair suggests an Eastern influence. *The Year One* also featured two objects from the first century BCE, which depict Herakles and various marine deities from ancient Gandhara (now Pakistan) (fig. 4). These artefacts betray the influence of both ancient Greek sculptural forms and Indian iconography. This is unsurprising, Gandhara having been ruled by the Mauryas (India), Alexander the Great, and a combination of Scythians and Parthians between the fourth and first centuries BCE.

Lost Kingdoms comprised 170 works of art documenting the dissemination of artistic styles and iconographies in the first millennium CE along land and seafaring routes through Hindu and Buddhist kingdoms from Pyu (in modern Myanmar) to Śrīvijaya (in western Indonesia, Malaysia, and southern Thailand). This process is often referred to as the 'Indenisation' of Southeast Asia, that is, the adoption and adaptation of Indic ideas 'providing a conceptual and linguistic framework for new ideals of kingship, state, and religious order'.[8] One sees this in an impression of a clay seal (fig. 5) depicting a ship at sea, which was made in India, found in central Thailand, and dated to the fourth or fifth century CE. The ship

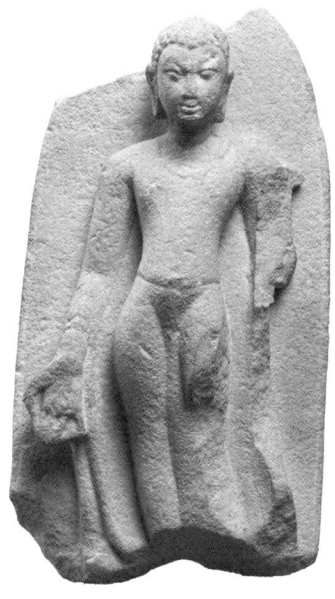

Figure 6. Buddha Granting Boons, first half of the 6th century CE. Northern India (Uttar Pradesh, Sarnath). Sandstone. H. 6 ½ in. (16.5 cm); W. 3 ¹⁵⁄₁₆ in. (10 cm); D. est. ¹³⁄₁₆ in. (2 cm); approx. Wt. 2.2. National Museum, Bangkok, Thailand. (Plate 6, p. 230) Art Resource, NY (ART586838) © The Metropolitan Museum of Art.

is an ocean-going vessel. Similar ships are found on sculptural reliefs in India, on a stupa from the Mauryan Period (first century BCE) in Bharhut, Madhya Pradesh, and on coins that circulated along the Coromandel Coast of Andhra Pradesh in the first century CE. That the clay impression was found in central Thailand is evidence of maritime trade across the Indian Ocean early in the first millennium CE. Perhaps the most compelling evidence of this trade and the dissemination of religious ideas and iconography throughout the region, though, is established by comparing a fifth-century-CE sculpture of the Buddha Śākyamuni from Sarnath, India (fig. 6) with a seventh-century sculpture of the Buddha Granting Boons, found in southern Thailand (fig. 7). The stylistic and iconographical commonalities between these two figures are only reinforced by many other formal similarities among Buddhist and Hindu figures found throughout Southeast Asia, which derive from earlier Indian sources.

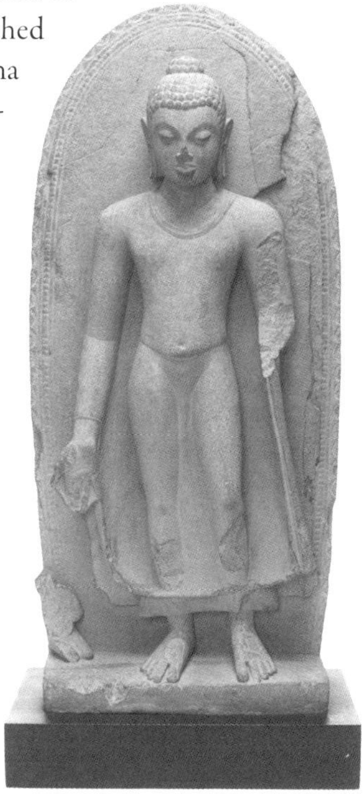

Figure 7. Buddha Śākyamuni Granting Boons, Sarnath region, Uttar Pradesh, northern India, c. 475, Sandstone. H. 34 ⅛ in. (86.7 cm), w. 17 ⅝ in. (44.8 cm), Asia Society, New York, Mr. and Mrs. John D. Rockefeller 3rd Collection (1975.5). (Plate 7, p. 230)
From *Lost Kingdoms Hindu-Buddhist Sculpture of Early Southeast Asia*, The Metropolitan Museum of Art, Yale University Press, © 2014 by The Metropolitan Museum of Art.

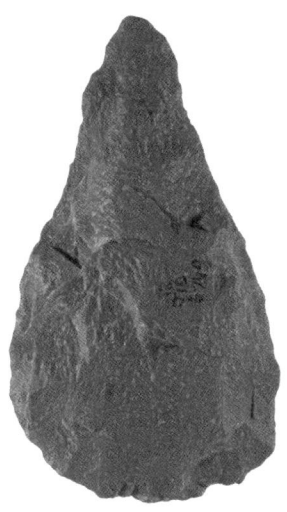

Figure 8. Lower Palaeolithic Hand-Axe, Quartzite, 1,700,000 –
1,070,000 years old, Attirampakkam, Tamil Nadu, India. Height:
13.5 cm / Width 7.6 cm / Thickness: 4 cm. Sharma Centre for Heritage
Education, Chennai (T8 6740). (Plate 8, p. 231)
From *India and the World, A History in Nine Stories*, Penguin Books, © CSMVS
(Chhatrapati Shivaji Maharaj Vastu Sangrahalaya, Mumbai).

The third exhibition, *India and the World*, was organised by two Indian museums and one British, with loans from these three institutions and more than twenty other collections across India. The purpose of the exhibition was to tell the story of India and its vast and rich artistic invention. It included objects spanning Indian history, from a hand-axe from Tamil Nadu made over a million years ago during lower Palaeolithic (fig. 8) to a contemporary sculpture, *Unicode*, made in 2011 by the artist L.N. Tallur, who was born in Kundapur, educated in India and Britain, and resides in India and Korea (fig. 9). It features a ball of concrete and money set within a traditional prabha or flaming halo. Concrete and money, the sculpture seems to suggest, represent new, Shiva-like Indian gods of time and destruction.

Sabyassachi Mukherjee, director general of Chhatrapati Shivaji Maharaj Vastu Sangrahalaya, the organising Indian museum, described *India and the World* as an experimental attempt 'to provide a model for museums to share their collections with people across the world'.[9] The aim is to 'give an opportunity to people from diverse countries and cultures to become partners in the world narrative' and motivate 'them to reclaim and reposition their own unique regional, national and global identities in the changing cultural landscape of the world'.[10] The project entails three art museums collaboratively conceiving and presenting exhibitions of objects borrowed from multiple collections. *India and the World* has been shown in venues that were unlikely to have seen such a range of objects before. In these contexts, the curators hope, the exhibitions will provoke curiosity about connections among peoples and cultures over time.

These entanglements are already evident from the very start of the exhibition, which opens with a group of hand-axes. One example, which was found in Olduvai Gorge, Tanzania, and is now in the British Museum, is between 800,000 and 400,000 years old. Another example dates back as many as a million years into the Lower Palaeolithic. Having been excavated in India at Attirampakkam in northwest Chennai, it is now in the collection of the Sharma Centre for Heritage Education, Chennai.

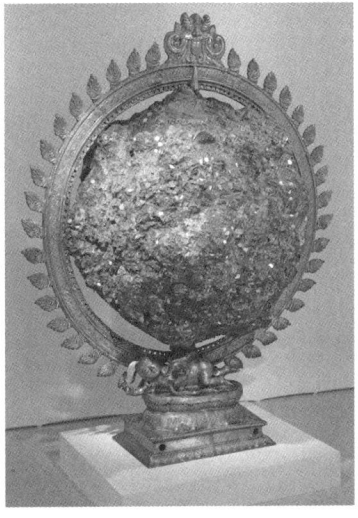

Figure 9. 'Unicode', by L.N. Tallur, AD 2011, Tallur Studio, Koteshwara, Karnataka, India, Bronze, coins and concrete. Height: 183 cm/ Width: 152 cm/ Depth: 117 cm. Kiran Nadar Museum of Art (33SCLNT001). (Plate 9, p. 232)
From *India and the World, A History in Nine Stories*, Penguin Books, © CSMVS (Chhatrapati Shivaji Maharaj Vastu Sangrahalaya, Mumbai).

These two objects not only remind us that humans lived a very long time ago. They also suggest striking continuities in human tools and practices—continuities that are all the more significant given that the two axes were separated by more than 5,400 kilometres. Indeed, these stones were cut and chipped in similar ways on two different continents and in two distinct eras. Both were fashioned to be more effective and efficient as a means of butchering animals, digging for root plants and water, chopping wood, and removing tree bark; both were constantly refined to be sharper and stronger; held more easily and firmly in the hand; and glint in the sunlight and enhance the play of colours across their surfaces.

The impulse to improve the human condition is evident throughout all three exhibitions. However distant the represented peoples or cultures may have been one from another, this urge—a defining feature of our species—remains constant.

The stories of these exhibitions, as with all exhibitions, are told through the objects they present. Moreover, those objects, like all objects, include evidence of the circumstances of their history: the history of their form and materials, imagery and iconography, discovery and subsequent ownership. It is fashionable to be critical of encyclopaedic museums on the grounds that they are colonial or imperial institutions with collections resulting from an imbalance of power. Certainly, objects bear the imprint of their histories. Many of those in the British Museum and the Louvre, for example, are inscribed with the evidence of empire, not only of the British and French empires but also of those of Assyria, New Kingdom Egypt, China, Rome, and the Mauryan and Mughal Empires of India, too. Political power is an aspect of the history of these objects that must be acknowledged. However, empire is no simple thing.

It is a truth about empire that, despite its violence, it has contributed and continues to contribute to the overlapping of territories and intertwined histories. In his book,

Culture and Imperialism, Edward Said reminds us that cultures, 'far from being unitary or monolithic or autonomous things',

> actually assume more 'foreign' elements, alterities, differences, than they consciously exclude. Who in India or Algeria today can confidently separate out the British or French component of the past from present actualities, and who in Britain or France can draw a clear circle around British London or French Paris that would exclude the impact of India and Algeria upon those two imperial cities.[11]

To Said, cultures are humanly made structures of 'both authority and participation, benevolent in what they include, incorporate, and validate, less benevolent in what they exclude'.[12] Or, as Sanjay Subrahmanyam, an Indian-born scholar who has lived and worked in Paris, Oxford, Los Angeles, and New York, has written: 'A national culture that does not have the confidence to declare that, like all other national cultures, it too is a hybrid, a crossroads, a mixture of elements derived from chance encounters and unforeseen consequences, can only take the path to xenophobia and cultural paranoia'.[13]

The importance of encyclopaedic art museums stems from the fact that they are the repositories of material evidence from which so much of the global history of the world can be written. Protecting, documenting, and sharing that history is the responsibility of such museums. The history of the world, they remind us, is inevitably a history of entanglements and networks, of the sharing and overlapping of economic, political, and cultural developments. And much like the two books with which I opened this chapter, these museums show how national histories are ineluctably intertwined with global history.

Notes

1 Quoted in Patrick J. Geary, *The Myth of Nations*, 25.
2 Geary, *The Myth of Nations*, 157.
3 Sebastian Conrad, *What is Global History?*, 3.
4 Conrad, *What is Global History?*, 3.
5 Conrad, *What is Global History?*, 7.
6 Conrad, *What is Global History?*, 9.
7 Conrad, *What is Global History?*, 5
8 John Guy, 'Introducing Early South Asia,' 3.
9 Trustees of the British Museum and Chhatrapati Shivaji Maharaj Vastu Sangrahalaya, 'Objects on display'.
10 Trustees, 'Objects on display'.
11 Edward Said, *Culture and Imperialism*, 15.
12 Said, *Culture and Imperialism*, 15
13 Sanjay Subrahmanyam, 'Golden Age Hallucinations'.

Works Cited

Conrad, Sebastian. *What is Global History?* Princeton: Princeton University Press, 2017.

Geary, Patrick J. *The Myth of Nations: The Medieval Origins of Europe.* Princeton: Princeton University Press, 2002.

Guy, John. 'Introducing Early South Asia'. In *Lost Kingdoms: Hindu-Buddhist Sculpture of Early Southeast Asia*, edited by John Guy, 3–14. New Haven: Yale University Press, 2014.

Said, Edward. *Culture and Imperialism*. London: Vintage Books, 2014.

Subrahmanyam, Sanjay. 'Golden Age Hallucinations'. *Outlook India Magazine*. Posted August 20, 2001. http://www.outlookindia.com.

Trustees of the British Museum and Chhatrapati Shivaji Maharaj Vastu Sangrahalaya, 'Objects on display'. *India & the World: A History in Nine Stories.* Posted in 2017. https://www.indiaandtheworld.org/objects-on-display.

Dialogue Among Cultures
A Challenge for Museums of the Future

Hartwig Fischer

In exploring themes that resonate across different cultures and across the ages, in establishing dialogues between works of art and objects of material culture from around the world, Louvre Abu Dhabi is making a major contribution to the development of the universal museum in the twenty-first century. As a way of marking its first anniversary, this short contribution discusses some of my own experiences working in a number of museums that share its aspiration towards universality, each in its own distinct way. In attempting to draw lessons for contemporary museology, I will pay particular attention to forms of global dialogue, encompassing both contemporary exchanges between museums and complex interactions among cultures over the course of world history. It is through fostering dialogues—at times difficult dialogues—with different institutions, audiences, and historical narratives, highlighting both the individuality of cultures *and* their interconnectedness, that museums can secure the future of universal history and the culture of the universal in the twenty-first century. Today any aspiration to the universal has to pass by the critical deconstruction of the very notion of the universal as a unifying, overpowering concept; it requires the participation of many to define and establish what we share.

Between 2012 and 2016 I served as Director General of the Dresden State Art Collections. In this role, I oversaw a conglomerate of fourteen museums covering a wide range of cultures, times, and regions. Trying to display and do justice to objects that represent a particular culture, one has to be aware that a museum is a highly charged place imposing its own methods and technologies that condition the narratives we create. Almost everything you find in a universal museum was not created to appear in a universal museum, or in any museum. We therefore have to address the tension not only among the objects themselves, but also between their past functions and meanings, and the ways in which they are displayed, interpreted and looked at today. It is important that you make the audience aware of the criteria you apply when you highlight these links and make comparisons, whether they are made on the basis of form, function, use, materiality, craftsmanship, history and provenance or any other criterion, and there are myriads, obviously. The major question we had to elaborate on in Dresden, was this: what is it that links these cultures and how can we help visitors understand these connections?

As custodians of objects and the narratives they encapsulate, we have to ensure that those who come to our museums have meaningful experiences and have the opportunity to engage with those connections without determining them in advance. For as much as we have to facilitate access to the works and objects in the collection and invite our visitors to enter into dialogue with them, we must also be careful not to hamper the free play of association. We must provide an open space for there to be both, studium and punctum, to borrow Roland Barthes' terms, systematic approach on the one hand, and the serendipity of revelation on the other, that sudden deep connection between an object and our inner self.

Since 2016, I have been the Director of the British Museum, which is perhaps the most comprehensive collection of world cultures, presented in direct proximity to each other under one roof. Visitors walk from Egypt to China, from China to Iran, and from Iran to South America, they are constantly drawn into a dialogue among these cultures, offering the possibility to explore the connections between them. And where there is no direct link, it is illuminating to look at structural similarities and disparities. Through exhibitions, research, and programmes, the British Museum has contributed significantly towards exploring the interconnectedness of cultures and towards rethinking what it means to present "the world in a museum". But so much more remains to be done!

For when it comes to the particular way in which we display objects in the collection, the British Museum is still fairly siloed: you have Egypt here, Assyria over there, and the Levante and Greece in other galleries, without helping visitors understand that each of these cultures shared one vast space of exchange, namely the Eastern Mediterranean and the Middle East. Just to give you one example, in October 2018, we opened the new Albukhary Foundation Galleries of the Islamic World. There, we realised that taking a global approach, which covers several continents and hundreds of years, is stimulating and provocative. Staging dialogues among cultures and regions, I believe, is the next step that institutions with large collections must take. We must make a contribution towards developing an understanding of the world as a complex whole. And we can only do that if we bring to bear different approaches, work together with scholars and communities from around the world to make different voices audible, different stories legible, different layers of meaning accessible.

Realising a museum of world cultures entails responsibilities not just to national publics, but to global audiences too. How can these responsibilities to such diverse and often distant publics be met? At one level, a museum of world cultures must function as a hub. It projects world cultures in a certain space—London, Abu Dhabi, New York, or St. Petersburg—to audiences that are local, national, and global. At another level, it has to reach out and work globally. The British Museum has exhibitions travelling to many parts of the world. We have partnerships on all continents with institutions and communities involving research, the preservation of cultural heritage, training, and skill-sharing. We invite colleagues to the Museum to learn from them and help us re-think collections, display, and research. Our greatest responsibilities is to participate in a world network and share collections with the widest possible audience.

The ways in which the British Museum is engaging with different publics around the world can be brought into focus by way of an example. In November 2017, our colleagues at the Chhatrapati Shivaji Maharaj Vastu Sangrahalaya (CSMVS) in Mumbai opened the exhibition *India and the World,* which grew out of a collaboration with the British Museum. Together we convened curators from both India and the UK to develop the concept, the narrative and its various chapters to explore the interaction between South Asia and other parts of the world across millenia. Everyone brought different frames of reference, experiences, cultural sensitivities, and methodologies to the table. With the exhibition on display at the CSMVS in Mumbai and subsequently at the National Museum in New Delhi, the notion of sharing was key: objects pertaining directly to the history of South Asia were lent by Indian collections, both public and private; those pertaining to the global context came from the British Museum. The exhibition can serve as a template. It was a huge success with the general public, and an opportunity for both venues to familiarise young audiences with their own past in a global context.

As we move forward, a global museum must assume the responsibility of making such sharing evident and visible. This entails circulating objects through direct loans. For all of us who are passionate about culture and collections, the encounter with the object itself is crucial. At the same time, we acknowledge that the digital will continue to transform how we display and relate to objects. The fact that digital technology not only allows us to record and preserve cultural heritage but enables us to reproduce it in ever more perfect replicas opens new ways of sharing on a global scale.

The question of how we reach out to global audiences is fundamental to the British Museum, which was founded by the British Parliament in 1753. The collections belong to neither the state nor the government. Parliament set up a Board of Trustees who have fiduciary custodianship. They hold these collections in trust for the public. That public is not just the British public, but every living person on this planet, as well as future generations. I think that this is an extraordinary basis on which to create a museum. It means that everyone has the right to access these collections.

Engaging with diverse audiences from around the world is clearly also important to Louvre Abu Dhabi, which like all major museums functions as an interface between high end research and a wide-ranging, diverse public. As with all major museums, however, visitors come with their own background, their own experience and codes. The museum has the task of mediating, of presenting specialized knowledge in intelligible and accessible ways. As such, it has an incredibly important role for public life, for our awareness of community—in fact it generates community.

The task of understanding the many cultures of the world in their own right and in relation to each other, and mediating that understanding present a considerable challenge, which cannot be addressed in isolation; it requires the collaboration of all major museums across the globe. But it cannot be done by museums alone either, nor by museums working with scholars and experts. This dialogue has to include communities that hail from and represent those cultures today.

In the discourse of museums, we often talk about dialogue and exchange among institutions and professionals from different parts of the world. Such dialogue does not work simply because we say we want to have a dialogue. A meaningful world dialogue, which would recognise and attend to the interconnectedness of cultures, requires that we truly listen and that we endure that which we do not understand. It acknowledges that being baffled, disoriented, or not knowing are what opens people up to another culture. This is what I wish museums realise on a global scale. The ways in which people look at objects in Japan differs from the ways in which people look at objects in Mexico or Nigeria. How do you bind these different backgrounds, traditions, customs and habits into one big, complex, and world-encompassing dialogue? How can museums help us to activate the cultures of the world, past and present, as our own personal resource. The answer, I would suggest, lies in genuine—that is, open and vulnerable—exchange among museums and those who visit them to explore the world. Bringing previously separate histories and cultural traditions into contact with one another, we might recognise connections and narratives that will help us to rewrite our shared complicated history as equals, and to shape a better future together.

Unity in Diversity

One Louvre Among the Three Louvres in the Twenty-First Century

Jean-Luc Martinez

From the perspective of the Louvre, I would like to present a number of challenges faced by both museum audiences and collections themselves in the twenty-first century. They pertain specifically to the difficulty of striking a balance between universality on the one hand and local or national culture on the other. Indeed, it seems that in the twenty-first century, the museum is a key site at which local and world cultures come together. As such, contemporary museums encapsulate the so-called 'glocal': that is, the local manifestation of globalising processes. Combining the local and global in this way, many museums contribute to an admirable goal: namely, that of developing an awareness that humans belong to a universal community that has its roots in local cultures but is not limited to them. Museums reinforce the notion of what unites rather than differentiates humanity.

Is the Louvre a universal museum?

Answering this somewhat provocative question will allow us to better understand what we are trying to do—not only with our Emirati partners in Abu Dhabi, but also in Paris and Lens. Each in their own way, these three different Louvres perform two essential functions. At one level, they exhibit a variety of different cultures, thus participating in the construction of a universal culture. At another, they have each fostered a special relationship with their local culture.

The first thing to emphasise is that the Musée du Louvre finds itself in a paradoxical position in relation to French art. It is interesting to note that the Louvre has never referred to itself as a 'French national museum'. Much like the Vatican Museum in Rome and The State Hermitage Museum in St Petersburg, the palace in which the Louvre is situated was once the centre of power in France. Being so closely wedded to the architecture of French nationhood in this way has allowed the Louvre to avoid the question of how it defines and relates to French national art. In 2012, however, the Louvre came out from behind its walls for the first time to settle in Lens. That compelled the museum's management to reflect on the Louvre's identity, beyond its affiliation with the palace and its history of power.

With that in mind, it is worth briefly going over the Louvre's complex history. The transformation of the Louvre Palace into a museum was contrived during the reigns of Louis XV and Louis XVI. Displaying the royal collections, it was hoped, might 'regenerate' French art, which was then thought to be in decline. Reinforcing knowledge of the great masters of the past was believed to be the key to stimulating French production in the present, which at the time was thought to be expressionless.

Yet, paradoxically, when the museum opened in 1793, in the midst of the Revolutionary period, the eighteenth-century French artists' dream of renewing French art led to much of that art being dismissed. Conceived and directed by artists, and primarily opened for the benefit of artists, the Louvre quickly re-established its link with power and underwent radical transformation. During the Napoleonic conquests, it came to house the artistic treasures of Europe. Indeed, from 1804 it was even called the Musée Napoléon.

Having been established in a historical seat of power, the museum was inevitably invested with political significance. Still, it refused to be a museum of French art. In fact, it contains relatively little French art. It contains neither French furniture nor French sculpture (which is presented in the Musée des Monuments Français, which Alexandre Lenoir set up in a former convent opposite the Louvre), and sent its collections of contemporary French painting to Versailles. Indeed, the Louvre did not exhibit new French painting; that mission fell instead to the Salon Carré, a brief annual exhibition. What was shown in the Louvre at the start of the nineteenth century, then? Essentially, it exhibited the nucleus of the royal collections, which is to say Roman sculpture (on the ground floor) and Italian painting (upstairs). Historically, therefore, the heart of the Louvre was Italian and this remains true today.

However, the range of the Louvre collections progressively expanded to encompass the world's different cultures. This was endorsed by academic research spurred in particular by the Académie des Inscriptions et Belles-Lettres, which promoted the work of the museum's curators. Research was therefore an important wellspring behind the Louvre's development. This can be seen in the museum's inclusion of Greek art. The arrival of the *Vénus de Milo* in 1821 announced the creation of the first gallery devoted to 'early Greek art.' In this way, the Louvre broke with the general notion of 'antique art' inherited from the Enlightenment. Then, in 1827, an Egyptian gallery was created followed by the world's first Assyrian gallery in 1847. It should be pointed out that the Louvre's opening up to Egypt and the Middle East was prompted by an interest in European culture's biblical roots. It was initially the Holy Scriptures and biblical archaeology, not a search for beautiful objects, that led the museum to dedicate new galleries to these first non-European cultures. Gradually this curiosity extended to embrace all world cultures, with the Louvre's collections broadening to include Mexican and American galleries.

During this same period, however, French art made its entry into the museum through two developments. The first was a profound change in the nature of the Louvre's collections during the nineteenth century. The closure of the Museum of French Monuments and the Museum of Contemporary Artists at the Luxembourg Palace meant that the Louvre came to accommodate their collections of French painting and sculpture. In addition, the Museum of Modern Sculpture was established in the Galerie d'Angoulême in 1824. From an administrative point of view, though, its independence was limited, for it remained accountable to the Antiques Department until 1893. Artworks were gradually moved from the Luxembourg Palace to the Louvre as their makers died. For an artist's work to be exhibited at the Louvre meant that they were welcomed into something of an artistic pantheon. The most famous example of this canonisation process was Delacroix's *Liberty Leading the People*, which was displayed in the Louvre in 1874. In consequence, the Louvre became the world's largest museum of French painting, sculpture, and *objets d'art*.

The second development was concomitant with, and even a result of, the broadened scope of the collections. I am referring to the progressive division of disciplines, which led to the creation of independent museums outside the Louvre Palace. This process of dispersal began in 1862, when Napoleon III announced his desire to establish the National Archaeological Museum in Saint-Germain-en-Laye. This underlines the fact that the Louvre has never represented all of the cultures that have existed on French territory under one roof. As such, it is quite unlike the remarkable Archaeological Museum in Madrid, which encompasses the broad variety of Iberian cultures. Indeed, due to a lack of physical space in the Palace, several of the Louvre's collections would be established elsewhere. Beginning at the end of the nineteenth century and continuing through the twentieth, some non-European collections were moved, followed by its holdings in modern art.

The history of the Louvre can thus be seen as a long process of pruning. Today, the non-European collections are held in the Musée du Quai Branly—Jacques Chirac de Paris and the Musée National des Arts Asiatiques Guimet (National Museum of Asian Arts Guimet, Paris). The creation of the Musée d'Orsay deprived the Louvre of the art of the second half of the nineteenth and early twentieth centuries, separating it definitively from contemporary and modern art. Ultimately, this long and complex history has, through this process of subtraction, come to delineate the sphere of the Louvre's collections and thus limit its claim to universality. The core of its Antiquities collection, for example, essentially pertains to the Mediterranean world. The Department of Near Eastern Antiquities extends, however, as far as Anatolia, Central Asia, and the Iranian plateau. Although the Department of Islamic Art brings together cultures from roughly the same territories, it includes little relating to Asian Islamic cultures—those of Indonesia, for example. Many of these gaps result from the progressive shrinking of the Louvre's collections, such that they now revolve around European art of the medieval and modern periods up until the seventeenth century. At its heart, the Louvre has three main areas of focus: the art of France, Italy, and the Low Countries (Flanders and Holland). We have to admit that, when it comes to the eighteenth and nineteenth centuries, the Louvre's collections are almost exclusively French.

The Louvre's claim to universality may be diminished, but this is compensated by the fact that today its visitors come from around the world. In 2018, we welcomed over ten million visitors, of whom less than a third were French. Breaking down the range of nationalities, it would appear that the Louvre is an important destination for Americans, with more than a million visitors arriving from the United States each year. The second and much more recent phenomenon, which hardly existed ten years ago, is the large presence of Chinese people. Currently we receive 800,000 visitors from China annually. It is also an important museum for Brazilian, British, German, and Spanish visitors, among others. This international public often questions the universality of the Louvre. Our Brazilian and Chinese visitors ask, "But where is the Chinese/Brazilian art in the Louvre, the universal museum?" What they discover instead is a palace, a centre of French power that represents part of the history of France's relationship with the world.

The former president Jacques Chirac was acutely aware of the museum's diminished universality. So aware of it, in fact, that he sought to reestablish the Louvre's global scope. In 2000, he requested the creation of a museum of the arts of the cultures of Africa, Oceania, Asia and the Americas, within the Louvre Palace. This is now a branch of the Musée du Quai Branly and housed in the Pavillon des Sessions, which is one of the most beautiful parts of the Musée du Louvre. With it, President Chirac wished to restore 'the equal dignity of cultures', to use his rather political expression. The advertising campaign for this new venture was very interesting. It showed individual objects alongside the tag 'Je suis au Louvre', as though the objects themselves were speaking. 'I represent this culture', they seemed to say, 'and I have the right to be displayed in the Louvre'.

Louvre-Lens, or, the Louvre differently

To conclude, I would like to relate an experience that had a very powerful effect on the Louvre's staff: the creation of a museum in Lens, a city about 200 kilometres to the north of Paris. For the first time, the goal was to present the Louvre's collections outside of the Palace. This provided the opportunity for us to ask ourselves: does the Louvre exist outside of the Louvre Palace? How might it change when removed from its proximity to French political power and its architectural expression? These questions found a reply, first in Lens and then in Abu Dhabi. And the very idea of what the Louvre is has been transformed in the process.

Lens lies in a very distinct part of France, the Hauts-de-France region, which has been badly affected by deindustrialisation and poverty. The city has a high rate of unemployment. What did it entail to create a museum with claim to universality in an area that has been lacerated industrially, socially and economically? The danger to be avoided, of course, was condescension and arrogance, the suggestion that a Parisian institution rather than the local population was imposing its vision of what the city needed The conception of the project was thus complex but stimulating. We presented collections from the Louvre in a single and completely open space of 3,000 square metres that we call the "Galerie du Temps" (Time Gallery). All of the Louvre's collections are represented there, so that the presentation forms a small Louvre of about 200 objects. Many challenges had to be met: how should objects made from different materials and to a variety of scales be presented together? How should works requiring different conservation conditions be presented in the same way and with the same lighting? How is it possible to bring out the links between works from different cultures that are usually exhibited separately? How, for example, should one accentuate the relations between Egyptian art and the Assyrian, Greek, and Roman civilisations? In addressing these questions, we searched for what unites the cultures presented at the Louvre rather than what differentiates them. Composing a continuous art historical narrative in a single gallery required a completely new selection from and presentation of the Louvre's collections.

Can a museum exist without collections? Can a museum exist without a narrative? In the Louvre in Paris, such fundamental questions are no longer asked. In Lens, however, we needed to establish a history of art that, far from being composed of divisions, revealed continuities. Showing Islamic art in all its wealth and beauty required display-ing its relations with Europe, but also with the art of Central Asia, Africa, and China—areas that do not feature prominently in the Louvre's holdings. Accordingly, in bringing this narrative of art historical continuities to light, we presented numerous examples of the reuse or recurrence of artistic motifs and the diffusion of techniques.

During this exercise, it became apparent to us that the heart of the collections in the Musée du Louvre dates from the period between 1630 and 1670: the generation of Rembrandt, Rubens, Poussin, Velázquez, and other great artists. During the creation of many museums in the eighteenth century, this period was singled out as a golden age of European art. When we statistically represented the collections in a single space of the Louvre-Lens, this over-representation of the mid-seventeenth century was very ev-ident. This prominence of early modern art is the outcome of a political desire to make Poussin and his generation a high point of European art on the part of Louis XIV and traditional historians of French art. In constructing the new museum at Lens, we had to remain conscious of the fact that the museum's collection was the product of this particular history.

Another challenge was to tell that history in a very distinct regional site. This was not a simple task. Indeed, the Louvre's collections come to a halt in the mid-nineteenth cen-tury: the exact moment that the city of Lens grew into an industrial centre, stimulated by coal mining. Leaving that historical coincidence aside, we responded to the challenge of engaging with Lens by setting up the exhibition programme. A geographical cross-roads, Lens has a long history marked by exchange and conflict. The city lies in a densely populated basin, with Luxembourg, much of Belgium, and parts of the Netherlands and England all within a 200-kilometre radius. Building on these broad European con-nections, Louvre-Lens put on an exhibition titled *The Europe of Rubens*. It presented the Flemish artist's life and work, following his travels between courts in Italy, Paris, and London. Similarly, another exhibition named *The Disasters of War*, focused on the bloody history shared by these lands during the first and second world wars. Both exhi-bitions emphasised the importance of world heritage as it has been created or conserved in the region. In addition, the Glass Pavilion has hosted a cycle of exhibitions organised by local curators so as to highlight the region's distinct cultural legacies.

It was only with this experience of establishing the Louvre-Lens behind us that the Agence France-Muséums took up the challenge of meeting the expectations of our Emirati partners in our conception of Louvre Abu Dhabi. Clearly, in the absence of ei-ther the central Louvre or Louvre-Lens, Louvre Abu Dhabi would have turned out very differently. In prompting us to display our collections into relation a markedly different region, for the first time, the Louvre-Lens helped us define what the Musée du Louvre is without reference to the Palace and at the service of a completely different territory. In Paris, Lens, and Abu Dhabi, the Louvre has had the opportunity to give three different responses to the challenges faced by the museum world in the span of less than thirty years. Three places, three collections, three buildings, and three different audiences, but the same question: how can universality be served by highlighting local heritage and cultures?

PART 2

GLOBALISATION

AND

SOCIETIES

Introduction

Universality, Globalisation, and Museums: Narratives of Material Cultures

Rose-Marie Mousseaux

Acting as interfaces among conserved artefacts, knowledge gained from research, and the curiosity of museum visitors, museum professionals have seen their role evolve over the past few decades. As H. E. Shaikha Mai bint Mohammed al Khalifa rightly reminds us, this change has to do with the fact that cultural administrators must now take account of new behavioural trends associated with globalisation. Today, more people travel the world than ever before. When it comes to providing access to information and culture, then, the appetites of diverse multicultural communities must be accommodated. Mai bint Mohammed Al Khalifa is the President of the Bahrain Authority for Culture and Antiquities, which has played a pioneering role in developing cultural policy in the Gulf region over the past few decades. Indeed, the Sultanate of Bahrain stands as a strong example of how to construct a well-thought-out approach to navigating the relationships among heritage, the local community, and global tourism.

The chapters presented in this second part of the volume explore the ways in which globalisation processes have reshaped research on past societies, especially with regard to historical interlinkages among heritage sites at both the local and international levels. Tracing ceramics trading networks during Roman and modern periods, Martin Pitts reveals how artefacts constitute a crucial vector in the dissemination of cultural practices. Studying trade and objects-in-motion in this way highlights how societies are interconnected, whether that be from a spatial perspective, in that Pitts indicates trade links between continents, or a temporal perspective, in that past forms of globalisation shed light on the present.

Looking back on the history of museums over the centuries, Hervé Inglebert analyses the ways in which museums have constructed narratives of universal, world, and global history. Told by means of selecting artefacts and artworks and exhibiting them in specific geographical and historical contexts, these narratives inevitably reflected the cultural assumptions and conceptions that prevailed at the time. Informed by cultural comparisons and theories of global history, Inglebert's conceptional analysis of universal museums underlines the singularity of Louvre Abu Dhabi, which is based on an inclusive, indeed universal vision of the history of the arts.

In bringing interconnected material cultures into contact with both one another and viewers, contemporary museums must address the fundamental problem of how to construct narratives of globalisation and material culture that will be understood. When addressing a multicultural audience, museum professionals must weave a narrative that communicates both accurate information about an artefact and kaleidoscopic interpretations of its significance. The process of exhibiting an artefact must be multifaceted if it is to occasion education and experience, pleasure and wonder, surprise and recognition in its viewers. Indeed, if set up in this way, physical encounters with museum artefacts can trigger forms of curiosity, questioning, and intellectual openness appropriate to the contemporary period of global intercultural connection.

Preserving Pasts, Investing in Futures

The Developing Landscape of Bahrain's Museums

H.E. Shaikha Mai bint Mohammed Al Khalifa

Culture reminds people of their shared heritage, reaching across social divides. It is also an engine that drives economic growth. For these reasons and more, the Arabian Gulf is fortunate to host such a large number of museums. Most recently, Louvre Abu Dhabi has become an exciting new tourist destination in the region. A feat of architectural engineering, the museum is a monument to world heritage, preserving and celebrating art and cultural traditions relating to all peoples and regions of the planet.

I am proud, therefore, to mark the first anniversary of this important new museum by contributing to this book. I take this essay as an occasion to reflect on the distinctive landscape of Bahrain's museums. The Bahrain National Museum, the country's first national museum, celebrated its thirtieth anniversary in late 2018. The collections move through the successive periods of Bahrain's history, from Dilmun hegemony, through the Hellenistic period, to the Portuguese incursions of the sixteenth century. Built to international standards, the museum showcases archaeological discoveries pertaining to these and a range of other periods.

Yet museums should do much more than simply present artefacts and host exhibitions. One of the most fruitful ways to approach museums, I would suggest, is to see them in terms of *experiences*. From the beginning of my work in the administration of cultural heritage, whether at the national, regional, or global level, I have emphasised how museums should seek to bring together and actively involve everyone with a stake in the cultural field. Indeed, as President of the Bahrain Authority for Culture and Antiquities, I am keen to stress that if museums are to function as major cultural hubs, then they must develop a variety of outreach activities and host diverse visiting exhibitions. With this approach in mind, the Bahrain National Museum has initiated a series of visiting exhibitions, sending significant portions of the collection—some dating back as far as Dilmun civilization—to Saint Petersburg's State Hermitage Museum, the Arab World Institute, and other museums. This forms part of Bahrain's wider plans to open up and present its cultural treasures to the world. Bahrain may be geographically small, but it is rich in history and antiquities. Given the remarkable concentration of Bahraini history and culture, we have sought to extend it to a wider set of locations. Indeed, the Bahrain National Museum is far from being the only destination available to those interested in the history of Bahrain and the wider region. Thanks to an ambitious programme of investment in culture, the country now hosts a variety of cultural sites.

The first round of investment in the cultural sector began a decade ago. In collaboration with banks and other private companies, Bahrain set out to develop its local cultural infrastructure. The first project, the Qala'at Al-Bahrain (Bahrain Fort) Site Museum, opened in 2008. The reason that it is referred to as the Qala'at Al-Bahrain site is that the fort in itself is less important than the archaeological site on which it rests. Indeed, the hill presents a kind of palimpsest or layered archive of the region's successive historical periods, including ruins that still lie deep underground. I should stress—as all those concerned with antiquities would—that what we have discovered Qala'at Al-Bahrain so far represents a mere five percent of the treasures still to be unearthed at the site.

Our work with museums, then, focuses on archaeological sites. Indeed, following the opening of the Qala'at Al-Bahrain Site Museum, the Authority for Culture and Antiquities established two further museums. The first is a small museum in the city of Riffa, which also has a historical fort; the second is based in the Khamis Mosque, which dates back to the third century AH and displays artefacts from the Islamic periods. We are trying to move forward with one museum project, for example, on the site of the Saar Settlement, which dates back some 5,000 years. The Japanese architect Tadao Ando has designed a museum building for the site, which has the potential to serve as a major destination for those interested in the early Dilmun period, especially given its proximity to the Arab Regional Centre for World Heritrage, established as a UNESCO Category 2 Centre in 2008. As such, Bahrain now serves Arab countries in the fields of urban heritage conservation, antiquities, and conservation at large.

Inevitably, museum visitors have varied tastes. A suite of flexible and engaging cultural activities are therefore crucial in attracting different audiences. As part of its diversification strategy, the Bahrain Authority for Culture and Antiquities launched the Food is Culture initiative, which put renowned artists and chefs in dialogue with one another. The results were showcased in public spaces at the Bahrain National Museum, thereby attracting a new group of visitors to the museum. We also put on a music festival in the Bahrain National Museum. In this way, we hoped to signal that the museum, far from being restricted to displaying antiquities or hosting historical exhibitions, can serve as a centre for a broad range of cultural activities, targeted at diverse audiences. Community engagement is key for museums. Museum facilities, such as a café or boutique, also help attract certain audiences. Providing visitors with accessible information and engaging experiences, such amenities are a key part of what tempts people to visit museums.

In seeking to engage communities, the Authority for Culture and Antiquities is also looking to build new museums. One key project currently under development is a children's museum, which is intended to teach new generations about love, community, and a wider set of themes to prepare them for the future. Above all, it will show them that culture can be a form of resistance and source of inspiration. Through culture, societies can promote beauty, progress, knowledge and education as well as compassion for one another and mutual understanding across cultures. Through culture, people and communities can present their desired image to the world, reaching out across national differences to promote a more vibrant future. Hence the need for museums to foster cultural awareness and engage energetically with new groups of visitors.

This leads to my central theme: the importance of investing in culture and museums. One of the most recent and striking examples of such investment in Bahrain is the Pearling Path Visitor Centre. Inaugurated in 2018, this new museum is devoted to the history of the Bahraini pearling industry. Perhaps the region's largest open-air museum, it extends over three-and-a-half kilometres. It tells the story of pearling, beginning with the underwater *hayrat* (oyster beds), which divers once scoured for pearls. The path then leads visitors through a series of urban heritage buildings and elements that were once engaged in different aspects of pearling. The Nukhidhah House belonged to Jassim Ajaj, the captain for a pearling vessel; the Al-Ghous House was home to generations of divers; the Badr Ghulum House was home to a practitioner of folk medicine. Along the path are also a number of buildings reflecting the rich and diverse cultural heritage of Bahrain, such as Dar al-Muharraq dedicated to the pearl diving music known as *Fdjiri*. Indeed, music was an essential source of entertainment for the divers, who were often away from their homes and families for three months at a time.

With its distinctively weightless architecture and openness to the elements, the Pearling Path Visitor Centre is a significant new addition to Bahrain's museal landscape. As such, it is a boon to the Authority for Culture and Antiquities, especially in its efforts to promote Bahraini cultural heritage at global events, such as the World Expo in Dubai in 2020. Investing in museums does not always mean the erection of new institutions, however. On the contrary, it is just as crucial that museums renew and enhance existing collections. With this in mind, the Bahrain National Museum recently initiated plans to renovate its galleries. Of these, we hope that the Hall of Dilmun Graves, the first display of archaeological models of the burial mounds, listed as a World Heritage site and thus recognised as a key destination for cultural tourism. The evidence suggests that this would boost cultural tourism by twenty-five percent.

Naturally, investment decisions in the cultural sector are driven by economic as well as cultural rationales. In promoting and developing museums and other historical sites, the Authority for Culture and Antiquities aims to attract visitors who are especially interested in cultural tourism. People in this group not only spend money in the countries they visit; they are also likely to share their experiences of cultural heritage sites as they travel the world. When Cambodia renovated the world-famous temple Angkor Wat, for example, it attracted 10,000 visitors daily, thus rejuvenating the surrounding area's economy. Accordingly, in developing cultural sites we strive to revive both historical landmarks and the neighbourhoods that have grown up around them. We hope that this will be the case with the Pearling Path Visitor Centre. It is the communities living and working in proximity to historical sites who will ultimately reap the returns on Bahrain's investment in museums and culture. If ancient cities are to retain their significance in the twenty-first century, then they must become attractive destinations in the global cultural economy.

In this short essay, I hope to have conveyed the Authority for Culture and Antiquities' key emphases and concerns in developing Bahrain's cultural landscape. Through an ambitious investment programme, involving the foundation of a range of new museums and renovation of existing ones, we have sought to engage diverse new visitors and boost local economies. In this way, cultural policy plays a crucial role in positioning Bahrain in relation to history, culture, and economy of the wider region, indeed the world.

Premodern Globalisations

Cultural Connectivity and Objects-in-Motion in Ancient Worlds

Martin Pitts

Objects are at the heart of both museal practice and historical thought more generally. To a very significant degree, historical narratives and explanations rest upon the interpretation of commodities, documents, tools, and other material remains—in a word, *objects*—received from the past. With the exception of oral testimony and architectural form, objects are the very matter of history. This was the case in the nineteenth and twentieth centuries, when scholars and curators were engaged primarily with national histories, and it remains true today as they turn towards questions of cross-cultural contacts and world heritage. No exploration of current forms of museology would be complete, it follows, without a reflexive account of the place and significance of objects in the contemporary practice of history.

In this context, this chapter makes the case for a new, object-orientated practice of global history. Critically applying ideas of globalisation, it places objects and connectivity at the centre of historical analysis. I begin with a brief summary of research on the relationship between globalisation and history, before considering the advantages of thinking about ancient societies and their material culture through the lens of globalisation. This is followed by a discussion of some examples, which illuminate what is at stake for thinking about and visualising objects-in-motion in the connected past.

Rethinking globalisation in deep history

What is globalisation? What are its effects? Can a relatively recent concept, coined to describe developments in the last century, have relevance for the more distant past? To answer these questions, it is instructive to look at three key definitions of globalisation proposed by social scientists shortly after the concept's rise to prominence in popular and academic discourse in the 1990s:

> the intensification of worldwide social relations which link distant localities in such a way that local happenings are shaped by events occurring miles away and vice-versa.[1]

> a social process in which the constraints of geography on economic, political, social and cultural arrangements recede, in which people become increasingly aware that they are receding and in which people act accordingly.[2]

> a world of disjunctive flows [that] produce problems that manifest themselves in intensely local forms but have contexts that are anything but local.[3]

These three definitions describe a common set of effects. In essence, globalisation entails connections among hitherto separate or poorly integrated regions, the overcoming of physical obstacles posed by distance through technological development, the creation of new relationships, and fostering of global consciousness. In turn, these effects result in a series of changes that are manifest in different ways in local societies and cultures. Whereas much of the social scientific literature on this topic links globalising processes to the modern or postmodern periods, this does not mean that these phenomena did not exist in the past. Indeed, there are numerous examples in historical written sources that attest to the existence of very similar processes long before the inventions of the motor car and the jet airliner. Take this passage from Polybius, for example, which describes the implications arising from the Roman victory over Carthage in the Second Punic War at the end of the third century BCE:

> ...in earlier times the world's history had consisted, so to speak, of a series of unrelated episodes, the origins and results of each being as widely separated as their localities, but from this point onwards history becomes an organic whole: the affairs of Italy and of Africa are connected with those of Asia and of Greece, and all events bear a relationship and contribute to a single end.[4]

The effects that Polybius sets out here, which follow the 'global moment' of Rome's military success in dominating the Mediterranean, are remarkably similar to recent definitions of globalisation. In emphasising how local events are shaped by those taking place in distant localities, the passage chimes especially with Giddens's account. These transhistorical resonances underline how globalisation specialists working in fields such as sociology, geography, and economics often reason from a perspective of historical myopia. Their implicit assumptions about the connectivity unique to modernity are not critically examined. Having joined the globalisation debate late in the game, historians and archaeologists are now scrutinising the concept afresh with their own data and beginning to forge different views.[5]

Can we really talk about globalisation in ancient history? There are many conflicting views as to when globalisation began, often depending on the academic discipline to which a given scholar belongs.[6] The three main positions are these.[7] The first perspective is that of the 1990s social scientist, who understands globalisation as a unique characteristic of the modern or contemporary world. This position allows little room for temporal depth, envisioning globalisation as beginning sometime between the 'discovery' of the Americas in 1492 and the 1970s. It also assumes that globalisation must be literally 'global,' that is, it should encompass or affect the whole planet. There are several weaknesses to this position. Above all, it is incredibly *presentist*, paying little attention to the origins of globalising processes or analogous developments in the past. Indeed, it overlooks historical civilisations and systems that, despite not being literally 'global,' had a significant pan-regional reach.

Position two, which is much more helpful in looking at ancient societies, examines the phenomenon in the terms established by world-systems analysis.[8] These approaches emphasise the deeper historical genealogies of globalisation, sometimes going back as far as the origins of civilisation and urbanism. However, there is often an attempt to draw a single evolutionary lineage of globalisation from antiquity to modernity. The implication that globalisation is a constant evolutionary force is also problematic. In particular, it is a hinderance when trying to account for diverse historical circumstances and outcomes, especially periods in which connectivity was eroded by tendencies towards regionalism and the collapse of unifying world empires.

Position three, which is inherently more helpful for archaeologists and historians, is to think about not just one process of globalisation, but rather multiple, plural globalisations. This perspective is premised upon the argument that world history is punctuated by surges in connectivity of such intensity and scale that they produce similar effects and experiences to those of modern globalisation, as described in the quotes at the beginning of this paper: the fostering of new forms of 'global' or pan-regional culture and consciousness.[9] This position provides a more critical perspective on globalisation and has a greater historical depth. When considering Roman and Mediterranean history, for example, we might conceive the period from c. 200 BCE to 200 CE as an especially striking 'punctuation of connectivity.' This phase of trans-regional contact was of no small significance in world history; indeed, it transformed a wide range of societies. Still, not all instances of premodern connectivity meet the criteria set by globalisation theory. We should be cautious, then, about building equivalent narratives of globalisation in the more distant past without sufficient evidence for long-distance exchange and meaningful participation in forms of 'global' culture.

The methodological advantages of globalisation thinking

Accepting that we can apply ideas of globalisation to ancient history and the deep past, what are the benefits of doing so? Although my observations in this section are confined to the Roman period, the implications are wide-ranging. Indeed, I would suggest that notions of globalisation are eminently good to think with when studying any period, whether they apply directly or not.

Long before the term globalisation was coined, historians and archaeologists of ancient Rome developed the concept of *Romanisation*. For the most part, it was used to help explain the cultural, political, and religious changes that took place in conquered and annexed provinces of the Roman empire. In essence, the concept of Romanisation posits Rome as the centre and standard against which all other cultures and contexts are assessed. It envisions change as spreading uniformly outwards from Rome to its conquered provinces, like the ripples formed when a stone is dropped into a pond. This deliberately simplistic characterisation of Romanisation emphasises its centre-periphery logics; few would subscribe to this way of thinking in the twenty-first century. More nuanced perspectives prevail in contemporary scholarship. Andrew Wallace-Hadrill's metaphorical account, for example, has Rome functioning as a 'heart' for the 'circulation system' of its empire.[10] This model begins with a diastolic phase, much like a heart drawing in blood from the body, in which Rome sucks in a large part of the wealth, commodities, objects, and ideas from across its newly founded empire. Crucially, this phase acknowledges the essential formative influence of the 'periphery' on the 'centre,' especially when it came to the eastern empire, including Greece and Egypt. This way of thinking helps to explain how what we call 'Roman culture' came into being through constant internal and external dialogues, rather than appearing suddenly fully-formed. A second systolic phase sees the oxygenated and unified 'Roman' blood pumped back out to the provinces in the form of 'Romanisation.' There, societies engage with it in different ways, producing a plurality of experiences of 'becoming Roman.'[11] Both patterns of circulation occur constantly through Roman history, ensuring that what is understood as 'Roman', in both the centre and periphery, underwent constant transformation.

What is wrong with this metaphor, and how can globalisation improve on the model? Despite its complexities and sensitivity to historical change, the heart metaphor is flawed in the key respect that it entails a centre-periphery dynamic. Rome retains its place as *the* essential mediating nexus for all kinds of cultural changes. Globalisation adds a new dimension to our understanding by decentring Rome. This is especially productive when it comes to studying how cultural change occurred in provincial societies and at the fringes of empire, as well as important transformations in the realm of objects and material culture. Decentring Rome essentially entails thinking about the entire Roman world and its neighbours as a *polycentric periphery*.[12] In this light, every centre in the empire can be seen as a mini-heart in its own right. From cities to villages, each node has some capacity for influence, albeit in a more limited and localised sense. This reconceptualisation allows for significant interactions that took place outside Rome's core sphere of influence, recognising a wide variety of periphery-periphery interactions alongside the established centre-periphery dynamic.

In addition to decentring Rome, a second major benefit of thinking in terms of globalisation is that it moves beyond the influence of methodological nationalism in studies of the Roman world. Again, this has particular ramifications for how objects from the period are interpreted and understood. In archaeology, material from the Roman provinces is approached first and foremost from a national or provincial perspective. Take the example of 'Roman Britain'. For many decades, 'Roman Britain' has formed a convenient unit of historical analysis. In part, this arose from the practicalities of national legislative and curatorial systems for objects found in the modern administrative area of the United Kingdom. The term also has a substantive basis in that it recognises how in the Roman period, too, Britain was also administered as a distinct island-province, namely Britannia. The situation is similar in many other parts of the Roman world. Despite the convenience of treating Roman provinces as discrete units in this way, it makes little sense from the point of view of historical reality. Indeed, in the closely connected Roman empire, there were no hard borders between provinces that constrained movement in the modern sense. Thinking through the lens of globalisation, then, helps regain a sense of the bigger picture. Moving away from the idea of isolated societies and sites loosely impacted by distant Rome, it instead draws attention to vibrant networks of connected localities.

A third major advantage to thinking in terms of globalisation is that it allows objects to take centre stage. Decentring Rome entails taking objects-in-motion and their impacts on societies seriously. In turn, this creates new perspectives for seeing and exploring myriad cultural networks and movements of people and objects in the past.[13] This object-centred perspective challenges prevailing ideas of imperialism in (Roman) history and archaeology, in which the state and military are often accorded disproportionate importance.

Objects-in-motion and globalisation

Moving in the second half of this chapter, I wish to give a couple of examples that illuminate the role of objects-in-motion as both indicators and drivers of globalisation. My first example comes not from the Roman period, but from modern northwest Europe. In particular, I have in mind Chinese export porcelain tea cups and saucers, and their impact on European culture from the seventeenth century. Today, many of us take tea cups and saucers for granted. From a historical perspective, however, our modern experience may be seen as a long-term consequence of global histories defined by objects-in-motion. Investigating the origins of the mass consumption of cups and saucers in European societies in terms of globalisation, it follows, requires looking at the long-term circulation and consumption patterns of Chinese export porcelain. Through this export market, tea cups and saucers were permanently introduced into European objectscapes. Figure 1 is derived from the records of the Dutch East India Company in the seventeenth century. It shows a snapshot of the various kinds of Chinese export

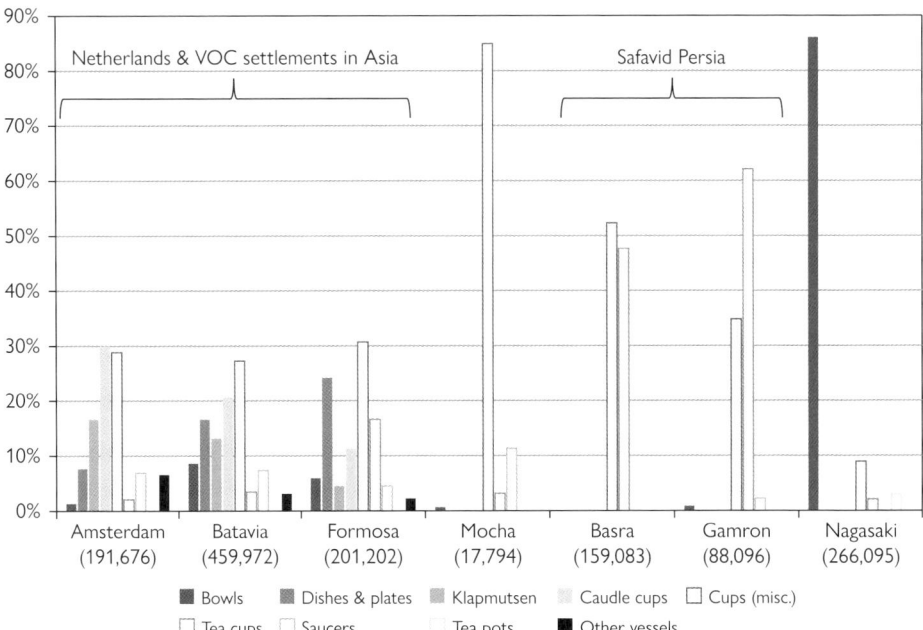

Figure 1. Chinese porcelain shipped by the Dutch East India Company c. 1640-1649 (total no. of vessels per location given in brackets). Data from Volker (1954).
© Martin Pitts.

porcelain that the Dutch were shipping to various localities around the world, including Amsterdam and Dutch-controlled territories in the Far East, but also Nagasaki and locations in the Middle East.

The records illustrate how, in a connected world, mass-produced commodities such as porcelain in a series standardised shapes and styles can illuminate the distinct characters of different consumer societies. Indeed, they show that in Europe and the Dutch-controlled Asian bases, the Dutch are importing every kind of porcelain shape they can get their hands on: china-mania is in full swing and traders are not really privileging particular kinds of vessels at this time. The company records indicate that in the Middle East, though, the Dutch are selling tea cups and saucers, vessels that are predominantly concerned with the consumption of tea and, perhaps, coffee. Similarly, different shapes of porcelain are preferred in Japan, likely to cater for the distinct needs of the Japanese tea ceremony. By contrast, cups and saucers specified for tea make up a very small proportion of the total number of vessels imported into Amsterdam and elsewhere in northwestern Europe at this time. In large part, this is because tea had only just begun to be imported as a bulk commodity, and tea drinking had yet to be established as a middle-class pursuit.[14]

When porcelain first appeared in the Netherlands, consumers were less interested in what we now think of a quintessentially European practice of drinking tea than in acquiring and displaying Chinese porcelain from the other side of the world. Figure 2 shows that archaeological 'assemblages' or deposits of ceramics from Dutch towns in

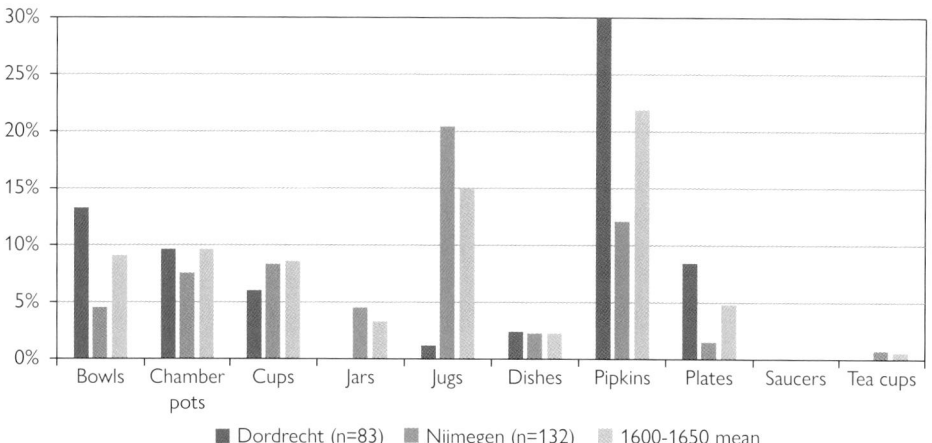

Figure 2. Ceramic assemblages from Dutch cities, c. 1600-1650. Data from Bartels (1999).
© Martin Pitts.

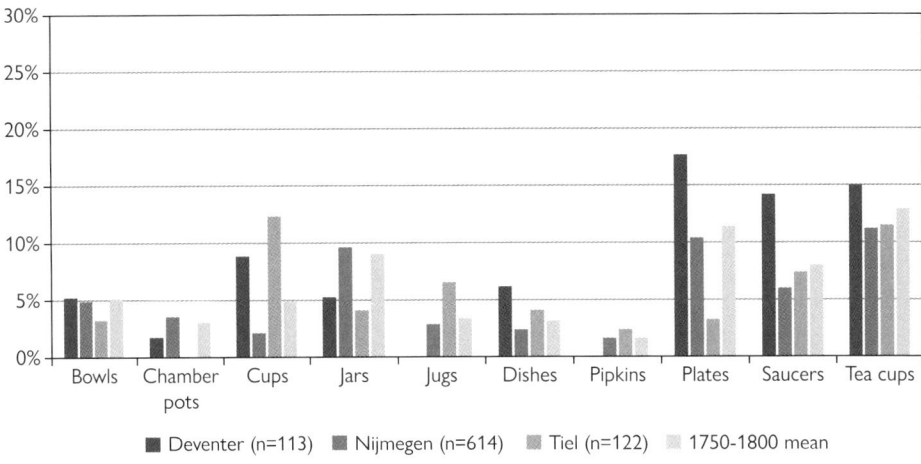

Figure 3. Ceramic assemblages from Dutch cities, c. 1750-1800. Data from Bartels (1999).
© Martin Pitts.

the early seventeenth century were statistically dominated by crude locally fashioned wares. Chamber pots, jugs, jars, and cooking vessels (tripod pipkins), these objects were well suited to consumption practices still rooted in the medieval era. Porcelain tea cups and dinner services do not really register. This is due partly to their limited availability at the time, and partly to their prestige status, which meant that they were better looked after. As such, porcelain items were less often broken and discarded alongside cheaper, more readily replaceable local pottery. If we fast-forward 100 to 150 years, however, a big transformation has taken place (fig. 3). Coarse local- and regionally-made vessels, which dominated the early seventeenth-century assemblages, are now in the minority. Together, plates, saucers, and teacups are now the biggest ceramic categories in urban assemblages.

How and why did this shift from coarse locally made pottery shapes to more refined plates, tea cups, and saucers come about? In the first place, we must consider that this transition would not have been possible in the eighteenth century without the circulation and importation of Chinese porcelain. Many of the new cups, saucers, and plates are, in fact, Chinese porcelain themselves. At this time, only a small proportion of vessels were made locally by European porcelain industries. In part, this was down to the fact the production process was still very expensive, although cruder wares imitating Chinese and Japanese porcelain (such as Delft wares) helped fill an important share of the mass market. This shift at the drinking end of the ceramic repertoire saw an increase in interest in tea cups and saucers, rather than the more diverse plethora of cups originally imported in the seventeenth century. A major clue as to why can be found by returning to figure 1. It shows how a preference for using the cup-and-saucer ensemble was already well established in the Middle East (most strikingly so at Mocha in contemporary Yemen, where it was probably used for coffee drinking). Further insights are hinted at, tantalisingly, by Dutch records from 1645, before the word 'saucer' properly entered European vocabularies. Seemingly dealing with early orders of saucers deemed likely to sell in Yemen, they highlighting their use for tea drinking among Turks:

> 50,000 flat small dishes as large as a tasting-dish without foot, some with and also some without a small rim as thick as a straw at the base, to be used to hand over thereon the small, fine, newly-devised tea-cups which nowadays is a habit among the Turks; together with the coffee-cups they could bring in 3 R. p.c., or 7500 reals.[15]

By the eighteenth century, it seems that the practice of cup-and-saucer use had been gradually appropriated by Europeans. Gradually, over the centuries, it came to be regarding as quintessentially European. This is just one example of how attending to objects can illuminate globalisation, and how objects-in-motion can have significant and long-lasting impacts on societies over the longer term.

For my second example I shall return to northwestern Europe in the Roman period to explore the possibility that objects-in-motion might have had analogous impacts in a different kind of globalising scenario. Although the northwestern Roman provinces of Britannia, Gallia Belgica, and Germania Inferior had more limited long-distance connections than Europe of the seventeenth and eighteenth centuries, a case can nevertheless be made for a surge in connectivity in the Roman period, as compared to the preceding Iron Age. What happens if, as in the case of Chinese porcelain in Europe discussed above, we explore the impact of objects-in-motion and pan-regional connections in the Roman context?

While nothing exactly like porcelain existed in the Roman world, a close analogy can be drawn with standardised and mass-produced *terra sigillata*, also known as Samian ware. Like porcelain, Samian ware was distributed extensively, well beyond its core production areas. Initially it spread through Italy in the last decades of the first century BCE, before large-scale production shifted to southern France in the early to mid-first century CE, most notably at La Graufesenque. The spread of *terra sigillata* has been seen as a major part of a new consumer revolution in the Roman northwest, in a manner comparable with the global cultural changes brought on by Chinese porcelain exports. In the course of this revolution, new objects enabled the spread of new kinds of social display (in this case dining practice), as an integral side-effect of a given society 'becoming Roman.'[16]

To explore the initial impact of *terra sigillata* in northwestern Europe, let us consider the contents of a cremation grave from St. Albans in southern Britain (fig. 4). The grave, which included the remains of a young adult of indeterminate sex, dates to the period between c. fifteen BCE and thirty CE, just before the region was formally conquered by Rome under the emperor Claudius in forty-three CE. The grave is modestly furnished. Indeed, at face value its contents are not especially remarkable, apart from a *terra sigillata* plate made in Lyon, which was particularly scarce in Britain at the time. However, closer inspection reveals that all four of the ceramic grave offerings owed something to connectivity: two beakers are local imitations of the very latest standardised designs in circulation from Gaul and Italy, while a third is an import from Reims in northern France. Taken together, these finds present a globalising scenario in which the design, production, and selection of objects were anything but local, deriving instead from multiple, distantly connected localities.[17] At the same time, it would be unreasonable to claim that the objects represent a conscious attempt by the buriers to present the dead as typically Roman. The dominance of large beaker vessels in this grave suggests instead that the buriers were emphasising the conspicuous consumption of alcohol (probably locally made beer), which was popular amongst many pre-Roman societies in northern Europe. As with the example of porcelain, moving objects do not always foster the spread of new practices straight away, especially when novel designs appear for the first time.

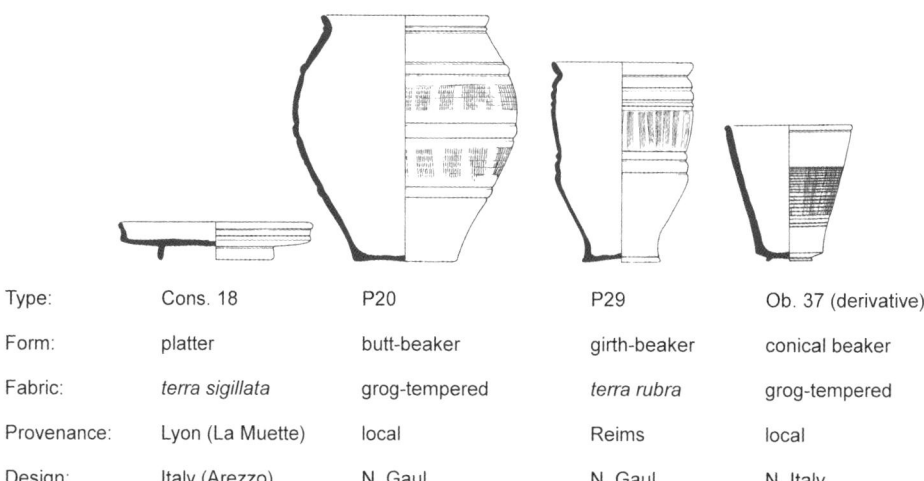

Type:	Cons. 18	P20	P29	Ob. 37 (derivative)
Form:	platter	butt-beaker	girth-beaker	conical beaker
Fabric:	*terra sigillata*	grog-tempered	*terra rubra*	grog-tempered
Provenance:	Lyon (La Muette)	local	Reims	local
Design:	Italy (Arezzo)	N. Gaul	N. Gaul	N. Italy

Figure 4. Finds from grave 328 at King Harry Lane, St. Albans (after Stead & Rigby 1989, 364).
© Martin Pitts.

Moving forward in time, I would like to juxtapose this burial with an analogous grave dug roughly a century later. The grave in question (fig. 5), which comes from a roadside cemetery just outside the city of Bavay, features the remains of an unsexed adult dating to the period between c. seventy and ninety CE. This time, the grave finds overwhelming suggest that the process of 'becoming Roman' is in full swing: three of the pottery vessels (two cups and a plate) are in *terra sigillata*, with a further plate of Mediterranean genealogy in locally-made *terra nigra*. In addition, there is a Roman-style grinding bowl or *mortarium*, in addition to an oil-lamp and glass flask, which may have originally contained perfumes.[18] Placed in a wider connected context, these objects align the grave ensemble with others around the Roman northwest in this period, in which local elites and their subordinates sought to appropriate styles of consumption previously associated more exclusively with Roman military communities in the region. A consideration of all of the finds in the grave, however, illustrates that a wholesale shift in identity had not yet occurred. The inclusion of fibulae or brooches was very much a hangover of later Iron Age funerary practice. This was scarce among grave ensembles associated with Roman colonial populations. Likewise, the black-grey *terra nigra* vessels (especially the jars of local genealogy) would certainly have been out of place at the dining tables of the top provincial elite at the time. In this way, the contents of the Bavay grave reflect not so much a desire to 'become Roman,' but rather slower rates of change among sub-elites, which drew upon elements of the circulating repertoire of 'global' objects, alongside material culture associated with more traditional forms of display.[19] This example further underlines the importance of studying the impacts of objects-in-motion as part of larger objectscapes. This enables historians and other scholars to appropriately characterise the effects of globalising processes in a given historical moment.

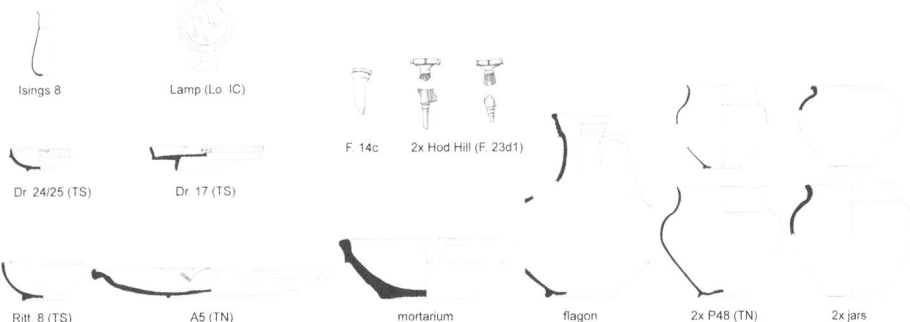

Figure 5. Objects from grave 135, Fache des Près Aulnoys cemetery, Bavay (after Loridant & Deru 2009, 160, Fig. 63). TS = *terra sigillata*; TN = *terra nigra*.
© Martin Pitts.

Conclusions

This paper has made three arguments: first, that it is possible to apply ideas of globalisation to the distant past, provided that it is done in a sensitive and critical manner; second, that doing so brings major conceptual and methodological benefits, especially in providing new insights into how past societies worked within wider connected cultural systems; and third, that to do justice to the idea of past globalisations we must put objects and material connections at the forefront of historical analysis. The examples I have discussed the second half of the chapter demonstrate not only how attending to objects-in-motion illuminates the fine-grain detail of ancient connectivity in a given historical moment. What is more, it shows how such objects drive longer-term changes in objectscapes and culture in their respective local societies. In both instances, an initial surge of interest in new kinds of objects, produced far away, eventually resulted in new kinds of objectscapes and practices centuries later. Although these new objects closely resembled items imported in the first major phases of cultural contact, they do so in innovative ways that demonstrate significant local agency. These patterns raise the provocative question of whether objects, rather than people, are the real catalysts of change in the connected past.

Notes

1   Anthony Giddens, *The Consequences of Modernity*, 64.
2   MalcomWaters, *Globalization*, 5.
3   Arjun Appadurai, 'Grassroots globalization and the research imagination', 6.
4   Polybius, *Histories,* 1.3.
5   On early modern history, see for example A. G. Hopkins, *Globalization in World History*; on Roman history and archaeology, see Martin Pitts and Miguel John Versluys, *Globalisation and the Roman World*; on world archaeology, see Tamar Hodos, *The Routledge Handbook of Archaeology and Globalization*.
6   This diversity of perspectives is usefully summarised in Nederveen Pieterse, *Globalization and Culture*, 7–25.
7   Here I following Jennings 2011, 3–18. See also Pitts and Versluys, 'Globalisation and the Roman world', 15–18.
8   See for example contributions in Barry K. Gills and William R. Thompson, *Globalization and Global History*.
9   Jennings 2011, 13–17; Pitts and Versluys, 'Globalisation and the Roman world', 15–18.

10   Andrew Wallace-Hadrill, *Rome's Cultural Revolution,* 361.

11   Woolf, *Becoming Roman.*

12   Nederveen Pieterse, 'Ancient Rome and globalisation'.

13   See in particular Versluys, 'Understanding objects in motion'; Pitts, *The Roman Object Revolution.*

14   Pitts, 'Globalization and China'.

15   T. Volker, *Porcelain and the Dutch East India Company*, 100.

16   Greg Woolf, *Becoming Roman*, 181–205.

17   Pitts, *The Roman Object Revolution*, 3.

18   Isings, 8.

19   Pitts, *The Roman Object Revolution*, 166–71.

Works Cited

Ancient sources
Polybius, *Histories*. Translated by Ian Stanley Scott-Kilvert. London: Penguin, 1979.

Modern sources
Appadurai, Arjun. 'Grassroots globalization and the research imagination'. In *Globalization*, edited by Arjun Appadurai, 1–21. London: Duke University Press, 2001.

Bartels, Michiel. *Steden in scherven. Vondsten uit beerputten in Deventer, Dordrecht, Nijmegen en Tiel (1250-1900)*. Zwolle: Stichting Promotie Archeologie, 1999.

Giddens, Anthony. *The Consequences of Modernity*. Stanford: Stanford University Press, 1990.

Gills, Barry K., and William R. Thompson, eds. *Globalization and Global History*. London: Routledge, 2006.

Hodos, Tamar, ed. *The Routledge Handbook of Archaeology and Globalization*. London: Routledge, 2017.

Hopkins, A. G., ed. *Globalization in World History*. London: Pimlico, 2002.

Loridant, Frédéric, and Xavier Deru. *Bavay. La nécropole Gallo-Romaine de 'La Fache des Près Aulnoys'*. Paris: Revue Du Nord, 2009.

Nederveen Pieterse, Jan. *Globalization and Culture: Global Mélange*. 3rd ed. Lanham: Rowman and Littlefield, 2015.

———. 'Ancient Rome and globalisation: Decentring Rome'. In *Globalisation and the Roman world: World history, connectivity and material culture*, edited by Martin Pitts and Miguel John Versluys, 225–39. Cambridge: Cambridge University Press, 2015.

Pitts, Martin, and Miguel John Versluys, eds. *Globalisation and the Roman world: World history, connectivity and material culture*. Cambridge: Cambridge University Press, 2015.

———, and Miguel John Versluys. 'Globalisation and the Roman world: perspectives and opportunities'. In *Globalisation and the Roman world. World history, connectivity and material culture*, edited by Martin Pitts and Miguel John Versluys, 3–31. Cambridge: Cambridge University Press, 2015.

———. 'Globalization and China: Materiality and Civilité in Post-Medieval Europe'. In *The Routledge Handbook of Archaeology and Globalization*, edited by Tamar Hodos, 566–79. London: Routledge, 2017.

———. *The Roman Object Revolution: Objectscapes and Intra-Cultural Connectivity in Northwest Europe*. Amsterdam: Amsterdam University Press, 2019.

Stead, Ian Mathieson, and Valery Rigby. *Verulamium: The King Harry Lane site*. London: English Heritage, 1989.

Versluys, Miguel John. 'Understanding objects in motion. An archaeological dialogue on Romanisation'. *Archaeological Dialogues* 21, no. 1 (2014): 1–20.

Volker, T. *Porcelain and the Dutch East India Company*. Leiden: Brill, 1954.

Wallace-Hadrill, Andrew. *Rome's Cultural Revolution*. Cambridge: Cambridge University Press, 2008.

Waters, Malcom. *Globalization*. 2nd ed. London: Routledge, 2001.

Woolf, Greg. *Becoming Roman: The Origins of Provincial Civilization in Gaul*. Cambridge: Cambridge University Press, 1998.

Universal History, Global History, and Universal Museums

Hervé Inglebert

Introduction

This volume celebrates the first anniversary of the inauguration of Louvre Abu Dhabi. As such, it is first and foremost a contribution to contemporary museology. Louvre Abu Dhabi, though, aspires to be a universal museum, a museum that exhibits a universal history of artistic forms. *Worlds in a Museum*, it follows, has implications not just for scholars of contemporary art, but for historians of all periods.

As a specialist in the cultural evolution that occurred during Late Antiquity, I have studied Greek and Roman histories that describe the totality of the past and Christian universal histories.[1] As a historian living in the twenty-first century, I am interested in current debates over global history and its relations with universal history. I have been struck by the fact that much of the discourse surrounding global history is conducted in English, ignoring German, the language that dominated the study of universal history between 1770 and 1970. Furthermore, research on global history is generally led by specialists in modern or contemporary history, who have no great interest in the realities of Antiquity or the Middle Ages. Admittedly, these periods were little or less globalised, especially with regard to their traditions of history-writing. Nevertheless, the absence of premodern periods in this debate prompted me to write *The World, History* (2014), a historiographical enquiry into the ways in which the past has been described from Antiquity to the present day.[2]

Since that book was published, my thinking has progressed in two directions. First, I have more accurately grasped the relations between universal and global history.[3] Second, studying the historiography of universal history in the nineteenth and twentieth centuries encouraged me to suppose that there may be parallels between the writing of universal history and the idea that museums should aspire to universality, whether they focus on the fine arts, applied arts, or ethnography. Each of these developments raises the same methodological problems. In approaching knowledge or artefacts drawn from all periods and all cultures, one must develop a rationale for explaining them and a unified narrative able to assimilate their diversity. Still, comparing universal histories and universal museums, it appeared to me, would make it possible to describe a fundamental conception that was common to both histories and museums at the start of the twentieth century. What it more, it would bring into focus another conception of what the past was and means, a conception that underlies accounts of global history and certain contemporary museums, such as Louvre Abu Dhabi, the early twenty-first century.

To test this hypothesis, an international research project titled 'Universal Histories and Universal Museums' was launched in partnership with Sandra Kemp at the Victoria and Albert Museum, André Delpuech at the Musée du Quai Branly, and the LabEx 'Pasts in the Present' programme coordinated by the Université Paris Nanterre.[4] We organised three workshops ('The evolution of the museum in the 19th century', 'Comparative museologies: case studies from Asian art', and 'Museum universalities in Western cultural capitals in the 19th and early 20th centuries') and a symposium ('Notions of universality in universal museums'). The proceedings of these exchanges are due to be published. This project should then lead to the writing of a book on affinities between the writing of universal history and conceptions of universal museums in the West, but also elsewhere in the world, since the eighteenth century.

Here I will develop a few remarks on the theme of 'Universal history, global history, and universal museums'. My focus will be the question of universal history around 1900, the links between universal history and global history, and the question of universal museums in the contemporary era of globalisation.

I.   The '1900 conception' of universal history

It is important to distinguish accounts of the past in its entirety (at least those that were considered memorable and significant) from the modern concept of history. Accounts of what were considered the dominant characteristics of history as a whole have been written for a very long time. They figure in very different civilisations, including the Mesopotamians more than four thousand years ago, and the Greeks, Romans, and Chinese a little over two thousand years ago. They feature in Late Antiquity and the Middle Ages and during the modern period among the Chinese; Western Christians (in Latin and the vernacular languages); Byzantines (in Greek); Syriacs (in Aramean); and Muslims (in Arabic, Persian, and Turkish). Such accounts are still produced today in the West, Russia, Japan, and China.[5] However, before the mid-eighteenth century in Europe and the nineteenth century elsewhere, these accounts of the past neither claimed to be exhaustive nor believed that they were able to provide a general sense of the present or past (save for a few exceptions, each of which focused on particular themes, namely political theory for Polybius, civilisation for Ibn Khaldûn, communications and sea trade for António Galvão, and knowledge for Loys Le Roy and Daniel Morhof[6]).

In Europe around 1750, the emergence of the concept of History—considered as a unified process of evolution comprehensible to humans—completely overturned received understandings of the past.[7] For the first time, it was thought that there was an explanation for the totality of the evolution that had begun in the past, was continuing now, and would stretch into the future. For the first time, humans imagined that they could access the significance of events from the beginning to the end of time, which had hitherto been understood only by God the Creator. From that moment onward, it was thought that a common thread ran through time, unifying the process of evolution and endowing human history with significance. This thread was no longer that of a transcendental history—the Christian history of salvation or Muslim history of prophets and kings. Nor was it a history of domination, such as the Chinese history of the succession of dynasties or European history of empires. Rather, this thread was made up of themes shared by all humanity, based on new ideas and developments that had surfaced during the second half of the eighteenth century. These included notions of scientific and technical progress; commercial and economic development, first during the eighteenth century and then in the Industrial Revolution; discourses of political freedom that had been initiated by the American and French revolutions; and burgeoning ideas of democratic equality.

This conception of history as progress gave rise to the 'universal history' that was first articulated in philosophy between 1770 and 1870. In Germany, it was presented by Herder, Kant, Hegel, Schlegel, and Marx; in France it was put forward by Condorcet. During the same period, history was developed as a university subject, first in Göttingen from 1750, then in Berlin from 1810. This development precipitated research into all domains of the past, principally political and cultural. The publication of documents (such as European medieval accounts and archival sources in the *Monumenta Germaniae Historica* or Roman inscriptions in the *Corpus Inscriptionum Latinarum*); decipherment of hieroglyphic and cuneiform scripts; opening of institutional archives; contributions made by archaeology; discovery of non-European worlds (often as a result of colonialism); and invention of Prehistory all meant that by 1850 the field of universal history had become too vast for a single historian, even a Michelet or Leopold von Ranke, to survey. The academic tradition of the great university and public collections of universal history were established, first in Germany after 1870, then elsewhere in the West after 1918, and then all around the world after 1945.

In spite of these developments in knowledge, between 1770 and 1980 a great majority of Western philosophers, historians, archaeologists, and politicians shared a set of
Eurocentric beliefs. They held that universal history was a process of progress that had
begun with the origin of civilisation (between 1750 and 1850 this was considered to
have occurred in the Far East; after 1850 it was thought to have taken place in the Fertile
Crescent). From there it had run continually up and into the present, which was dominated by Western liberal values in the fields of economics, politics, and social issues.
After 1850, the spread of the idea of evolution led intellectuals to position the various
cultures of the world known to nineteenth-century Europe on the chronological line
that represented universal history. So-called 'primitive' peoples, for example, were cast
as the vestiges of Prehistory, China and India were thought to denote Antiquity, while
Islam were seen as traces of the Middle Ages. Only Europe had become modern. This
conviction was dependent on the industrial and colonial successes of the countries of
Europe and the United States. It is important to point out, though, that the Marxist
mindset that developed in the USSR after 1917 was equally Eurocentric, for it stressed
how European societies alone among historical peoples had advanced through the full
range of modes of production (developing through primitivism, slavery, feudalism, and
bourgeois capitalism, before arriving at socialism).

Whereas ethnologists agreed with this evolutionist conception during the nineteenth century, in the twentieth they generally shifted away from it due to the rise of
diffusionist, functionalist, and structuralist models.[8] It was similarly rejected by great
travellers such as Wilfred Thesiger, who was too aware of cultural differences to be
convinced of a unitary and progressivist conception of history.[9] Still, such deviating
voices remained a minority in the West.

This '1900 conception' of universality embodied by the West concerned more than
just history however. In the nineteenth century, the universality of modern science, industrial technology, and art was also asserted. During the latter half of the century, it
was celebrated in the World's Fairs. These universal expositions, it should be recognised,
were closely linked to the urban planning of the great cities that organised them. They
were also bound up with the creation of new museums, which reused the buildings constructed and collections assembled for the World's Fairs. Indeed, museums took over
exhibition venues in a number cases. London held the Great Exhibition of the Works
of Industry of all Nations in 1851. Having acted as consultant for its organisation, the
civil servant Henry Cole went on to advise on the South Kensington Museum of Art
and Science, which was founded in 1857. Vienna hosted the Weltaustellung in 1873,
resulting in the construction of the Ringstrasse (a grand boulevard), Naturhistorisches
Museum (the Natural History Museum, inaugurated in 1889), and Kunsthistorisches

Museum (the Art History Museum, opened in 1891). Paris put on the Expositions Universelles twice: first in 1878, leading to the opening of the Musée d'Ethnographie du Trocadéro (the Trocadéro Ethnography Museum) in the Palais de l'Industrie in 1882, and again 1900, after which the Petit Palais became the Palais des Beaux-Arts de la Ville de Paris (the Palace of Fine Arts, opened in 1902). Chicago held the World's Columbian Exposition in 1893. The exhibition's Fine Arts Building later became the Columbian Museum of Chicago, which was renamed the Field Museum of Natural History in 1905. Brussels hosted the Exposition Internationale of 1897 and opened the Musée du Congo Belge in 1910.

The nineteenth century saw the creation of a number of museums (sometimes in association with one another) claiming a universal approach. Whether sited adjacently to one another or distributed more widely, museums of art, natural history, archaeology, civilisation, the applied arts, ethnography, and the sciences and technology accumulated in large cities. This made possible the emergence of 'metropolitan universalities' with the goal of demonstrating an encyclopaedic knowledge of the world. Around 1900, the most successful of these endeavours were to be found in Europe (London, Paris, Berlin, St Petersburg, and Vienna) and North America (New York, Chicago, and Washington, D.C.). If academic universal histories, universal expositions, and universal museums (or rather metropolitan clusters of museums with universal designs) after 1870 were based on the same conception, then, they offered an inventory of the world based on Eurocentric universalism.

What is particularly striking is that art museums exhibited (and, for the most part, continue to exhibit today) a view of the history of civilisation that began in Egypt and Mesopotamia, continued into Graeco-Roman Antiquity, and was followed by the European Middle Ages, Renaissance, and modern age. This approach is the fossilised remnant of a late-nineteenth-century conception of universal history, which continues to convey the historic fantasy of a 'Western' history. At the time (and still today in most cases), artefacts of other cultures were usually exhibited in other museums: museums of art (Asian art in the Musée Guimet in Paris, for example); applied art (Indian art at the Victoria and Albert Museum in London, for instance); and ethnography (the Musée d'Ethnographie du Trocadéro in Paris or the Museum für Völkerkunde or 'folk art' in Berlin from 1873). This marginalisation of other cultures was reflected in the structure of books on universal history (in which they were either neglected, treated in separate volumes, or mentioned only in relation to certain periods); stands at World's Fairs (where they were absent, presented under the heading of colonies, or marginalised in the case of independent nations like Persia and Japan); and the reality of international relations dominated by European and US imperialisms. As such, there was a correlation between world political and economic realities, books written by historians on the past and present, and the way in which collections were presented in museums. The notion that universality was Western remained dominant until the 1970s.

II.   Universal history and global history

After 1945 it became increasingly difficult to justify a Eurocentric universal history; eventually, it proved impossible. The longstanding template for this vision of history was rendered obsolete by a number of factors, including the end of the colonial empires (most of which crumbled between 1947 and 1962); the tensions surrounding multi-culturalism in US society during the 1960s; the development of postcolonial studies in India around 1970; the emergence of new economic centres in Asia around 1980; the collapse of the USSR around 1990 (which had offered a variant form of Eurocentrism in understanding history); and, since 1990, the intensification of the process of globali-sation and burgeoning of knowledge of culture around the world.

This shift away from universal history was reflected in the emergence of world history around 1945 and global history from 1980. World history covered the history of all the world's regions. Nevertheless, in emphasising how the modern world-system originated in West European empires, it maintained Europe as the dominant force in the unifica-tion of the world from the fifteenth century onwards.[10] After 1985, historians criticised this theory, shifting both the chronology of the world-system, such that it was thought to begin before 1492, and their geographical focus, insisting on the importance of the Mongol Empire during the thirteenth century;[11] demographic and economic growth of Song China from the year 1000; the significance of the Indian Ocean in world history since the Abbasids; and the primacy of Europe over Qing China during the nineteenth century.[12] In turn, this altered approach led historians to consider Europe as marginal not only before 1500 but even during the incipience of the modern age. The debate over the importance of Europe's role in modern history continues between those who uphold the theory of a European world-system that came into being in the sixteenth century, adherents of the view that globalisation began early in Asia, and advocates of a globalisation process driven by Europe from the eighteenth century.

Today, many historians think that global history will replace what was once universal history. Three limits to this approach, however, suggest that this may not transpire.

First, global history often foregrounds the history of economic globalisation. Sometimes this is supplemented by other transnational factors, whether ecological, technological, cultural, or religious. This conception is often teleological, in that diverse historical situations are seen as leading inexorably towards our present. What is more, these new accounts contradict and claim to transcend national histories; this development is not accepted the world over. In Russia and China, for instance, global history is widely perceived as a Western-centric history that bolsters US ideology and policy.

Second, global history must confront the question of how and when globalisation began. There is no agreement on this. Instead, we have at least fifteen different theories. Some espy the origins of globalisation from as early as the Big Bang or formation of the Earth (big history) or the appearance of hominids (deep history). Others foreground the collapse of the USSR and creation of the World Wide Web around 1990 (new global history) or accept multiple dates for the origin of the world-system, from the Neolithic, Christopher Columbus's voyages, or the Industrial Revolution of the nineteenth century. The best recent texts generally agree that, although globalisation has become fully effective only since 1945, there was a proto-globalisation related to Europe. This development, however, would only have set in during the eighteenth century, not around 1500.[13]

Lastly, as a method global history applies not only to global factors (such as climate, ecology, economics, and world cultures). They also bear upon local structures and practices, which they put in a global perspective, whereupon they are described as 'glocal'. At both global and local levels, stress is laid on the existence of networks and connections. Though interesting, this new approach forgets that in the past such exchanges were often of little significance, especially in Antiquity and the Middle Ages. Hence, insisting on the importance of extensive exchange distorts the past, for the limited connections that did exist were not extensive enough to represent a form of structural globalisation.[14]

In short, global history's thematic, chronological, and methodological limits mean that cannot replace universal history. Although it cannot represent the totality of the past, it can complement universal history and greatly reduce its Eurocentrism.[15]

I also need to describe the consequences of global consciousness for museums (not just art museums). In this respect, we can discern a 'global turn' in museology.

The first point to make is that different global museums might reflect differing theories of the beginnings of the globalisation process. The exhibition *A History of the World in 100 Objects* developed by Neil MacGregor from the collections of the British Museum is a fine example. Founded on the periodisation advanced by deep history, it has travelled the world since 2016.[16] Other approaches are equally possible.

Next, collections that already exist in universal museums can be presented in a different manner by integrating concepts stemming from global history. This has already been done in the galleries dedicated to the medieval and modern periods at Louvre Abu Dhabi. This is the approach taken in exhibitions that emphasise global themes or global circulation of objects relating to other themes. Recent examples include the exhibition *Infinite Blue* at the Brooklyn Museum in New York and *Globes: Visions of the World* at Louvre Abu Dhabi, both of which were held in 2018.

Lastly, museum collections relating to a particular cultural area can also be presented in a different light by adopting a glocal perspective, which shows how local actualities are defined by global connections. This can be seen, for example, in the exhibition *India and the World*, which was held in Mumbai in 2017. Hence, it is possible to recast the models of global history at work in the museum world. Doing so, however, entails establishing a critical distance from their concepts and methods.

III.   Universal museums in an era of globalisation

All museums reflect the mentalities of their era; this is as true today as it was in 1900. Given this, it is unsurprising that the global turn that occurred at the end of the twentieth century shaped museums' mission and purpose. At least six aspects of this shift warrant mention here.

The first is the emergence of a global contemporary art in which artists from around the world are usually seen as having an equal standing. This situation has existed at least since the exhibition *Les Magiciens de la Terre*, which was held in Paris in 1989. Today it can be seen everywhere, in theory at any rate. In fact, regional and cultural arts scenes have their own logic, which are not necessarily egalitarian. This state of affairs, however, is partly offset by political correctness, which has pushed arts institutions to cover a greater variety of artists than ever before. The same principle holds true for the question of gender.

Next, ethnological museums have evolved along two different lines. According to the first, some museums have emphasised their artefacts' aesthetic characteristics over their ethnographic aspects, thereby transforming the way in which they are considered. The question of aesthetic value was posed in 1954 with the creation of the Museum of Primitive Art by Nelson Rockefeller in New York. The new museum prompted heated debate, at the heart of which was the question of whether it was right to describe this art as 'primitive'. This question was acutely felt in Paris after 1995, when the closure of the Musée de l'Homme (Museum of Man) and the Musée National des Arts d'Afrique et d'Océanie (National Museum of the Arts of Africa and Oceania) prompted a discussion of the place of the 'primitive arts'. This debate led to the opening of a new department in the Pavillon des Sessions du Louvre in 2000, which was named 'des Arts d'Afrique, d'Asie, d'Océanie et des Amériques' (the Arts of Africa, Asia, Oceania, and the Americas, also called the department 'des Arts premiers', which translates as the 'first' or even 'primal' arts). It also resulted in the creation of a new museum in 2006, the Musée du Quai Branly – Jacques Chirac de Paris, which is dedicated to the arts and civilisations of Africa, Asia, Oceania, and the Americas. Two problems are salient in these developments. First, these young museums often attribute aesthetic and bourgeois values to ethnographic objects. Second, the collections of the former museums were distributed among the Musée du Quai Branly and Musée des Civilisations d'Europe et de Méditerranée de Marseille (the Marseille Museum of the Civilisations of Europe and the Mediterranean). Even today, at the start of the twenty-first century, this allocation of artefacts reproduces a problematic Eurocentric distinction between the West and the Rest.

Following another line of evolution, other ethnological museums have chosen to first highlight the decisive influence that European representations have had on other cultures and then deconstruct them. These institutions have largely done away with the title ethnographic museum, instead choosing names considered more suited to contemporary concerns. This was the case with the Museum Fünf Kontinente (Five Continents Museum) in Munich and Weltmuseum (World Museum) in Vienna, both of which were renamed in 2014. This shift has been much more successful in Vienna than in Munich: whereas the latter museum scarcely acknowledges or criticises Eurocentric approaches, such critique is central in the Weltmuseum, which has been completely renovated to incorporate this outlook.

The third point is the creation of new departments within traditional universal museums. Their aim is to bolster the notion of the museum's universality by incorporating cultural areas that had been hitherto neglected. Consider, to cite two examples, the departments of Islamic art established in the Louvre between 2003 and 2012, or extensively renovated in the Metropolitan Museum in 2011.

I must also mention the foundation of museums dedicated to non-Western civilisations in non-Western contexts. These include the Asian Civilisations Museum in Singapore, which was established in 1997, and the Museum of Islamic Civilisation in Sharjah, which opened in 2008. Theoretically, these new museums should enable the emergence of different, non-Eurocentric approaches to the cultural areas they cover. However, the curators of these museums studied in the West and reproduce the templates they learned there. There is nothing abnormal about this, for the blueprint of the museum—like that of history—was invented in Europe in the eighteenth and nineteenth centuries. Very often the discourse that accompanies museum exhibitions remains modelled on Western paradigms in terms of both content and form. A certain degree of Eurocentrism, it seems, is insurmountable. Nevertheless, Chinese museums such as the National Art Museum of China in Beijing devote a lot of space to calligraphy, a non-European art.

Fifth, I wish to point to a debate around the notion of the universal or encyclopaedic museum that has emerged since 2002 in the wake of arguments advanced by Neil MacGregor and James Cuno.[17] This partly ideological debate reveals how a museal universalism of a European (though putatively 'universal') origin has diverged from postcolonial localisms or nationalisms, which argue that this universalism is in fact a Western neo-imperialist concept. The purpose of universalist rhetorics in contemporary museums, adherents of this postcolonial perspective suggest, is to prevent objects being returned to their place of origin, which some consider justified and others see as unwarranted.[18]

The last thing to note is the ongoing debate about new types of universal museums. The best current example is Louvre Abu Dhabi, which attempts to offer a universal account of art history by taking into account methodological concepts offered by global history, especially in approaching the medieval period. The comparisons that the museum makes in Room 3 (which is devoted to ancient empires and civilisations) and the viewpoint it assumes in Room 5 (on Asian trade routes) serve to integrate the contributions of universal history (with its focus on all the great civilisations) and global history (in particular, its emphasis on the significance of the Indian Ocean and trans-Asian overland trade, which are not just recent phenomena). Hence, Louvre Abu Dhabi's collection—which, though limited in quantity, contains outstanding works—is organised according to a comprehensible and consistent rationale. The curators who conceived and created it are to be congratulated.

To bring this chapter to a close, I want to emphasise how today, as in 1900, the writing of history and organisation of museums are linked. Both arise from the same wellspring of representation. Yet the '2000 conception' has replaced the '1900 conception'. Universal history remains the best framework with which to account for humanity's past and productions, of which art is one key domain. Of course, its Eurocentric dimension needs to be limited as much as possible, but not eliminated altogether. To do so, historians and curators should attempt to take into account all of the world's cultural areas, as occurs in traditional universal museums of art (such as the Metropolitan Museum of Art), the applied arts (such as the Victoria and Albert Museum), and ethnography (such as the Musée du Quai Branly). But we can also utilise beneficial aspects of global history, which enables both a synchronic and diachronic presentation, as at the Galerie du Temps (Gallery of Time) at Louvre-Lens, or an emphasis on global exchanges, as at Louvre Abu Dhabi.

Indeed, Louvre Abu Dhabi successfully combines cultural universality and globality in a universal history of art and civilisations. It is to art what the Weltmuseum in Vienna is to ethnology: a museum that carefully considers its ethos. Although they are very different in conception (the Viennese museum being a reinterpretation of an earlier museum, Louvre Abu Dhabi a new creation), today these institutions are two outstanding examples of museums for the twenty-first century.

Notes

1 Hervé Inglebert, *Les Romains chrétiens face à l'histoire de Rome* and *Interpretatio Christiana*.
2 Inglebert, *Le Monde, l'Histoire*.
3 Inglebert, *Histoire universelle ou histoire globale?*
4 For summaries of this project, see LABEX, 'Histoires universelles et musées universels: une comparaison transnationale' and Universal Histories & Universal Museums, 'Home'.
5 Inglebert, *Le Monde, l'Histoire*.
6 On Polybius's study of political theory, see Adriana Zangara, *Voir l'histoire*; on Ibn Khaldûn's study of civilisation, see Gabriel Martinez-Gros, *Ibn Khaldûn et les sept vies de l'Islam*; on communications and sea trade, see António Galvão, *Tratado dos descobrimentos antigos, e modernos, feitos ate a era de 1550*; on knowledge and civilisation, see Loys Le Roy, *De la vicissitude ou variété des choses en l'univers et concurrence des armes et des lettres*; Daniel Morhof, *Polyhistor, sive de auctorum notitia et rerum commentarii*.
7 Reinhart Kosselleck, *Futures Past*.
8 Nonetheless, a principally Anglo-Saxon neo-evolutionism emerged from 1940 and become increasingly important since 1960. See Carneiro, *Evolutionism in Cultural Anthropology*; Claessen, *Structural Change*; and Testard, 'La question de l'évolutionnisme dans l'anthropologie sociale'.
9 Wilfred Thesiger, *Arabian Sands*.
10 Fernand Braudel, *Civilisation matérielle, économie et capitalisme* and Immanuel Wallerstein, *The Modern World-System*.
11 Janet L. Abu-Lughod, *Before European Hegemony*.
12 On the growth of Song China, see Eric Jones, *Growth Recurring*; on the Indian Ocean in world history, see Kirti Narayan Chaudhuri, *Asia Before Europe* and Philippe Beaujard, *Les Mondes de l'Océan Indien*; on Europe's assertion of dominance of China only in the nineteenth century, see Roy Bin Wong, *China Transformed*; André Gunder Franck, *ReOrient*; and Kenneth Pomeranz, *The Great Divergence*.

13   This is the case with the six-volume collection *Die Geschichte der Welt* edited by Akira Iriye
       and Jürgen Osterhammel, which has been translated in English as *A History of the World*.
14   Conrad, *What is Global History?*
15   On the impossibility of avoiding a certain degree of Eurocentrism, on account of the fact
       that the conception of History as a unified development (as opposed to history as the writing
       of the past) appeared in Europe around 1750, see Inglebert *Histoire universelle ou histoire
       globale?* (note 2) 1109–1131 and Inglebert 2018 (note 3) 54–58 and 127–128.
16   MacGregor, *A History of the World in 100 Objects*.
17   For MacGregor's view, see the British Museum, 'Declaration on the Importance and Value
       of Universal Museums'. For Cuno's see his *Who Owns Antiquity?*; *Whose Culture?*; and
       Museums Matter.
18   Geoffrey Lewis, 'The Universal Museum: A Special Case?'; Mark O'Neill, 'Enlightenment
       Museums: Universal or Merely Global?'; and Isaac Kaplan, 'The Case against the Universal
       Museum'.

Works Cited

Abu-Lughod, Janet L. *Before European Hegemony: The World-System A.D. 1250-1350*. New
       York: Oxford University Press, 1989.
Beaujard, Philippe. *Les Mondes de l'Océan Indien*. 2 vols. Paris: A. Colin, 2012.
Braudel, Fernand. *Civilisation matérielle, économie et capitalisme*. 3 vols. Paris: A. Colin,
       1967–1979.
The British Museum. 'Declaration on the Importance and Value of Universal Museums'.
       International Council of Museums News, 1 (2004): 4.
Carneiro, Robert. *Evolutionism in Cultural Anthropology: a Critical History*. Boulder, C.O.:
       Westview Press, 2003.
Chaudhuri, Kirti Narayan. *Asia Before Europe: Economy and Civilisation of the Indian Ocean
       from the Rise of Islam to 1750*. Cambridge: Cambridge University Press, 1990.
Claessen, Henri J. M. *Structural Change: Evolution and Evolutionism in Cultural Anthropology*.
       Leiden: Universiteit Leiden, School of Asian, African and Amerinidian Studies, 2000.
Conrad, Sebastian. *What is Global History?* Princeton: Princeton University Press, 2015.
Cuno, James. *Museums Matter: In Praise of the Encyclopedic Museum*. Chicago: University of
       Chicago Press, 2011.
———. *Who Owns Antiquity? Museums and the Battle over our Ancient Heritage*. Princeton:
       Princeton University Press, 2008.

———. *Whose Culture? The Promise of Museums and the Debate over Antiquities*. Princeton: Princeton University Press, 2009.

Franck, André Gunder. *ReOrient: Global Economy in the Asian Age*. Berkeley: University of California Press, 1998.

Galvão, António. *Tratado dos descobrimentos antigos, e modernos, feitos ate a era de 1550*. Lisbon: 1563.

Inglebert, Hervé. *Histoire universelle ou histoire globale?* Paris: Presses Universitaires de France, 2018.

———. *Interpretatio Christiana. Les mutations des savoirs (cosmographie, géographie, ethnographie, histoire) dans l'Antiquité chrétienne (30-630 après J.-C.)*. Paris: Institut d'Études Augustiniennes, 2001.

———. *Le Monde, l'Histoire. Essai sur les histoires universelles*. Paris: Presses Universitaires de France, 2014.

———. *Les Romains chrétiens face à l'histoire de Rome: histoire, christianisme et romanités en Occident dans l'Antiquité tardive (IIIᵉ-Vᵉ siècles)*. Paris: Institut d'Études Augustiniennes, 1996.

Iriye, Akira, and Jürgen Osterhammel, eds. *Die Geschichte der Welt*. 6 vols. Munich: C.H. Beck, 2013.

———, eds. *A History of the World*. 6 vols. Harvard, The Belknap Press, 2014–2020.

Jones, Eric. *Growth Recurring: Economic Change in World History*. Oxford: Clarendon Press, 1988.

Kaplan, Isaac. 'The Case against the Universal Museum'. *Artsy*, April 26, 2016. https://www.artsy.net/article/artsy-editorial-the-case-against-the-universal-museum.

Kosselleck, Reinhart. *Futures Past: On the Semantics of Historical Time*. New York: Columbia University Press, 2004.

LABEX. 'Histoires universelles et musées universels: une comparaison transnationale'. *Les Passés dans le présent*. http://passes-present.eu/fr/histoires-universelles-et-musees-universels-une-comparaison-transnationale-33541.

Le Roy, Loys. *De la vicissitude ou variété des choses en l'univers et concurrence des armes et des lettres par les premières et plus illustres nations du monde depuis le temps où a commencé la civilité et mémoire humaine jusques à présent*. Paris: 1575.

Lewis, Geoffrey. 'The Universal Museum: A Special Case?' *International Council of Museums News*, 1 (2004): 3.

MacGregor, Neil. *A History of the World in 100 Objects*. London: Allen Lane, 2010.

Martinez-Gros, Gabriel. *Ibn Khaldûn et les sept vies de l'Islam*. Arles: Actes Sud-Sindbad, 2006.

Morhof, Daniel. *Polyhistor, sive de auctorum notitia et rerum commentarii*. Lübeck: 1688.

O'Neill, Mark. 'Enlightenment Museums: Universal or Merely Global?' *Museum & Society*, 2. no. 3 (2004): 190–202.

Pomeranz, Kenneth. *The Great Divergence: China, Europe, and the Making of the Modern World Economy*. Princeton: Princeton University Press, 2000.

Testard, Alain. 'La question de l'évolutionnisme dans l'anthropologie sociale'. *Revue Française de Sociologie*, 33, no. 2 (1992): 155–187.

Thesiger, Wilfred. *Arabian Sands*. London: Longman, 1959.

Universal Histories & Universal Museums. 'Home'. *Universal Histories & Universal Museums*. http://wp.lancs.ac.uk/universalhistories/.

Wallerstein, Immanuel. *The Modern World-System*. 4 vols. Berkeley: University of California Press,1970–2011.

Wong, Roy Bin. *China Transformed: Historical Change and the Limits of European Experience*. Ithaca: Cornell University Press, 1997.

Zangara, Adriana. *Voir l'histoire. Théories anciennes du récit historique, IIe siècle avant J.-C. – IIe siècle après J.-C.* Paris: Éditions de l'École des hautes Études en Sciences Sociales, 2007.

PART 3

GLOBAL/LOCAL

TENSIONS

Introduction

Local and Global: A Complex Field of Tension

Guilhem André

To what extent is the art world truly global and what are the interactions with a supposedly local artistic sphere? The landscape of artistic practices and museums has certainly undergone a dramatic process of diversification and diffusion since the end of the Cold War, with new artistic voices, initiatives as well as institutions springing up around the world. Not only have new museums of a western model opened across Asia and the Middle East; the twenty-first century has also witnessed the emergence of new artistic scenes in parallel with global art fairs as key forums of artistic display. This emphasis on global connectedness has fed into the substance of artistic practice itself, with countless artists hybridising motifs culled from once distant regions and cultural traditions.

However, the globalisation of art has also precipitated a countervailing turn towards the local. Artists mainly inspired by their millennial local traditions are still active, while others from the global trend, perhaps in search of roots, began to install works or mount performances that were indissociable from particular places. This situational trend cuts against the predominance of global concerns and emphases in contemporary art: just when the art world appeared to be globalising, artists embraced locality.

In different ways, each of the following three chapters attests to the fact that the globalisation of the art world, far from simply erasing local artistic scenes, has opened up a complex field of tension between the local and the global. To show how these tensions bear upon the formation of artistic canon, Cecilia Hurley's chapter analyses the correspondence between the distinguished art historian Ernst Gombrich and the scholar and potter Quentin Bell. Whereas Gombrich was concerned with safeguarding the Renaissance legacy against the encroachment of what he perceived as lesser art, Bell underlined the need to recognise the value of not just craft, but art from beyond the West too. Unpacking this exchange, Hurley indicates how the global circulation of non-Western art has challenged the established artistic canon. Although it may once have been considered universally valid and very widely adopted, the Western canon is now perceived as one heritage among many, a local construct in a way.

Sylvie Ramond describes how museums are balancing an older aspiration towards universality with the imperative to engage with local contexts. Taking Lyon's museums as an example, her chapter traces how successive directors of the Musée des Beaux-Arts de Lyon acquired various collections relating to Ancient Egyptian, Islamic, Japanese, and other artistic traditions, only for these to be detached to form the nucleus of separate museums. Alongside this predilection for universality, though, the Musée des Beaux-Arts remained in touch with the culture of the Lyon region. Even recently, the museum has acquired works by significant artists linked to Lyon. Like Ramond, Nathalie Bondil's chapter reflects on how museums might navigate tensions among the global, metropolitan, and local scales in a 'multipolar' world. She describes how the Montreal Museum of Fine Arts, while mindful of global trends, has increasingly focused its attention on engaging with local communities. Through ambitious education and outreach programmes, Bondil argues, museums can raise pressing social issues and instill visual literacy among diverse publics. Hence, whereas Hurley's chapter indicates how globalisation challenges local perceptions of art, Ramond's and Bondil's contributions propose ways in which museums might bridge the global and the local.

Connecting Canons

Critiques of the Western Canon in Recent Art Historiography

Cecilia Hurley

The discipline of art history has been notoriously wary about questioning, let alone gainsaying, its own basic tenets.[1] The established account of the canon of art is but one example of this circumspection. Even now, at the end of the second decade of the third millennium, we art historians pluralise all too seldom the canon, speaking more readily of 'the canon of art' than of 'the canons of art'. However, this does not mean that we have eschewed all debate on artistic canons and their formation; some art historians have long been critically questioning prevalent formulations of the canon of art. Fortunately, this questioning still continues today.

In September 2017, a press release announcing the forthcoming opening of Louvre Abu Dhabi made a welcome contribution to this debate, stating that: 'The dialogue between works from different geographical territories, sometimes far apart, highlights similarities between the canons despite each having its own mode of expression'.[2] In Louvre Abu Dhabi, multiple canons interacting with each other, would offer fresh insights into art and cultural history. The exhibition galleries have upheld this promise, juxtaposing objects from different cultures, artistic traditions, and media.

A canonical debate

This essay will not provide a comprehensive survey of the art-historical literature about the canon and its formation. Instead, it will focus on a number of important contributions to the debate made over the last fifty years. The starting point is an illuminating episode, a weighty discussion between two notable art historians that predates our ongoing exchanges by several decades. In 1973, Sir Ernst Gombrich gave the prestigious

Romanes Lecture in the Sheldonian Theatre at the University of Oxford.[3] In the lecture, which was subsequently published as *Art History and the Social Science*s, Gombrich expressed his faith in the canon of art history; he illustrated his comments on values in the arts by referring to a number of examples, including the painting on the ceiling of the Sheldonian Theatre.[4] Executed by Robert Streater, a competent if secondary history painter of the seventeenth century, the painting was completed in 1668-1669.[5] By 1670 it had already inspired a poem by Robert Whitehall, a fellow of Merton College in the same university, whose concluding couplet reads:

> That future ages must confess they owe
> To Streeter more than Michael Angelo.[6]

Local pride and institutional interests and pride were clearly in play here: Whitehall claimed that Oxford was an artistic counterpart (or even rival) to the Urbs aeterna. To this end, the Sheldonian ceiling offered the perfect example for a clever comparison, which served to vaunt the merits of local artists. Basing his argument on the traditional notion of the artistic canon, Gombrich commented that Whitehall was sorely misguided, and that some questions could not be decided by appealing to relativism. In particular, the canon should be understood as an arbitrary construction that reposes on objective rather than subjective standards. For these reasons, he concluded, Streater could never be included among the canon of great artists, let alone be presumed to dislodge Michelangelo.[7]

This essay will not dispute Gombrich's conclusions, not least because Whitehall's position is particularly difficult to defend. Instead, it will focus on a discussion that was provoked by these ostensibly incontrovertible pronouncements by an art historian who had recently retired from the directorship of the Warburg Institute. The lecture was published and Gombrich dispatched copies to selected friends, including Quentin Bell, an eminent art historian and potter. Bell picked up the gauntlet thrown down by Gombrich, offering his opinion on the canon in a letter. The two men thereafter engaged upon a lively epistolary exchange (published in *Critical Inquiry* in 1976), concerning the canon, its unity, its unicity, its rigidity, and its characteristics.[8]

Bell proved to be a tough opponent for Gombrich, questioning and even refuting many of his hypotheses. Much as Jakob Burckhardt had done over one century earlier and in remarkably similar terms, Gombrich asserted on several occasions in this correspondence that an art historian's duty was to receive, conserve, and transmit the canon untouched to future generations. Bell was of a very different opinion. He addressed the problem analytically, asking: 'what does one mean by a canon, and what does one do with it when one has it?'[9] Here he seems here to be suggesting that we can—and indeed should—meddle and fiddle with the canon. A few lines later, he reinforced this idea when he stated

> a canon [in Gombrich's sense] is too rigid, too absolute a structure to be accommodated to the catholicity of human taste. We must have an entity which will serve as a guide, but we cannot altogether accept it.[10]

Bell thus questioned the canon. Like the literary historians who were also opening a debate about the literary canon during the 1970s, he requested that art historians should examine other cultures, other civilisations, and other arts.[11] Unfortunately, he left one question unasked and therefore unanswered. Is there one canon or are there many? On this, he had nothing to say.

Global canons: the museum as showcase

Over recent years, these and similar discussions have become increasingly important, particularly in the wake of the 'global turn' that has interested art historians just as it has scholars working in the other humanities and social sciences. Many of our certitudes have been questioned: our methods, categories, taxonomies, perspectives, and reliance on a Eurocentric canon.[12] Given its ambitions and the scope of its collections, an encyclopaedic museum is an ideal place for debate and experiment on canons, their formation and their display.

Founded in the eighteenth, nineteenth, and early twentieth centuries, and holding collections across a wide range of disciples and drawn from around the world, survey or universal museums (the adjective 'encyclopaedic' will be used here) reflected the encyclopaedic spirit of their times. Over the course of time, they were shaped by various factors, including the publics they sought to attract (artists, amateurs, laymen, regular, and occasional visitors); the purposes they were intended to serve (chiefly artistic, educational, and leisure); the provenance and type of their collections; and, more generally, the prevalent political, social, educational, and historical discourses. The display and organisational principles developed in these institutions during these years and decades reflected these concerns.

At the turn of the twentieth century, a geographical classification and organisation of collections had become accepted practice in encyclopaedic museums throughout Europe. The model was also being discussed for use American museums. There are several reasons for this, originating both within and outside the museum. First, by the closing decades of the nineteenth century, paintings were almost always hung according to schools and periods. This had first been implemented in Vienna in 1780 and was subsequently adopted with greater or lesser alacrity in collections throughout Europe and America over the nineteenth century; it was also increasingly being used in displaying sculpture.[13] Its authority was so great that at the beginning of the twentieth century it could even be proposed as a model for organising collections of plaster casts. Wilhelm Klein, professor of classical archaeology in Prague, suggested this in a programmatic article on plaster cast collections that he wrote for the journal *Museumskunde* in 1912.[14]

Second, archaeological collections had greatly increased in both number and scope. Throughout the nineteenth century, Western governments financed many large-scale archaeological expeditions; on the whole, the results of these endeavours were brought back to Europe and deposited in museums, where they were generally organised in departments bearing the names of the areas or civilisations that had been excavated. Greek and Roman antiquities, Egyptian, and Mesopotamian collections occupied distinct spaces in the museum.[15] Third, the nascent ethnology museums also left their imprint on the universal museum—in these institutions, departments were often arranged according to civilisations and cultures.[16]

The fourth reason is the authority of the 'universal' exhibitions or World's Fairs in the second half of the nineteenth century. At regular intervals, over a period of months, many of the world's nations displayed their industrial might, their arts, history, architecture, and culture; the works, the products, and the goods were on show in vast exhibition halls, or even in national pavilions constructed in entire quarters of the host city.[17] Given the close links between the applied arts, the museums, and the World's Fairs or universal exhibitions (for example, the South Kensington Museum was built using the proceeds from the 1851 Great Exhibition), it is surprising that applied arts collections were among the last to be organised according to region or culture. For many years, the collections in South Kensington and similar institutions were organised by materials or techniques. Objects were therefore grouped into categories such as bronze, glass, ivories, or enamels. Within the major material categories, geographical or regional subdivisions were sometimes permitted. By the end of the century, however, dissenting voices were being heard. Perhaps the spirit of intense industrial rivalry among dominant nations was beginning to abate; perhaps the utility of these collections as models to encourage industrial production was increasingly being called into question. For whatever reason, the material and technical qualities of the industrial, applied, and decorative arts were no longer considered their most important features. Artistic, aesthetic, stylistic or historic characteristics were what interested scholars and the public alike, and the museums could therefore do away with their earlier system of display and experiment with new ones, for example along geographic and chronological lines. In his survey of 'Current theories of the arrangement of museums of art as applied to museums of fine arts', the curator and scholar Matthew Stewart Prichard is quite clear when explaining this new curatorial practice. Drawing on his study of European museums, he states that, when considering a cultural artefact or work of art, 'the material embodying the idea is negligible—almost accidental; it is the form and style that are essential'.[18]

By the turn of the twentieth century, therefore, the overwhelming majority of collections were organised along geographical lines, with clear distinctions drawn between different cultures and civilisations. This was an essentialist vision of the world, based on the theory that each nation or civilisation possesses its own, unique cultural characteristics, a reflection of its spirit and identity. Artistic and industrial art productions obey these same rules; they can therefore be organised into national or regional departments in the museum. In moving from one department to the next, museum visitors travelled the world. This is hardly surprising, given that the museum institution was experimenting with theories that were being developed outside its walls. In the *Ideen* (*Ideas on the Philosophy of Human History*), published in four parts between 1784 and 1791, the German philosopher Johann Gottfried Herder elaborated his theory of a *Volksgeist*.[19] This 'national spirit', he claimed, shaped national cultural development. During the nineteenth century, the theory gained acceptance from a wide public and from many authors in German and elsewhere; the era was profoundly marked by the birth and emergence of nation states. Art history, like many other disciplines, applied Herder's model. General or universal histories of art written during this period—and for many decades into the twentieth century—found a convenient organisational framework in political and physical geography; parallel narratives of artistic and cultural production, each centred on a country, a region, or a continent, were juxtaposed to form the basis of works by art historians from Franz Kugler and Carl Schnaase, to Roger Peyre, and right though into the 1980s.[20] Connections among cultural regions were seldom established; even if they were attempted it was often on a comparative basis, highlighting the differences rather than the similarities.

Art history, canons, and blind spots

It is undoubtedly an institution organised along these lines, on models inherited from the nineteenth century, that Mary D. Sheriff has in mind when, at the beginning of her introduction to a collection of essays on culture and contact, she invites her readers to imagine visiting an encyclopaedic museum. In this institution (which she does not identify), the Western fine arts—European and American painting, sculpture, engraving, and drawings—take pride of place, whereas the other arts, as well as the arts of non-Western cultures, are pushed out from the centre of the building into peripheral positions.[21] This antithetical couple of centre and periphery is familiar; it is a model developed in an article by Carlo Ginsburg and Enrico Castelnuovo at the end of the 1970s and which has since been used regularly in discussions of artistic geography.[22] Sheriff hastens to add that it is not only the museum that is guilty of privileging Eurocentric narratives of art and art history. Textbooks, and thus by extension lectures and classroom debates, are equally marked by these typically nineteenth-century attitudes.[23]

Sheriff believes that a number of our traditional methods impede our understanding of globalising interconnections; it is noteworthy that throughout her discussion she never explicitly refers to the canon. She identifies a number of what she calls 'blind spots' in art-historical discourse.[24] First, studies of Western art tend to overlook a number of Western artists. They are forgotten, she proposes, because they hail from countries that are commonly overlooked in 'universal' or 'general' or 'survey' texts. She specifically identifies Croatia, Denmark, Portugal, Sweden, and Switzerland. All these countries and their artists are studied by national and local historians, but they are not included in overarching narratives.[25] It is thus not difficult to surmise, by extrapolation, that art historians are guilty of omitting many other artists from countries in less familiar regions.

The second blind spot that Sheriff detects in our art-historical narratives results from what she calls the divorce between 'high' art and 'decorative' art.[26] Unfortunately, her argument on this point appears to be a rather clumsy conflation of two major polarities that have become tenets of the discipline of art history. It would be advisable to distinguish between, on the one hand, the debate about 'fine' arts and 'decorative' or 'applied' arts (as expounded in Kristeller's theory of the 'modern system of the arts') and, on the other hand, the distinction between 'high' and 'low' art (questioned in Roger Chartier's work on representation and appropriation).[27] Disentangling this knot adds clarity and force to Sheriff's discussion.

The third blind spot singled out by Sheriff, is a refusal to engage sufficiently with ethnographic objects; art historians tend, she suggests, to prefer art to artefacts.[28] Despite the material turn inspired by the increasing attention paid to anthropological theories by art historians, this attitude persists. The fourth blind spot is art history's loyalty to 'an assumed dichotomy between formal properties and subject matters'.[29] As a result, on the few occasions when scholars do work with objects from several cultures, this 'assumed dichotomy' encourages them to prefer superficial formal analyses and comparisons to more profound investigations, which would take into account not only formal borrowings across cultures, but also semantic shifts, questions relating to contextualisation, social and historical criteria. Sheriff's text may have been written ten years ago, but much work still remains to be done if art historians are to find ways of avoiding these blind spots.

Canonising the overlooked

Although Sheriff's introduction does not refer to the correspondence between Gombrich and Bell, there are several points of similarity between her contribution and the earlier debate. Bell was not only an eminent art historian but also, very importantly for him, a talented potter.[30] His artistic practice was to have a profound effect on his view of art history. Prior to his debate with Gombrich, he had already addressed the question of the canon. In a lecture given at the University of Cambridge in 1973—the same year as Gombrich's Romanes Lecture at the University of Oxford—he had leapt to the defence of the Pre-Raphaelites, whose work was sadly overlooked at that time.[31] Bell suggested that their works should be considered as equally important as those of the most famous artists of their time. Some years later he continued this campaign, publishing an important volume devoted to the Pre-Raphaelites, more than a decade before their reputation was rehabilitated by scholars.[32]

In his discussion with Gombrich, Bell introduced two proposals that, for the period, were even more outrageous than his advocacy of the Pre-Raphaelites. Having recently visited the British Museum, he had been struck by the beauty of a group of Egyptian preparatory (he calls them 'off duty') drawings assembled in a display case. He praises them, saying that they are 'rapid, expressive, sensitive', and he wonders why they rarely figure in histories of Egyptian art.[33] He concedes that they cannot rival with the mummies and sphinxes. Nor are they the first works that come to mind when one thinks of Egyptian art. They are, nevertheless, often far superior to the officially commissioned works of art. Above all, these examples of 'underground' artistic production, he claims, prove that there are often two (or more) currents of art at work in a civilisation at any one time.[34] Bell is maybe in this passage adumbrating the theories about 'popular culture' or 'high' and 'low' art. Then, following a different line of reasoning, he states that it would be worthwhile to associate the 'useful' (by this he surely means 'applied' or 'decorative') arts with the accepted canon.[35] An obvious candidate for this 'canonisation' of a 'useful' art, he suggests, would be ceramics, buttressing his argument with the observation that a potter can be an artist of the 'highest genius'.[36]

Great ceramic ware, therefore, is on a par with great paintings or sculptures. Bell's assertion is surprising, given that the potter's craft has all too often been relegated to the status of a 'useful' art. To counter this, Bell urges that it should now be elevated to a higher rank. However, he insists that this rehabilitation should not merely serve to glorify pottery, but rather force us to reassess our understanding of the canon in general. It should also oblige us to question the figure of the artist, which was largely inherited from the Romantic conception of the artist as genius. This conception clashes sharply with the history of pottery, since, as Bell points out, 'the canon here is of course composed not of the work of great individuals but of great collective achievements'.[37]

Bell has here identified a surprising and troubling fact about the artistic (as opposed to the literary) canon: we tend to articulate the artistic canon around figures—hence around artists—rather than works. In the Gombrich-Bell debate, for example, few works are mentioned and appreciated. The discussion revolves instead around the figure of the artist, not his or her production. This reality remains a constant feature in many of the more recent debates about the artistic canon. We canonise artists, not their masterpieces. Indeed, it can be tempting to believe that a canon is closer to a pantheon than to a masterpiece room.[38] But, as Bell points out, pottery is often a collective art, with creators' names obscured or forgotten. This raises a fundamental question regarding the canon: can—or indeed should—the canon or canons that we construct admit anonymous works, which we cannot link to a biographical narrative?

The museum in the new canonical debate: theory's material turn

The questions raised by Sheriff, and earlier by Gombrich and Bell, assume a new relevancy and urgency in the context of our globalised world and in the light of the global turn. In their wake has come a series of series of new concepts that have become part of the *lingua franca* of art history over the last few years: globalisation, migration, circulation, contact, hybridity, transnationalism, transculturation, connected and intertwined histories, *métissage*.[39] These terms are not merely a new academic jargon. Objects bear witness to many of the ideas expressed by these terms. Objects are moved, they circulate, they come into contact with and are appropriated by other cultures. Museums offer an ideal stage for the production of new discourses around these themes. In so doing, they breathe new life into familiar artefacts and force us to question our ideas and preconceptions concerning our arsenal of terms and concepts.

In these circumstances, the question remains as to how museums should display singular or plural canons and the overlaps and connections between them. A recent exhibition set out to do just this. Curated by the philosopher and art theoretician Wolfgang

Scheppe, the exhibition *Die Dinge des Lebens, Das Leben der Dinge* (*The Things of Life, the Life of Things*) was held in the State Collections in Dresden in 2014.[40] The visitor who entered the rooms on the piano nobile of the Castle of the Electors of Saxony, encountered a series of ninety-nine black and white photographs making up the Italian photographer Franco Vimercati's 'Soup Bowl' cycle. Opposite the photographs, on the other side of a narrow gangway, and arranged in a single row along a simple, bare, white counter, was a series of ninety-nine bowls selected from the Dresden State Collections. The presentation was stark; its minimality was heightened by the fact that there appeared to be none of the material that traditionally accompanies exhibits in a show, such as labels or texts.

The bowls ranged from a very simple form, fashioned out of vine leaves, to an ornate, seventeenth-century cup on a silver foot; from a bowl-object created in Switzerland in 2013 to another hewn out of stone thousands of years ago in Papua New Guinea.[41] Many were in ceramics, some in paper, yet others in metal, wood, and various other materials. They share some common features, namely their basic shape and their most elementary functions. Despite these common features, nonetheless, each bears its own characteristics, and stands as a token of a period, a region, a social group, a series of inherited and transmitted customs and uses. Laid out in a row—without any attempt on the curator's part to impose a narrative, whether based on chronology, geographic origins, symbolism, style or ritual function—these vessels encouraged visitors to create their own narratives.

After wandering along the gangway, examining the bowls and trying to make sense of them, visitors rounded a corner to find an installation by Mario Klingemann, which took the form of a series of visualisations inspired by George Kubler's book *The Shape of Time* (1962).[42] In a series of five 'network diagrams', the artist plotted connections among the ninety-nine bowls. He selected five headings: creation, form, decoration, function, and provenance. Klingemann mapped the data in large diagrams and matrices, which schematically represent the connections among the bowls, their geographical circulation, the development of their formal characteristics, and their diverse functions (ritual, civic or domestic).

These schematic diagrams drew much of their inspiration from the work of Kubler. He was a noted historian of Spanish, Portuguese, Iberian colonial, and pre-Colombian art. From the 1940s onwards, he addressed in his texts the question of artistic geography and developed a model for explaining artistic forms, their evolution and the appearance of variations of them in terms of centre and periphery.[43] In the *Shape of Time*, he took these ideas further, offering a radical rereading of the history of art. He replaced the notion of style with the model of historical sequences based on continuous change:

objects and images evolve in response to changes in the world surrounding them. Before Bell or Sheriff, he questioned the validity of art-historical narratives that draw too heavily on artists' biographies; instead, he pleaded for a history of things. He believed that only this new art history, whose narrative would be built on a matrix of objects, could accommodate both art and artefacts. It could also find a place for techniques and genres that were all too often neglected in conventional art histories. Kubler was adamant on one point: these hitherto overlooked and undervalued techniques and genres would not supplant the great works of the Western figurative tradition, pushing them in turn into oblivion. Rather, he thought, the acquisition of new knowledge, the willingness to investigate new and different forms and artistic practices could offer stimulating new perspectives and comparisons: 'For example, the recent advent of Western action painting has prompted the re-evaluation of a similar tradition in Chinese painting since the ninth century—a tradition to which the West was insensitive until recent years'.[44]

Kubler thus anticipated a number of central issues in recent debates over global canon(s). He advocated a more open and critical understanding of art history: an approach to the discipline that would question the canon and stress the importance of material objects. His ambitions are best seen in the following, highly programmatic passage:

> Our choice of the 'history of things' is more than a euphemism to replace the bristling ugliness of 'material culture.' This term is used by anthropologists to distinguish ideas, or 'mental culture,' from artifacts. But the 'history of things' is intended to reunite ideas and objects under the rubric of visual forms: the term includes both artifacts and works of art, both replicas and unique examples, both tools and expressions—in short all materials worked by human hands under the guidance of connected ideas developed in temporal sequence. From all these things a shape in time emerges. A visible portrait of the collective identity, whether tribe, class, or nation, comes into being. This self-image reflected in things is a guide and a point of reference to the group for the future, and it eventually becomes the portrait given to posterity.[45]

Canons of art, canons of objects: the plurality of the canon is now generally accepted in the discipline of art history. Even so, much work remains to be done. Over the last few pages, I have been discussing the museum: its organisational principles, its responses to a new global world, its work with newly defined canons, its awareness of the challenges posed by postcolonialism, by transnational history, and by connected and intertwined histories. The objects summoned up as examples throughout this essay spring from what we now call 'world cultures'. And yet the methods adopted here to analyse them as well as the authors cited are Western, indeed European. (The possible exception is Kubler, who was born in the United States but grew up in Europe before returning to the States to write his doctorate and teach). Furthermore, the concepts of art and artefact, canon and masterpiece are all expressed in language and by means of an epistemological apparatus that are irretrievably tied to late twentieth-century Western thought. They are therefore both geographically and chronologically bounded. These limits do not invalidate the work already done—far from it—nor should they dishearten art historians. Rather, they should incite the discipline to weave new narratives, engaging critical transcultural outlooks and opening transnational dialogues. They should also encourage art historians to investigate semantic problems and to query the translatability or otherwise of many of our notions and concepts. There is a risk that new blind spots will be discovered; on the other hand, the existing ones will be avoided, even if not entirely eradicated, and our canons and our canonical concepts will be more connected.

Notes

1   Monica Juneja, 'Circulation and Beyond', 59.
2   The Louvre Press Room, 'Louvre Abu Dhabi to welcome visitors from November', unpaginated.
3   Ernst Gombrich, *Art History and the Social Sciences*.
4   Gombrich, *Art History*, 25.
5   Richard Jeffree, 'Robert Streater'; Anne Thackray, 'Robert Streater'; and Timothy Wilson and Catherine Whistler, 'The Sheldonian Theatre'.
6   Robert Whitehall, *Urania, or A description of the Painting of the Top of the Theater at Oxon, as the Artist Lay'd his Design*, 7.
7   Gombrich, *Art History*, 26, 39–40.
8   Ernst Gombrich and Quentin Bell, 'Canons and Values in the Visual Arts'.
9   Gombrich and Bell, 'Canons and Values', 407.
10 Gombrich and Bell, 'Canons and Values', 408.
11 Lucie Robert, 'Canon, Canonisation'; Frank Kermode, 'The Argument about Canons'; Jan Gorak, *The Making of the Modern Canon*; John Guillory, *Cultural Capital*; Wendell V. Harris, 'Canonicity'; Kermode, *The Classic*; Lee Morrissey ed., *Debating the Canon*; Robert von Hallberg ed., *Canons*; Harold Bloom, *The Western Canon*; W. J. T. Mitchell, 'Canon'; and Jan Gorak ed., *Canon vs. Culture*.

12　David Damrosch, 'World Literature in a Postcanonical, Hypercanonical Age'; and Michael Camille, Zeynep Çelik, John Onians, Adrian Rifkin, and Christopher B. Steiner, 'Rethinking the Canon'.

13　Debora Meijers, *Kunst als Natur*; Carol Duncan, *Civilizing Rituals*; and Andrew McClellan *The Art Museum from Boullée to Bilbao*, chapter 4.

14　Wilhelm Klein, 'Die Aufgaben unserer Gipsabguss-Sammlungen', 9: 'Die Zeit in die es gehört, die Schule und Richtung, der es entstammt, bestimmt seinen Platz in derselben Art, in der unsere modernen grossen Gemäldegalerien vorangegangen sind [...]'.

15　Stephanie Moser, *Wondrous Curiosities*; Mirjam Hoijtink, *Exhibiting the Past*; Christopher Whitehead, *Museums and the Construction of Disciplines*; and Shawn Malley, *From Archaeology to Spectacle in Victorian England*.

16　H. Glenn Penny, *Objects of Culture*; and Han F. Vermeulen, *Before Boas*.

17　Pieter van Wesemael, *Architecture of instruction and delight*; and Wolfgang Friebe, *Architektur der Weltausstellungen*.

18　Matthew Stewart Prichard, 'Current Theories of the Arrangement of Museums of Art and their Application to the Museum of Fine Arts', 11.

19　Johann Gottfried Herder, *Ideen zur Philosophie der Geschichte der Menschheit*. On Herder, see Thomas DaCosta Kaufmann, *Toward a Geography of Art,* 46–48. On museums and nationalism in this period, see: Peter Aronsson and Gabriella Elgenius, *National museums and Nation-building in Europe, 1750-2010*.

20　Kaufmann, *Toward a Geography*, especially chapters 2 and 3.

21　Mary D. Sheriff, 'Introduction', 1.

22　Enrico Castelnuovo and Carlo Ginzburg, 'Centro e periferia'.

23　Sheriff, 'Introduction', 1.

24　Sheriff, 'Introduction', 4–9.

25　Sheriff, 'Introduction', 5.

26　Sheriff, 'Introduction', 5–6.

27　Paul Oskar Kristeller, 'The Modern System of the Arts'. On Kristeller, see Claire Farago, 'The Classification of the Visual Arts in the Renaissance'; Larry Shiner, *The Invention of Art: A Cultural History*; James I. Porter, 'Is Art Modern?'; and Cecilia Hurley, 'Putting Art in its Place'. Roger Chartier, 'Le Monde Comme Représentation', especially 1511–1512, 'Culture populaire'; and 'Preface'.

28　Sheriff, 'Introduction', 7. On this problem, see Arthur Danto, *Art/Artifact*; and Ruth B. Phillips, 'The Museum of Art-Thropology', 8–19.

29　Sheriff, 'Introduction', 8.

30　Meißner, Günter, Andreas Beyer, Bénédicte Savoy, and Wolf Tegethoff, *Saur allgemeines Künstler-Lexikon*, 8, 415.

31   Quentin Bell, *The Art Critic and the Art Historian*.

32   Bell, *A New and Noble School: the Pre-Raphaelites*.

33   Gombrich and Bell, 'Canons and Values', 404.

34   Gombrich and Bell, 'Canons and Values', 404.

35   Gombrich and Bell, 'Canons and Values', 405.

36   Gombrich and Bell, 'Canons and Values', 405.

37   Gombrich and Bell, 'Canons and Values', 405.

38   Paul Hetherington, 'Pantheons in the *Mouseion*', 215–228; Richard Wrigley and Matthew Craske, *Pantheons*; Alain Bonnet, 'Une Histoire de l'art illustrée'; Stephen Bann, 'Paul Delaroche à l'hémicycle des beaux-arts'; and 'Pre-histories of Art in Nineteenth-Century France'; France Nerlich, 'Palette contre plume.'

39   For an overview of the literature that has been published on these various terms and their use in art history, see the contributions in Thomas DaCosta Kaufmann, Catherine Dossin, and Béatrice Joyeux-Prunel, *Circulations in the Global History of Art*; Diana Newall, *Art and its Global Histories*; Anne Gerritsen and Giorgio Riello, *The Global Lives of Things*; Jill H. Casid and Aruna D'Souza, *Art History in the Wake of the Global Turn*; Hans Belting, *Global Studies*; and James Elkins, *Is Art History Global?*

40   Wolfgang Scheppe, *Die Dinge des Lebens – das Leben der Dinge*.

41   The various bowls on show are included in the second volume of the exhibition catalogue: Scheppe, *Die Dinge des Lebens – das Leben der Dinge, 2*.

42   George Kubler, *The Shape of Time*.

43   Kaufmann, *Toward a Geography of Art*, chapter 7. For some of Kubler's major works, see 'Two Modes of Franciscan Architecture'; *Mexican Architecture of the Sixteenth Century*; (with Martin Soria), *Art and Architecture in Spain and Portugal and their American Dominions*; *The Art and Architecture of Ancient America*; and *Studies in Ancient American and European Art*.

44   Kubler, *The Shape of Time*, 123.

45   Kubler, *The Shape of Time*, 9.

Works Cited

Aronsson, Peter, and Gabriella Elgenius, eds. *National museums and Nation-building in Europe, 1750-2010: Mobilization and Legitimacy, Continuity and Change*. London: Routledge, 2015.

Bann, Stephen. 'Paul Delaroche à l'hémicycle des beaux-arts: l'histoire de l'art et l'autorité de la peinture'. *Revue de l'art* 146 (2004): 21–34.

———. 'Pre-histories of Art in Nineteenth-Century France. Around Paul Delaroche's Hémicycle des beaux-arts'. In *The Art Historian: National Traditions and Institutional Practices*, edited by Michael F. Zimmermann, 25–40. New Haven: Yale University Press, 2003.

Bell, Quentin. *The Art Critic and the Art Historian*. London: Cambridge University Press, 1974. Reprinted in: Quentin Bell, 'The Art Critic and the Art Historian'. *Critical Inquiry* 1, no. 3 (1975): 497–519.

———. *A New and Noble School: The Pre-Raphaelites*. London: Macdonald, 1982.

Belting, Hans, ed. *Global Studies: Mapping Contemporary Art and Culture*. Ostfildern: Hatje Cantz, 2011.

Bloom, Harold. *The Western Canon: the Books and Schools of the Ages*. New York: Harcourt Brace, 1994.

Bonnet, Alain. 'Une Histoire de l'art illustrée: l'hémicycle de l'École des beaux-arts par Paul Delaroche'. *Histoire de l'art*, 33/34 (1996): 17–30.

Camille, Michael, Zeynep Çelik, John Onians, Adrian Rifkin, and Christopher B. Steiner, 'Rethinking the Canon'. *The Art Bulletin* 78, no. 2 (1996): 198–217.

Casid, Jill H., and Aruna D'Souza, eds. *Art History in the Wake of the Global Turn*. Williamstown: Sterling and Francine Clark Art Institute and Yale University Press, 2014.

Castelnuovo, Enrico, and Carlo Ginzburg. 'Centro e periferia'. In *Storia dell'arte italiana, I. Materiali e problemi, I. Questioni e metodi*, edited by Giovanni Previtali, 285–352. Torino: Einaudi, 1979.

Chartier, Roger. 'Culture populaire'. In *Dictionnaire des sciences historiques*, edited by André Burguière, 174–179. Paris: Presses Universitaires de France, 1986

———. 'Le Monde Comme Représentation'. *Annales. Histoire, Sciences Sociales* 44, no. 6 (1989): 1505–1520.

———. 'Preface'. In Lawrence W. Levine, *Culture d'en haut, culture d'en bas: l'émergence des hiérarchies culturelles aux États-Unis*. Translated by Marianne Woollven and Olivier Vanhée. Paris: Éditions la Découverte, 2010.

DaCosta Kaufmann, Thomas. *Toward a Geography of Art*. Chicago: University of Chicago Press, 2004.

Damrosch, David. 'World Literature in a Postcanonical, Hypercanonical Age'. In *Comparative Literature in an Age of Globalization*, edited by Haun Saussy, 43–53. Baltimore: Johns Hopkins University Press, 2006.

Danto, Arthur. *Art/Artifact: African Art in Anthropology Collections*. New York: Center for African Art and Prestel Verlag, 1988.

Duncan, Carol. *Civilizing Rituals: inside Public Art Museums*. London: Routledge, 1995.

Elkins, James, ed. *Is Art History Global?* New York: Routledge, 2007.

Farago, Claire, 'The Classification of the Visual Arts in the Renaissance'. In *The Shapes of Knowledge from the Renaissance to the Enlightenment*, edited by Donald R. Kelley and Richard H. Popkin, 23–48. Dordrecht: Kluwer, 1991.

Friebe, Wolfgang. *Architektur der Weltausstellungen: 1851 bis 1970*. Stuttgart: Kohlhammer, 1983.

Gerritsen, Anne, and Giorgio Riello, eds. *The Global Lives of Things: the Material Culture of Connections in the Early Modern World*. London: Routledge, 2016.

Gombrich, Ernst. *Art History and the Social Sciences*. Oxford: Clarendon Press, 1975.

———, and Quentin Bell. 'Canons and Values in the Visual Arts: A Correspondence'. *Critical Inquiry* 2, no. 3 (1976): 395–410. Reprinted in: Ernst Gombrich, *Ideals and Idols: Essays on Values in History and in Art,* 167–183. Oxford: Phaidon, 1979.

Gorak, Jan, ed. *Canon vs. Culture: Reflections on the Current Debate*. New York and Abingdon: Routledge, 2016.

———. *The Making of the Modern Canon: Genesis and Crisis of a Literary Idea*. London: Athlone Press, 1991.

Guillory, John. *Cultural Capital: The Problem of Literary Canon Formation*. Chicago: University of Chicago Press, 1993.

The Louvre Press Room. 'Louvre Abu Dhabi to welcome visitors from November'. Posted November 11, 2017. https://presse.louvre.fr/louvre-abu-dhabi-to-welcome-visitors-from-november/.

Hallberg, Robert von, ed. *Canons*. Chicago: University of Chicago Press, 1984.

Harris, Wendell V. 'Canonicity'. *PMLA* 106 (1991): 110–121.

Herder, Johann Gottfried. *Ideen zur Philosophie der Geschichte der Menschheit*, 4 vols. Riga: Johann Friedrich Hartknoch, 1784-1791.

Hetherington, Paul, 'Pantheons in the *Mouseion*: An Aspect of the History of Taste'. *Art History* 1, no. 2 (1978): 215–228.

Hoijtink, Mirjam. *Exhibiting the Past. Caspar Reuvens and the Museums of Antiquities in Europe, 1800–1840.* Translated by Wendie Shaffer, Donald Gardner, and Kate Williams. Turnhout: Brepols, 2012.

Hurley, Cecilia. 'Putting Art in its Place: the 'Modern System of the Arts' in Bibliographies and 'Bibliothecae''. *Perspective: actualités de la recherche en histoire de l'art 2* (2016): 87–110.

Jeffree, Richard. 'Robert Streater'. In vol. 29 of *The Dictionary of Art*, vol. 29, edited by Jane Shoaf Turner, 766–767. London: Macmillan, 1996.

Juneja, Monica. 'Circulation and Beyond – the Trajectories of Vision in Early Modern Eurasia'. In *Circulations in the Global History of Art*, edited by Thomas DaCosta Kaufmann, Catherine Dossin, and Béatrice Joyeux-Prunel, 59–77. Aldershot: Ashgate, 2015.

Kermode, Frank. 'The Argument about Canons'. In *The Bible and the Narrative Tradition*, edited by Frank McConnell, 78–96. Oxford: Oxford University Press, 1991.

———. *The Classic: Literary Images of Permanence and Change*. London: Faber, 1975.

Klein, Wilhelm. 'Die Aufgaben unserer Gipsabguss-Sammlungen' *Museumskunde* 8 (1912): 1–10.

Kristeller, Paul Oskar. 'The Modern System of the Arts: a Study in the History of Aesthetics'. In *Journal of the History of Ideas* 12, no. 4 (1951): 496–527 and 13, no. 1 (1952): 17–46.

Kubler, George. *The Art and Architecture of Ancient America: The Mexican, Maya, and Andean Peoples*. Harmondsworth, Middlesex: Penguin Books, 1962.

———, and Martin Soria. *Art and Architecture in Spain and Portugal and their American Dominions: 1500 to 1800*. Harmondsworth: Penguin Books, 1959.

———. *Mexican Architecture of the Sixteenth Century*, 2 vols. New Haven: Yale University Press, 1948.

———. *The Shape of Time: Remarks on the History of Things*. New Haven: Yale University Press, 1962.

———. *Studies in Ancient American and European Art: the Collected Essays of George Kubler*, edited by Thomas F. Reese. New Haven: Yale University Press, 1985.

———. 'Two Modes of Franciscan Architecture: New Mexico and California'. *Gazette des beaux-arts*, 23 (1943): 39–48.

McClellan, Andrew. *The Art Museum from Boullée to Bilbao*. Berkeley & Los Angeles & London: University of California Press, 2008.

Malley, Shawn. *From Archaeology to Spectacle in Victorian England: the Case of Assyria, 1845-1854*. Farnham: Ashgate, 2011.

Meijers, Debora. *Kunst als Natur: die Habsburger Gemäldegalerie in Wien um 1780*. Translated by Rosi Wiegmann. Vienna: Kunsthistorisches Museum and Skira, 1995.

Meißner, Günter, Andreas Beyer, Bénédicte Savoy, and Wolf Tegethoff eds. *Saur allgemeines Künstler-Lexikon: die Bildenden Künstler aller Zeiten und Völker*, Vol. 8. Munich: Saur Verlag, 1991.

Mitchell, W. J. T. 'Canon'. In *New Keywords: a Revised Vocabulary of Culture and Society*, edited by Tony Bennett, Lawrence Grossberg, and Meaghan Morris, 20–22. Oxford: Blackwell, 2005.

Morrissey, Lee, ed. *Debating the Canon: A Reader from Addison to Nafisi*. New York: Macmillan, 2005.

Moser, Stephanie. *Wondrous Curiosities: Ancient Egypt at the British Museum*. Chicago: University of Chicago Press, 2012.

Nerlich, France. 'Palette contre plume: peindre l'histoire de l'art: le cas de Paul Delaroche et de Johann Friedrich Overbeck'. *Histoire de l'art* 79/2 (2016): 11–24.

Newall, Diana, ed. *Art and its Global Histories: A Reader*. Manchester: Manchester University Press, 2017.

Penny, H. Glenn. *Objects of Culture: Ethnology and Ethnographic Museums in Imperial Germany*. Chapel Hill: University of North Carolina Press, 2002.

Phillips, Ruth B. 'The Museum of Art-Thropology: Twenty-First Century Imbroglios'. *RES: Anthropology and Aesthetics* 52 (2007): 8–19.

Porter, James I. 'Is Art Modern? Kristeller's 'Modern System of the Arts' Reconsidered'. In *British Journal of Aesthetics* 49, no. 1 (2009): 1–24.

Prichard, Matthew Stewart, 'Current Theories of the Arrangement of Museums of Art and their Application to the Museum of Fine Arts'. In Museum of Fine Arts Boston, Vol. 1 of *Communications to the Trustees*, 3-25. Boston: Museum of Fine Arts Boston, 1904.

Robert, Lucie. 'Canon, Canonisation'. In *Le dictionnaire du littéraire*, edited by Paul Aron, Denis Saint-Jacques, and Alain Viala, 74–76. Paris: PUF, 2002.

Scheppe, Wolfgang, ed. *Die Dinge des Lebens – das Leben der Dinge*. 1. *Die Dinge des Lebens – das Leben der Dinge: Proposition I. Franco Vimercati & George Kubler*; 2. *Die Dinge des Lebens – das Leben der Dinge: Eine Formsequenz aus 99 Schalen: 99 Schalen aus den Staatlichen Kunstsammlungen Dresden*; 3. *Die Dinge des Lebens – das Leben der Dinge: Franco Vimercati, der Terrinen-Zyklus, 1983 – 1992*. Köln: König, 2014.

Sheriff, Mary D. 'Introduction: cultural contact and the making of European art, 1492-1930'. In *Cultural contact and the making of European art since the age of exploration*, edited by Mary D. Sheriff, 1–16. Chapel Hill: University of North Carolina Press, 2010.

Shiner, Larry. *The Invention of Art: A Cultural History*. Chicago: University of Chicago Press, 2001.

Thackray, Anne. 'Streater, Robert (1621–1679), painter.' *Oxford Dictionary of National Biography*. 23 Sep. 2004; Accessed 29 Mar. 2020. https://www.oxforddnb.com/view/10.1093/ref:odnb/9780198614128.001.0001/odnb-9780198614128-e-26657.

Vermeulen, Han F. *Before Boas: the Genesis of Ethnography and Ethnology in the German Enlightenment*. Lincoln: University of Nebraska Press, 2015.

Wesemael, Pieter van. *Architecture of Instruction and Delight: A Socio-historical Analysis of World Exhibitions as a Didactic Phenomenon (1798-1851-1970)*. Rotterdam: 010 Publishers, 2001.

Whitehall, Robert. *Urania, or A description of the Painting of the Top of the Theater at Oxon, as the Artist Lay'd his Design*. London: Thomas Ratcliffe and Thomas Daniel, 1669.

Whitehead, Christopher. *Museums and the Construction of Disciplines: Art and Archaeology in 19th-Century Britain*. London: Duckworth, 2009.

Wilson, Timothy, and Catherine Whistler. 'The Sheldonian Theatre'. *Apollo* 145 (1997): 20–22.

Wrigley, Richard, and Matthew Craske. *Pantheons: Transformations of a Monumental Idea*. Aldershot: Ashgate, 2004.

Universal Museum, Global Museum

The Example of Lyon

Sylvie Ramond

Global, universal, local: for some twenty years now, museums have been looking to define themselves on the basis of space and scale, as represented in their collections and reflected in the publics that they address. Although museums have long developed in the context of rivalries among the regional, national, and universal, the balance between these scales seems to have shifted over the last two decades, such that the global is increasingly prominent. This shift has been a key issue in my thinking and decision making over the last decade and a half working in Lyon, where I direct the Musée des Beaux-Arts (Lyon Museum of Fine Arts) and, more recently, the pôle des musées d'art, which includes the Musée d'art contemporain (Lyon Museum of Contemporary Art).

In this chapter, I discuss the theme of spatial scales in museums as they bear upon the case of Lyon. First, I survey the history of Lyon's Musée des Beaux-Arts and Musée d'Art Contemporain within the more general context of the development of Lyon's public collections. Then, I show how, as Lyon's collections have developed over the years, an ever-greater emphasis has been put on striking a balance between the local and other domains, whether they relate to France or other parts of the world. Lastly, I discuss issues pertaining to the concepts of the universal and global museum. Taking Lyon's museums as a case in point, I shall attempt to draw some general conclusions.

The development of Lyon's Musée des Beaux-Arts and public collections

The Musée des Beaux-Arts de Lyon was originally founded as a consequence of the French Revolution. As from 1791, an initial collection was installed in a former royal Benedictine convent, the Abbaye des Dames de Saint-Pierre. Built in 1659 in the Italian style, it remains one of the city's most outstanding historical buildings (fig. 1). Early

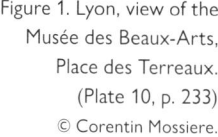

Figure 1. Lyon, view of the Musée des Beaux-Arts, Place des Terreaux. (Plate 10, p. 233) © Corentin Mossiere.

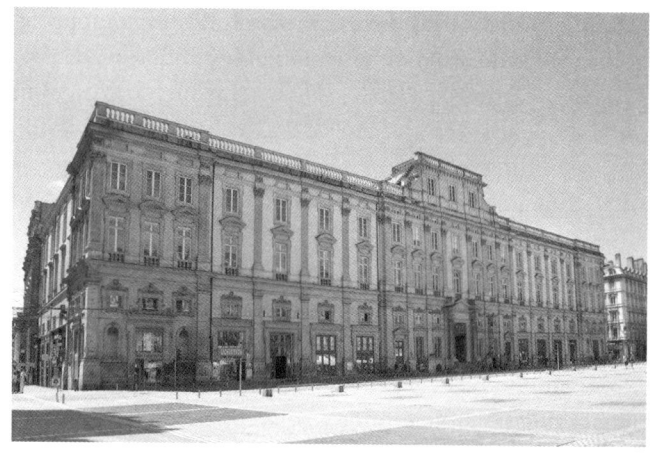

on, the project's founders took to the idea of addressing the collection to a universal audience, thereby making the place 'a temple of universal knowledge together with the expression of genius'.[1] The museum was the first in the region to be mentioned in the Chaptal Decree of 1801, which redistributed works of art seized from churches and foreign territories during the revolution and subsequent wars. This greatly enhanced the collection. Still, at this time the museum was riven by contrary purposes. Given its large collection, it functioned as a second Musée des Monuments Français[2] and second Louvre. At the same time, it was also engaged with the traditional local silk industry and all the tasks related to training craftsmen and educating taste that this implied.

Between 1808 and 1810, the museum began to develop an independent programme. This period, perhaps, represents the true emergence of the Musée des Beaux-Arts de Lyon. The curator, François Artaud, acquired two new collections. One belonged to an M. Tempier from Nîmes. It included the famous Athenian statue, the *Koré*, which at the time was thought to represent the ancient Egyptian god Isis (fig. 2). The other was the Marquis de Migieu's collection, which contained over one thousand artworks stemming from the Middle Ages and Renaissance.

During this period, Lyon's collection was unique in France, unmatched by even the Louvre. The 1816 catalogue of the museum's antiquities conveys an idea of the sheer range of works it contained: Egyptian artefacts, antiquities from the Indies, Etruscan figures, Gallic antiquities, Greek vases and sculptures, Roman antiquities, and 'foreign curiosities', meaning works from even further afield. Another catalogue, compiled between 1855 and 1857, listed objects such as a 'Saracen vase', discovered in the River Saône in Lyon in 1843. Made of metal, it bore a dedication to the just, scholarly, and

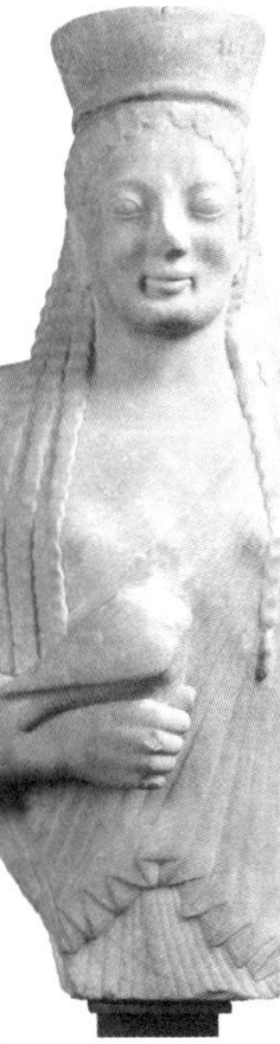

Figure 2. Athens, *Koré*, c. 540 BCE, Marble. (Plate 11, p. 234)
Inv. H 1993. Lyon, Musée des Beaux-Arts. © Lyon MBA – Photograph by Alain Basset.

pious El Malek Al Aschraff, the son of the Sultan Salah ad-Din (widely known today as Saladin). Indeed, the Islamic arts became increasingly important as the collection developed in the nineteenth century.

With the support of the art patron Édouard Aynard (who served as president of the museum's board of directors from 1878 to 1897), Jean-Baptiste Giraud (one of the museum's curators) decided to enlarge the collection to include further Islamic objects. In Aynard's own words, he wished to establish 'a more complete history of all the arts'[3]. As a result of their efforts in this direction, today the Musée de Lyon possesses the second-largest collection of Islamic art in France, second only to the Louvre's (fig. 3). Considered in this light, the museum resembles those early encyclopaedic museums that liked to think of themselves as universal.

Certainly, each gap in the collection's non-European works underlined the difficulty of maintaining this pretence of universality. Nevertheless, the very ideal was beneficial in that it allowed the collection to venture into other historical and cultural eras and areas, before and beyond the modern West.

This openness to the world was fostered equally by two great directors of the museum. The first was Henri Focillon, an immense figure and one of the twentieth century's leading art historians. He died in exile in the United States in 1943, having challenged

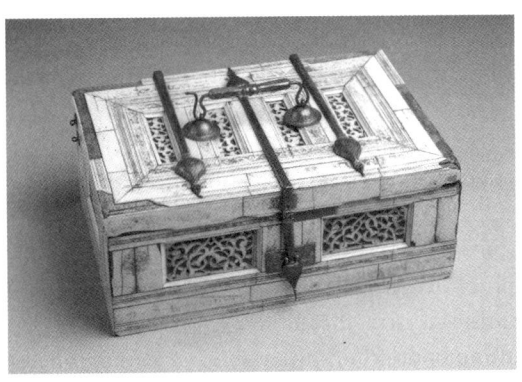

Figure 3. Islamic Art, Grenada, Casket, 14th century. Cedar wood from the Atlas, sculpted bone, engraved and painted. (Plate 12, p. 235)
Inv. D 378. Lyon, Musée des Beaux-Arts. © Lyon MBA – Photograph by Alain Basset.

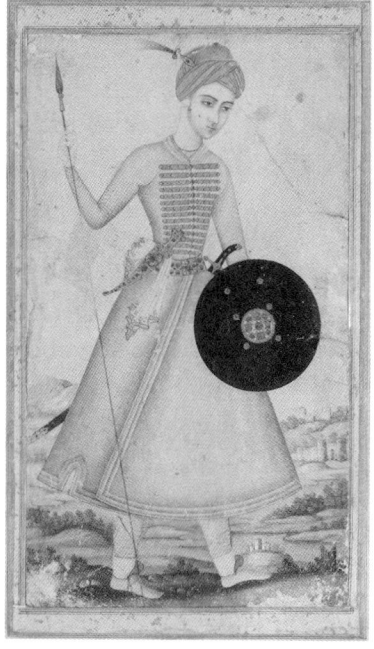

Figure 4. Ispahan, Ali Qoli (styled after), *An Indian Prince armed with a spear and shield*, c. 1660. Ink, gouache and watercolour on paper. (Plate 13, p. 236)
Inv. E 585-a. Lyon, Musée des Beaux-Arts. © Lyon MBA – Photograph by Alain Basset.

Figure 5. Islamic Art, Andalousia, Body of a jar, 14th – 15th century. Ceramic with green moulded glaze. (Plate 14, p. 237) Inv. D 557. Lyon, Musée des Beaux-Arts. © Lyon MBA – Photograph by Alain Basset.

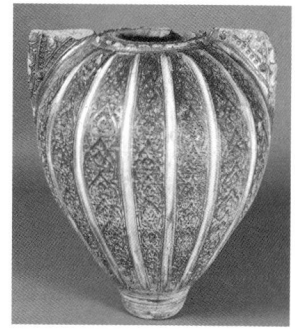

the armistice that France signed with Germany in 1940 and announced his support for the Free French Forces. During his directorship of the Musée des Beaux-Arts de Lyon between 1913 and 1924, Focillon acquired popular ceramics from Transylvania, Moldavia, and Wallachia; organised the procurement of a small set of beautiful Persian miniatures (figs. 4 and 5); and added a series of Iranian ceramics to the collection of Islamic arts. In 1917 he ensured the acquisition Raphaël Collin's exceptional collection of more than 400 pieces of Japanese, Chinese, and Korean ceramics (fig. 6). This is one of the great collections formed during the period of Japanism in the second half of the nineteenth century, which was characterised by the enthusiastic consumption of Japanese cultural products in Europe. Its addition further extended the geographical and cultural scope of the decorative arts collection. Of course, Focillon's universalism is rather dated: it was the universalism typical of a student trained at the École Normale Supérieure during the Third Republic, a socialist influenced by Ruskin, and French representative at the League of Nations (along with the author Paul Valery) from 1925. Focillon wished to include the popular arts in museums. His universal vision included Asian cultures but ignored other realms of art history, such as those represented by Africa, Oceania, and South America. The fact remains that in his work, friendships, and professional struggles, Focillon embodied something related to the universal.

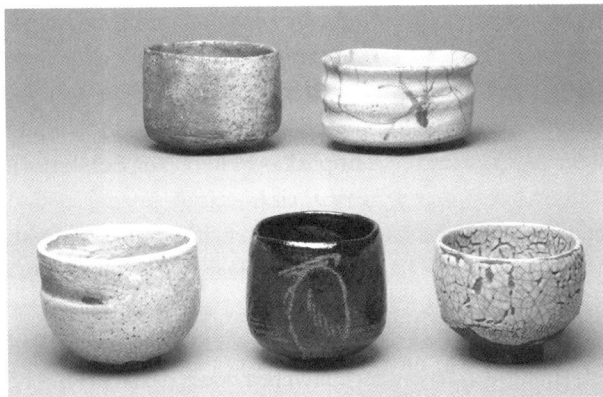

Figure 6. Japan, Bowls, 16th-18th century. Stoneware. Collection Raphaël Collin. (Plate 15, p. 238) Inv. E 554-175, Inv. E 554-152, Inv. E 554-151, Inv. E 554-438, Inv. E 554-345. Lyon, Musée des Beaux-Arts. © Lyon MBA – Photograph by Alain Basset.

Another remarkable figure was Léon Rosenthal, an art historian, activist, and critic at the daily newspaper *L'Humanité* (an organ of the French Communist Party). Before being appointed curator at the museum in Lyon, Rosenthal developed a social and educational doctrine for the museum, which he considered an 'instrument of comprehensive education'.[4] For Rosenthal, there was no contradiction between a local and universalist outlook. Quite the contrary, he saw these perspectives as fully compatible. He also saw universalism as inseparable from a concern for popular education, which was the condition of possibility for museums being able to speak to the 'crowd'. (This last term, it should be noted, is that used by Rosenthal himself, for whom it was in no way derogatory.) To me, this explicitly universal theoretical legacy is an essential aspect of the museum and is still valid today. Perhaps more than collections themselves, it is these dreams and doctrines that still entitle the museum to assert its universality.

Throughout its 230-year history, the Musée des Beaux-Arts has gradually achieved an international reputation. Three main departments came to coexist: the antiquities collection, which covers the Mediterranean world and edges of the Middle East; the paintings and sculpture collections, which are essential to a museum of French and European art; and the decorative arts collection, which encompasses works from the Islamic world and Far East.

As it was accumulating works and extending into the Palais Saint-Pierre, the Musée des Beaux-Arts assisted in the creation of neighbouring institutions that would come to house some of its collections. First was the Musée des Tissus et des Arts Décoratifs (the Textile and Decorative Arts Museum), which was instigated by an influential collector, Édouard Aynard and originally overseen by the Lyon Chamber of Commerce. Then came the Musée Gallo-Romain (Gallo-Roman Museum), which was established on the hill of Fourvière in 1975. This new venture absorbed the fine arts museum's collection in this specific field. This transfer of the Gallo-Roman collections was preceded by the arrival at the Musée des Beaux-Arts of the Egyptology collections of the Musée Guimet in 1969, which was followed by the Institut universitaire Loret's Egyptology collection (named after the French Egyptologist Victor Loret). Another institution established in Lyon is the Musée d'Art Contemporain. When it was founded in 1984, this museum was situated in the Palais Saint-Pierre as part of the Musée des Beaux-Arts; since 1995 it has been sited at the Cité Internationale (fig. 7). Lastly, Lyon's newest museum, the Musée des Confluences (named after its location at the confluence of the Saône and Rhône rivers), was founded in 2014. Housed in a spectacular building designed by the Austrian studio Coop Himmelb(l)au, its collections cover the natural sciences, humanities, science, and technology. It inherited the wonderful natural history collection from the Musée d'Histoire Naturelle de Lyon (the Lyon Natural History Museum). In addition to *naturalia*, this collection includes a fine set of objects and works from the Far East stemming from the Musée Guimet. All of these transfers are critical to understanding how the city of Lyon and its museums have tackled the concepts of universalism and globality, both historically and today. Lyon can pride itself not only on having a series of outstanding museums and collections; what is more, the history of these museums indicates how they have successfully shared collections.

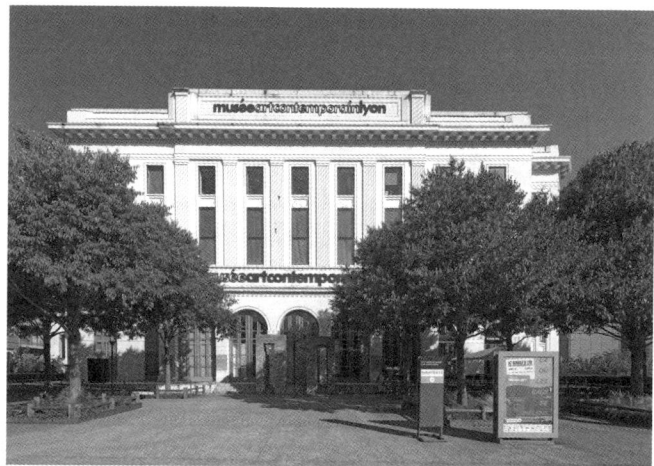

Figure 7. View of macLyon.
(Plate 16, p. 239)
Photograph by Blaise Adilon.

Balancing the local, national, and global

Let us now consider the question of the 'local', by which I mean works and objects that are representative of a museum's surrounding area or proximate culture (which, I realise, are not quite the same thing). Very early on, the Musée des Beaux-Arts assigned an important place to antiquities discovered during excavations in the city and its wider region. Local painters and sculptors were well represented, with their works being acquired both during their lifetime and posthumously. Among others, these artists included Jacques Stella, Jospeh Chinard, and Paul Chenavard. The emphasis placed on these artists, however, ultimately proved awkward. In the building in which the museum is housed—an ancient convent—the collections are displayed according to the principle of the *galleria progressiva*. As such, they were presented chronologically from Antiquity to the twenty-first century. In the admirable renovation carried out between 1989 and 1998, the former director Philippe Durey sought to avoid altering this traditional model, which allowed artistic developments to progress chronologically through seventy rooms. Where the collections made it possible, objects and works could also be displayed according to geographical and/or cultural areas or artistic schools. In this arrangement, the Lyon artists, principally of the nineteenth century, formed a distinct school. Although there was no question of challenging the strictly historical procession of the exhibition galleries, for years the curators and I have attempted to organise the works in ways that introduce different historical narratives and readings. I feel that inventing new practices of looking at the same body of works is the best way of reconsidering these Lyonnais artists.

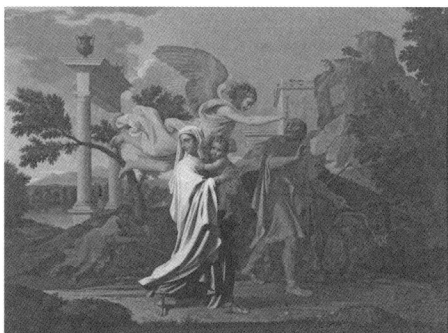

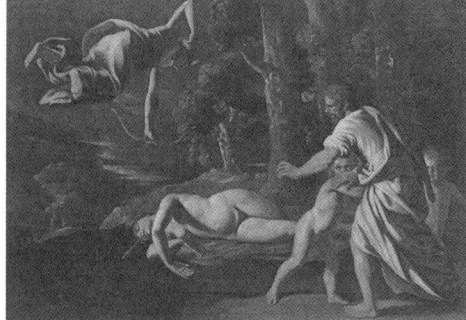

Figure 8. Nicolas Poussin, *Flight into Egypt*, 1657. Oil on canvas. (Plate 17, p. 240) Inv. 2004.5.1. Lyon, Musée des Beaux-Arts. © Lyon MBA – Photograph by Alain Basset.

Figure 9. Nicolas Poussin, *Death of Chione*, 1619-1622. Oil on canvas. (Plate 18, p. 241) Inv. 2016.1. Lyon, Musée des Beaux-Arts. © Lyon MBA – Photograph by Alain Basset.

Consider two examples of the innovations we put forward. In 2008, the Musée de Lyon, in collaboration with the Louvre, acquired a late work by Poussin, the *Flight into Egypt* (1657) (fig. 8). Poussin had been a glaring omission in the museum's otherwise outstanding collection of seventeenth-century paintings. In 2016, we were able to acquire another painting by Poussin, an extraordinary early work titled *Death of Chione* (fig. 9), which was painted around 1622 in Lyon for a collector named Silvio I Reynon. When we considered where we should hang the paintings, we decided not to situate them among works of French Classicism, which include paintings by Laurent de la Hyre, Simon Vouet, and Jacques Blanchard. Instead, we chose to create a dedicated room in which the Poussins would hang next to other artists closely linked to Lyon.

Alongside Jacques Stella and Jacques Blanchet, this room also hosts works by Louis Cretey, an artist who was rediscovered some twenty years ago by Gilles Chomer and Pierre Rosenberg (fig. 10). We had already given Cretey his first large solo exhibition, which finally inducted him into the inner circle of French artists who made their careers in Italy in the seventeenth century. A native of Lyon who arrived in Rome around 1660 (at the very end of Poussin's life), Cretey worked for influential clients and developed a form of tenebrism that sometimes borders on the extravagant. The hanging of the room dedicated to artists associated with Lyon reflects a wish to offer unconventional and unexpected aesthetic juxtapositions. Although these may have been disconcerting for art lovers, our choices remained grounded in the history of art.

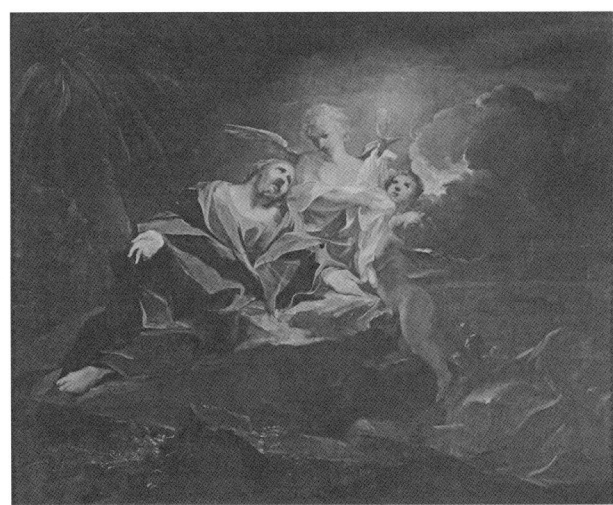

Figure 10. Louis Cretey,
Jesus in the Garden of Olives,
c. 1683. Oil on canvas.
(Plate 19, p. 242)
Inv. 1976-1. Lyon, Musée des
Beaux-Arts. © Lyon MBA –
Photograph by Alain Basset.

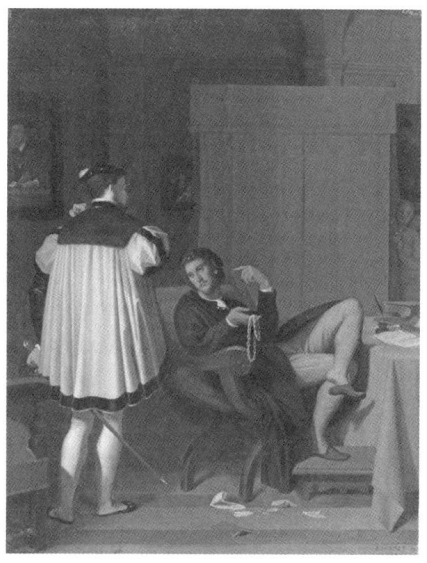

Figure 11. Jean-Auguste-Dominique Ingres, *Aretin and the Envoy of Charles V*, 1848. Oil on canvas. (Plate 20, p. 243) Inv. 2013.1.1. Lyon, Musée des Beaux-Arts. © Lyon MBA – Photograph by Alain Basset.

The second example of the new approaches trialled at the Musée des Beaux-Arts concerns the Lyon School during the nineteenth century. This school encompasses a diverse range of painters, including Fleury François Richard and Pierre Henri Révoil, who, having trained in the studio of Jacques Louis David, worked in the troubadour style; Victor Orsel and Louis Janmot, who belonged to the Philosophical or Spiritual School so disliked by the French poet Charles Baudelaire (who was schoolboy in Lyon from 1832 to 1836); and the brothers Jean Hippolyte Flandrin and Paul Flandrin, who were pupils of Jean Auguste Dominique Ingres. Again, we tried to create associations among these works, many of which are of great beauty, and others, such as the painting *L'Arétin et l'envoyé de Charles Quint* (1848) by Ingres, who had shared a studio with Révoil and François Marius Granet (figs. 11 and 12).

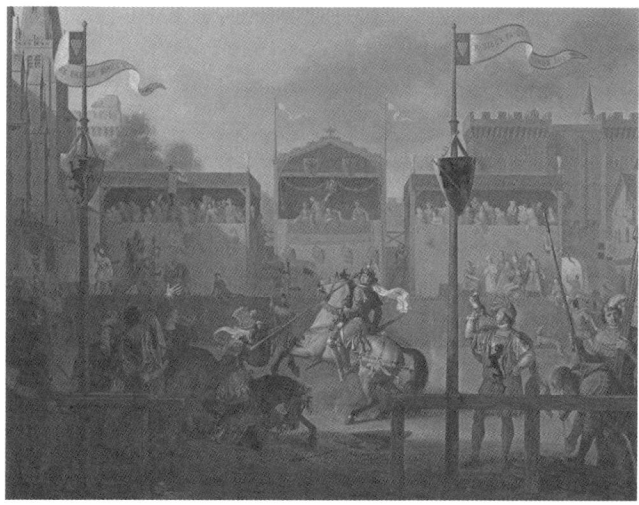

Figure 12. Pierre Révoil, *A Tournament*, 1812. Oil on canvas. (Plate 21, p. 244) Inv. A 164. Lyon, Musée des Beaux-Arts. © Lyon MBA – Photograph by Alain Basset.

Figure 13. Louis Janmot, *Flower of the Fields*,.
1845. (Plate 22, p. 245)
Inv. B 502. Lyon, Musée des Beaux-Arts. Image © Lyon
MBA – Photograph by Alain Basset.

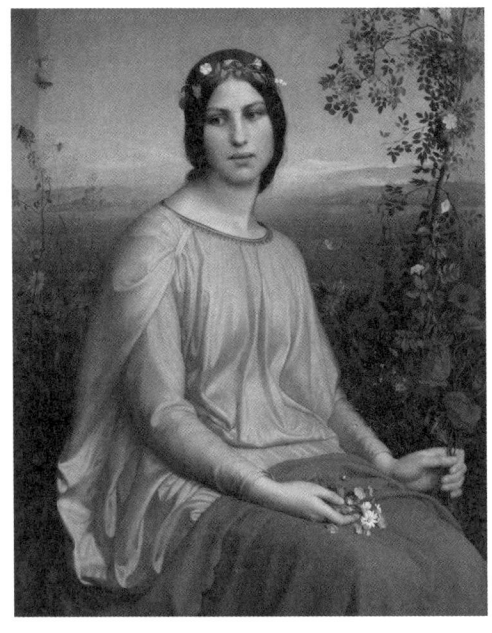

Going deeper, I tried to highlight the common ground between this school and other European movements—such as the Nazarenes and the Pre-Raphaelite—that shared the same mysticism and enthusiasm for Primitivism. These links have been demonstrated by art historians such as Henri Dorra and Daniel Ternois. In the museum rooms, however, the Lyonnais artists were still to be situated in relation to supra-national European trends. Two manifesto exhibitions devised with Stephen Bann made it possible to present all of these affinities. By establishing connections between artists in the permanent exhibition, where this was possible, they disrupted long worn-out categories, hierarchies, and narratives, which had seemed set in stone. By giving shape to these propositions in the museum space, it was possible to bring an increasingly large public to understand and appreciate that Janmot's *Flower of the Fields* (1845) (fig. 13) is one of the museum's greatest masterpieces and an emblematic work.

I could continue by giving further examples of new approaches tried out at the Musée des Beaux-Arts: each period and region covered by the museum offers us ample opportunities for this type of experimentation. In all probability, the vision that I had of this collection and what I wished to do with it was determined, to a great extent, by my experiences visiting German museums. Having begun my career in Colmar in Alsace, I had colleagues in charge of collections on the German side of the Rhine, which I used to regularly visit. Their approach to the nineteenth century, and the question of how to represent supposedly 'local' cultures, was very different to that which had developed in France. Among the things I learned was that the idea of scale—ranging from the irreducibly local to the global, passing through many other significant levels along the way—offers a fertile approach to deciding how to hang works. This remains true, although it sometimes entails running counter to, or even breaking with, the great chronological narrative that still underlies encyclopaedic museums, such as that in Lyon.

Now let us turn to contemporary art. The Musée d'Art Contemporain was created in 1984 under the directorship of Thierry Raspail and installed in a wing of the Musée des Beaux-Arts before it was transferred to the Cité Internationale area in Lyon. Originally conceived as an anti-museum that eschewed all 'overbearing' narratives and did not present a permanent collection, the institution has always resembled a *Kunsthalle*. The museum has won itself great renown over its thirty years, which has been heightened by its links with the Lyon Contemporary Art Biennale, one of the most important in the world.

The Musée d'Art Contemporain was conceived at a moment when two very different models of the museum were competing: on one side was the fine arts museum; on the other was the contemporary art museum. A wider set of oppositions clustered around this contest: Eurocentric versus global, tradition versus experimentation. The Musée d'Art Contemporain was founded on these contrasts, all of which are no longer current. The world's fine arts museums have modernised, gradually coming closer to the doctrines and operating procedures of contemporary art museums and accepting that established accounts of art history should be challenged. Although of course the new museal doctrines can be criticised, the fact remains that the old divisions have given way to a differently balanced environment.

When the twentieth century came to an end, curators in Lyon as elsewhere raised the question as to how its art should be represented in both fine art and contemporary art museums. At the request of Lyon's mayor, I was appointed director-general of the city's art museums. While both of these museums will maintain a significant degree of independence, it is clear to me that the purpose of this new grouping is to create a broader and more global foundation for the two collections. Moving forward, it is essential that the Musée des Beaux-Arts covers the breadth of art history right up until the present, while the Musée d'Art Contemporain must present work in a way that is both enduring and continuously experimental.

From the universal museum to the globalised museum

In directing the Musée de Beaux-Arts de Lyon for more than ten years, I have attempted to both ensure that the museum is engaged with its local context and open it up to a global scale. I will outline five ways in which the museum has addressed global issues and audiences.

Exhibiting works abroad

It seems to me that organising exhibitions of the museums' collections abroad is not simply a matter of institutional logistics or 'international policy'. Such transfers invite curators and audiences to draw new connections among works, prompting people see museal artefacts and the museums that host them in a different light.

International exhibitions may also turn out to be valuable testing grounds for new ideas. With this in mind, we presented an exhibition *Body Image in the 20th Century* as part of the 2010 World's Fair held in Shanghai. It brought together the large museums in the Rhône-Alpes regions, including the Musée des Beaux-Arts, Musée d'Art Contemporain, Institut d'Art contemporain de Villeurbanne (IAC), Musée d'art moderne et contemporain – Saint-Étienne Métropole, and Musée de Grenoble. The exhibition was shown again in a significantly different form at the Standard Bank Gallery in Johannesburg in 2012. A few years later, the collection of Lyon's Musée des Beaux-Arts made another large exhibition possible. Titled *Los Modernos* in 2015–16, it was held at Mexico City's Museo Nacional de Arte (MUNAL) and the Museo de las Artes (Museum of the Arts) at Guadalajara University. The idea behind the *Modernos* exhibition was to put the twentieth-century art collections belonging to the Musée des Beaux-Arts and MUNAL in dialogue with one another. In this way, it sought to highlight—and question—the transfers, connections, and equivalencies between arts practices in Europe and Mexico.

Other exhibitions have required cooperation between Scotland's National Galleries in Edinburgh, the Kunsthalle in Karlsruhe, and the Musée des Beaux-Arts de Lyon. The objective of this partnership, which was founded on these three collections, was to organise exhibitions that would alternately visit the three cities. The first exhibition created as part of this association was *Self-Portraits: From Rembrandt to the Selfie* (2015–16). Going against the logic underlying blockbuster shows, we are adopting a resolutely experimental perspective for these exhibitions, which reconsider how art history might merge into an anthropology of images. We intend to pursue this type of arrangement elsewhere in the future and are currently in discussion with possible partners in Asia, North America, and Latin America.

Exhibition themes of global flows and cultural transfers

Increasingly, Lyon's museums reflect histories of cultural transfers and the mobility of people, works, and ideas across the world. This point can be illustrated by way of reference to several exhibitions. Consider, for example, *Repartir à Zéro* (*Starting from Scratch*, held in 2008), which was formulated and mounted in collaboration with Éric de Chassey. It showed how, in the period immediately following 1945, US and European artists returned to an elemental grammar of forms, signs, and standpoints. This return to a primal plane of visual expression represented a reversion to basics in the face of the traumas wrought during the Second World War. In the same way, the exhibition *Joseph Cornell and Surrealism in New York* (2013) was an opportunity for presenting Surrealism's displacement across the Atlantic while also delving into the art of Cornell, one of the most interesting figures in the Surrealist milieu.

At this juncture, I would also like to describe another exhibition that was particularly important to me: *Islamophilia* (2011). Curated by Remy Labrusse and Salima Hellal, it considered the Islamic arts from the perspective of how they have been received by Western scholars and artists in the nineteenth and twentieth centuries. The Musée des Beaux-Arts' substantial Islamic collection allowed us to investigate the relations between Islamic culture and the West in depth. To a certain extent, this exhibition was a continuation of a lecture and seminar on Arab science and the Italian Renaissance given by Hans Belting, which had been organised by the museum and University of Lyon 2. Published under our patronage, the text of this lecture was a prelude to Belting's important book *Florence and Baghdad: Renaissance Art and Arab Science* (2011).

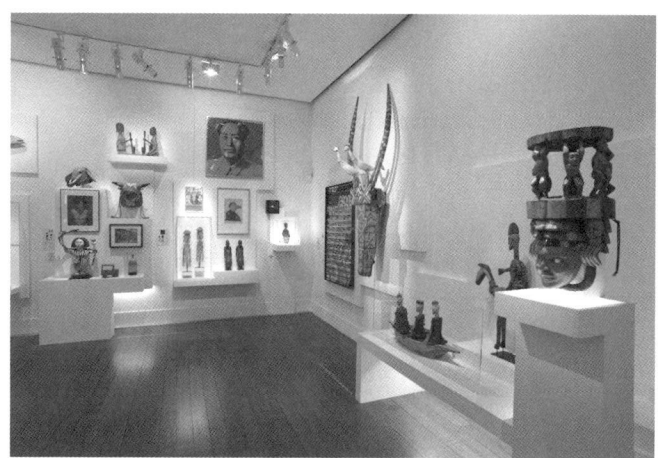

Figure 14. View of the exhibition *Métissages* at the Musée des Beaux-Arts de Lyon, 2013. (Plate 23, p. 246) © Lyon MBA – Photograph by Alain Basset.

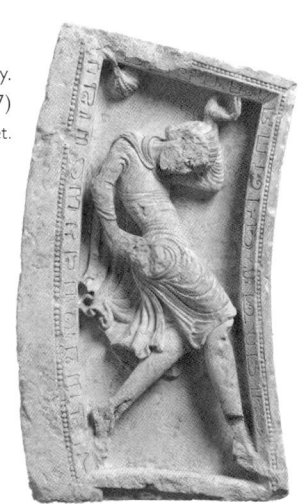

Figure 15. Unknown, *Juggler*, France, Last quarter of the 12th century.
(Plate 24, p. 247)
Inv. D. 140. Lyon, Musée des Beaux-Arts. © Lyon MBA – Photograph by Alain Basset.

Highlighting culturally hybrid objects

The last exhibition that I wish to mention is *Métissages* (*Hybridism*, mounted in 2013) (fig. 14). Based on a private collection in Lyon, it brought together diverse objects and works, such as everyday items from Africa, urban art, and contemporary ceramics. This disparate body of works was brought together on the grounds not just that they reflected their owners' taste, but above all by the fact that they blended elements of different cultural origins.

The exhibition's title, the word *métissages*, meaning hybridism or interbreeding is borrowed from the historian Serge Gruzinski (1999), whose work emphasised forms of cultural intermixing in Central America. As this exhibition showed, his ideas extend far beyond their initial subject matter.

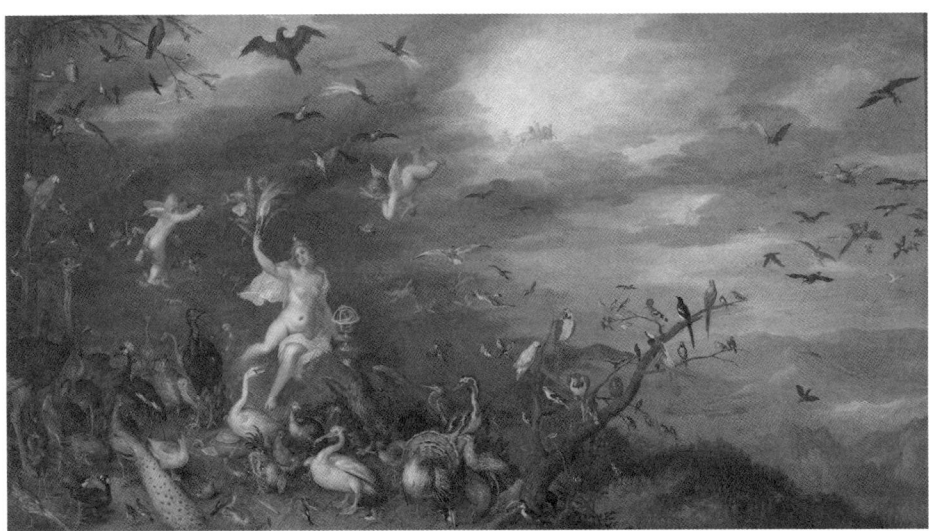

Figure 16. Jan Brueghel the Elder, *Air*, 16th-17th century. Oil on wood. (Plate 25, p. 248)
Lyon, Musée des Beaux-Arts. © Lyon MBA – Photograph by Alain Basset.

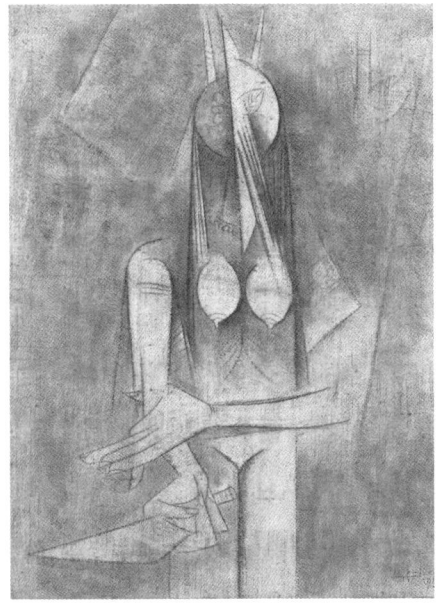

Figure 17. Wifredo Lam, *Woman with a Knife*, 1950. Oil on canvas. (Plate 26, p. 249)
Inv. 1997-37. Lyon, Musée des Beaux-Arts. © Lyon MBA – Photograph by RMN / Ojéda – Le Mage; © Adagp, Paris, 2019.

In attempting to highlight the cultural hybridity of the works in our collection, we have begun to draw up an inventory of works that are hybrid or expressive of distant cultures. An example is the famous *Juggler* from Bourges (fig. 15) that so fascinated the art historian Henri Focillon. A splendid Romanesque relief, whose frame bears approximate inscriptions in Kufic script that were inspired, no doubt, by objects imported from the East and held in abbeys from the early Middle Ages onwards. There is also a set of four paintings representing the four elements by Jan Brueghel the Elder (fig. 16). In fact, they indicate how the sheer variety of the animal kingdom loomed into view with the great discoveries of the late fifteenth and early sixteenth centuries. Brueghel's paradisal landscapes constitute a historical response to the newly globalised world of the early modern period. I could go on almost indefinitely. Consider one of the two works by Wifredo Lam in Jacqueline Delubac's collection (fig. 17), or *Cultural Melting Bath*, a spectacular installation by Cai Guo Qiang that was exhibited at the Musée d'Art Contemporain (figs. 18 and 19). This

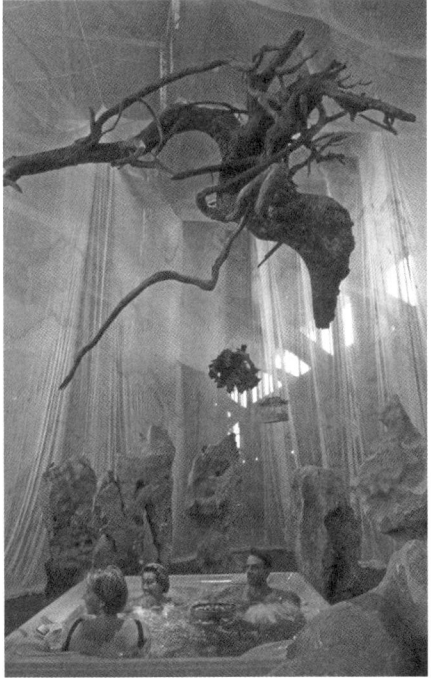

Figure 18. Cai Guo Qiang, *Cultural Melting Bath: Projects for the 20th Century, 1997.* View of the Lyon Contemporary Art Biennial, 2000. (Plate 27, p. 250)
© Cai Studio – Photograph by Blaise Adilon.

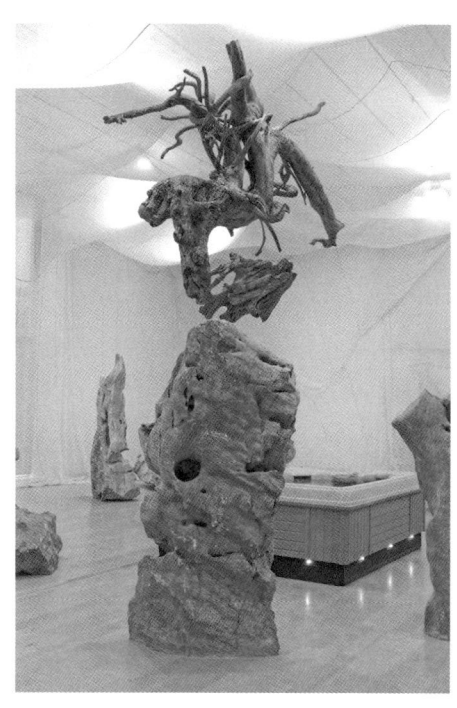

Figure 19. Cai Guo Qiang, *Cultural Melting Bath: Projects for the 20th Century, 1997.* View of the exhibition in2016 in maclyon. (Plate 28, p. 251) ©Cai Studio – Photograph by Blaise Adilon.

last piece might be considered a manifesto for a wider aspect of the contemporary art collection. It is important to stress, though, that works treating 'connectivity' among cultures, to use an academic term, demand careful curation to ensure that all of their implications and meanings are made comprehensible.

Contemporary art

From its opening onwards, the Musée d'Art Contemporain has presented works from contemporary art scenes around the world, such as those of China and India, to mention just two examples. Accordingly, in this context, my aim of broadening the Lyon museums' scope to a global scale had to be approached differently. With regard to the city's biennial exhibitions, I must mention one organised by Jean-Hubert Martin with Marc Augé in 2000. Titled *Partage d'Exotismes*, it was as large as the *Magiciens de la Terre* (one especially notable exhibition mounted at the Pompidou Centre in 1989). To me, *Partage d'Exotismes* was remarkable for the connections that it established among globalised, multicultural contemporary art and anthropology. In the future, it will be necessary to show works stemming from other art scenes and involve foreign curators in developing exhibitions, including some that will draw from the Musée d'Art Contemporain's collection.

Hanging the permanent collection

For some years we have been working on ways of foregrounding another dimension of the collection, namely the circulation of motifs and forms among cultural areas over the long term. The new display in the decorative arts department clearly tends towards a globalised or interconnected history of objects, forms, and motifs. In this, we were inspired

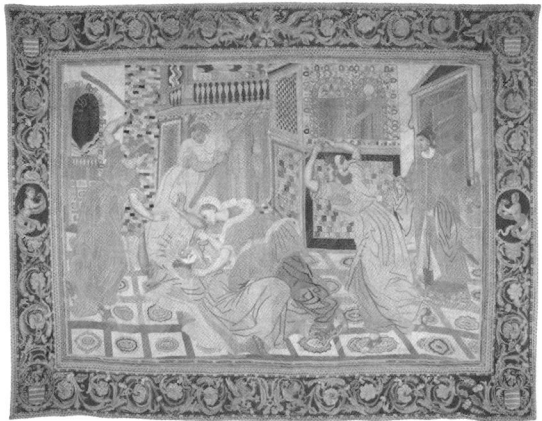

Figure 20. *The Vengence of Hecube*,
Macao, 17th century. Silk embroidery,
gold thread and painted satin.
(Plate 29, p. 252)
Inv. 1970-537. Lyon, Musée des Beaux-Arts.
© Lyon MBA – Photograph by Alain Basset.

by Lisbon's Museo de Oriente (Orientalism Museum) and the exhibition *Beyond the Nile* put on at the Getty in 2018, which situated Egyptian art as part of a vast space of cultural circulation around the ancient Mediterranean. Among the key works in the decorative arts section are two outstanding large embroideries from Macao, both of which illustrate episodes from Ovid's *Metamorphoses* (figs. 20 and 21). Probably inspired by engravings made in Lyon, the two embroideries are part of a set of four large compositions: three are kept in the New York Metropolitan Museum, another in a private collection.

The challenge for the future will be to organise the display of the works so as to accentuate cultural exchanges without turning away from the museum's original mission of conservation of cultural heritage. In the end, the challenge is to have different and contradictory conceptions of and approaches to museal practice coexisting in a single institution. With its overarching formal narrative, the encyclopaedic and ordered museum must be able to enter into dialogues with the globalised museum, to establish productive relations with new ephemeral and interpretative approaches, and to engage in experiments and anthropological questioning.

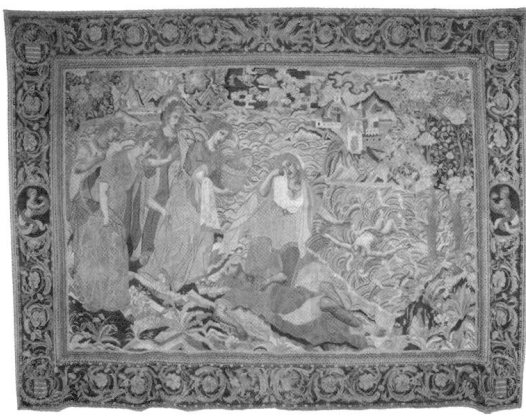

Figure 21. *The Death of Polydoros*,
Macao, 17th century. Silk embroidery,
gold thread and painted satin.
(Plate 30, p. 253)
Inv. 1970-538. Lyon, Musée des Beaux-Arts.
© Lyon MBA – Photograph by Alain Basset.

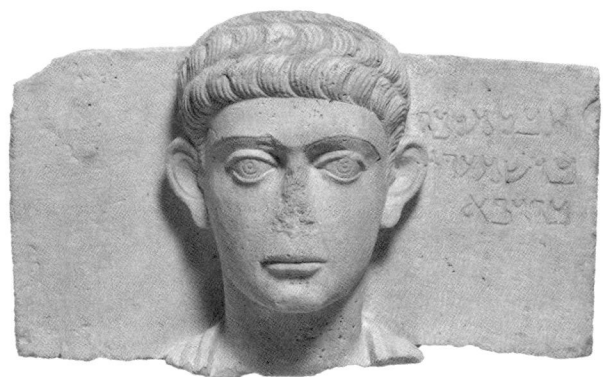

Figure 22. Bas-relief of Maliku,
Palmyre, Roman period,
2nd century. Limestone.
(Plate 31, p. 254)
Inv. 2011.11.2. Lyon, Musée des Beaux-
Arts. © Lyon MBA – Photograph by
Alain Basset.

I will bring this chapter to an end with a face (fig. 22). It is that of a young man whose name—Maliku—is given in the inscription on the relief. He entered Lyon's collection in 2013, a year before the destruction unleashed by the Islamic State in Palmyra, from whence he comes. Following the Islamic State's atrocities, visitors will probably view this work and its eternally youthful face differently. Inevitably, I too look on it differently. To me, when questioning and wondering about the destiny of this work, the idea of universality seems inescapable.

Notes

I would here like to express my warmest thanks to Gérard Bruyère and Léna Widerkehr for their assistance.

1   The expression 'a temple of universal knowledge united by the voice of genius' is used in a decree promulgated by the representatives of the people of Boisset, Borel, and Cadroy. Addressed to the departments of Ain, Isère, Loire, Rhône, and Saône-et-Loire, it was dated 16 May 1795 (27 Floréal year III on the French Republican calendar). The decree called for the creation of a museum in the 'house known as St Pierre'. See Representatives of Boisset, Borel, and Cadroy, 'Decree'.

2   The first Musée des Monuments Français was founded in 1795 by Alexandre Lenoir in the former ancient convent of the Augustinians (which was also once the site of the École nationale supérieure des Beaux-Arts).

3   This ambition is articulated in a report of 1887, in which Aynard writes that 'our administration, which always operates with limited means with regard to the proliferation of all works of art, is above all committed to building or completing our collections, to filling in the all-too conspicuous gaps, so that the Palais Saint-Pierre offers a slightly more complete history of all the arts'. Édouard Aynard, *Les Musées de Lyon*, 11–12.

4   Léon Rosenthal, 'La résurrection des villes', 3.

Works Cited

Aynard, Édouard. *Les Musées de Lyon, leur état actuel, leur avenir: rapport au maire de Lyon sur l'emploi du legs Chazière.* Lyon: De Mougin-Rusand, 1887.

Gruzinski, Serge. *La Pensée métisse.* Paris: Librairie Arthème Fayard, 1999.

Representatives of Boisset, Borel, and Cadroy. Decree of 16 May 1795, document number 1 L 1073, Departmental Archives of the Rhône and City of Lyon.

Rosenthal, Léon. 1915. 'La résurrection des villes. Musées régionaux et musées locaux'. *L'Humanité,* 28 August 1915, 3.

Which Worlds Belong in a Museum?

A Manifesto for a Humanist Museum

Nathalie Bondil

> We can say that postcolonial thought is, in several respects, a world thought …
> But postcolonial thought is also a dream: the dream of a new form of human-
> ism, a critical humanism founded above all on the divisions that, this side of
> the absolutes, differentiate us. It's the dream of a *polis* that is universal because
> ethnically diverse.[1]
> —Achille Mbembe

Atlas Fractured and the circulation of worlds

The video artist Theo Eshetu was born in 1958 London, has lived in Senegal and
Ethiopia, and is now based in Rome. Drawing on this distinctly pan-national experience, his perspective foregrounds the global dimensions of art. Presented at Documenta
2017, the video installation *Atlas Fractured* projected human portraits onto ancient
masks conserved in the Ethnologisches Museum in Berlin. Some of the projected images were portrait photographs; others showed the faces of sculptures of human figures. In
combining faces and masks from around the world, Eshetu questions the geopolitics of
borders. 'Cultural identities cannot be fixed and defined', he writes:

> They are in constant flux, created and moulded by political projections, erected and
> destroyed by historical events, and fluctuate with the displacement of cultural ob-
> jects and the migration of populations.

This vision of fluid global identities chimes with developments in postcolonial theory.
Achille Mbembe, a key postcolonial critic, writes that 'another cultural geography of the
world is setting in'. In this new dispensation, 'Europe is no longer the gravitational centre

of the world. There is no longer a peripheral art scene'. The emergence of this newly de-centred world history of the arts, he argues, should be accompanied by a 'circulation of worlds' in which cultural practices would interpenetrate without losing their specificity.

How can a museum be a vector of social progress as recommended by the Organisation for Economic Cooperation and Development (OECD) and International Council of Museums' (ICOM) new guide, *Culture and local development: Maximizing the impact – Guide for local Governments, Communities and Museums*? How can it retain the essential aspects of its traditional missions with regard to its collections? How can we imagine a global citizenship that equally addresses the challenge of current issues such as sustainable development, community harmony and protection of diversity? How can we exhibit our networks of artifacts in an open and dynamic manner? How do we avoid ideological and systemic constraints? What is our ideal vision of a universal *polis*? Mbembe has also said "post-colonial criticism is also dream thinking: the dream of a new form of humanism (...) It is the dream of a polis that is universal because it is cross-pollinated."

Cultural policy in a globalising world

At the Earth Summit in Rio de Janeiro in 1992, 173 heads of state formulated Agenda 21, a plan for global sustainable development in the twenty-first century. Among a broad variety of topics, the plan tackled cultural development, which was henceforth to be 'defined at the level of cities and local governments', with commitments to 'human rights, cultural diversity, participatory democracy and creating conditions for peace'.[2] Although a range of social initiatives and economic models are available for pursuing these ends, the advantages offered by the cultural sector remain largely unknown. The broad set of debates relating to migration, integration, and multiculturalism, for example, are each animated by cultural dynamics. Regardless of this, in many contexts (not least in the province of Quebec, where my museum is located) spending on culture represents scarcely a single percent of state expenditure.

More than ever before, in the twenty-first century culture and education (its Siamese twin) will play a leading role in maintaining forms of coexistence in our 'global village'.[3] When it comes to legislation, culture does not fit neatly into any one ministry, but answers to different mandates, including education, family, immigration, health, economics, infrastructure, and tourism. In consequence, any cultural policy has to address how culture—in a 'glocal' era defined by intergenerationalism and interculturalism—might contribute to inclusion and the retention of populations; wellbeing and pride among different sectors of society; and economic development.

How might culture contend with the issues of the twenty-first century? Indeed, many might suppose that pressing contemporary challenges would be better faced by investing in the fields of ecology, biodiversity, education, local and global economics, civil democracy, and sustainable development. I would suggest, however, that culture embraces these fields too. I am referring to culture, here, in the sense of civilisation, which UNESCO has defined as:

> the set of distinctive spiritual, material, intellectual, and emotional features of society or a social group, and … encompasses, in addition to art and literature, lifestyles, ways of living together, value systems, traditions and belief.

Notice how encompassing this definition is: the dominance of forms of entertainment and spectacle in the contemporary era should not blind us to culture's primary significance as a way of life and conception of the world. Humanity, I would venture, is as much *homo aestheticus* as *homo festivus*.

The Montreal Museum of Fine Arts (MMFA) is situated in a world city: in 2013, one third of Montreal's population were immigrants. Two hundred languages are spoken in the city, which hosts 120 cultural communities. More than half of its population is either foreign born or has at least one foreign-born parent. In the future, international immigration will be the principal driver of the city's demographic growth. Founded in 1860, the MMFA is a multidisciplinary space, featuring five pavilions, a concert hall, and a cinema. Both a museum of historical artefacts and a gallery of artworks, its collection is encyclopaedic. Not subject to a restrictive mandate or mission, the museum has the advantage of being able to pursue innovative and ambitious projects. With a centre for education and art therapy, cinema, and concert hall, the MMFA offers one of the largest educational and cultural complexes in a North American art museum.

It is through providing an array of diverse services, many of which actively reach out to museum publics, that cultural institutions such as the MMFA are able to help fulfil the mission outlined in Agenda 21. Many museums work hard to make culture accessible to schools, families, and other members of the public. This stems from a longstanding Anglo-Saxon tradition, which has taken hold strongly across North America, of striving to attract diverse publics. As a key point of contact between Europe and America, drawing on both indigenous legacies and English and French colonial histories, Quebec is especially well placed to foster cultural hybridity. This has been boon to the MMFA in reaching out to a variety of demographics.

Rethinking the collections: our works are the words in a dictionary of the world

More than ever, education is seen as crucially important in achieving societal goals. Although classical education entails learning to read and write, visual literacy is also of paramount importance. This is more than just a matter of acquiring formal knowledge: to understand images, we need to learn not only how to see but also how to feel—to nurture and articulate the emotions inspired by cultural works.

At the MMFA, our educational practice places greater emphasis on understanding our state of being than on knowing how to act. Over and above our cognitive and intellectual understanding, it is important that we teach perceptiveness. This quality, above all others, differentiates humans from robots, our emotional intelligence from their artificial intelligence. Research on perceptiveness grows each day. Bringing together the humanities and sciences, two spheres that are traditionally separated in a sterile dualism, this approach to education will help future generations better understand the complexities of culture and much else besides. If cultural institutions are to retain their relevance, they must adopt such alternative approaches. Mutually called upon to address emerging challenges, the arts and sciences have more things in common than ever before.

As part of this attempt to rethink education through art, MMFA has collaborated with a group of designers and creators to build a free, open access digital platform named EducArt (https://www.mbam.qc.ca/en/education-wellness/educart/). Linked to a variety of teaching programmes, the platform makes the MMFA's collections available to the outside world. This ambitious pilot project, which has been supported by Quebec's Digital Cultural Plan, allows users to approach the museum's works from all disciplinary perspectives, encompassing the social sciences, mathematics, languages, ethics, religious studies, and more. During my involvement with this project, I had four key questions and concerns in mind. These are:

1. How should we bequeath our collections to future generations? EducArt's innovative approach is to prise open art historian's and critic's quasi monopoly over the interpretation of art so as to allow experts in other fields (which were previously considered irrelevant) to have their say.

2. Recognising that teachers are often overworked and that museum initiatives aimed at schoolchildren are seldom taken up, I wanted to engage experts to work for the benefit of teachers. Having these experts has helped the Museum incorporate its artworks in schools' educational programmes, forming a mutually creative partnership.

3. To encourage teachers and curriculum builders working outside Montreal to use our collections, I developed seventeen pilot projects produced in partnership with Quebec's seventeen administrative regions.

4. If no disciplinary boundaries are imposed on our encounters with art, it speaks to everyone. The diversity of our collections means that they relate to all disciplines and social issues, beyond art history as it has been defined hitherto. Does the word 'encyclopaedic' not mean 'complete instruction', evoking the image of an encompassing circle?

These specific concerns raise the wider point that, if the MMFA is to reach out to publics and connect with pressing contemporary issues, then it must adopt a holistic approach to education. When we learn to read and write, we also learn to see: each of these skills are necessary in approaching multifaceted artworks. Works of art are symbolic, historical, stylised, material, technical, physical, chemical, neurobiological, and much more besides. The plurality of perspectives required to grasp their complexity only heightens their polysemic and ultimately humanist character.

Rethinking our collections means that we must open the museum's doors to other disciplines and accept that different perspectives on artworks and their complexity are just as legitimate as established interpretations. Above and beyond art history, or indeed any one discipline, the works have to be considered from all points of view. By encouraging unrestricted analysis, it becomes possible to unlock their complexity and diverse meanings. Every work of art contains a world.

Rethinking museums' relevance in a multipolar world

Do fine arts museums question and act upon key contemporary issues? Do they not tend to leave such questions to other museums, which deal specifically with science or society? In the twenty-first century, culture and education are key in easing forms of cultural coexistence in an increasingly globalised world. In this, it is essential that museums reach across generations and cultures. This open approach encourages forms of collaborative creativity with experts in other fields. It also raises provocative new questions about agency, looking, and meaning in museums. Consider Bénédicte Savoy's challenging idea that objects have the right to present themselves. Whether artworks or other culture artefacts, objects in museums have endured through time. As objects are displaced or move through space, they knit together formerly discrete times, creating a concertina of temporalities.

Insofar as they hail from distant contexts, of which we as museumgoers have little idea, objects in museum collections can provoke anxiety: works of art challenge our intellectual security. Manifesting traces of obscure histories and perspectives, they destabilise our sense of the world. How might ethnological objects, for example, be approached aesthetically? How have the so-called 'primitive' arts found a place in the artistic pantheon? Who among contemporary artists has a place in the artistic canon? How might we interpret historical objects today? The exhibition *From Africa to the Americas: Face-to-Face with Picasso, Past and Present* tackled such questions—posed by Picasso among others—by adopting a historical, contextualising, and ethnological approach. It enabled contemporary artists from Africa, or of African origin, to propose new readings of cultural appropriation. In this way, the exhibition increased the number of viewpoints on the power dynamics at play in the formation of the modernist canon. It also challenged the received Eurocentrism of art historical narratives, which have long marginalised the 'decorative' arts and art from non-Western cultures.

During the interwar period, various terms were used interchangeably to encompass the art of Africa, Oceania, and the Americas: Fénéon wrote of the 'distant arts', the Surrealists of the 'magical arts', Malraux of the 'primordial arts'. Many commentators spoke of the 'Negro arts'. Having come to be recognised as pejorative, these terms gave way to the 'primitive arts'. Still, in evoking the notion of origins, these terms insidiously inferred that the 'primitive arts' were simplistic and rudimentary. As 'primitive arts' too fell by the wayside, new terms took in its place as critics began speaking of the 'ethnic arts' and 'tribal arts'. Although Jacques Kerchache's suggestion—'*arts premiers*' or the 'first art'—was included in the French Dictionary, the scholarly community came to prefer 'non-Western arts', 'non-European arts', or 'extra-European arts'. All of these, however, remained Eurocentric. As no one of these terms was satisfactory, the most acceptable ways of naming the diversity of artistic cultures around the world was simply to indicate the arts of Africa, the Americas, Asia, and Oceania geographically.

To counter prevailing assumptions in the history of art, the exhibition *From Africa to the Americas* foregrounded some of the key material and spiritual principles of traditional cultures. Above all, it challenged the idea of the supposed universality of art. The cliché that great art is timeless persists even as art itself evolves. Not only are organic materials perishable, but artworks were not necessarily made to last. Indeed, in many situations artworks are produced only to be downgraded or destroyed (if their effectiveness was contested), or abandoned (following their owner's death). Against the prevailing artistic paradigm, traditional cultures raise the possibility that art need not have an artist—at least in the Western sense of the word. Whereas for a long time collectors had little regard for the pedigree of artworks, which were acquired without consideration for their context. The information gathered to accompany such works was limited to the name of their acquirer or collector; the culture in which they were made; their school; and perhaps individual master under whose direction the work was produced. By attributing works to known figures, historians and curators have often been able to eschew their ignorance of past artists' true names, which have come down to us only in a few exceptional cases.

An engaged museum, committed to togetherness and social peace

"We must change the imaginations of humanities" wrote Édouard Glissant[4]. With our new wing for One-World, I have chosen the name in reference to the poet and philosopher who explained: "I call 'One World' our universe as it changes and persists through our interactions." – thus expanding upon the generous ideas of one of the most important Post-Colonial theorists. Glissant's native West Indies formed the bedrock of his writings. An extraordinary setting of languages and cultures (European, American, African, Asian, Francophone, Creole, etc.), it created the conditions for a plural identity that is open to the world: "No island dominates; each develops its identity in relation to the others, through differentiation." In this unique primary setting, our human cultures are simultaneously in contact with each other. This accelerated development forces us to shed our former absolutes. Glissant anticipated a world where our identities exist in relation to each other: "When I am asked to draw a tree, I paint a forest." He interpreted modernity as a relational process between all peoples. We cannot live together without a convergence of memories.

One other point of reference in this venture was UNESCO, for which 'diversity does not exist between cultures, but is inherent to the very idea of culture and is thus a constituent part of cultures'. In representing the cultures from all around the world, the One World collection offers an outstanding tool for discovering and understanding cultural diversity. The second largest museum collection in Canada, the wing contains over 10,000 artworks from all continents and periods, and measures 1,000 square metres. Its purpose is to enhance visitors' knowledge and understanding of other cultures in an age in which cultural coexistence is a fact of everyday life. In curating this collection, we wanted to emphasise the longstanding connections among different cultures, both historically and today. In adopting these dynamic values—the same values, I might add, that prevail in Montreal, Quebec, and Canada at large—the wing fosters an outlook that is more *inter*cultural than *multi*cultural. Our Policy for Diversity as well as our high profile Committee for Togetherness and our Intercultural Arts curator reinforce our commitment at each level of the institution.

In today's increasingly hybrid societies, what can museums offer their visitors with various intercultural backgrounds? People learn to live together through forms of cultural exchange. Take the case of Montreal. The majority of the immigrants who come to Quebec live in Montreal. This city's population makes for a distinctly 'hot' society, in Lévi-Straussian sense of a society oriented towards future evolution. This cosmopolitan city grows by drawing in people and ideas, and making them its own. As a creative hub, Montreal is fuelled by immigration and a large contingent of students. Indeed, it is both one of North America's leading knowledge-based cities and a key consular city. With its complex assortment of nationalities, Montreal benefits from an excitingly composite culture and society that values tolerance, defined by Lévi-Strauss in the following terms:

> Tolerance is not a contemplative attitude, dispensing indulgence to what has been or what is still in being. It is a dynamic attitude, consisting in the anticipation, understanding and promotion of what is struggling into being. We can see the diversity of human cultures behind us, around us, and before us.[5]

Accepting difference—not to mention anticipating difference, as Lévi-Strauss prompts us to here—requires constant effort. When it comes to tolerance, all forms of progress require continual reinforcement. 'It's easier to break the atom than to destroy prejudice', said Einstein. In this century of economic and climate migration, in which stereotypes predominate (not least on social media), it is difficult to ensure a tranquil society. I propose that we should aim to live not in a society that is fractured like a mosaic, but rather in a society of exchange.

"It is often the way we look at other people that imprisons them in their own narrowest allegiances. And it is also the way we look at them that may set them free" wrote Amin Maalouf. Can museums become this place where thoughts of the world encounter one another? How do we avoid shared spaces and instead create a space of sharing? Collections are constantly evolving and (de)constructing. We have added contemporary works created by international artists to ancient art, but also commissioned Canadian culturally diverse local artists. This experience of discovery and questioning, with as many shared inter-subjectivities, is neither a teleological story nor theoretical argument.

From cultural appropriation to cultural exchange

To promote interculturalism rather than multiculturalism (that 'mosaic society' I mentioned above) it is crucial that cultural institutions find ways of avoiding combative identities and populist tendencies. They must promote debate, not conflict. In this vein, consider *Once Upon a Time… The Western*, a multidisciplinary exhibition on representations of the American West, one of the twentieth century's most enduring myths of identity. First, I wanted to show how history and cultural representation come together to fabricate myths—in this case that of the Western frontier. Second, I was concerned to emphasise how artists have engaged this mythology to challenge macho values, racist stereotypes, land annexation, genocide, and a culture of violence, all of which unfortunately remain present in contemporary North American culture.

This concern with fostering interculturality is also evident in a performance produced with the MMFA named *Another Feather in Her Bonnet* (2017, https://www.youtube.com/watch?v=h43qO5gYobc). The result of an unlikely partnership between fashion designer and writer Jean-Paul Gaultier and Cree-Irish painter Kent Monkman, it enacted a symbolic ritual of friendship. The two creators proposed this performance as a way of overcoming divisions. In it, Monkman played his alter ego Miss Chief Eagle Testickle, playing on stereotypes of exotic indigenous women as perceived through the colonial gaze. He wore a headdress of white feathers that Gaultier, inspired by the First Nations people of the plains, had designed for a haute-couture wedding dress.[6] Traditionally worn only by men, the headwear was imbued with spirituality. Gaultier's stylistic borrowing of the headdress contributed to debates over cultural appropriation.

Developing a culture of partnership

To bolster innovation, it is important that museums build creative partnerships with experts, schools, NGOs, associations, institutes, universities, and so forth. Nourishing interdisciplinary approaches is key to creating an active and creative culture. In such partnerships, each participant can draw on the strengths of his or her own field. By implementing a comprehensive partnership policy, the MMFA hopes to ground its work in mutual development and collaboration, not competition. Such flexible alliances make possible new ways of thinking, invention, and experimentation. This interactive approach allows museums to reach greater publics, especially those who do not have access to cultural activities. Community organisations, intermediaries, and volunteers can develop and implement activities outside the museum's walls. Counting

450 partnerships with associations, clinics, hospitals, faculties, and other institutions, the MMFA's outreach programme is making a difference in society. Along the way, it has confronted racism, homophobia, and ageism, in addition to discrimination against physical and mental disabilities; illiteracy; high school drop outs; poverty; and itineracy. Often, this discrimination takes the form of intimidation, violence, radicalisation, and social exclusion.

As means of developing cross-sector partnerships, the MMFA offers expert contributions to over fifty university research programmes in areas including art-therapy, restorative justice, museum mediation, the use of technology in colleges, art education in multicultural environments, prevention of radicalisation, acceptance of mental disabilities, acceptance of migrants, and so forth. The Museum also contributes to breaking down loneliness among the elderly, those suffering from physical and mental health problems in disadvantaged environments, and victims of abuse.

Museotherapy, our new concept for Museum and health

Our need for 'beauty', or at least for aesthetic emotion, is not just philosophical or cultural, but *physiological* too. As artificial intelligence becomes more intrinsic to societies, interest in emotional intelligence grows. The neurosciences trace complex circuits that link our emotional and sensational being with our intellectual and rational being. Culture provides an environment in which to explore these connections, in which awareness and feeling link up with our emotional being. Much like love and friendship, aesthetic emotion is therefore able to stimulate positive feelings and enhance wellbeing. Art represents a form of 'soft power' through which people cultivate empathy.

As virtual technologies proliferate, more and more value will be placed on physical experience. In the face of an increasingly dematerialised culture, people will seek out sensory and emotional experiences. The word 'aesthetic' derives from the Greek word *aisthesis*, meaning 'sensation'. Research, in the neurosciences in particular, attests to the benefits of aesthetics for our wellbeing and its utility in therapy: the circuits that connect human biology with our responsiveness to culture are coming into greater focus.

The Art and Health Advisory Committee, which is chaired by Quebec's Chief Scientist, has given the MMFA the green light to develop innovative pilot projects with its partners. Their aim is to analyse how visiting museums and participating in workshop activities impact upon individuals. Visiting museums, this research suggests, influences processes of healing with respect to a number of conditions: Alzheimer's disease; suicidal tendencies; cardiac problems; autism; anorexia and other eating disorders; mental health; post-traumatic stress disorder; and war trauma. The MMFA mounts exhibitions in medical centres and is a founding partner of the Chair in Research, Art, Culture, and Wellbeing created at the University of Quebec in Montreal. This artistic and scientific committee includes experts in the fields of education, health, research, social services, and university and community environments.

Recognized as a pioneer and major player, our Museum seeks to become a vehicle for individual and social well-being. This is why we have hired the first full time art therapist in a museum. In 2018, we also launched the very first medical Museum Prescriptions in partnership with the Médecins francophones du Canada. In our *International Atelier for Education and Art Therapy*, we have set aside physical spaces dedicated to therapy with a medical consultation room. Those facilities provide an unprecedented practice framework for medical and community professionals. We are involved in the training of future physicians by offering McGill University medical student workshops. Our *Art Hive* space includes a full-time art therapist (a museum first) which offers supervised activity for people of wide socioeconomic backgrounds and cultures, in a safe and user-friendly setting that fosters a spirit of community. Reflecting on these path-breaking initiatives, we have created a new concept for wellness through the arts, *Museotherapy* because art has beneficial effects at both the social and individual levels.

I am convinced that in the twenty-first century, culture will be as important to health as sport was in the twentieth. Culture stimulates discussion of the issues underlying our intercultural era. Although the current museum environment around the world offers support to artists and art history, this is not enough.

I am convinced that an understanding of our emotional intelligence is as essential as artificial intelligence. Over and above our cognitive and intellectual knowledge, it is essential to create a school of perception. It is what differentiates human beings from robots. This field of research is growing daily as the humanities meet up with the sciences.

I am convinced that aesthetics could encourage understanding between human beings. It is our belief that aesthetics can play an immense role in fostering understanding and reconciliation. As such, contributing to harmony in our society becomes part of our mission too.

I am convinced we can participate in building a better global citizenship whose objective is to address our current issues like togetherness, biodiversity and sustainable development. We are in a global age when all humanity shares a common destiny. We aim to redefine the role of the fine arts museum in society. Our innovative, socially engaged vision has been brought into the limelight by the Organisation for Economic Cooperation and

Development (OECD) and International Council of Museums (ICOM) in their guide *Culture and Local Development: Maximising the Impact – Guide for Local Governments, Communities and Museums* (2018). Those studies commissioned by OECD-ICOM have been conducted providing a roadmap for local governments and museums on how to jointly define a development agenda. This recognition of our numerous actions supports our vision of the Museum as a vector of social progress. As such, this validation by international economic and cultural institutions enables to expand the definition of the museum with "inclusion" and "well-being".

I am convinced of a civic-spirited museum. Museums are a tool of cultural diplomacy. The cohabitation of cultures has never before been brought about so rapidly, driving a necessary thinking of the world as a whole.

Notes

1   Mbembe, Achille, Olivier Mongin, Nathalie Lempereur, and Jean-Louis Schlegel. 'Qu'est-ce que la pensée postcoloniale? Entretien avec Achille Mbembe'. Eurozine. Posted January 9, 2008. https://www.eurozine.com/what-is-postcolonial-thinking/. See also: *Penser par éclairs et par la foudre*, entretien d'Achille Mbembe par Seloua Luste Boulbina, Collège International de Philosophie, Rue Descartes, n°83, 2014, p. 97-116 and *Sortir de la grande nuit. Essai sur l'Afrique décolonisée*, Paris, La Découverte, 2010.

2   Culture 21. 'Committee on Culture'. *agenda21culture.net*. Posted in 2017. http://www.agenda21culture.net/who-we-are/committee-on-culture.

3   McLuhan, Marshall, and Bruce R. Powers. *The Global Village: Transformations in World Life and Media in the 21st Century*. Oxford: Oxford University Press, 1989.

4   See Édouard Glissant: *Poétique IV: Traité du Tout-Monde,* Paris, Gallimard, 1997; *Une nouvelle région du monde, Esthétique I*, Paris, Gallimard, 2006; *L'imaginaire des langues: entretiens avec Lise Gauvin (1991-2009),* Paris, Gallimard, 2010.

5   Lévi-Strauss, Claude. *Race and History*. Sacramento: Creative Media Partners, LLC, 2014, p. 46.

6   The headdress is part of Gaultier's collection *Les Hussardes*, 2002–03.

PART 4

CENTRE

AND

PERIPHERY

Introduction

Centre and Periphery or Circulation and Dialogue?

Sophie Mouquin

"Centre and periphery". The core-periphery metaphor is well known to economists, and commonly used in the fields of geography and political sociology. Such a model implies a hierarchical or dependent relationship. As its basis stems from Imperialist or Capitalist theory, the periphery is considered to be subordinated to the centre. Nevertheless, this worldview is debatable. Great scholars have shown its limits due to the complex interactions between politics, sociology and economy that it glosses over. The model might be satisfying for the rational mind but is often over-simplifying[1]. "The problem of combining socio-economic space with geographic or Euclidean space in one theory or model has for long been a key problem for all economists"[2]. Historians are also dealing with the adequation of the core-periphery model to their object of studies: "Re-Mapping Centre and Periphery" is clearly a necessity[3].

However, art historians have demonstrated how accurate the centre-periphery concept can often be. Regarding the art market, it's a commonly accepted fact that Paris grew to prominence in the 1800s after a large domination of Amsterdam and Antwerp in the previous century, but was superseded by London at the turn of the 19th century, which was then overtaken by New York after the Second World War. These phenomena of centre or epicenter displacements are well known. But over the last 50 years, scholars, such as Ginzburg and Castelnuovo, have highlighted the necessity of avoiding a simplistic use of the core-periphery concept in art history. Based on Italian art, their study proves that the time has come for a mindset shift: rather than being viewed through the lens of domination, the links in between centre and periphery should be viewed in terms of circulation and dialogue in a multifaceted approach[4].

This kind of reexamination of previously accepted notions has become, in the past decades, more common: globalization has brought a term to both the system and the vision scholars and specialists have of it. Therefore, for museums, the centre-periphery model has become nearly irrelevant, or should at least be challenged.

The amazingly rich spectrum of museum directors in this chapter, hailing from a wide range of places and contexts, is the perfect demonstration of such a shift. Anne-Marie Maïla-Afeiche (The National Museum of Beirut, Lebanon), Kennie Ting (Asian Civilisations Museum, Singapore) and Henry Kim (Aga Khan Museum, Toronto) call into question the relevance of these concepts in relation to contemporary museology. These museum leaders' diverse and far-reaching experiences are the basis for enriching contributions that prove how circulation and dialogue are at the core of culture and its multiform representations today.

Notes

1   See Andre Gunther Frank, *Dependent Accumulation*, New York: University Press, 1979.
2   Nigel McKenzie, "Centre and Periphery: The Marriage of Two Minds", *Acta Sociologica,* vol. 20, n° 1, 1977, p. 55–74 (p. 56).
3   Teresa Hauswedell, Axel Körner, Ultrich Tideau, *Re-Mapping Centre and Periphery: Asymmetrical Encounters in European and Global Contexts,* London: UCL Press, 2019.
4   Carlo Ginzburg et Enrico Castelnuovo, "Domination symbolique et géographie artistique dans l'histoire de l'art italien", *Actes de la Recherche en Sciences Sociales*, 1981, n° 40, p. 41– 72. See also Christophe Behnke, Cornelia Kastelan, Valérie Knoll and Ulf Wuggenig, *Art in the Periphery of the Centre,* Berlin: Sternberg Press, 2015; Esther Peeren, Hanneke Stuit and Astrid van Weyenberg, *Peripheral Visions in the Globalizing Present: Spaces, Mobilities, Aesthetics*, Leiden: Brill, 2016.

Centering Nationhood

Centrality and Peripherality in the Museal Culture of Contemporary Lebanon

Anne-Marie Maïla-Afeiche

In reflecting on the worlds of museology today, my contribution to this volume explores the question of how museums evolve in relation to one of the key structuring dynamics of the contemporary world: allocations of centre and periphery. At first glance, understanding museology in terms of 'centre' and 'periphery' might be taken to entail comparisons among more or less important museums or an analysis of how collections discovered in remote areas inevitably end up being exhibited in major museums. My discussion in this chapter, though, explores strategies for challenging established hierarchies between 'central' and 'peripheral' museums and collections at a national scale. To do so, I foreground the importance of *geography* in museological policy. Almost invariably, national museums were located in national capitals. Promoting today national museums in the peripheries of a given country, I want to suggest, serves to balance out the centre and thereby foster a more distributed and accessible museal culture.

Given my position as Director General of the General Council of Museums and former director of the National Museum of Beirut, my discussion hones in on the Lebanese national context. Rather than attempting a global survey, this chapter covers state museums in Lebanon administered by the Ministry of Culture. Since Lebanon is relatively small, I do not think that we can speak of a conflict between centre and periphery in contemporary Lebanese museums. It is important to note, however, that a suite of new private museums have arisen in the country over the last decade. In broaching the tensions between the centrality of established Lebanese museums and the peripherality of those currently under development, I first present the National Museum of Beirut before briefly outlining the new vision for museums in Lebanon today. The chapter closes by discussing how dynamics of centre and periphery play out in some new projects currently being developed in Lebanese museums.

The National Museum of Beirut

I shall start with the centre, by introducing the National Museum of Beirut (fig. 1), which was the first collection of antiquities assembled to narrate the history of Lebanon. Although its construction only began in 1930, the museum was first envisioned in 1919. In the 1930s, founding a national museum was a political decision. Indeed, the museum would provide a symbol of nascent national unity, cementing the population around a common history and cultural heritage. As this cultural process of nation-building gathered momentum, Lebanon was still governed under the terms of the League of Nation's Mandate for Syria and the Lebanon, according to which France administered most of the region. By the time of its inauguration in 1942, the National Museum had come to symbolise national pride and unity. Indeed, it not only housed national treasures, but bore witness to Lebanese national history and identity. Significantly, Lebanon gained independence in 1943, the year following the National Museum's inauguration; in Lebanon's national history, museology preceded politics by a year.

Located in Beirut, Lebanon's capital, the museum aimed to establish a central narrative of Lebanese history. In only displaying archaeological objects that were unearthed in Lebanon, the museum's three floors sought to represent the history of the whole country. The collection grew throughout the twentieth century, as excavations

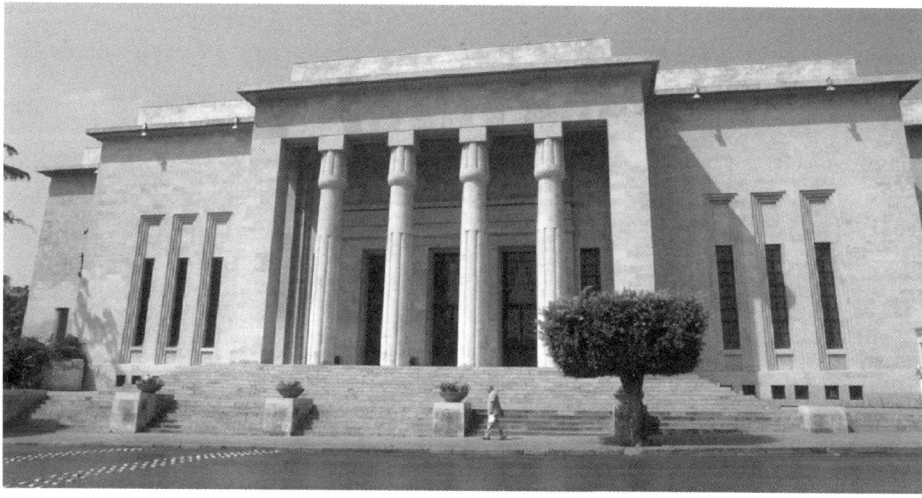

Figure 1. The National Museum of Beirut. (Plate 32, p. 255)
©Ministry of Culture/Directorate General of Antiquities of Lebanon/National Museum of Beirut.

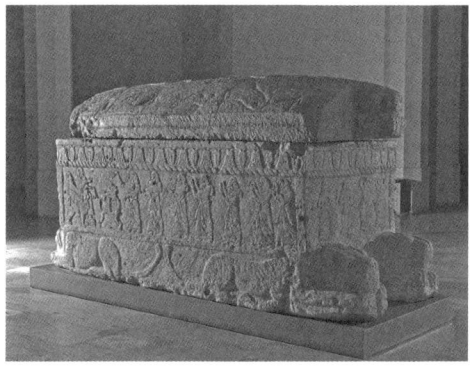

Figure 2. The sarcophagus of King Ahiram
10th century B.C. (Plate 33, p. 256)
©Ministry of Culture/Directorate General of Antiquities
of Lebanon/National Museum of Beirut.

revealed more and more of Lebanon's past from Prehistory to the Ottoman period. Hundreds of new artefacts were added to the exhibits. To name just two masterpieces, the Ahiram sarcophagus, which contained the remains of the king of Byblos bears a carved Phoenician inscription dated to the tenth century BCE (fig. 2). Or a Roman mosaic showing the Seven Wise Men (fig. 3). Discovered in Baalbeck, it is now displayed at the entrance of the museum.

The museum was severely damaged during the Civil War that devastated Lebanon between 1975 and 1991 (fig. 4). After a process of reconstruction, during which the building was repaired and the archaeological collection restored, two floors were reopened in 1999. At that point, it was decided that some of the damage sustained by the building should be preserved so as to bear witness to the destruction wrought by the war. Inside

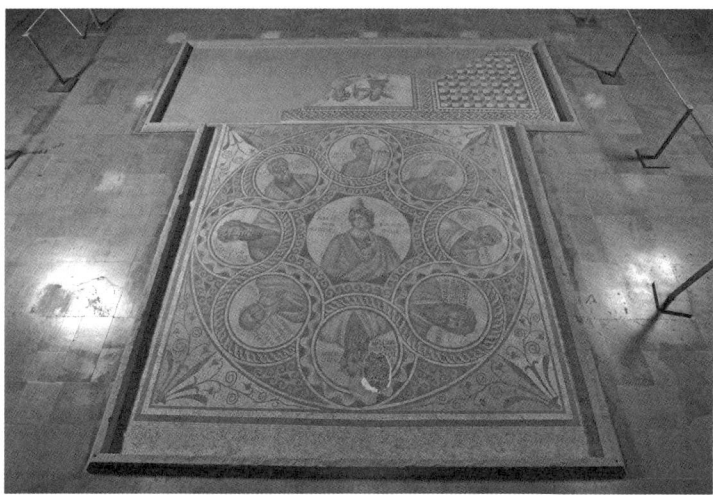

Figure 3. Roman mosaic of the Seven Wise Men, Baalbeck. (Plate 34, p. 257)
©Ministry of Culture/Directorate General of Antiquities of Lebanon/National Museum of Beirut.

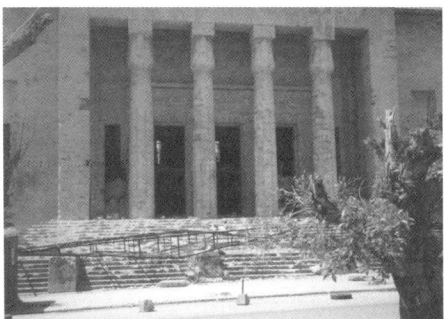

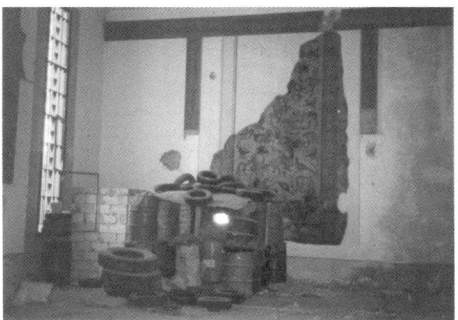

Figure 4. The National Museum of Beirut at the end of the war (1993). (Plate 35, p. 258)
©Ministry of Culture/Directorate General of Antiquities of Lebanon/National Museum of Beirut.

Figure 5. The Byzantine "mosaic of the Good Shepherd" showing the sniper hole. (Plate 36, p. 259)
©Ministry of Culture/Directorate General of Antiquities of Lebanon/National Museum of Beirut.

the museum, the collection retained damaged artefacts. In displaying their treasures' fragility and survival in this way, the curators underlined the importance of safeguarding cultural heritage in times of crisis. The traces of warfare are especially vivid in the case of a fifth-century Byzantine Mosaic named 'The mosaic of the Good Shepherd'. Sometime during the 1980s, a sniper took position inside the museum and made an opening in the mosaic. Through this aperture, he shot at people in the street who were attempting to cross the so-called 'green line' that separated Beirut into two sectors (fig. 5). Today, visitors to the museum can learn about the institution's history (including its reconstruction) through guided tours[1] and a short documentary titled *Revival*. The film[2] tells the story of the museum, beginning with its foundation, progressing onto the damage it sustained during the war, before charting its reconstruction. Viewers see how its floors were successively inaugurated, from the ground and first floors in 1999 to the basement in

Figure 6. The National Museum basement floor. (Plate 37, p. 260)
©Ministry of Culture/Directorate General of Antiquities of Lebanon/ National Museum of Beirut.

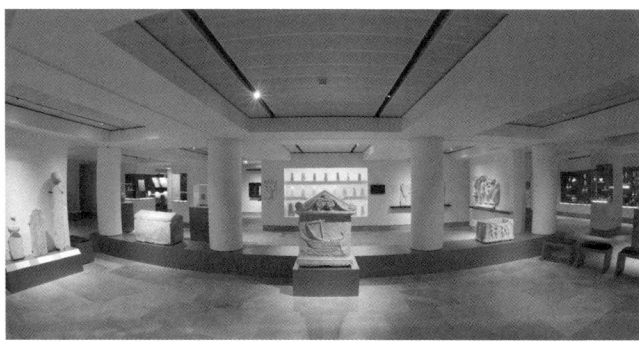

2016. Reopened a full forty years after the outbreak of the war, the National Museum's basement (fig. 6) is dedicated to funerary art. Chronologically, the new museography ranges from Prehistory through to the Ottoman period. In encompassing so much of Lebanese history, this collection emphasises how the museum continues to flourish to-day, specifically through the regular or salvage archaeological excavations undertaken in the country. This is further underlined by the addition of a new building[3]: an annex that will host temporary exhibitions, events, and a cafeteria (fig. 7).

Alongside its more traditional roles of preservation, research, and delectation, the National Museum of Beirut has another overarching mission: that of receiving and con-solidating Lebanese history. From this perspective, Lebanese people endow the muse-um with a specifically national significance. The museum is a focal point in Beirut, the nation's capital. It is notable to observe, for instance, that major social demonstrations often start, or end outside the museum. The National Museum, then, can be said to function as a national unifier. This justified the idea of the museum's centrality, at least in the national context, in which its plays a major, indeed central role.

National site museums

Lebanon's Ministry of Culture has long adopted a policy of cultural proliferation. From 1990 onward, several relatively small museums have been founded outside Beirut, each with its own distinct focus. These so-called 'site museums' are located within areas of particular archaeological interest, such as the cities of Byblos and Baalbek, an eight-eenth-century palace in Beiteddine, and a medieval castle in Tripoli. These museums aim to introduce visitors to a given cultural heritage site, and allow them to understand its history and environment. They were established to highlight archaeological remains

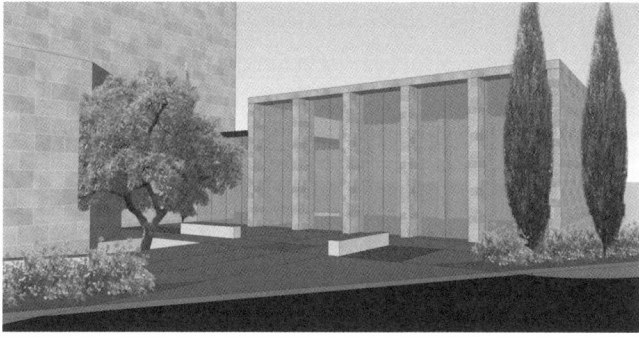

Figure 7. The new annex project. (Plate 38, p. 260)
©Raed Abillama architect.

Figure 8. The Tomb of Tyre.
(Plate 39, p. 261)
©Ministry of Culture/Directorate
General of Antiquities of Lebanon/
National Museum of Beirut.

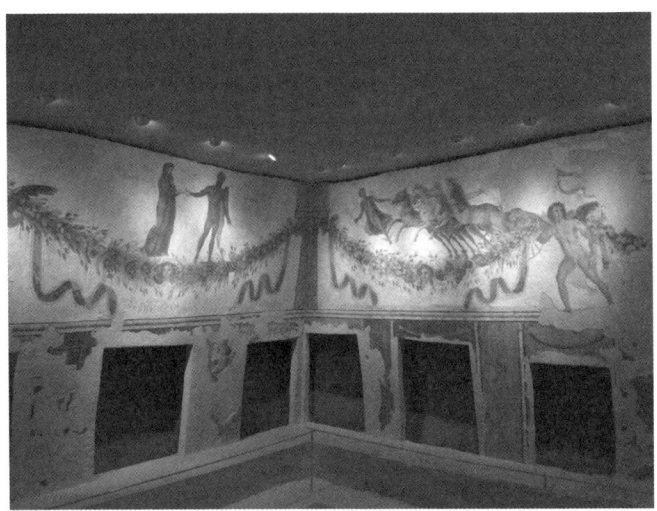

and historical buildings and to enhance regional collections. Their exhibits focus on various periods, themes, and events, and house some highly significant historical objects.

Here, I would like to hone in on an archaeological find from the twentieth century. In 1937, a peasant digging in his field in Tyre (south Lebanon) discovered a Roman tomb. A square hypogeum about two meters below the soil, it was probably a family tomb built in the second century BCE. The tomb was marked out by the outstanding frescoes covering its four walls. In lavish detail, they depicted scenes from Greek mythology, luscious vegetation, and illusionistic architectural similes or *trompe-l'oeil*. Maurice Dunand, a French archaeologist started excavating the hypogeum in 1939. Before long, the pictorial layers coating the four walls were transferred to the National Museum of Beirut. A dedicated room in the museum's basement was built to display the frescoes. Its dimensions were designed so as to match the hypogeum's exactly. At the time of the museum's inauguration in 1942, the Tomb of Tyre was one of its central masterpieces. During the civil war, though, the National Museum's basement was beset by flooding and humidity, which damaged the frescoes. The wall paintings were eventually restored between 2010 and 2011, thus insuring their long-term preservation (fig. 8). A professional museography project was also implemented[4].

What would happen were such a discovery to be made today? Would the Ministry of Culture transfer the frescoes and display them 85 kilometres away from their native archaeological context? Or would it keep them *in situ* and create a museum around them? Displaying these works of funerary art in their original setting would certainly have attracted visitors to Tyre, which would in turn have supported economy and tourism in the region. This thought leads us to question future museal policy in Lebanon, especially given that a national Council of Museums has recently been established.

The General Council of Museums is a new independent seven-member board within the Ministry of Culture. Its mission is to develop existing museums, create new ones, and promote and preserve collections. As part of this mandate, it seeks to establish museums in all regions of the country, so as to preserve and raise awareness of regional differences. As such, the council attempts to strike a more equitable balance between centre and peripheries in the museal culture of contemporary Lebanon. Among the challenges entailed in this venture is the need to involve local communities and ensure that museums offer enjoyable experiences, regardless of their collections' size or significance. Other issues arise from the fact that these museums—particularly Lebanese State museums— cannot succeed without the involvement of civil society and private donations. More pressingly still, a common legal framework for the management of these museums has yet to to be defined. In facing up to these challenges, the Ministry of Culture has developed a series of new projects, many of which purposefully seek to redirect flows of attention and resources from the centre to the peripheries. In closing this chapter, I shall briefly describe four key new ventures.

The first is the Byblos Museum, which will be in a traditional Lebanese house on the coast inside the archaeological site. The Ministry's planning for this new museum, in coordination with the Louvre Museum's Department of Oriental Antiquities, and the Directorate General of Antiquities has been ongoing since 2016. The exhibits are set to reveal the course and causes of Byblos's historical development, from Neolithic settlements to the modern city. The museum will also underline the city's shifting interactions with the Mediterranean world.

The second project is a museum that is currently being constructed in the old city of Saida. The site was expropriated by Lebanon's Directorate General of Antiquities in the 1940s on account of the density of archaeological structures it contains. A Lebanese-British team has been excavating the site for more than twenty years, funded by the British Museum. The Saida museum location, on top of the archaeological site, will therefore focus, as in the case of Byblos, on the urban development from the Bronze Age to the Ottoman period, with a special emphasis on creating *in situ* exhibits beneath the ground.

Third is the Tyre Museum, a site museum aiming to help visitors to appreciate Tyre's rich past. Through an exceptional collection of objects uncovered over the last few decades, the museum will enhance the antique city's initial development before turning to its expansion during the Phoenician period.

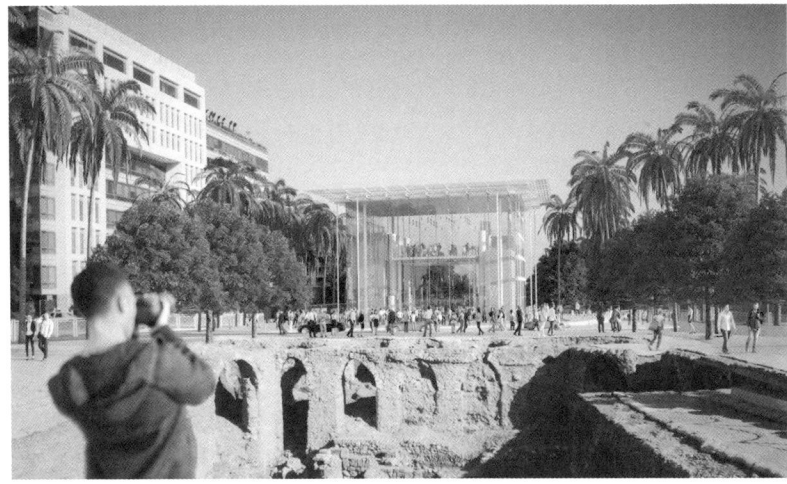

Figure 9. Beirut History Museum. (Plate 40, p. 262)
©RPBW-architects

Lastly, I would like to mention the Beirut History Museum. Located in downtown Beirut, this new museum was envisioned by architect Renzo Piano (fig. 9) to tell the story of the city and its inhabitants. Through archaeological artefacts and historical exhibits, the museum will shed light on transformations in the urban landscape across several major historical periods as well as Beiruti people's historical beliefs, cultural practices, and relations with the environment. It will also present the results and analyses of the excavations that took place between 1995 and 1999, in what was then the largest urban archaeological field.

Through this ambitious set of projects, a more equitably distribution of museal resources could be implemented across the cities and regions of Lebanon. No longer will artefacts simply move from the peripheries to the capital, conceived as the epicentre of national culture. Indeed, my hope is that in the museal culture currently being incubated in Lebanon, notions of 'centre' and 'periphery' will become increasingly redundant.

Notes

1   Available on the free Smartphone application: 'National Museum of Beirut'.
2   Directed by Bahige Hojeij.
3   Thanks to the National Heritage Foundation initiative and funds.
4   By the Italian architect Antonio Giammarusti.

Interstitial Identities

Reimagining the Asian Civilisations Museum

Kennie Ting

Writing from a Singaporean perspective, I would like to say from the outset that I do not quite understand theories of centrality and peripherality. Certainly, I do not subscribe to them, for in Singapore, we do not see ourselves—nor wish to be seen—as either central or peripheral. Rather, as a port city, we exist in an interstitial, liminal condition: a hybrid position between fixed allocations of centre and periphery. In reflecting on the place and significance of the art museum under the shifting conditions of contemporary globalisation, this chapter will return, again and again, to these notions of 'liminality', 'interstitiality', and 'hybridity'.

I am the Director of the Asian Civilisations Museum, one of four main national museums and galleries in Singapore. We used to be a somewhat more traditional Asian art museum in that our collections were organised geographically, with permanent galleries dedicated to East Asia, South Asia, West Asia, and Southeast Asia. Over the last seven years, however, the museum has been undergoing a long and painful, transition towards a thematic organisation of the collections, which is still ongoing. As an entirely new museum, curated from the outset according to a thematic rather than geographical framework, Louvre Abu Dhabi holds out a model for this museological configuration. The Asian Civilisations Museum, however, could not start over again from scratch: our greatest challenge was to fundamentally reorganise an existing collection. This chapter reflects on both the pain and new possibilities thrown up in that process.

Some seven years ago, my predecessor sat down with the museum's board of managers and curators to reflect broadly on the institution in our custody. One of the questions posed then was the basic, indeed existential question: 'Why does Singapore have an Asian art museum?' Stepping back from the daily concerns of collection management in this way, we were struck by the unlikeliness of the Asian Civilisations Museum. Why should an Asian city host a museum specially dedicated to Asian art? Is Singaporean art not always already Asian by definition? As Hervé Inglebert has suggested, the answer to

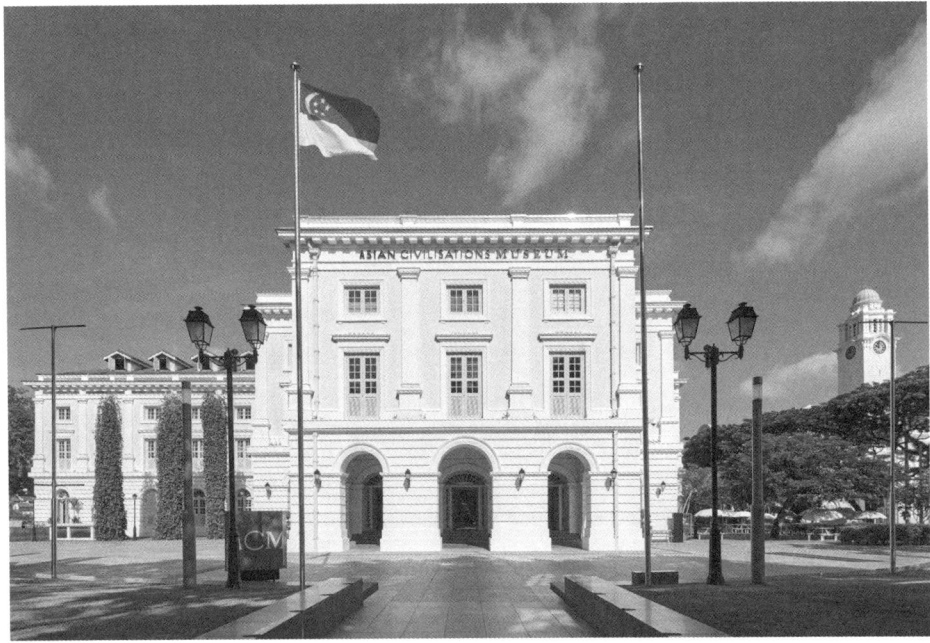

Figure 1. Asian Civilisations Museum, Singapore. (Plate 41, p. 263)
Image courtesy of Asian Civilisations Museum.

these questions seems to be that Singaporeans rarely identify themselves as being particularly Asian, at least in any exclusive sense. Often, they imagine and present themselves instead as a blend of East and West. It is on account of this distinctive hybridity,
according to which Singapore belongs to no one cultural or even continental tradition
of artistic practice, that it makes sense for the city to have a separate Asian art museum
(as San Francisco also does).

Gathered in our meeting room, the board and my predecessor worked through various possible strategies for linking the museum more closely to Singapore, both spirit-
ually and in terms of the museum's social roles. This is not the place in which to reca-
pitulate our deliberations. Suffice it to say that, at length, it was decided that a thematic
organisation of our collections would allow the museum to engage very directly with
the diverse historical and cultural trajectories that clash and converge in the city. The
rationale we agreed upon in developing our new, thematic approach is as follows. The
Asian Civilisations Museum is Singapore's Museum of Asia. Paying particular attention to the museum's emplacement in the city of Singapore, our manifesto emphasises

interconnections both among civilisations in Asia and between Asia and the world. Our permanent galleries are now organised thematically, focusing on networks and flows rather than borders and boundaries. Just as Singaporeans themselves are essentially mixed, so many of the objects in our collections are hybrid, whether they combine East with West or East with East. In and through this thematic approach, our message is that Singapore, like Asia at large, has always been cross-cultural. No culture, Asian or otherwise, has ever existed in isolation; cultures have always interacted with and mutually enriched each other.

It is worth making two further points in relation to our renewed programme. First, I would be lying if I neglected to mention that this reconfiguration of our galleries was driven by a wish—perhaps an anxiety—to be more relevant to Singapore's national identity. It was national identity, indeed a kind of national imperative, that drove us to rethink and reorganise the museum. However, it is important to bear in mind Singapore's distinctiveness as both a nation state and port city, situated at a historical crossroads among various shifting empires and cultures. In the case of Singapore at least, then, this 'national imperative' opens up onto broader, indeed *trans*national themes and connections. Ideas of globalisation and world cultures, then, are inseparable from Singaporean national identity. As such, they must figure centrally in the curation of its artistic heritages.

The second point I want to make relates to our collections and change in approach. As I have emphasised above, we specialise in collecting hybrid things. At the heart of the museum are forms in which East and West—and indeed East and East—have merged indissociably. This is what we mean by 'cross-cultural'. In their new configuration, our galleries and collections are organised according to three overarching themes: trade, faith, and design. The themes of trade and faith are close to the pulse of Singaporean identity and history, Singapore being a multicultural, multifaith, multiethnic Asian port city and trading centre. Trade and religious conviviality are deeply

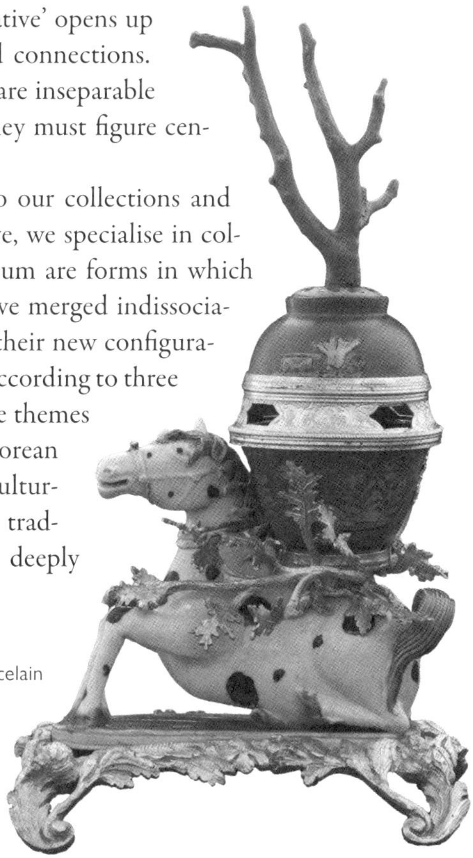

Figure 2. Mounted incense burner, Europe, 18th century. Porcelain (China, Jingdezhen, c. 1700), gilded bronze mounts (France, mid-18th century), lacquer bowls (Japan, 18th century), red coral, Height 26.2 cm. (Plate 42, p. 264)
2014-00706, Asian Civilisations Museum, Singapore.

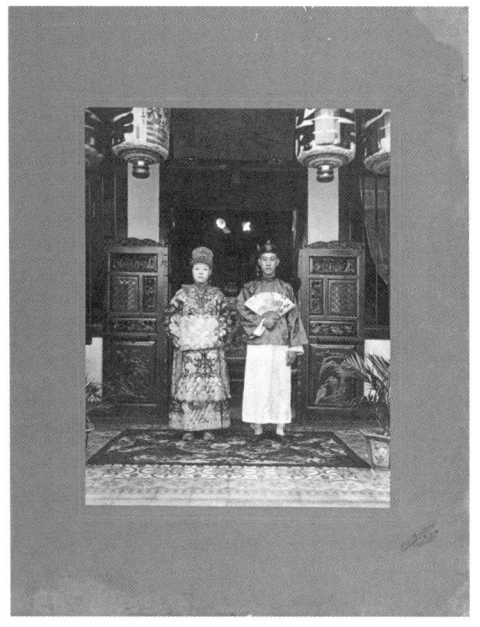

Figure 3. Untitled. Lee Brothers (李昆昌), Singapore, around 1920s. Gelatin silver print, 45.6 × 35.2 × 0.2 cm. (Plate 43, p. 265) 2015-00886, Peranakan Museum, Singapore. Gift of Mr and Mrs Lee Kip Lee.

patterned into the city's heritage. At the same time, though, we are the first to acknowledge that trade and faith are hardly the special preserve of Singaporean history. Far from it: commerce and spirituality are major historical driving forces. Both historically and today, they have fuelled the global movements of peoples, cultures, goods, and ideas that traverse and shape transnational hubs such as Singapore.

With regard to our third theme, design, the Asian Civilisations Museum is distinguished by its preference for artefacts that relate to hybrid communities. Such objects fall into two subcategories. First are artefacts that have been produced in, or shaped by, contexts of cultural encounter among different communities in Asia: East/West or East/East. Second, and to my mind most interesting, are objects derived from the material cultures of mixed-race and multicultural communities. We have a very beautiful term in Malay that refers to this: *peranakan*, meaning 'of the soil'. Peranakan designates people who, though descended from non-Malay communities, were born in the Malay Archipelago and have absorbed aspects of Malay culture into their own cultures. In displaying the heritage of this and other similarly hybrid communities, the museum can draw on

Figure 4. Ewer, China, probably Gongxian kilns, c. 830s. Stoneware, height 104 cm. (Plate 44, p. 266) 2005.1.00900, Asian Civilisations Museum, Singapore. The Tang Shipwreck was acquired through the generous donation of the Estate of Khoo Teck Puat.

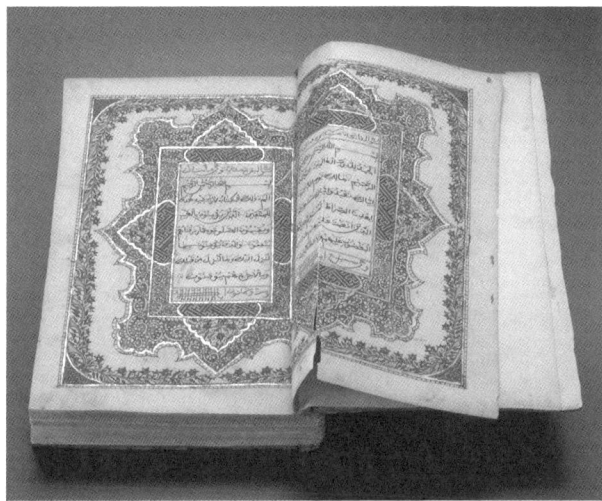

Figure 5. Quran, Central Java, late 19th or early 20th century. Paper, ink, coloured pigments, leather binding. Inscription: Quran 1: 1–7 (Surah al-Fatihah, The Opener), 2: 1–4 (Surah al-Baqarah, The Heifer). (Plate 45, p. 267) 2005-01608-001, Asian Civilisations Museum, Singapore.

extensive collections relating to the material culture of Eurasians in Southeast Asia, for example, or the Straits Chinese, who have been in the Malay world for some 300 or 400 years.

But how do our three overarching themes translate into actual collections? The museum has three floors, each of which aligns with the topic of either trade, faith, or design. On the ground floor we present our collection of Asian art produced for export between the ninth and early twentieth centuries BCE. We have export art from China, India, Southeast Asia, and also Japan. Especially important is our Tang Shipwreck collection, which comprises the cargo carried by a dhow (a traditional Arabic sailing ship) that sank off Indonesia in the ninth century BCE. Now recovered and restored for public display, the collection includes gold, silver, and some 55,000 ceramics that were made in China for the Middle Eastern market.

Our second floor is devoted to another broad area in which we specialise: what we call sacred and ritual art. As one might expect, our collections feature artistic traditions related to Buddhism, Hinduism, Islam, Christianity, Taoism, Confucianism, and other systems of faith. Alongside these established world faiths, though, we also curate artefacts belonging to the many indigenous forms of ancestor veneration and worship in Southeast Asia. In this area too we foreground the syncretic or hybrid: pieces of devotional art that blend different religions. The material culture of Javanese Islam, for one example, is often syncretic because its articulation of Islam retains elements derived from an earlier Hindu-Buddhist culture. In the same way, our collections include instances of

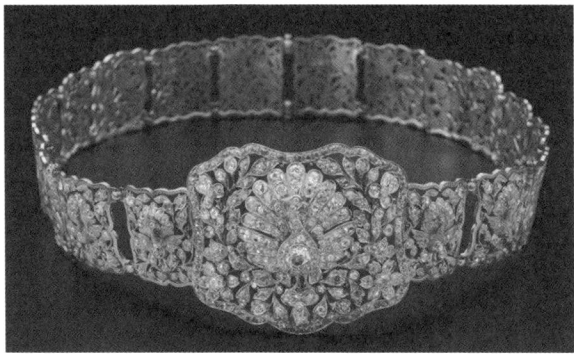

Figure 6. Peacock belt, Singapore,
c. 1900. Gold, diamonds,
Buckle: 7 × 8.3 × 2.8 cm;
Belt: 68.5 × 4 × 0.7 cm.
(Plate 46, p. 268)
2015-01994, Peranakan Museum,
Singapore, Gift of Mr Edmond Chin.

Christian art that are situated within the tradition of Islamic Mughal visual culture. These works depict the Madonna or Biblical scenes in rich, possibly intercultural ways that prompt us to wonder how these motifs made their way into Mughal visual culture in the first place. Finally, on the third floor—which will open in 2020—we have a collection of pan-Asian fashion, textiles, and jewellery. As with the other themes, here we emphasise hybridity and the syncretic.

Summarising all of this, the Asian Civilisations Museum has undertaken three key changes over the last seven years. First, it has moved from a geographical to a thematic organisation of its collections. Second, it has established new conceptual premises, focusing not on discrete civilisational heritages but rather on peranakan or hybrid transactions among cultures. Third, it has substituted its received ethnographic mindset for a new art historical approach. Indeed, the reader will have noticed the very beautiful objects from our collection that illustrate this chapter. These images embody our move away from ethnography, indicating how we at the museum now understand, curate, and display even traditionally ethnographic pieces as works of art.

When we first shifted our approach, we imagined (perhaps optimistically) that publics and critics alike would laud our initiative and farsightedness. Instead, the changes were met with cries of protest. Clearly, today methodologies of Asian art history often remain siloed and geographically oriented. A number of curators felt uncomfortable working within the new parameters and left the museum. What is worse, our once supportive public hated the changes and left in droves. Indeed, our footfall halved in the few years following our change in approach. We first explored our new approach in a series of special exhibitions, one of which actually prompted a death threat. The surprising thing, though, is that while our existing audiences turned away, we started attracting younger visitors: people who were more familiar with ideas of networks and flows. The idea that cultures interact and depend on one another came very naturally to this younger audience, which was already globally connected and aware through its use of social media. Accordingly, the median age of visitors to the museum has markedly dropped. Before our new curatorial vision came into effect, on average visitors were in their mid-forties. Now they are in their early thirties. That said, even today former volunteer guides, all of whom were passionately devoted to the museum, sometimes entreat me to restore the museum to its former glory. Although I apologise for their sense of loss, I nevertheless insist that the old museum is dead. A new vision stands in its place.

After joining the Asian Civilisations Museum in 2016, I spent the first year consulting with various stakeholders. Taking groups of students, elderly people, or anyone else I could find through the exhibits and galleries, I wanted to understand what people actually respond to in museums. Ultimately, I realised that what the curators and I were grappling with was the issue of positioning. How do we position art historical ways of thinking about the world and museums in a way that engages with very specific audiences in Singapore? I must have spoken with about 400 people, from academics to high

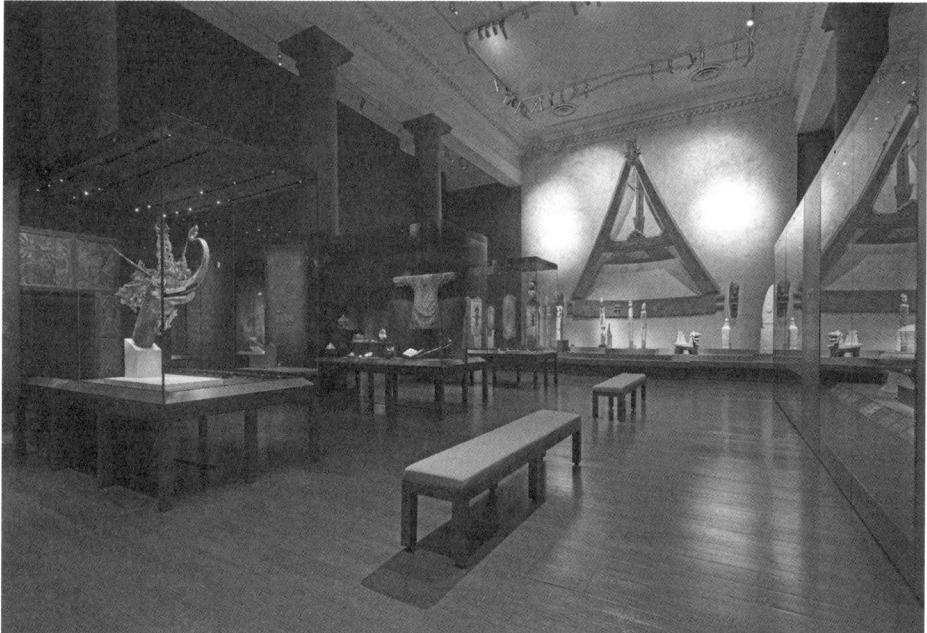

Figure 7. Ancestors & Rituals gallery at the Asian Civilisations Museum Singapore. (Plate 47, p. 269)
Image courtesy of Asian Civilisations Museum.

school students. It was through these conversations that we arrived at our overarching themes (trade, faith, design) and our new positioning of seeing Asia through the lens of Singapore. That is a positioning with which all of our audiences seem to agree.

Adopting a thematic approach has been tremendously beneficial for us as a museum, I claim, in that it has allowed us to explore new perspectives on old things. A strange place like Singapore, I would venture, presents a particularly apt context for this revaluation of the past. For example, consider an exhibition the museum mounted in late 2016. It focused on cosmopolitan port cities in Asia: Manila, Goa, Batavia (present-day Jakarta), Canton (present-day Guangzhou), Nagasaki, Saigon, Rangoon (present-day Yangon), and, of course, Singapore. In accordance with the centre-periphery model that I mentioned in opening this chapter, most art histories hone in on centres of elite production and imperial courts. Indeed, in Asian contexts, peripheral cultures and creators are often dismissed as 'foreign barbarians' that occasionally invade or otherwise intrude into Asian history. These port cities, however, are profoundly interstitial. They are in between: that is, reducible to neither Imperial court nor 'foreign barbarian', but including aspects of both. Chaos and messiness arise at these the crossing points among cultures, along with that spirit of innovation that, at least to us at the museum, embodies the meaning of Singapore. This was the first exhibition anywhere to explore Asian port cities.

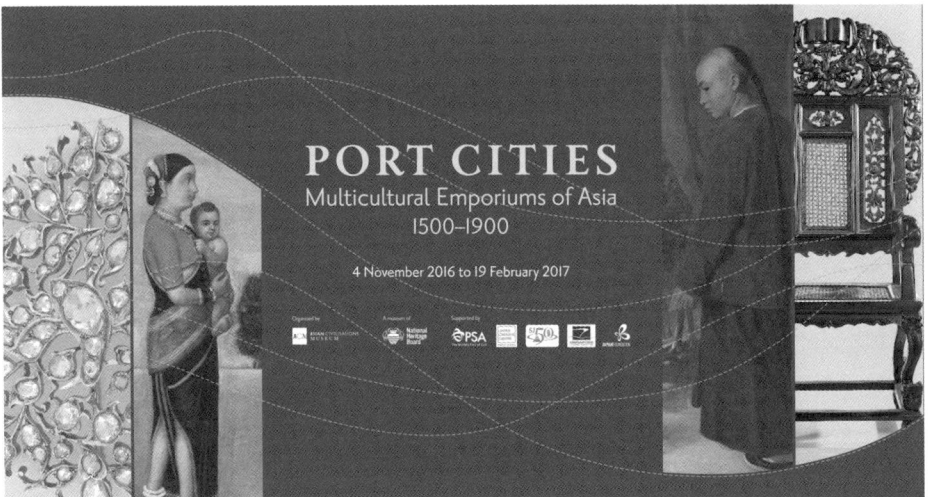

Figure 8. *Port Cities: Multicultural Emporiums of Asia 1500-1900* exhibition banner (Plate 48, p. 270)
Image courtesy of Asian Civilisations Museum.

In focusing on encounters, we have also been able to explore colonial history. Singapore in general, and the Asian Civilisations Museum in particular, are among the few places in Asia that can address the colonial past in a distanced and deliberative manner. This is due to Singapore's distinctive relationship to its colonial past, which differs markedly from other imperial legacies in Southeast Asia and Asia. This came out clearly through an exhibition held the Asian Civilisations Museum, on which we collaborated closely with the Musée National des Arts Asiatiques Guimet (National Museum of Asian Arts Guimet, Paris). It surveyed aspects of the history of Angkor (in present-day Cambodia), presenting not only Khmer arts and heritage, but also artefacts relating to the French colonisers' encounter with Angkor. Every exhibition we host is accompanied by an international symposium, to which we invite experts on the exhibition's theme. In the case of the Angkor exhibition, we had the pleasure of hosting a number of world-renowned authorities in their fields, from Mr Kong Vireak, the director of the National Museum of Cambodia, through Pierre Baptiste from Musée Guimet, to a wider array of expert archaeologists from America, Asia, Australia and Singapore. Nobody is better placed to address pressing questions in the curation of colonial history, from 'what do you do with colonial collections?' to 'how do you represent them in a contemporary context?' Extending our engagement with colonial history, in February 2019 the Asian Civilisations Museum undertook a major exhibition in collaboration with the British

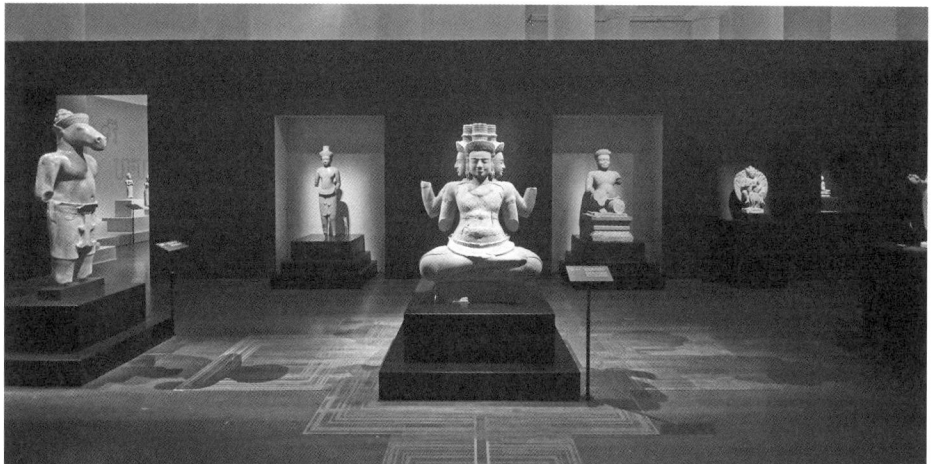

Figure 9. *Angkor: Exploring Cambodia's Sacred City* exhibition at the Asian Civilisations Museum Singapore. (Plate 49, p. 271)

Image courtesy of Asian Civilisations Museum.

Museum, loaning some works from museums in Indonesia and The Netherlands. *Raffles in Southeast Asia* explored the British encounter with the Malay world in the nineteenth century. This project, too, broached questions of how colonial collections should be put to use in the present.

Casting forward to the museum's future development, it has occurred to me that there is a gap in our collection, which relates specifically to how West Asia has long been both a marketplace and producer of luxury goods for export to the rest of the world. True, the Tang Shipwreck bears upon the idea of West Asia being a marketplace: its cargo was part of a transcontinental trade in luxury goods during the ninth century BCE. Still, much remains to be explored in the history of the region's global export markets. With this in mind, our museum hopes to work towards an exhibition on interactions between West Asia and Southeast Asia across our signal themes of trade, faith, design—of course, emphasising hybridity and the syncretic along the way.

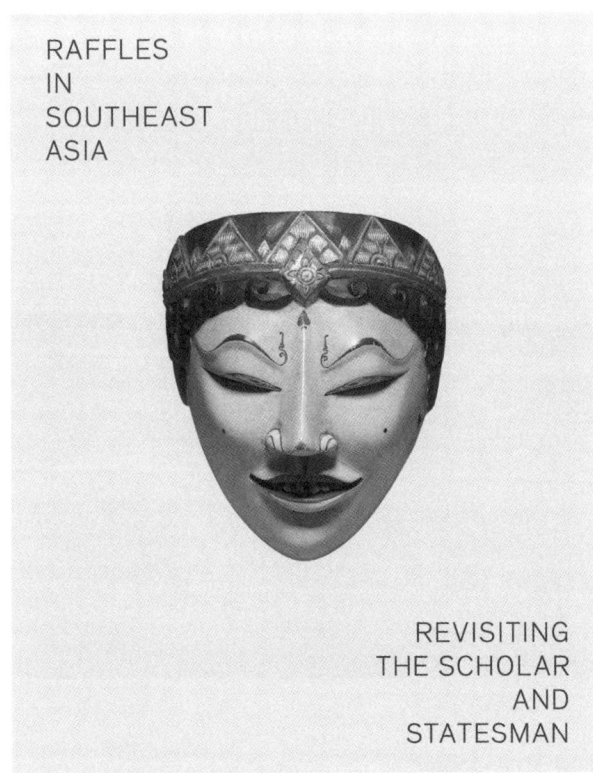

Figure 10: *Raffles in Southeast Asia* exhibition catalogue cover
(Plate 50, p. 272)
Image courtesy of Asian Civilisations Museum.

Curating across Cultures

Globalising Dynamics in Contemporary Museal Practice

Henry Kim

This chapter addresses the relationship between two distinct yet overlapping topics in contemporary museal practice. One is the issue of globalisation and global perspective; the other is the question of centre versus periphery. Ideas of centrality, peripherality, and the global are of particular interest to me personally. Indeed, I have been involved in two museums that, despite being located in very different contexts and focused on very different themes, have taken markedly similar approaches to interpreting and displaying objects in their collections. In this chapter, I want to suggest that these convergent approaches speak to global trends that are coursing through museums today and bridge perceived distinctions among centres and peripheries.

Before my current position as director of the Aga Khan Museum, I worked at the Ashmolean Museum in Oxford. At one time, the Ashmolean was the most traditional of traditional museums. This is unsurprising, for it prides itself on being the oldest museum in the world. The Ashmolean figures a prime example of a museum based on a universal model. In the past, its plentiful collections were organised into discrete cultural lineages, which were kept quite separate from one another. One might explore its collections by looking first at Greece, then at Rome, China, India, and so forth, each in isolation from the others. The collections created divisions within the museum, divisions that made sense based on the specialisms of the time. When I first became involved in the Ashmolean, it was very traditional. By reinterpreting its vast collections in ways that made cross-cultural connections among artefacts and sections, I had the chance to help transform it into a modern museum. From 2009, though, the old purist structure was dissolved. In its place, we took a much broader, cross-cultural approach. This proved a very successful way of reinvigorating a collection that, despite being world-class in terms of the range and significance of the objects it contained, was falling behind in terms of how people perceived it.

A few years after my work at the Ashmolean, I became the first director of the Aga Khan Museum in Toronto, a new museum of Islamic art that opened in 2014. Whereas the Ashmolean has a very broad collection, the Aga Khan Museum's is very specific. The museum is devoted to the arts of the Muslim world. Although this might lead one to suppose that the museum is narrowly focused, this is not the case. Maintaining a level of specialisation without becoming merely niche was a difficult balance to strike. We rose to the challenge by exploring cultural connections both within and beyond the Muslim world. In considering Islamic art, we did not limit our focus to artefacts made within Muslim states, regions, and cultures. Rather, we chose to look at the historical connections that drew cultures together. This allowed for greater dialogue between our collection and broader historical narratives, and underlined the museum's relevance for contemporary audiences.

Both the Ashmolean and Aga Khan museums, then, adopted a cross-cultural approach to the curation of their collections. They arrived at their similar strategies, however, for completely different reasons. The Ashmolean sought to modernise a museum that was steeped in traditional museal rhetorics of universality. The Aga Khan Museum, in contrast, meant to put its specialty subject matter in a broader perspective. These two institutions are not alone in opting for a new transcultural view of their collections. In modernising their practice and addressing these issues, a range of other museums are also taking similarly global approaches. This is a very real trend shaping contemporary museal worlds.

Although this is one of the most interesting dynamics at work in museums today, the globalisation of curatorial perspectives and practices has taken twenty to thirty years to emerge. This is notable, given that in universities cross-cultural perspectives emerged and matured a good generation earlier, in the 1970s and 80s. It was only in the 2000s and onwards that museums finally grasped this approach and began looking at their collections in another light. There are two reasons for this, I would suggest. First, it takes time for scholarship to develop and for the novel to become orthodox. Second, museums are the cargo ships of the cultural world. They are big, indeed massive. It takes a long time for a museum to change course. Quite often change comes about through a new build or redevelopment, which creates an impetus for new approaches. In the context of institutional shifts and reorganisations, fresh ideas finally see the light of day. This comes out strongly in the case of the museum created by the Louvre in Lens and what you have here in Abu Dhabi. Both were built from scratch and both have explored the broad issues of global connections and cross-cultural histories. The lesson to be learnt here is that museums can seize the moment of change. They can catch up with leading scholarly trends. The resources required, however, are sometimes massive. The questions to be posed are: 'can you afford the cost of making the change?' followed by 'can you afford not to?'

Now I would like to turn to the question of centre and periphery. There is little doubt that museums and the contemporary art world are far more global than they were thirty or forty years ago. One of the primary dynamics at work in this process, I would suggest, is that the art world has expanded markedly. No longer concentrated in New York, the US more generally, Europe, or Japan, the art world now involves much of the rest of the world. Museums and the arts are proliferating around the world. One of the central drivers of this process is contemporary art, in which many key trends can be spotted early.

Does the idea of centres and peripheries provide a sort of model with which to explain these shifts towards the cross-cultural and the global? For myself, I do not think that it does. Actually, I am much more sympathetic to chaos theory. I believe in neither a central controlling force nor the idea that there are paradigmatic examples of the museum or artistic practice that can be franchised throughout the world. I hold that there are other, complex factors propelling the globalisation of contemporary curatorial perspectives. For a variety of reasons, ideas prevailing in the art world are now travelling outwards from their traditional geographical 'centres' into new markets that might once have been cast as 'peripheral'. In the remainder of this chapter, I would like to put forward four ideas that might help grasp the spread and mutation of contemporary museal practice, such that it is increasingly assuming a global aspect.

The first is the concept of emulation. If you have something that works, others will replicate it. Biennials are a good example of this. The 1895 Venice Biennale inaugurated the format, precipitating a spread of similar festivals throughout the world. Toronto is going to host a biennial next year. Biennials are also springing up across South Asia. In the last twelve months, I have been to one in Lahore and Karachi. This new venture joins two longer-standing South-Asian biennials, the Dhaka Art Summit and Kochi Biennale. Over the last two decades, biennials have sprung up like mushrooms in a field after a rainy night. The reason, simply, is that the biennial is a wonderful idea. Biennials are the fulcrums around which the global art world gathers to celebrate the arts in a given set of cities. As such, the idea is enthusiastically emulated. Interestingly, though, differences that are now beginning to appear in how biennials are conceived. Whereas some cities simply try to emulate one of the bigger biennials, such as that held in Venice, others seek local significance. I find these latter events especially interesting. Under the model of emulation, local actors (those responsible for a biennial) adapt an internationally established model to their local circumstances. This is neither a hub-spoke nor a centre-periphery schema. Rather, it entails one of emulation, imitation, and adaptation.

The second force shaping contemporary museums is the spread and sharing of ideas. The Louvre Lens and Louvre Abu Dhabi are extremely well-executed examples of how to reinterpret world history by looking at cultures both diachronically and across geography. However, this approach did not originate with either project, but developed elsewhere at different points in time. The Ashmolean in Oxford from 2009 onwards is one instance of this; the Kelvingrove in Glasgow from 2006 is another. In fact, precursors of contemporary cross-cultural curation can be traced back an entire century to the 1880s and 90s. Museums such as the Pitt Rivers Museum in Oxford have preserved this approach unchanged. This is made possible by the fact that museum professionals, much like publics at large, continually communicate and visit one another's museums. Far from being simply local, museums are viewed by international audiences and form nodes in a global dialogue.

The third development that I want to indicate is the rise of private initiatives and private institutions. Recent discussions in museology, I would suggest, have put too much emphasis on the role of national or civic museums in the globalisation of museal practice. This is not to deny their significance in driving this trend. Nevertheless, it is important to acknowledge that globally there are far more private museums than national or civic ones. Private initiatives, it seems, power much of the change unfolding through museal worlds today. Many of these organisations are highly specialised and focused on a particular mission. They cover one area in depth. This intensity is a source of great strength. Indeed, private museums can often promote the study or appreciation of their speciality much more effectively than larger museums, which, by their very nature, have to look at the bigger picture. Private initiatives can afford to focus narrowly on their core mission. Looking beyond museums to the wider art world, it is clear that private initiatives and foundations will remain a crucial shaping force well into the future.

The final factor to consider in this context is the local meanings and embeddedness of museal practice. I equate this with 'relevance'. For national, local, and private museums alike, relevance is absolutely crucial. Relevance requires that curators and museum directors do not think simply in terms of top-down approaches. 'If I build it, they will come. If I have this idea, people will appreciate it': this mantra is dead, or least residual. As more and more museums listen to audiences in an attempt to understand what they are looking for, what is significant locally is going to affect how museums and galleries programme major events. Listening to publics might involve anything from exhibitions in which curators talk with community groups to exhibitions created by communities themselves. In her contribution to this volume, Nathalie Bondil describes how these listening exercises and participatory projects are now seen as good practice in Montreal.

Such dialogues and collaborations with local communities, I expect, will decisively impact future art programming.

It follows from this that although themes of transnationalism and cross-cultural connection may be emulated globally, they will be interpreted very differently from institution to institution in view of their different local audiences. This dynamic ensures that the globalisation of contemporary museums will remain unpredictable and exciting. True, museal ideas and discourses spread globally. The ways in which they are concretely articulated in actual curatorial practice, however, differs markedly depending on the local community being addressed or involved.

I am unconvinced by the explanatory potential of thinking in terms of centres and peripheries (Kennie Ting takes a similar position in his chapter). Things are driven along, I believe, by many other more passive and unobtrusive structures and forces. But as I look at the art world and museums today, I certainly see that there is a trend to organise and narrate collections not as the exclusive legacies of discrete peoples, but in terms of cross-cultural themes. Received approaches, according to which one would select and survey a civilisation in isolation from all others, are falling by the wayside. The future of most museum practices lies in themes and relevance.

Conclusion

Navigating Universality in the Museums of the Twenty-First Century

François-René Martin

In concluding *Worlds in a Museum*, I do not mean to summarise the foregoing contributions, still less to offer my commentary on echoes and diverges among them. Instead, I mean to reflect on the volume's overall ambitions, picking out some especially generative questions and topics and suggesting how they might push forward current thinking about museology in relation to globalisation and universality.

This volume has endeavoured to put in dialogue, and perhaps even marry, curation and academia, or Museum and University: two cultures that do not always talk to one another sufficiently. As Claire Barbillon pointed out in the introduction, the École du Louvre has long been a site at which these two communities overlap and engage in sustained discussions and common projects. *Worlds in a Museum*, I hope, attests to the continuing fecundity of that overlap. Still, our central aim in assembling this volume goes beyond this. In bringing together key voices from a variety of fields and institutions, this volume turns on the question of how museums that were initially founded upon a traditional aspiration towards universality might—or perhaps should—approach contemporary conditions of globalisation. In an inevitably incomplete and conditional fashion, we have endeavoured to step back and assess the trajectories of contemporary museology between the claims of universality and globalizing forces, the power of centres and distinctiveness of peripheries, long-established conventions and emergent curatorial practices.

In this short conclusion, then, I appraise what I see as some key questions, themes and concepts that pertain to the concerns articulated in this volume. Still, it is important to remember that the foregoing reflections on museology and globalisation were occasioned by the first anniversary of the opening of Louvre Abu Dhabi. With that in mind, I would like to describe my first impressions of the museum, which I imagine will resonate with others' experiences. Visiting Louvre Abu Dhabi is a rare pleasure. Outside, one is struck by the beauty of the building; inside one is captivated by the range and significance of the works on show. Room after room, I was taken by the lucidity of the curatorial choices, especially the pairings of particular works. Above all, this museum is unique in that was created in a single stroke, in much the same way that certain modernist urban developments were constructed in one fell swoop. Indeed, the idea of designing and building an institution from scratch is an abiding dream among architects, a topos that has recurred across the history of architecture, especially its modernist strains. This dream was vividly expressed by the architect Tony Garnier, who fantasied about designing an entire city all at once, on a *tabula rasa*, in his book *La Cité Industrielle* (1917).

Only rarely have such dreams been realised: Louvre Abu Dhabi is one such case. It was constructed in just ten years. By comparison with the lifespans of established universal museums, this is little more than the blink of an eye. And yet now the museum stands complete, receiving visitors. This sense of simultaneity—which infuses Louvre Abu Dhabi's display of its collections as much as its architecture—cuts against the impression of many museum collections, which retain traces of their accretion over centuries. Indeed, so often our perception of collections is 'layered' in that it is inflected by our awareness of chronological development and institutional histories. We will have to wait and see whether this invigorating sense of simultaneity remains in thirty year's time, when the loaned works currently on display will have been replaced by new acquisitions. This is important, for I would suggest that, along with its representation of diverse cultures and periods, Louvre Abu Dhabi's distinctive temporality, the consequence of its rapid coming into being, may turn out to be a key ingredient of its universality.

This notion of 'universality' immediately raises tricky terminological issues that have figured prominently in this volume. Enlightenment museum, encyclopaedic museum, universal museum, national museum, imperial museum, global museum—each of these categories arose in response to different historical and political circumstances. In navigating the problems and possibilities thrown up by this cloud of terms, each of which comes with its own specific baggage, contemporary museums will likely want to hedge their bets and combine different curatorial approaches. I would suggest that there are at least two principal paradigms of museological practice on offer today. The first, historical model is based on migration, cultural contacts and transfers, and the hybridisation of forms. The second, aesthetic or formal model prioritises iconography and visual form above histories and contexts. In drawing connections among formal practices from disparate periods, this model challenges received constructions of artistic canons in a manner that recalls Cecilia Hurley's contribution to this volume or Malraux's dream of an imaginary museum.

As they strive to reconcile received ideas of universality with newer discourses of globalisation, many museums draw on both approaches, simultaneously situating works in cultural traditions and historical narratives, and setting up an interplay of formal affinities. Something of this balance can be seen in recent exhibitions. Amsterdam's Rijksmuseum, for example, recently put on a spectacular exhibition in which seventeenth-century ceramics and wardrobes were displayed alongside Rembrandt's paintings. Interaction does not only occur between cultures, it would seem, but among artistic media too. This example also suggests that some of the most ambitious and farsighted museums—Louvre Abu Dhabi included—are precipitating what I would venture to call a change in taste. Through this shift, the decorative arts and other previously neglected areas of cultural practice are coming to the fore. Indeed, they are being treated with such seriousness as to challenge even great masterpieces of painting and sculpture.

One crucial topic broached in the foregoing contributions was the role of the public in relation to museums. This is an old and revolutionary question. First posed by the founders of the Musée du Louvre in 1789, the question of the museum public goes to the heart of debates surrounding notions of universality and the global in museology today. Indeed, it is only through engaging with diverse publics that a cultural institution can plausibly lay claim to universality. Whether from across the street or the other side of the world, it is a museum's visitors that stimulate and justify its preoccupation with the universal. But then again, visitors only come because they expect to encounter works that embody or speak to their concerns. In constructing an approach to the universal, then, museums should not privilege publics at the expense of collections or vice versa. Again, the need to strike this balance leads back to old questions concerning what museums are and who they are for. Contemporary museums, such as that headed by Nathalie Bondil in Montréal, are posing these queries anew in response to the specific circumstances of the twenty-first century. Indeed, today the question of the public is an important part of the politics of museums, whether in relation to colonial histories and the postcolonial present; gendered relations and representations; and other domains in which people are seeking to alter their relationship with museums.

Just as important as the question of the public, though, are the trajectories through which people arrive at the museum and the cultural frames they bring to the encounter. In this vein, James Cuno's and Martin Pitts' contributions to this volume foreground the theme of journeys. These journeys need not necessarily be those undertaken by people; museum collections are also concerned with, and constituted by, what Pitts calls 'objects in motion.' Indeed, for Cuno, museums attest to the journeys undertaken by (and encoded in) objects themselves. Museums, I would suggest, are the point of confluence between these two species of journey; in museums, travelling objects are met by visitors who have all journeyed in one form or another, whether across the world or to visit the local collection. Indeed, in contemplating objects and works from distant places and periods, museum visitors set off on mental journeys of an altogether imaginative and poetic kind.

To conclude, I want to invoke another relevant idea. Like several of the questions and issues broached above, it is long established. I am referring to the notion of the *Kunstkörper* or 'art-body', as formulated by Goethe in 1798. By 'art-body', Goethe meant an artistic site or territory, which could be either geographical (a physically existing space) or ideal (a spiritual or conceptual construct). In formulating this concept, Goethe was responding specifically to the plundering of Italian art during the Napoleonic conquests. In this context, he had two specific 'bodies' in mind. The first was the territory in which these works of art were created. For Goethe writing in 1798, Italy was the original art-body, the terrain that had given rise to a great artistic tradition. He contrasted this to a second body, an 'ideal body of art,' namely the new ensembles in which works of art are placed, having been torn from their original context. As an ideal art-body, a museum endows ostensibly miscellaneous collections of artworks with a new unity. Indeed, displayed together in a new site, what initially seem like fragments of former worlds and traditions come to cohere, almost like an organic body. In the Romantic conception of both the Schlegel brothers and Goethe, the Louvre was potentially an ideal art-body, despite being built on the pillaging of Italy, that great former art-body.

Far from being theoretical or remote, these early nineteenth-century discussions remain central to thinking about museums today. Indeed, although it does not feature in the contributions to *Worlds in a Museum*, this notion of the art-body is both useful and disconcerting when posed in relation to contemporary museology.   In particular, it brings into focus the relations among the sites at which artworks are produced and the museums in which they are ultimately exhibited. What is more, the corporal metaphor resonates strongly among curators. Consider the sense of loss that attends Jean-Luc Martinez's contribution to this volume. Read in the light of Goethe's concept, Martinez's description of how the Louvre has been gradually 'pruned' down as works are sent elsewhere, or simply of gaps in its collection, strongly evokes bodily incompleteness, a dismembered art-body. Indeed, I have heard him speak of how the Louvre's lack of Chinese art feels like 'missing an arm'. As an art historian, it is interesting to see how a successor to Vivant Denon—the Louvre's first director and direct beneficiary of the Napoleonic spoils—has become something of a Quatremère de Quincy, grieving over the museum's irreparable incompleteness.

This leads to my final point. For Goethe, the art-body that is the museum may be composite and may be incomplete. However, as a defined segment of the world, it confers a kind of unity on the fragments it corrals together. To the outside world, then, the museum might well appear coherent and complete. An ideal art-body, composed of fragments of former art-bodies, Louvre Abu Dhabi can therefore rest assured in the knowledge that, in the end, coherence, completeness, and perhaps even universality are all in the eye of the beholder.

Abstracts (Arabic)

الجزء الأول: المتاحف والعولمة

التاريخ العالمي والمتاحف الفنية

جيمس كونو

إن القصص التي ترويها المعارض الفنية إنما ترويها من خلال القطع التي تعرضها للزوار. وتحمل هذه القطع، كما هي حال كل الأشياء، بصمات تاريخها، مثل تاريخ شكلها وموادّها، وتاريخ رسومها وأشكالها الرمزية، ثم تاريخ اكتشافها وملكيّتها المتعاقبة. وقد شاع انتقاد المتاحف الموسوعية بوصفها مؤسسات استعمارية أو إمبريالية تمتلك مجموعات وصلت إليها نتيجة اختلال في موازين القوى. والعديد من القطع المعروضة في المتحف البريطاني أو اللوفر تحمل أدلة تشير إلى الإمبراطورية دون أن تقتصر على الإمبراطورية البريطانية بل كذلك إمبراطوريات آشور والمملكة المصرية الحديثة والصين وروما والإمبراطوريّتَين المغولية والماورية في الهند. ورغم أنّه ينبغي الاعتراف بالسلطة السياسية بوصفها أحد جوانب تاريخ هذه التحف، إلّا أنّ الإمبراطورية عمومًا ليست بالمسألة البسيطة.

والحقيقة بخصوص الإمبراطوريات أنّها على الرغم من عنفها، فقد ساهمت وتساهم في تقاطع الأقاليم وتشابك تواريخها. فكما يذكّرنا إدوارد سعيد في كتابه «الثقافة والإمبريالية»: «إن الثقافاتُ بعيدة كل البعد عن كونها وحدوية أو متجانسة أو مستقلة ذاتيًا، بل إنها تكتسب في الواقع عناصر «أجنبية» وتناوبات واختلافات تفوق ما تقوم باستبعاده عن وعي. من يستطيع في الهند أو الجزائر اليوم أن يعزل بكل ثقة المكوّن البريطاني أو الفرنسي للماضي عن الحقائق الراهنة؟ ومن في بريطانيا أو فرنسا يستطيع أن يرسم دائرة واضحة حول لندن البريطانية أو باريس الفرنسية تستبعد تأثير الهند أو الجزائر على هاتين المدينتَين الإمبراطوريتين؟»[1] فالثقافات بنيات صنعها البشر، على حد تعبير سعيد، «كل من السلطة والمشاركة، مطبوعتان على حب الخير فيما تشتملان عليه وتضمّانه إليهما وتمنحانه المصداقية، لكن حبهما للخير أقلّ فيما تستبعدانه»[2]. أو كما كتب سنجاي سوبرهمانيام المولود في الهند والذي عاش وعمل في باريس وأكسفورد ولوس أنجلوس ونيويورك: «الثقافة الوطنية التي ليس لديها الجرأة بأن تعلن كما تفعل كل الثقافات الوطنية الأخرى، بأنها بدورها مهجّنة وأنها نقطة التقاء ومزيج من العناصر المستمدة من لقاءات عَرَضية والعواقب غير المتوقعة، لا يمكن إلّا تسلك طريق كراهية الأجانب وجنون العظمة الثقافي.»

هذا هو الدرس الذي تقدّمه المتاحف الموسوعية وهنا تكمن أهميتها: فهي مستودعات الأدلة المادية التي يمكن أن يُكتب انطلاقًا منها جزء كبير من التاريخ العالمي للعالم.

فحماية ذلك التاريخ وتوثيقه ومشاركته تقع ضمن مسؤولية هذه المتاحف: إنها تذكّرنا بأنّ تاريخ العالم هو بالضرورة تاريخ شبكات وتشابكات، وتاريخ تبادل التطورات الاقتصادية والسياسية والثقافية وتداخل بعضها مع بعض، وأنّ تاريخ شعب ما متشابك بالضرورة مع التاريخ العالمي.

1   إدوارد سعيد، الثقافة والأمبريالية. دار الآداب 2014. ط. 4. ترجمة كمال أبو ديب ص. 85.

2   إدوارد سعيد، المصدر المذكور، ص. 85.

حوار بين الثقافات: تحدٍّ لمتاحف المستقبل

هارتويغ فيشر

أضحى المتحف العالمي ضروريًا أكثر من أي وقت مضى، وهناك مجموعة متنوعة من المؤسسات التي تروي قصة تاريخ العالم بطرق جديدة مثيرة. إلّا أنّ مهمة تمثيل ثقافات من كل أرجاء العالم تطرح على المتاحف وأمنائها عددًا من التحديات. وينبغي للمتاحف بوجه خاص أن تُنصف الأعمال الفنية القادمة من سياقات ثقافية خاصة للغاية. وقد تكون هذه المهمة صعبة للمتاحف العالمية التي تحتوي على قطع من مختلف التقاليد والأمكنة. وهكذا تواجه المتاحف العالمية مهمة رئيسية تتمثل في إدارة التوتّرات ما بين أعمال فنية متباينة ثم بناء رواية شاملة انطلاقًا من قصص مختلفة.

لا توجد طريقة واحدة تصلح لمعالجة هذه المسائل، بل هناك في المشهد المتحفي المعاصر كمٌّ هائل من الأساليب المختلفة لصياغة رواية عالمية في القرن الواحد والعشرين. تتألف المجموعات الفنية الحكومية لمدينة درِيسدن من أربعة عشرة مؤسسة، وقد ركّزت على شرح الروابط القائمة بين متاحفها مع الحرص في الوقت نفسه على ألّا تحدد تجربة الزوار مسبقًا. وبفضل مجموعاته الشاملة، يمثّل المتحف البريطاني عالمًا مصغّرًا من الثقافات من كل الحقب التاريخية وكل أقاليم العالم. وعلى هذا النحو، فهو يسلّط الأضواء على العديد من الروابط الرئيسية والتأثيرات المتبادلة التي تركت أثرها على ثقافات العالم على امتداد التاريخ. ومع ذلك، ما زال المتحف البريطاني يقدّم الثقافات بوصفها كيانات منفصلة. وهكذا تظلّ مجموعاته مجزّأة بعض الشيء. وعلى الرغم من ذلك، ففي قاعة مؤسسة البخاري الخاصة بالعالم الإسلامي يعتمد المتحف طرقًا تبيّن كيف تساهم الحضارات في مناطق إقليمي واسع دون أن تكون هناك حدودا دقيقة تفصل بين مختلف التقاليد.

ومع ازدياد الترابط العالمي، ينبغي للمتاحف العالمية ألّا تكتفي بالتوجه إلى الجماهير المحلية بل إلى الجماهير العالمية كذلك. وسعيًا من المتحف البريطاني لإتاحة مجموعاته الفنية لأكبر عدد ممكن من الجماهير، شارك في مجموعة من المعارض مع متاحف تقع في أماكن أخرى من العالم. فكان معرض «الهند والعالم» (2017-2018)، على سبيل المثال، ثمرة جهود مشتركة بين المتحف البريطاني ومتحف شهاتراباتي شيفاجي مهاراجا فاستو سنغراهالايا في مومباي. أقيم المعرض في موقعين مما أتاح له الوصول إلى جماهير عريضة جديدة.

وسيكون الحوار بين المؤسسات أمرًا حاسمًا بينما تسعى المتاحف لتحسين طرق جذبها للجماهير العالمية وعرضها لثقافات العالم. ومن ثمّ، فإن وجهات النظر الثابتة لا تجدي نفعًا عندما يتعلق الأمر بتفسير تاريخ العالم بأسره وتراثه الثقافي. وعوضًا عن ذلك سيكون الانفتاح وتغيير التوجهات ضروريًا للتطور المستقبلي للمتحف العالمي.

في التنوّع وحدة: متحف لوفر واحد من بين متاحف اللوفر الثلاثة في القرن الواحد والعشرين

جون لوك مارتينيز

يمكن للمتاحف المعاصرة من خلال جمعها بين الثقافات المحلية والعالمية أن تسهم في تعزيز الوعي بانتماء الشعوب إلى مجتمع عالميٍّ متجذّر في التقاليد المحلية. ويتّسم اللوفر بعلاقته التناقضية بالثقافة الفرنسية، فهو متحفٌ عالميٌّ وهو في الوقت نفسه موقعٌ تاريخيٌّ شهير في العاصمة الفرنسية. وعلى غرار اللوفر في باريس، كان على اللوفر في مدينة لنس واللوفر أبوظبي أن يجدا التوازن الدقيق بين التواصل مع سياقهما المحلي الخاص من جهة وسرد رواية عالمية لثقافة العالم من جهة أخرى.

وعلى الرغم من موقعه داخل قصر اللوفر الذي كان المقرّ التاريخي للسلطة في فرنسا، فإنّ متحف اللوفر لم يقدّم نفسه أبدًا بوصفه متحفًا وطنيًّا فرنسيًّا. وخلال حملات نابليون امتلأ المتحف بكنوز ثقافية من كل أرجاء أوروبا. وعلى امتداد القرون حصلت تقسيمات جديدة بين مختلف المجالات المعرفية وظهرت مجالات أخرى علاوة على ظهور متاحف متخصصة أكثر فأكثر، وكل ذلك أدّى تدريجيًا إلى تشتيت مجموعات اللوفر. في سنة 1862، سُحبت من متحف اللوفر أعمال فنية كبرى تتعلق بالتاريخ الفرنسي كي تصبح نواة المتحف الأثري في سان جرمان آون لاي. وخلال القرن العشرين نُقلت المجموعات غير الأوروبية إلى متحف رصيف برانلي — جاك شيراك في باريس، كما نُقلت عدة أعمال فنية عائدة لأواخر القرن التاسع عشر وبدايات القرن العشرين إلى متحف أورسيه. ونتيجة لعمليات النقل المذكورة، فإن اللوفر اليوم لا يحتوي إلّا على القليل من الأعمال الفنية الفرنسية.

ونشهد هذا التوتّر ما بين الثقافة المحلية والعالمية في اللوفر-لنس وفي اللوفر أبوظبي كذلك. تقع مدينة لنس في المناطق العليا من شمال فرنسا وقد تأثرت للغاية من موجات تراجع التصنيع والبطالة. ورغم كون اللوفر-لنس عالمًا مصغّرًا للوفر في باريس، فإنه استضاف معارض تتناول تاريخ مدينة لنس بوصفها ملتقى الطرق لشمال غرب أوروبا. فمعرض «أوروبا روبنس»، على سبيل المثال، رسم خريطة أسفار الرسام بيتر بول روبنس عبر بلاطات اوروبا، بينما ركّز معرض «كوارث الحرب» على تصوير الأعمال الحربية بطرق تتناغم مع هذه المنطقة التي مزّقتها الحروب على مر التاريخ. ويسعى اللوفر أبوظبي بدوره إلى التواصل مع جمهوره الوطني والإقليمي. وهكذا نرى أنّ كل متحف من هذه المتاحف الثلاثة يتواصل مع مجتمعه المحلي دون أن يفقد التركيز على الثقافة العالمية. في الواقع، إنّ وجود ثلاثة متاحف لوفر في ثلاث مناطق مختلفة للغاية من العالم يعكس اهتمام هذه المتاحف المشترك بسرد رواية التاريخ العالمي.

الجزء الثاني: العولمة والمجتمعات

الحفاظ على تراث الماضي، والاستثمار في المستقبل: تطوّر متاحف البحرين

معالي الشيخة مي بنت محمد آل خليفة

من خلال المحافظة على التراث الثقافي، تسعى المتاحف المعاصرة أكثر فأكثر إلى جسر الهوة الاجتماعية وتحفيز النمو الاقتصادي. وتمتلك مملكة البحرين قطاعًا متحفيًا نشطًا، لاسيما بعد أن أنشأت هيئة للثقافة والتراث بهدف تنمية متاحفها ومواقعها التراثية والترويج لها. قد تكون البحرين صغيرة في مساحتها لكنّها غنية بتاريخها وآثارها. يحتل متحف البحرين الوطني مكانة بارزة في صميم التراث البحريني. وتشمل مجموعاته التاريخ البحريني بدءًا من حضارة دلمون القديمة مرورا بالعصر الهلينستي ووصولاً إلى الحقبة المتأخرة للحكم البرتغالي. افتتح المتحف عام 1988، وقد قام مؤخرًا بتجديد قاعة المقابر، كما أنه يقيم باستمرار معارض متنقلة في عدة متاحف في كل أرجاء العالم.

تعمل هيئة البحرين للثقافة والآثار بالتعاون مع البنوك ومؤسسات القطاع الخاص، وقد استثمرت بكثافة خلال العقد الماضي في البنية التحتية الثقافية المحلية. فأنشأت عبر برنامج الاستثمار الطموح المذكور مجموعة من المتاحف والمواقع الأثرية الجديدة. وكان متحف موقع قلعة البحرين أوّل هذه المشروعات الذي افتتح عام 2008. وهو معلم رائع ليس بسبب القلعة فحسب بل كذلك بسبب الموقع الأثري الذي تقع فيه القلعة والذي عمّره الإنسان لما يزيد على أربعة آلاف سنة. أمّا أحدث هذه المشروعات فهو طريق اللؤلؤ الذي افتتح عام 2018، والأرجح أنه أكبر متحف في الهواء الطلق، وهو مكرّس لتاريخ صيد اللؤلؤ في البحرين. يضمّ المتحف أحواض قواقع المحار وسلسلة من المباني خصّص كل واحد منها لجانب من جوانب صيد اللؤلؤ. وهناك مشروعات أخرى بصدد التطوير منها إنشاء مركز تراثي في مستوطنة سار التي تعود لخمسة آلاف سنة مضت وتمثّل مركزًا مهمًا في حقبة دلمون المبكرة.

وإذا كانت المؤسسات التراثية تسعى للعمل كمراكز ثقافية كبرى، فينبغي لها أن تتفاعل بقوة مع مختلف الفئات الاجتماعية الجديدة. وبناء على ذلك، يستضيف متحف البحرين الوطني أحداثًا مختلفة ويقوم بمجموعة من الأنشطة المتنوعة لأغراض التوعية والتواصل مع المجتمع، منها مبادرة «ثقافات فن الطبخ» التي شملت علاقات تعاونية بين الفنانين والطهاة، ومهرجان دولي للموسيقى. وبالإضافة إلى ذلك، تعتزم هيئة البحرين للثقافة والآثار إنشاء متحف يستهدف خصيصًا الأطفال. ومن خلال الاستثمار في قطاعها الثقافي وتواصلها مع مختلف الجماهير، سعت البحرين لجذب الزائرين للمنطقة وتحفيز النمو الاقتصادي المحلي والعمل على وضع البحرين في قلب التراث العالمي.

العولمة في عصور ما قبل الحداثة: الترابط الثقافي والتّحف المتنقّلة في العصور القديمة

ماتن بيتس

تُبرز هذه الدراسة الفوائد الناجمة عن وضع مفهوم الترابط والتّحف الفنية في صميم الدراسات الجديدة حول التاريخ العالمي، وذلك من خلال الاستئناس بأمثلة من خزفيات العالم الروماني وأمثلة أخرى من الفترات التاريخية الأحدث. هل يمكن أن تقدّم لنا أفكار العولمة وجهات نظر جديدة حول الأدوار التي أدّتها التحف في الماضي؟ أرى أنه من منظور التاريخ وعلم الآثار الرومانية، توفّر لنا العولمة إمكانيات هائلة. فهي تحفزنا في المقام الأول على تفكيك المراكز الكبرى مثل روما في عملية كتابة تاريخ العالم، وعلى إيلاء العالم الروماني اهتمامًا أقلّ من منظور المركز والأطراف ومنحه مزيدًا من الاهتمام بوصفه إمبراطورية متعددة المراكز في حوار مع الحواضر والحضارات المجاورة. أما الفائدة الثانية المتأتية من العولمة، فتتمثل في مساعدتنا على تخطّي القومية المنهجية للأبحاث التاريخية القديمة التي غالبا ما تحصر فهمنا للتحف الفنية ضمن سياقات محدّدة بالحدود الإدارية الحديثة. تشجّعنا العولمة على دراسة المدى الكامل لهجرات التحف على الصعيدَين الإقليمي والعالمي، كما إنها تركّز الاهتمام على التأثيرات التحويلية لنقل التحف ضمن سياقات ثقافية محلية مختلفة. ومن ثمّ، يبدو أنّ أعظم فائدة للعولمة تتمثل في توفير الإطار اللازم لتفسير التحف المتنقّلة في البحوث التاريخية، وذلك بوصفها المحفّزات الحقيقية للتغيير في الماضي المتّصل بعضه ببعض.

التاريخ الكوني والتاريخ العالمي والمتاحف العالمية

هيرفيه إنغلبيرت

إنّ الروايات التاريخية لحلقات مكتملة من التاريخ التي تُعدّ مهمة وقيّمة قد كُتبت منذ ما يزيد على أربعة آلاف سنة في حضارات مختلفة جدًّا (بلاد الرافدين، واليونانية والرومانية، والصينية، والأوروبية، والبيزنطية، والمسيحية السريانية، والعربية الإسلامية، والغربية، والروسية واليابانية). غير أنّ مفهوم التاريخ بوصفه عملية نشوء وتطور موحّدة ومفهومة لدى البشرية كلها لم يظهر إلّا قرابة عام 1750 في أوروبا. ومنذ عام 1770 إلى عام 1980، كانت لدى الفلاسفة والمؤرّخين الغربيّين القناعة نفسها، ومفادها أنّ التاريخ الكوني للحضارة يهيمن عليه تاريخ أوروبا، وأنه انتهى بانتصار القيم الليبرالية في المجالات الاقتصادية والسياسية والمجتمعية. وقد استناد هذا الاعتقاد إلى نجاح التصنيع والاستعمار اللذان نشآ في أوروبا والولايات المتحدة، كما اتّسمت الرؤية الماركسية للتاريخ بدورها بالمركزية الأوروبية.

في القرن التاسع عشر، ترسّخت العالمية الثلاثية للتاريخ والتكنولوجيا والفن. وبعد عام 1850، تضاعفت المعارض العالمية (لندن وباريس) وتكاثرت المتاحف أو مجموعات المتاحف التي ادّعت العالمية في رؤيتها للتاريخ الإنساني (لندن وباريس وبرلين ونيويورك وسان بطرسبورغ وفيانا). ومع بداية القرن العشرين، عرضت متاحف الفنون والآثار الخطوط العريضة لتاريخ إنساني بدأ في مصر وبلاد الرافدين، وتواصل في العصر القديم الروماني الإغريقي، ثم في العصر الوسيط الأوروبي، تبعه بعد ذلك عصر النهضة، وأخيرًا العصر الحديث في أوروبا. أمّا منتجات الحضارات الأخرى فقد عُرضت بوجه عام في أماكن أخرى، في متاحف الفنون المتخصصة والفنون التطبيقية وعلم الأعراق البشرية.

وبداية من عام 1980، بدأ تاريخ العالم يشكّك في جلّ المفاهيم التي طغت عليها المركزية الأوروبية التي ورثناها من القرن التاسع عشر. فقد شجّعت نهاية الإمبراطوريات الاستعمارية، والطبيعة متعددة الثقافات لمجتمع أمريكا الشمالية، وإخفاق النموذج السوفياتي، وصعود أقطاب اقتصادية جديدة خاصة في آسيا، وتطور ظاهرة العولمة، على أخذ تاريخ الجميع في الاعتبار. غير أنّ القيود المنهجية والموضوعاتية والزمنية للتاريخ العالمي تحول دون اعتباره تاريخا يشمل الجميع ومن ثم حلوله محلّ التاريخ الكوني.

تظلّ المتاحف انعكاسات لعقليات عصرها اليوم وكما في عام 1900. وعلى مدى الخمسة عشرة سنة الماضية، احتدّ التباين بين الكونية الغربية المزعومة والحركات القومية/المحلية التي ظهرت بعد الفترة الاستعمارية، متخذًا شكل نقاش حول مفهوم المتحف العالمي الذي أطلقه آرثر ماك غريغور. وعلاوة على ذلك، من الملاحظ أنّ هذه المرحلة العالمية الحاسمة قد أدّت إلى تأثيرات مختلفة في عالم المتاحف كان أوّلها ظهور فنّ عالمي معاصر. وتمثّل ثانيها في تطوير متاحف الأصول العرقية التي أضفت بُعدًا

جماليًا على أعمالها (متحف رصيف برانلي) أو أوضحت أعمالها الأوروبية بناءً على ثقافات أخرى (ميونيخ وفيينا). وكان التأثير الثالث إضافة أقسام إقليمية جديدة داخل «المتاحف العالمية» التقليدية (المتروبوليتان واللوفر)، بينما تمثّل التأثير الرابع في إنشاء متاحف إقليمية تركّز على الحضارات غير الغربية (سنغافورة والشارقة). وتجلى آخر هذه التأثيرات في النقاش الذي أثير حول النماذج الجديدة من المتاحف العالمية على غرار اللوفر أبوظبي. فقد شمل هذا المتحف الذي يقع خارج الفضاء الغربي بعض الجوانب من التاريخ العالمي في إطار رواية للتاريخ العالمي تميزت بابتعادها عن المركزية الأوروبية أكثر من قبل، وهو توجّه لا يسعنا إلاّ أن نشيد به.

الجزء الثالث: توتّرات عالمية/محلية

مرجعيات مترابطة: نقد المرجعية الأدبية الغربية في دراسات تاريخ الفنّ الحديثة

سيسيليا هورلي

على امتداد فترة طويلة اعتُبرت الروائع الفنية والقوانين المرجعية عناصر أساسية — أي نقاط ثابتة في الواقع — في منظومة القيم التي تبني وتؤثّر في ممارستنا وفهمنا لتاريخ الفن، وذلك في قاعات المحاضرات وفي المتحف على السواء. وقد حاول هارولد بلوم أن يضع قانونًا أدبيًا مرجعيًا في مؤلفه الهائل بعنوان «المرجعية الأدبية الغربية: مؤلفات ومدرسة العصور» الصادر عام 1994. وقد كانت الكتب ومدارس العصور الزمنية غالبًا محل نقاش واسع، لاسيما على ضوء التطورات التكنولوجية والأكاديمية الحديثة. ويبدو أنّ التواصل بين البشر والعولمة والإنترنت تدحض على نحو متزايد هذه القوانين الإرشادية كلها أو تقلّص بدرجة كبيرة من صلاحيّتها. فهل ينبغي لنا بدورنا أن نتخذ موقفا نقديًا تجاه تلك القوانين الفنية؟ هل علينا تكييفها أو كما ينادي البعض، تدميرها؟ ينبغي لنا في المقام الأول أن نشكّك في إصرارنا على قانون فني واحد بعينه، كما إنه علينا التفكير في طريقة لفتح قوانينا الفنية وجعلها متعددة وقابلة للقياس والمقارنة. وممكن للمتحف الموسوعي أو العالمي أو المسحي أن يقوم بذلك من خلال توفيره بوتقة مثالية تتواجد فيها مختلف الثقافات الفنية والتاريخية وتخضع للتقييم. فمن خلال سرد قصة الحضارات الإنسانية على أساس تزامني وغير تزامني، وإتاحة الفرصة للجميع لمشاهدة الفنون التي أبدعتها كل الثقافات، يمكن للمتحف الموسوعي أن يوفر مساحات يمكن فيها إعادة النظر في الروايات التقليدية لتاريخ الفن التي تقوم على سِير المبدعين، أو على أساس التقسيمات الإقليمية والقومية، أو المسائل الأسلوبية أو التصويرية الرمزية أو الأيقونية، بل يمكن أيضا تعديل هذه الروايات أو حتى رفضها. وعلى هذا الأساس يمكن للمتحف الموسوعي أن يؤدّي دورًا نشطًا في إعادة صياغة المفاهيم وفي التشجيع على كتابة تاريخ جديد مترابط ومتشابك للفن يضع الشبكات وعمليات النقل والتبادل والحدود القابلة للاختراق في المقدّمة.

المتحف الكوني، والمتحف العالمي: متحف ليون نموذجًا

سيلفي راموند

يعدّ متحف ليون للفنون الجميلة نموذجًا ممتازًا للأوجه المتعددة التي يمكن من خلالها التعبير عن مفهوم العالمية في مؤسسة ثقافية. صُمّم المتحف إبّان الثورة الفرنسية بوصفه أكبر متحف خارج باريس وأطلق عليه مسمى «اللوفر الصغير» تقديرًا لتشكيلة أعماله المتنوعة، فقد عُرف متحف ليون للفنون الجميلة على مر الزمان بمجموعاته الكبيرة التي تشمل القرون الممتدة من العصر القديم إلى الحركات الطليعية والفن المعاصر الراهن.

وعلى مدى تاريخه، تشكّل هذا النموذج المتحفي بوصفه متحفًا كونيا وديمقراطيا بإدارة هنري فوسيّون، ثمّ بوصفه متحفا عالميا وشعبيا بإدارة خلفه ليون روزنطال. وخلال العقود الثلاثة الأخيرة، اكتسب مصطلح «الكونية» المعقّد دلالات جديدة. فقد بات يجسّد فكرة معيّنة عن العولمة في الفنون دون أن يغفل عن الحلم طويل الأمد المتمثل في إتاحة هذه الفنون للجمهور الأوسع.

تحديد مركز القومية: المركز والأطراف في الثقافة المتحفية للبنان المعاصر

آماري مايلا عفيش

لديّ قناعة أنه خلال القرن الواحد والعشرين ستكون أهمية الثقافة للصحة بنفس أهمية الرياضة لها خلال القرن العشرين. فالفنّ نافع على المستويَين الاجتماعي والشخصي. تُنشّط الثقافة الحوارات حول القضايا المهمة في عصرنا الجديد متعدد الثقافات. ورغم أنّ الدعم المقدَّم للفنانين ولتاريخ الفن يكمن في صميم رسالة الممارسة المتحفية، فإنّ على المتاحف أن تفعل أكثر من ذلك بكثير.

1. نشاط تربوي يشجع الحياة الجمعية والوئام الاجتماعي

في القرن الواحد والعشرين، تمثّل الثقافة وقرينتها التربية أدوات تماسك اجتماعي تؤدي دورا رياديا في تشجيع الحياة المجتمعية في «قريتنا العالمية». كما يمثّل التفاعل بين الأجيال وتعدد الثقافات مفهومَين رئيسيين لتطوير مجتمع شامل للجميع في عالمنا الكوني والمحلي. ويحتل التعليم صدارة أولوياتنا. ومع أن تعلّم القراءة والكتابة مسألة أساسية، إلاّ أنّ تعلّم الرؤية والشعور أمرًا أساسًا بدوره. نحن بحاجة إلى فكّ شفرة المعاني الواردة في الصور وفي أحاسيسنا، وعلينا الانتباه لأنّ وعينا بصدد الغرق في المعلومات. وبفضل ورشة ميشال دو شونيار الدولية للتعليم والعلاج بالفن، وقاعته السينمائية وقاعة الحفلات الموسيقية الجديدة، يعتزّ متحف الفنون الجميلة بمونتريال بامتلاكه لأكبر مركّب تعليمي وثقافي مقارنة بأي متحف من متاحف أمريكا الشمالية.

2. إعادة التفكير في جدوى المؤسسة: المتحف النشط اجتماعيًّا

هل تستكشف متاحف الفنون الجميلة قضايا عصرها وتشارك فيها؟ أم أنها تميل إلى ترك هذه المسائل إلى متاحف العلوم والمجتمعات؟ في هذا الصدد، يتميّز متحف الفنون الجميلة بمونتريال بتنوّع واتساع نطاق نشاطه في المجال الاجتماعي، إذ لديه 450 اتفاقية شراكة على مستوى الخبراء ويرتبط بأكثر من 50 برنامجًا جامعيًا مكرّسًا للأبحاث في مجالات الصحة والتعليم والمجتمع.

3. الإبداع المشترك! تطوير ثقافة الشراكة

يتيح هذا النهج التفاعلي والمتعاطف الوصول إلى المزيد من الجماهير ولا سيما أولئك الذين لا يمكنهم المشاركة في الأنشطة الثقافية. علينا أن نشجّع الشراكات الخلّاقة المشتركة ليس بغرض التعايش بل بغية التطور المشترك. إنّ تحفيز مفهوم التخصصات المتعددة وتعزيزه يجري في عروق المتحف «النشط والإبداعي».

4. إعادة التفكير في المجموعات الفنية

سعيًا للابتعاد عن احتكار المؤرخين والمتخصصين شبه الكامل لتفسير مجموعات المتاحف، يتمثل النهج الجديد في الاستماع إلى وجهات نظر خبراء في مجالات تبدو دخيلة من أول وهلة وحتى غير متوافقة، فتشجيع تعددية وجهات النظر من شأنه أن يبرز الطبيعة الإنسانية والمتعددة الدلالات للمجموعات الفنية. ويعود إلينا القرار في اعتماد نهج شامل حتى تخاطب أعمالنا الفنية جماهيرنا بخصوص القضايا المهمة للمجتمع المعاصر.

5. متحف من أجل صحة أفضل!

من المهم أن نعيد النظر في المتطلبات البيولوجية والتجريبية لزوّارنا. فالحاجة إلى «الجمال» أو على الأقل إلى إحساس جمالي هي حاجة فيزيولوجية وليست فلسفية أو ثقافية فحسب. والمتحف مدرسة للإحساس والمكان الذي نتواصل فيه مع وجودنا العاطفي. وفي إطار دوره كمتحف ومختبر في الوقت ذاته، فإنّ متحف الفنون الجميلة بمونتريال يعدّ رائدًا في التواصل مع الخبراء في مجالات التعليم والصحة والبحوث والخدمات الاجتماعية والأوساط الجامعية والمجتمعية، وذلك بدعم من الشركات والناشطين في مجال العمل الخيري.

6. منظور يتّسم بالمزيد من التواصل المشترك بين الثقافات والتعدد الثقافي

في إطار مجتمع يزداد فيه الاختلاط بين الثقافات، يشجّع متحف الفنون الجميلة بمونتريال الحوار الثقافي من خلال تعزيز الوعي العابر للتاريخ والثقافات، وذلك بغية تحفيز الأفراد والجماعات على الالتقاء والحوار. ومن أجل تحقيق اللامركزية في نظرتنا العرقية، علينا أن نتعلم النظر إلى ما هو أبعد من آفاقنا التقليدية وتحفيز الحوار مع الآخرين. وتمثّل المتاحف المكان الأنسب لاحتضان هذا النشاط وتعزيزه مع الحفاظ على الحيادية.

عُرف متحف الفنون الجميلة بمونتريال بممارساته المبتكرة وأنشطته الواعية بقضايا المجتمع، وقد شارك المتحف في دراسة أنجزتها منظمة التعاون الاقتصادي والتنمية حول كيفية مضاعفة تأثير المتاحف في الثقافة والتنمية المحلية.

الجزء الرابع: المركز والأطراف

تحديد مركز القومية: المركز والأطراف في الثقافة المتحفية للبنان المعاصر

آنماري مايلا عفيش

تؤدّي المتاحف دورًا ملحوظًا في إبراز الهوية الوطنية. وبوصفه متحف الدولة، فإنّ متحف بيروت الوطني أسهم إلى حد كبير في تغذية الشعور بالاعتزاز بالممتلكات الوطنية منذ إنشائه عام 1942. ولا يعدّ عرض القطع الأثرية القادمة حصريًا من التراب اللبناني وسيلة لإظهار الكنوز الوطنية فحسب، بل هو أيضا وسيلة لمشاهدة التاريخ الوطني. ونظرًا لتدمير المتحف جزئيًا خلال الحرب ما بين عامَي 1975 و1991، فإنه تقع على عاتقنا مسؤولية عرض عمليات إعادة البناء بوصفها حالة بقاء على قيد الحياة في زمن الأزمات ومثالاً على إحياء متحف.

إضافة إلى ذلك، اعتمدت الوزارة سياسة نشر الثقافة، فأنشأت عدة متاحف خارج بيروت لكل واحد منها خصوصيّته على غرار متحفَي طرابلس وبيت الدين وغيرهما من المتاحف الواقعة في الأماكن الأثرية مثل جبيل وبعلبك. وعلى سبيل المثال، يقع متحف طرابلس في القصر القديم للمدينة وقد تأسس ليُبرز هذا المعلم الأثري والمجموعة التي يضمّها على السواء. وعلاوة على لذلك، تغطّي المجموعة الفنية منطقة شمال لبنان بأكملها. وإلى جانب هذه السياسة الرامية إلى تعزيز الأطراف لخلق التوازن مع المركز، فإنّ أحد التحديات يكمن في إعادة تهيئة المتاحف وتحديثها، بينما يكمن التحدّي الآخر في إنشاء متاحف جديدة. وهكذا أنشئ في شهر أبريل 2018 مجلس المتاحف كهيئة مستقلة ضمن وزارة الثقافة. وتتمثل مهمة هذه الإدارة الفتيّة في إنشاء المتاحف الجديدة وتطوير المتاحف القائمة والنهوض بمجموعاتها الفنية والمحافظة عليها. وفي الوقت الحاضر، هناك مشروعات لمتاحف جديدة في كل من بيروت وصور وصيدا. وختامًا، للمتاحف دور في تلبية احتياجات السكان في البلاد بأسرها من خلال دعمها للاقتصاد المحلي واحترام تنوّعها وثراء تراثها الثقافي.

الهويّات الخلالية: تجديد متحف الحضارات الآسيوية

كيني تينغ

يعدّ متحف الحضارات الآسيوية متحف سنغافورة للفنون والآثار الآسيوية. وفي عام 2012، شرع المتحف في إجراء عملية تحديث كبيرة لروايتها المتحفية، متحوّلاً من تنظيم جغرافي لمجموعته وقاعاته الدائمة إلى تقسيم يعتمد على نهج موضوعاتي عابر للحدود والثقافات الوطنية يسلّط الضوء على موضوعين رئيسيّين: التجارة والمعتقد. ويستند هذان الموضوعان على طبيعة سنغافورة بوصفها ميناء متعدد الثقافات ومدينة تجارية في آسيا. كما أنّ التجارة والمعتقد هما محرّكان رئيسيان في التاريخ، فكلاهما قد غذّى تدفق الشعوب والثقافات والأفكار عبر آسيا وما بين آسيا والعالم. يقدم هذا العرض المزيد من التفاصيل حول النهج العلمي للمتحف اليوم وكذلك حول الفرص والتحديات والدروس المستفادة من هذا التحوّل المتحفي.

تنسيق المتاحف عبر الثقافات: عولمة القوى المحرّكة للتقاليد المتحفية المعاصرة

هنري كيم

بينما تركّز المناقشات حول «عولمة» الفنون بطبعها في أيّامنا الراهنة، على المبادرات الكبرى التي تتخذها كبريات المؤسسات وعلى سرعة انتشار التوجّهات والتيارات على نطاق واسع، فإنّ تأثيرات هذه التوجّهات داخل المؤسسات أو محليا لا تلقى الاهتمام ذاته. لقد شهدت المهرجانات والمعارض الفنية الكبرى انتشارًا سريعًا مثلما انتشر سريعا إنشاء المؤسسات الفنية الخاصة في السنوات

الأخيرة. وظهرت المتاحف في أماكن تعوزها التقاليد المتحفية بمبادرات من الحكومات المحلية أو الوطنية أو بمبادرات خاصة. كما ظهرت متاحف متخصّصة إلى جانب المتاحف التقليدية القائمة.

وعند وصفنا لهذه التوجهات بوصفها جزءًا من «عولمة» عالم الفن، فإن السؤال الذي يطرح نفسه هو إن كان ذلك يحصل بطريقة منظمة أم غير منظمة، ومدى إمكانية تطبيق نموذج المركز والأطراف. من وجهة نظري، أرى أنّ الانتشار قد حصل بطريقة غير منظمة بدافع من العوامل التالية على المستوى المحلي:

أ/ المحاكاة: الرغبة في الاستنساخ المحلي لما أُنجز بنجاح في أماكن أخرى

ب/ تطبيق الأفكار والممارسات الجيدة

ج/ قوة المبادرة الخاصة والمؤسسات الجديدة ذات الرسالة المحددة

د/ السعي وراء البروز المحلّي.

Abstracts (French)

Session 1

Histoire globale et musées d'art
James Cuno

Les histoires racontées par les expositions le sont au travers des objets présentés qui, comme tous les objets, portent la trace de leur histoire: celle de leur forme et de leurs matériaux, de l'imaginaire et de l'iconographie qui y sont liés, de leur découverte et de leurs propriétaires successifs. La tendance actuelle est à la critique des musées encyclopédiques en tant qu'institutions coloniales ou impériales, dont les collections sont le résultat d'inégalités de pouvoir. Nombre des objets du British Museum ou du Louvre sont empreints de la marque d'un empire. Pas seulement de l'Empire britannique, mais aussi de l'Empire assyrien, du Nouvel Empire d'Égypte, de l'Empire de Chine, de celui de Rome, ou encore des Empires maurya et moghol en Inde. Le pouvoir politique est un aspect de leur histoire qui doit être reconnu. Mais la notion d'empire est loin d'être simple.

Il est vrai que l'empire, malgré sa violence, a contribué, et contribue encore, aux chevauchements des territoires et à l'enchevêtrement des histoires. Edward Saïd nous le rappelle dans son livre, *Culture et Impérialisme*: « Loin d'être unitaires, monolithiques ou même autonomes, les cultures adoptent plus d'éléments «étrangers», d'altérités, de différences, qu'elles n'en excluent consciemment. Qui en Inde ou en Algérie peut aujourd'hui dissocier avec certitude les composantes britanniques ou françaises issues du passé des réalités actuelles, et qui, en Grande-Bretagne ou en France, peut tracer un cercle précis autour du Londres britannique ou du Paris français qui exclurait l'influence de l'Inde ou de l'Algérie sur ces deux villes impériales ? »

Les cultures sont des structures à l'image de l'humanité qui les bâtit, faites, selon les mots de Saïd, « à la fois d'autorité et de contribution, bienveillantes envers ce qu'elles incluent, intègrent et valident, moins envers ce qu'elles excluent » ou, comme l'a écrit Sanjay Subrahmanyam, intellectuel né en Inde et ayant vécu et travaillé à Paris, Oxford, Los Angeles et New York : « Une culture nationale qui n'est pas assez sûre d'elle pour déclarer que, comme toutes les autres, elle aussi est un hybride, un carrefour, un mélange d'éléments issus de rencontres fortuites et de conséquences imprévues, ne peut que prendre le chemin de la xénophobie et de la paranoïa culturelle. »

Voilà la leçon et l'enjeu des musées d'art encyclopédiques : ils sont les dépositaires des preuves matérielles à partir desquelles une part si importante de l'histoire globale du monde peut s'écrire.

Protéger, documenter et partager cette histoire est de la responsabilité de ces musées : ils nous rappellent que l'histoire du monde est inévitablement faite de croisements et de réseaux, de développements économiques, politiques et culturels en commun ou qui se recoupent, et que l'histoire d'une nation est nécessairement mêlée à l'histoire globale.

Dialogue entre les cultures : un défi pour les musées de l'avenir
Hartwig Fischer

À ce jour, le musée universel relève plus que jamais d'une nécessité vitale, avec une variété d'institutions narrant l'évolution de l'histoire du monde de manière novatrice et passionnante. Cependant, le projet de représenter les cultures du monde entier pose un certain nombre de défis, aux musées comme aux conservateurs. Les musées doivent notamment donner leur juste place à des objets anciens issus de contextes culturels très particuliers. Cet objectif pourrait se révéler difficile dans des musées universels abritant des objets en provenance d'une variété de traditions et de lieux. L'une de leurs tâches principales consiste alors à maîtriser les tensions entre les œuvres et à produire un récit en surplomb de la diversité de leurs histoires.

Il n'y a pas qu'une seule solution à ces problèmes. Le paysage des musées contemporains recèle une multitude d'approches différentes dans le but de produire un récit universel au XXIe siècle. Les Collections nationales de Dresde réunissent un conglomérat de quatorze institutions. Celles-ci ont œuvré à la clarification des liens entre leurs musées tout en veillant à ne pas prédéterminer l'expérience des visiteurs. Avec ses vastes collections, le British Museum est un microcosme de cultures de toutes les époques et régions du monde. En tant que tel, il met en évidence bon nombre d'interconnexions et d'influences mutuelles ayant façonné les cultures au cours du temps. Toutefois, il continue à présenter chaque culture comme une entité distincte. À ce titre, ses collections restent plutôt cloisonnées. Cependant, avec sa nouvelle Albukhary Foundation Gallery of the

Islamic World, le musée éclaire les manières dont les cultures et traditions historiques participent aux grands espaces régionaux d'échange, par-delà les frontières strictes qui les sépareraient.

Avec l'intensification de la connectivité mondiale, les musées universels doivent s'adresser non seulement à leurs publics nationaux, mais également à un public mondial. En partageant ses collections avec un public le plus large possible, le British Museum a contribué à des expositions coorganisées avec des musées ailleurs dans le monde. À titre d'exemple, l'exposition *India and the World* (« L'Inde et le monde », 2017-2018) fut le fruit d'une collaboration entre le British Museum et le Chhatrapati Shivaji Maharaj Vastu Sangrahalaya, à Mumbai. Présentée sur deux sites, elle s'adressa à de nouveaux publics élargis.

Le dialogue entre les institutions aura une importance fondamentale à mesure que les musées affineront leurs méthodes d'interaction avec un public international et exposeront les cultures du monde. Des perspectives déterminées une fois pour toutes se révèlent peu utiles pour la médiation de l'histoire et d'un patrimoine culturel issu du monde entier. Au contraire, l'ouverture d'esprit et les changements d'orientation joueront un rôle indispensable dans le développement futur du musée universel.

L'unité dans la diversité : un Louvre parmi les trois Louvres du XXIe siècle
Jean-Luc Martinez

En réunissant les cultures locales et mondiales, les musées contemporains peuvent contribuer à la prise de conscience que les individus appartiennent à une communauté universelle ancrée dans des traditions locales. Le Louvre entretient une relation paradoxale avec la culture française en ce qu'il est à la fois un musée universel et un site historique célèbre au cœur de la capitale française. À l'instar du Louvre de Paris, le Louvre-Lens et le Louvre Abu Dhabi ont dû trouver un équilibre délicat entre l'engagement dans leur contexte local particulier et la narration d'une histoire universelle de la culture mondiale.

Bien qu'il soit situé au palais du Louvre, siège historique du pouvoir en France, le Louvre ne s'est jamais qualifié lui-même comme musée national français. Pendant les conquêtes napoléoniennes, le musée s'est enrichi de trésors culturels de toute l'Europe. Au fil des siècles, de nouveaux partages entre les domaines de connaissance, comme l'émergence de nouveaux musées plus spécialisés, ont conduit à une dispersion progressive des collections du Louvre. En 1862, d'importantes œuvres liées à l'histoire de France ont été transférées au musée d'Archéologie nationale de Saint-Germain-en-Laye pour en former le premier noyau. Au XXe siècle, les collections non européennes du Louvre furent transférées au musée du quai Branly – Jacques Chirac de Paris, de même qu'une grande partie des œuvres d'art datant de la fin du XIXᵉ et du début du XXᵉ siècle prirent place au musée d'Orsay. Ce processus de soustraction explique la part relativement moindre de l'art français dans les collections du Louvre aujourd'hui.

Cette tension entre culture locale et culture mondiale est également visible dans le Louvre-Lens et le Louvre Abu Dhabi. Située dans les Hauts-de-France, au nord de la France, Lens a été durement touchée par la désindustrialisation et le chômage. Bien qu'à certains égards, le Louvre-Lens constitue un microcosme du Louvre de Paris, il a également su organiser des expositions portant sur l'histoire de Lens en tant que carrefour du nord-ouest de l'Europe. À titre d'exemple, *L'Europe de Rubens* a retracé les pérégrinations de Pierre Paul Rubens entre les cours européennes, tandis que *Les Désastres de la guerre* a exploré les représentations de la guerre en résonance avec cette région déchirée par l'Histoire. Le Louvre Abu Dhabi est, lui aussi, ouvert à son contexte national et régional. Chacun de ces trois musées se trouve donc impliqué dans son contexte local tout en mettant l'accent sur la culture mondiale. Leur appartenance à trois régions si différentes du monde met en évidence leur intérêt commun à narrer l'histoire universelle.

Session 2

Préserver le passé, investir dans l'avenir : le développement des musées de Bahreïn
S.E. Shaikha Mai bint Mohammed Al Khalifa

En préservant le patrimoine culturel, les musées contemporains cherchent de plus en plus à surmonter les clivages sociaux et à favoriser la croissance économique. Le royaume de Bahreïn dispose d'un secteur muséal particulièrement actif avec une Autorité pour la culture et les antiquités en charge du développement et de la promotion de musées nationaux et sites patrimoniaux. Bahreïn est peut-être petit en taille, mais il est riche en histoire et en antiquités. Son musée national est au cœur du domaine patrimonial. Ses collections couvrent l'histoire de Bahreïn, de l'ancienne civilisation de Dilmun, en passant par la période hellénistique et la dernière domination portugaise. Inauguré en 1988, le musée a récemment rénové sa galerie des cimetières et exporte fréquemment des expositions itinérantes vers des musées d'autres parties du monde.

En partenariat avec des banques et des entreprises privées, l'Autorité bahreïnie pour la culture et les antiquités a massivement investi dans les infrastructures culturelles locales au cours de la dernière décennie. Grâce à cet ambitieux programme d'investissement, elle a développé une variété de nouveaux musées et sites archéologiques. Le premier de ces projets s'est traduit par la création du musée du site de Qal'at al-Bahreïn (fort de Bahreïn), inauguré en 2008. Le lieu est remarquable non seulement pour l'édifice du fort qui héberge le musée, mais aussi pour le site archéologique sur lequel il repose, oc-cupé par les hommes pendant plus de quatre mille ans. Le projet le plus récent a consisté en la création du Centre de visiteurs de Pearling Path (« Promenade perlière »), qui a ouvert ses portes en 2018. Sans doute le plus grand musée en plein air du monde, il est consacré à l'histoire de l'industrie perlière de Bahreïn. Le musée abrite des parcs à huîtres ainsi qu'un ensemble de bâtiments dédiés autrefois aux différents aspects de l'activité perlière. D'autres projets sont en cours d'élaboration, comme la création du site patrimonial de Saar. Remontant à quelque cinq millénaires, il s'agit d'un centre de peuplement de première importance du début de la période de Dilmun.

Pour que les institutions patrimoniales fonctionnent comme des centres culturels majeurs, elles doivent s'engager avec force auprès de nouveaux publics diversifiés. Ainsi, le musée national de Bahreïn accueille une grande variété d'événements et propose une large palette d'activités de sensibilisation. Parmi celles-ci, citons notamment l'initiative Culinary Cultures (« Cultures culinaires ») qui fait collaborer artistes et chefs cuisi-niers et organise un festival international de musique. En outre, l'Autorité bahreïnie pour la culture et les antiquités prévoit la création d'un musée dédié aux enfants. En investissant dans son secteur culturel et en interagissant avec des publics vairés, Bahreïn souhaite attirer des visiteurs dans la région, favoriser la croissance économique locale et asseoir la place du pays au cœur du patrimoine mondial.

La globalisation prémoderne : La connectivité culturelle et les objets en mouvement dans les mondes anciens
Martin Pitts

L'objet de cet article est de donner un aperçu des bénéfices que peut apporter le fait de mettre la connectivité et les objets au centre des nouvelles études sur l'histoire globale, en s'appuyant sur les exemples de céramiques originaires du monde romain et d'époques plus récentes. Les principes de la globalisation offrent-ils de nouvelles perspectives in-téressantes sur le rôle des objets ? Du point de vue de l'histoire et de l'archéologie ro-maines, je soutiens que la globalisation a un immense potentiel. Tout d'abord, elle nous pousse à déplacer des centres aussi importants dans l'écriture de l'histoire globale que Rome, amenant ainsi à repenser le monde romain non plus comme un centre avec sa périphérie, mais plutôt comme un empire polycentrique dialoguant avec les régimes et les civilisations environnants. Le second bénéfice majeur de la globalisation de la pensée est de nous aider à aller au-delà du nationalisme méthodologique de la recherche tra-ditionnelle en histoire, qui enferme trop souvent la compréhension des objets dans des contextes définis par les frontières administratives modernes. La globalisation de la pen-sée incite à étudier toute l'étendue des diasporas des objets à l'échelle pan-régionale et globale, et focalise également l'attention sur l'effet transformateur que peuvent avoir des éléments en mouvement dans différents contextes culturels locaux. Ainsi, il semble que la globalisation manifeste son plus grand potentiel en tant que cadre d'interprétation de l'objet-en-mouvement dans la recherche historique, lui qui est le véritable catalyseur de changement dans ce passé connecté.

Histoire universelle, histoire globale et musées universels
Hervé Inglebert

Depuis plus de quatre millénaires, on a écrit, dans des civilisations très différentes (Mésopotamie, Grecs et Romains, Chinois, Européens, Byzantins, chrétiens syriaques, Arabes musulmans, Occidentaux, Russes et Japonais), des récits d'histoire sur des totalités du passé jugées mémorables et signifiantes. Cependant, le concept d'Histoire, pensé comme un devenir unifié et compréhensible par les humains, n'est apparu que vers 1750 en Europe. De 1770 à 1980, philosophes et historiens occidentaux ont partagé une même conviction : l'histoire universelle de la civilisation était dominée par celle de l'Europe et s'achevait avec le triomphe des valeurs libérales dans les domaines économiques, politiques et sociétaux. Cette conviction s'appuyait sur les réussites industrielles et le colonialisme des Européens et des États-Uniens ; le schéma marxiste développé en URSS, quoique différent, était tout aussi eurocentré.

Au XIXe siècle, on affirma la triple universalité de l'Histoire, de la Technique et de l'Art. Après 1850, les expositions universelles (Londres, Paris) et les créations de musées, ou d'ensembles de musées, à prétention universelle (Londres, Paris, Berlin, New York, Saint-Pétersbourg, Vienne) se multiplièrent. Vers 1900, les musées d'art et d'archéologie exposaient le schéma d'une Histoire qui commençait en Égypte et en Mésopotamie, se prolongeait dans l'Antiquité gréco-romaine puis dans un Moyen Âge européen suivi de la Renaissance et de la modernité européenne. Les productions des autres cultures étaient généralement exposées ailleurs, dans des musées d'art spécifiques, d'arts appliqués ou d'ethnographie.

Depuis 1980, l'histoire globale a remis en cause la plupart des conceptions eurocentrées héritées du XIXe siècle : la fin des empires coloniaux, la dimension multiculturelle de la société nord-américaine, l'échec du modèle soviétique, l'émergence de nouveaux pôles économiques, principalement en Asie, et le développement de la globalisation ont permis de prendre en compte l'histoire de tous. Cependant, les limites méthodologiques, thématiques et chronologiques de l'histoire globale l'empêchent d'être une histoire de la totalité et de remplacer l'histoire universelle.

Les musées sont des reflets des mentalités de leur époque, aujourd'hui comme en 1900. La tension entre un universalisme supposé occidental et des localismes/

nationalismes post-coloniaux s'exprime depuis quinze ans dans le débat sur la notion de musée universel proposée par Arthur MacGregor. Par ailleurs, on constate que le tournant global a eu diverses conséquences muséales. La première est l'émergence d'un art contemporain global. La deuxième est l'évolution des musées d'ethnologie qui ont attribué à leurs artefacts une dimension esthétique (musée du quai Branly), ou ont explicité les représentations européennes des autres cultures (Munich, Vienne). La troisième fut l'ajout de nouveaux départements régionaux au sein des « musées universels » traditionnels (Metropolitan Museum of Art, Louvre). La quatrième a été la création de musées régionaux consacrés aux civilisations non occidentales (Singapour, Sharjah). La dernière est la réflexion sur de nouveaux types de musées universels comme dans le cas du Louvre Abu Dhabi. Celui-ci, hors d'Occident, a intégré certains aspects de l'histoire globale dans un récit d'histoire universelle qui de ce fait est bien moins eurocentrée qu'auparavant. On ne peut que s'en réjouir.

Session 3

Des canons connectés : critiques récentes du Canon occidental dans l'historiographie de l'art
Cecilia Hurley

Depuis longtemps, l'œuvre d'art et le canon sont considérés comme des éléments essentiels (des constantes, en réalité) d'un système de valeurs qui structure et modèle notre pratique et notre compréhension de l'histoire de l'art, autant dans les amphithéâtres que dans les musées. Les tentatives de Harold Bloom de réguler le canon littéraire dans son livre percutant de 1994, *The Western Canon: The Books and School of the Ages* [*Le Canon occidental : Les livres et l'école des âges*], ont souvent été débattues, particulièrement à la lumière des récents développements technologiques et académiques : la connectivité, la mondialisation, Internet, tout, de plus en plus, semble rejeter radicalement, ou du moins réduire considérablement, la validité de telles listes prescriptives. Devrions-nous être aussi critiques du canon artistique ? Devrions-nous l'adapter ou même, comme certains le voudraient, le détruire ?

Plus que tout, c'est notre exigence d'un canon unique qu'il nous faudrait remettre en question ; nous devrions envisager d'ouvrir, pluraliser et rapprocher nos canons. Le musée encyclopédique universel en est capable, c'est un creuset idéal pour la confrontation et l'évaluation des différentes cultures artistiques et historiques. En relatant l'histoire des civilisations humaines de façon diachronique et synchronique, et en proposant un accès universel à l'art issu de toutes les cultures, le musée encyclopédique peut créer des espaces où les récits traditionnels de l'histoire de l'art, focalisés sur les biographies des créateurs, les regroupements régionaux et nationaux, ainsi que sur le style et les questions d'iconographie ou d'iconologie, peuvent être réexaminés, modifiés, voire rejetés. Il peut ainsi contribuer activement à redéfinir les concepts et à promouvoir une nouvelle histoire de l'art connectée ou croisée dans laquelle les réseaux, les transferts, les échanges et les frontières perméables sont mis au premier plan.

Musée universel, musée global : l'exemple de Lyon
Sylvie Ramond

Le musée des Beaux-Arts de Lyon offre un parfait exemple des multiples façons dont la notion d'universalité peut s'exprimer à travers une institution culturelle. Conçu au cours de la Révolution française comme le plus grand musée hors de Paris, surnommé « le petit Louvre » en reconnaissance de son large éventail de collections, le musée des Beaux-Arts de Lyon s'est toujours distingué pour son vaste patrimoine s'étendant sur plusieurs siècles, de l'Antiquité aux mouvements d'avant-garde et jusqu'à l'art contemporain.

Ce modèle typiquement français a pris forme au fil de l'histoire de l'institution : universel et démocratique sous la direction d'Henri Focillon ; cosmopolite et populaire sous son successeur, Léon Rosenthal. Au cours des trois dernières décennies, le terme complexe d'« universalité » a fini par revêtir de nouvelles significations en incarnant une certaine idée de la mondialisation dans les arts, sans perdre de vue le rêve déjà ancien de les rendre accessibles au grand public.

Quels mondes au musée ? Manifeste pour un musée humaniste
Nathalie Bondil

Je suis convaincue qu'au XXIe siècle la culture sera considérée comme bénéfique à la santé au même titre que le sport au XXe siècle. L'art est, en effet, bénéfique aux niveaux social et individuel. La culture ravive le débat sur les questions importantes de notre nouvelle ère interculturelle. Bien que le soutien apporté aux artistes et à l'histoire de l'art soit au cœur de la pratique muséale, les musées doivent accomplir beaucoup plus.
1.   Une activité éducative au service de la vie communautaire et de l'harmonie sociale
Au XXIe siècle, la culture et son pendant, l'éducation, sont des instruments de cohésion sociale qui jouent un rôle de premier plan dans l'équilibre de la vie communautaire au sein de notre « village planétaire ». Dans notre monde « glocal », l'intergénérationnalisme et l'interculturalisme sont des concepts clés dans le développement d'une société inclusive. L'éducation se trouve au cœur de nos priorités. Si apprendre à lire et à écrire se révèle fondamental, apprendre à voir et à ressentir le sera tout autant. Nous devons déchiffrer le sens des images et de nos émotions, sinon notre conscience sera noyée par

l'excès d'informations. Avec son Atelier international d'éducation et d'art-thérapie Michel de la Chenelière, sa nouvelle salle de cinéma et de concert, le Musée des beaux-arts de Montréal (MBAM) dispose du plus grand complexe éducatif et culturel parmi les musées nord-américains.

2.   Repenser la pertinence de l'institution : un musée socialement actif

Les musées des Beaux-Arts explorent-ils les questions de leur temps, s'impliquent-ils dans celles-ci ? Ou bien ont-ils tendance à laisser ces problématiques aux musées des sciences et sociétés ? Le MBAM se distingue par la diversité et la portée de son action sociale : il compte 450 partenariats avec des experts et il se trouve en relation avec plus de 50 programmes universitaires dédiés à la recherche sur la santé, l'éducation et la société.

3.   Cocréation ! Développer une culture du partenariat

Cette approche interactive et empathique permet de toucher davantage de publics, notamment ceux qui n'ont pas accès aux activités culturelles. Nous devons encourager les partenariats de cocréation, non à des fins de cohabitation, mais de coévolution. Stimuler et favoriser l'interdisciplinarité fait partie intégrante de l'ADN d'un musée « cré-actif ».

4.   Repenser les collections

Se détournant du quasi-monopole de l'interprétation des collections muséales par des historiens et des spécialistes, la nouvelle approche consiste à prendre les avis d'experts dans des domaines qui, à première vue, paraissent étrangers, voire incompatibles avec nos sujets. Encourager une telle pluralité de perspectives permet de faire ressortir la nature polysémique, multiforme et véritablement humaniste des collections. C'est à nous d'adopter une approche holistique pour que nos œuvres parlent à notre public des questions importantes pour la société contemporaine.

5.   Un musée pour une santé meilleure !

Il est important de repenser les exigences biologiques et expérientielles de nos visiteurs. Le besoin de « beauté », ou du moins d'émotion esthétique, n'est pas seulement de nature philosophique ou culturelle, il est aussi physiologique. Un musée est une école de sensibilité où nous pouvons nous connecter avec notre être émotionnel. En tant que musée-laboratoire s'adressant, avec le soutien d'entreprises et de philanthropes, à des experts dans les domaines de l'éducation, de la santé, de la recherche, des services sociaux et des milieux universitaire et communautaire, le MBAM est considéré comme un pionnier.

6.   Une perspective plus interculturelle et multiculturelle

Dans le cadre d'une société plus hybride, le MBAM encourage le dialogue culturel par la promotion de la conscience transhistorique et interculturelle, afin de favoriser le rapprochement des individus et des groupes. Dans l'optique d'une décentralisation de nos points de vue ethnocentrés, nous devons apprendre à voir par-delà nos horizons conventionnels et instaurer un dialogue avec les autres. Pour ce faire, les musées offrent un cadre accueillant, empathique et neutre.

Reconnu pour ses pratiques innovantes et ses activités attentives au social, le MBAM a participé à une étude réalisée par l'OCDE sur la manière d'optimiser l'impact des musées sur la culture et le développement local.

Session 4

Penser l'État : le centre et la périphérie dans muséologie du Liban contemporain
Anne-Marie Maïla Afeiche

Les musées jouent un rôle important de vitrines de l'identité nationale. Depuis sa création en 1942, le Musée national de Beyrouth, en tant que musée d'État, a largement contribué au développement d'un sentiment de fierté pour le patrimoine local. L'exposition et la mise en valeur d'objets archéologiques exclusivement issus du sol libanais permettent non seulement de montrer les trésors nationaux, mais également de témoigner de l'histoire du pays. Du fait qu'il a été en partie détruit pendant la guerre entre 1975 et 1991, il est de notre responsabilité de présenter son processus de reconstruction comme un modèle de survie en temps de crise et un exemple de renaissance de musée.

Par ailleurs, le ministère de la Culture a mis en place une politique d'expansion de la culture. Plusieurs musées ont été créés en dehors de Beyrouth avec chacun leur spécificité, comme à Tripoli et Beiteddine, ou sur des sites archéologiques comme Byblos et Baalbek. Le musée de Tripoli, par exemple, se trouve dans l'ancien château de la ville, où il a été installé pour mettre en avant un monument, mais également une collection, qui couvre par ailleurs toute la région du nord du Liban. Outre cette politique de promotion de la périphérie pour rétablir un équilibre avec le centre, deux défis se présentent : d'une part, réhabiliter et moderniser les musées, d'autre part en ouvrir de nouveaux.

C'est ainsi qu'en avril 2018 a été créé le Conseil des musées, un organisme indépendant au sein du ministère de la Culture. Cette jeune administration a pour mission de fonder des musées, de développer ceux qui existent déjà, ainsi que de promouvoir leurs collections et de les préserver. Actuellement, les villes de Beyrouth, Tyr et Saïda sont concernées par de nouveaux projets. Enfin, il appartient aux musées de répondre aux besoins des populations sur tout le territoire en soutenant l'économie locale et en respectant leurs disparités et la richesse de leur patrimoine culturel.

Identités interstices : une nouvelle approche au Musée des Civilisations asiatiques
Kennie Ting

Le Musée des Civilisations asiatiques est le musée d'art et d'antiquités asiatiques de Singapour. En 2012, il a entrepris de repenser radicalement son récit muséographique, passant d'une organisation géographique de sa collection et de ses galeries permanentes à une approche thématique, transnationale et interculturelle axée sur deux thèmes principaux : le commerce et la religion. Ces deux thèmes s'appuient sur la nature même de Singapour, à la fois ville marchande et port multiculturel et multiconfessionnel d'Asie. Le commerce et la religion représentent également deux forces motrices majeures dans l'histoire, tant ils ont contribué aux flux de populations, de cultures et d'idées à travers l'Asie, ainsi qu'à travers le reste du monde. Cette présentation apporte davantage de détails sur la politique actuelle de conservation du musée, ainsi que sur les opportunités, les défis et les enseignements auxquels il a pu être confronté au cours de cette transition muséographique.

Exposer à traverse des cultures : les dynamiques globales dans la museographie contemporaine
Henry Kim

Tandis qu'aujourd'hui les débats sur la « globalisation » des arts se focalisent naturellement sur les grandes initiatives prises par les principales institutions et sur la vitesse à laquelle des tendances ou des mouvements peuvent se répandre à grande échelle, les effets que ces tendances ont eu en aval à l'échelle locale sont moins largement communiqués. Les festivals artistiques, « biennales » et expositions se sont multipliés à vive allure, tout comme les fondations d'art privées créées en nombre ces dernières années. Des musées sont sortis de terre là où il n'y avait aucune tradition muséale, sous l'impulsion des autorités locales et nationales autant que d'initiatives privées. Des musées spécialisés sont apparus aux côtés de musées traditionnels établis.

Si l'on considère que ces tendances font partie de la « globalisation » du monde de l'art, la question se pose alors de savoir si tout cela se produit de façon structurée ou non, et jusqu'à quel point le modèle centre/périphérie peut s'appliquer. Je suggérerai que cette expansion s'est déroulée de manière non structurée, encouragée à l'échelle locale par les facteurs suivants :

a. L'émulation : le désir de créer localement ce qui a été mené à bien ailleurs,
b. La mise en application de bonnes idées et de bonnes pratiques,
c. La puissance de l'initiative privée et de nouveaux organismes à mission,
d. La recherche d'une signification locale.

About the Authors

H.E. Shaikha Mai bint Mohammed Al Khalifa
President of the Bahrain Authority for Culture and Antiquities, Kingdom of Bahrain
A leading figure in the Arab culture and art scenes, HE Shaikha Mai has spearheaded national efforts to develop the cultural infrastructure in the Kingdom of Bahrain for heritage conservation and the growth of sustainable tourism. The President of the Bahrain Authority for Culture and Antiquities, HE Shaikha Mai is the foremost public expert in the field, holding the unique portfolios of the Ministry for Culture & Information and the Ministry for Culture.

As the founder of the Shaikh Ebrahim bin Mohammed Al Khalifa Center for Culture and Research and Chair of its Board of Trustees since 2002, she works actively to preserve the traditional architecture of Bahrain. Major achievements include the 2005 and 2012 inscriptions of the Bahrain Fort and the Pearling: Testimony of an Island Economy as UNESCO World Heritage Sites; founding the Arab Regional Centre for World Heritage; the first laureate of the Colbert Prize for Creativity and Heritage in 2010; the Social Creativity Award by the Arab Thought Foundation; the Arab Women of the Year Award (2015); Watch Award (2015) by World Monuments Fund; the Légion d'Honneur, the Moroccan Order of Ouissam Alaouite (Grand Officer) and the Order of the Italian Star and the First Class Order of Merit from HM King Hamad of Bahrain. Bahrain was awarded Silver Pavilion Architecture Award, Expo Milan 2015 and HE Shaikha Mai became Special Ambassador of the International Year of Sustainability for Development, 2017-19 from the World Tourism Organization. She is also a renowned local historian with seven publications.

Mohamed Khalifa Al Mubarak
Chairman, Department of Culture and Tourism – Abu Dhabi, UAE
Mohamed Khalifa Al Mubarak is Chairman of Department of Culture and Tourism – Abu Dhabi, which oversees the conservation and promotion of Abu Dhabi's heritage and culture, leveraging them to develop distinctive Abu Dhabi experiences designed to enrich the lives of visitors and residents.

In 2016, he was additionally appointed Chairman of the Tourism Development & Investment Company (TDIC), master developer of major tourism, cultural and residential destinations in Abu Dhabi.

Al Mubarak is also Chairman of Miral Asset Management, an organisation responsible for creating and managing destinations in Abu Dhabi focused on building lifelong visitor value for the emirate. He is also CEO of Aldar Properties PJSC, Abu Dhabi's leading Property Development and Management Company. In addition, he is Chairman of Aldar Academies, one of the largest providers of modern private education in Abu Dhabi, and he is also Chairman of Image Nation Abu Dhabi.

Mohamed Khalifa Al Mubarak is a graduate of Northeastern University (USA), with a double major in Economics and Political Science.

Guilhem André
Chief Curator of Asian and Medieval Arts, Louvre Abu Dhabi, UAE
An archaeologist and art historian, Dr. Guilhem André began his career at the Musée des Arts asiatiques-Guimet. He joined the museum's Chinese Department at the time when it was undergoing renovation and contributed to its inaugural exhibition on the Steppes of Asia. While at the museum, followed by Agence France-Muséums, he helped organise numerous events in Europe, Asia, South America and the Gulf. Scientific manager on the French Archaeological Mission to Mongolia, he coordinated a large research programme that led him to edit several books and publish a number of articles and essays.

With a PhD from the Université Paris Sorbonne, he graduated from the École du Louvre and the Institut national des langues et civilisations orientales (INALCO) and then trained in China at Beijing University and Sichuan University. In France, he created the chair of History of the Arts of the Far East at the Institut Catholique de Paris, where he taught for several years. In 2013 and 2014 he chaired the programme of Far Eastern Arts at the École du Louvre. As Chief Curator at Louvre Abu Dhabi, he is currently responsible for the medieval section of the museum. As an expert in Asian arts, he has been key to the coordination of a scientific and cultural programme and to the creation of the museum's collection since 2009.

Claire Barbillon
Director, École du Louvre, Paris, France
Claire Barbillon is a university professor and has been director of the École du Louvre since December 2017. Her professional career has been divided between museums and universities. She spent fourteen years at the Musée d'Orsay, first as the head of the educational department, then as head of publications. After obtaining her doctorate on the subject of models of the human body in the 19th century (published by Odile Jacob editions, 2004), she was a resident at the Institut national d'histoire de l'art, then a lecturer at the universities of Bordeaux and Paris-Nanterre. She then joined the École du Louvre as director of studies, where she remained from 2004 to 2011.

After receiving accreditation to supervise research on the *Relief au croisement des arts au XIXe siècle* (published by Picard editions, 2014), Claire Barbillon was professor of contemporary art history at the university of Poitiers between 2014 and 2017. She is a specialist in the history of art during the 19ᵗʰ century, in particular sculpture and historiography. Her three most recent publications are the catalogue of the exhibition *Bourdelle et l'Antique, une passion moderne*, held at the Musée Bourdelle (3 October 2017- 4 February 2018), which she co-edited with A. Simier and J. Godeau, (Paris-Musées editions), the catalogue of the sculptures in the Musée des Beaux-Arts de Lyon, which includes twenty long essays and a concise catalogue, co- edited with C. Chevillot and S. Paccoud (Somogy, 2017), and a book *Comment regarder la sculpture?* (published by Hazan editions).

Nathalie Bondil

Director-General and Chief Curator, Montreal Museum of Fine Arts (MBAM), Canada
Art historian Nathalie Bondil has been the Director General and Chief Curator of the MMFA since 2007. Her original multidisciplinary exhibitions have been successfully exported internationally to 35 cities in ten years. Under her leadership, attendance has doubled (1.3 million visitors in 2017, making it the 8ᵗʰ most visited art museum in North America and 49ᵗʰ in the world). The museum's size has increased by 30% with the opening of two buildings: *The Claire and Marc Bourgie Pavilion for Quebec and Canadian Art* (2011), and *The Michal and Renata Horstein Pavilion for Peace* (2016). Au urban agora, the MMFA features a professional concert hall presenting 150 concerts annually and a cinema. The *Stéphan Crétier and Stéphany Maillery Wing for World Cultures and Togetherness* opened in 2019.

The author of a *Manifesto for a Humanist Museum*, Nathalie Bondil has tripled the educational spaces with the opening of the Michel de la Chenelière International Atelier for Education and Art Therapy (2016), one of the largest in a North American art museum. A Pioneer in social and community action, the MMFA collaborates with over 450 partners (schools, universities, associations, hospitals and medical research institutes). It launched the *Art & Health Committee* chaired by Quebec's Chief Scientist and several pilot projects and the very first medical prescriptions in 2017. Vice-Chair of the Canada Council for the Arts, Nathalie Bondil was awarded two honorary doctorates (McGill University and Université de Montréal) and appointed Member of the Order of Canada, Officer of the Ordre national du Québec, and Officer of the Ordre des Arts et des Lettres of the French Republic.

James Cuno

President and CEO, J. Paul Getty Trust, Los Angeles, USA
James Cuno took his BA degree in History from Willamette University in 1973, his MA in Art History from the University of Oregon in 1978, and MA and PhD degrees in Fine Arts (History of Art) from Harvard University in 1981 and 1985 respectively. He has held teaching positions at Vassar College, UCLA, Dartmouth, and Harvard and served as Director of UCLA's Grunwald Center of the Graphic Arts (1986-89), Dartmouth's Hood Museum of Art (1989-91), Harvard University Art Museums (1991-2002), Director and Professor of the Courtauld Institute of Art,

University of London (2002-04), and President and Director of the Art Institute of Chicago (2004-11). He assumed his current position as President and CEO of the J. Paul Getty Trust in August 2011.

He has lectured and written widely on museums and cultural and public policy. Since 2003, he has published three books with Princeton University Press: *Whose Muse? Art Museums and the Public's Trust* (author and editor), *Who Owns Antiquity: Museums and the Battle over Our Ancient Heritage* (author), and *Whose Culture? The Promise of Museums and the Debate over Antiquities* (author and editor)—and another with the University of Chicago Press, *Museums Matter: In Praise of the Encyclopedic Museum* (author). Cuno is a Fellow and International Secretary of the American Academy of Arts and Sciences. He serves on the Council at the Academy and on the Board of Trustees of the Courtauld Institute of Art, the Pulitzer Arts Foundation, and Willamette University.

Noëmi Daucé
Chief Curator for Archaeology, Louvre Abu Dhabi, UAE
A former student of the National Heritage Institute in Paris (INP), Noëmi Daucé is a graduate of Archaeology and Art History at the Pantheon-Sorbonne University (Paris I) and the École du Louvre. After teaching Near Eastern Archaeology at the École du Louvre, in 2010 she was appointed Curator for Archaeology in the French Museum of Fine Arts and Archaeology of Besançon. Daucé has been working closely with Louvre Abu Dhabi since 2014 when she joined Agence France-Muséums as the Curator for Archaeology. In her current role she manages the research policy and documentation centre of the museum and by managing loans has fostered international cooperation with other institutions in the UAE, Jordan, Oman and Saudi Arabia.

Daucé has conducted research on Near Eastern archaeology, the history of archaeology and the history of collections. Her main research has focused primarily on the Achaemenid architectural decoration in Susa, highlighting the creation process and technical aspects of a syncretic production that was inherited in the late Bronze and Iron Age in the Middle East. She was awarded the Jacques Morgan Award (Académie des Sciences, Arts et Lettres of Marseille) for her work coordinating the online publication of Roland Mecquenem's archaeological reports, the former Director of Archaeological Missions in Susa from 1912 to 1939 with a grant from the Leon Levy Shelby White Foundation Program for Archaeological Publication. Material studies, processes of creation and the history of collections are the main fields she is now developing at Louvre Abu Dhabi.

Hartwig Fischer
Director, British Museum, London, UK
Hartwig Fischer took up the post of Director of the British Museum in spring 2016. He gained his PhD in Art History at the University of Bonn in 1993 after studying in Berlin, Rome and Paris. He began his career in museums as a Research Assistant and then Curator of 19th Century

and Modern Art at the Kunstmuseum Basel, Switzerland before becoming Director of the Folkwang Museum, Essen in 2006. During his time as Director of the Folkwang Museum, he oversaw a major building project with the acclaimed architect David Chipperfield, as well as several blockbuster exhibitions and many key acquisitions.

In 2012 Hartwig Fischer was appointed Director General of the Staatliche Kunstsammlungen, Dresden (State Art Collections, Dresden), with responsibility for 14 museums and associated libraries, archives and research centres. As Director General of one of the foremost museums of the world, he led on the development of significant international exhibitions and research projects across the world as well as in Germany; he has also overseen several major building projects and renovations to the State Art Collection's estate in Dresden.

Hervé Inglebert
Professor of Roman History, Paris-Nanterre University, France

Hervé Inglebert is the Professor of Roman History at Université Paris Nanterre, where he specialises in the cultural and religious developments that occurred during Antiquity. On these themes he has published three books, an atlas and dozens of articles, and organised and edited several symposia. He has been both a junior and senior member of the Institut universitaire de France. He has spoken at many conferences and given lectures in Europe, North America and Asia (China, Japan). He edits the international *Revue de l'Antiquité tardive* and the Nouvelle Clio history collection at the PUF (Presses Universitaires de France). Inglebert also takes an interest in the epistemology of the human and social sciences, as well as the historiography of universal history, on which he has written two books: *Le Monde, l'Histoire. Essai sur les histoires universelles* (2014) and *Histoire universelle ou histoire globale ?* (2018).

Between 2016-18 he was co-director of a research project on the theme *Universal histories and universal museums* with Sandra Kemp (Victoria & Albert Museum) and André Delpuech (Musée du Quai Branly). It included three workshops: 'The evolution of museums in the 19th century', 'Museography compared: the example of the arts of Asia', 'The constitution of the different Western museum universalities in the great cultural capitals in the 19th century and early 20th century' and a conference 'What universality for universal museums?'. He is preparing a book giving an overview of the relations between the writing of universal history and the conceptions of universal museums.

Rose-Marie Herda Mousseaux
Chief curator for Early Modern Art, Louvre Abu Dhabi, UAE

Before joining Louvre Abu Dhabi, Rose-Marie Herda-Mousseaux was Curator for Archaeology at the Carnavalet Museum, where she was in charge of the Prehistoric and Roman collection, the archaeological storage spaces, the Archaeological Crypt in the Ile de la Cite and the Catacombs of Paris. She co-conceived the museographical redevelopment after a series of exhibitions that focused on the interpretations given to this archaeological site (*When Lutece became Paris*, 2010 and *Bygone Paris, Dreamlike Paris*, 2011).

As Director and Curator of Decorative Arts from 2013-18 at the Cognacq-Jay Museum, she curated the following exhibitions: *Enlightenment! Carte Blanche for Christian Lacroix*, 2014, *Tea, coffee or chocolate? Exotic drinks in the 18th century*, 2015, *Serenissima! Venetian feasts from Tiepolo to Guardi*, 2017 and *Manufacturing Luxury – Parisian marchands-merciers in the 18th century*. Her particular area of interest lies in the practices linked to cultural exchange and consumption, which has led her to work with international groups researching the transmission of material and social forms during the 18th century.

Cecilia Hurley

Director, Special Collections, Neuchâtel University, Switzerland, Research team, École du Louvre, Paris, France

Cecilia Hurley earned her MA degree in Literae humaniores form the University of Oxford, her doctorate in history from the University of Neuchâtel and her Habilitation à diriger des recherches in Art History from the University of Lyon II. She was formerly Curator of the Bibliothèque des Pasteurs in Neuchâtel (founded in 1540) and is now Director of Special Collections at the University of Neuchâtel. She is also a member of the Research Team and a Lecturer at the École du Louvre.

She has written widely on a number of subjects including Swiss artists (Léopold Robert, Aurèle Robert and Maximilien de Meuron), the history of museums, collecting and display, as well as the history of antiquarian thought and the history, classification and dissemination of art literature and art history. She has written *Monuments for the People* (2013, awarded a Gold Medal by the Académie des Inscriptions et des Belles-Lettres), co-edited two conferences: *Sammeln und Sammlungen im 18. Jahrhundert in der Schweiz* (2007) and *Le Catalogue dans tous ses états* (with Claire Barbillon, 2015), as well as various articles. Her forthcoming book, *Canons mobiles*, is a study of the tradition of masterpiece rooms in European fine-art museums during the long nineteenth century.

Henry Kim

CEO, Aga Khan Museum, Toronto, Canada

Henry Kim is Director and CEO of the Aga Khan Museum in Toronto, a museum whose mission is to foster a greater understanding and appreciation of the contribution that Muslim civilizations have made to world heritage. He joined the museum in 2012 and led the effort to develop the professional team and open the museum in 2014. An ancient historian and classical archaeologist by training, Mr. Kim joined the Aga Khan Museum from the University of Oxford where he taught, curated collections and managed capital projects at the Ashmolean Museum from 1994 to 2012.

Educated at Harvard and Oxford, he served as curator of Greek coins and university lecturer in Greek numismatics at the university. He is currently involved in art creation projects in Pakistan and is an advocate for the use of art objects in teaching.

Anne-Marie Maïla-Afeiche

Director, The National Museum of Beirut, Lebanon

A graduate of the École du Louvre, Anne-Marie Maïla-Afeiche has a Master's degree in the History of Art and Archaeology from the Université d'Aix-en-Provence, after graduating in the same subject from the Université Paris IV-Sorbonne.

Her involvement at the Direction Générale des Antiquités (Museums Section) began on her return to Lebanon in 1993, having spent several years abroad. At that time, she worked in a small team on the rehabilitation of the National Museum of Beirut, which had been seriously damaged during the war. She supervised the management of the archaeological collections and participated in the restoration of the museum and its re-opening in 1999.

In 2009 she became Curator of the National Museum of Beirut while also carrying out her duties as the Head of Studies and Publications, a position she had held since 2001. As editor of the journal BAAL (Bullétin d'Archéologie et d'Architecture Libanaises) published by the Ministry of Culture, Antiquities Department, she publishes the annual results of archaeological excavation and research in Lebanon.

In charge of the documentation and search for archaeological objects and of the reorganisation of the reserves of the National Museum, Afeiche is also responsible for the dossiers compiled on the illicit market in antiquities. Her extensive experience in the museum world allows her to run the course 'Museology and Heritage' at the Université Saint-Joseph in Beirut. In April 2018, she was appointed General Director and President of the Board of Governors of the National Council of Museums of Lebanon.

François-René Martin

Head of the Research Team, École du Louvre and Professor at the École des Beaux- Arts, Paris, France

François-René Martin is a professor of art history at the École nationale supérieure des Beaux-Arts of Paris. He has managed the research team at the École du Louvre since 2018. A doctor in political science and in art history, HDR, he is a former fellow of the Institut National d'Histoire de l'Art. Martin is an invited professor in the Deutsches Forum für Kunstgeschichte in Paris (2014-2015), guest researcher in the Getty Center (2018) and has published numerous studies on Grünewald, Ingres and the history of the methods of art history.

Jean-Luc Martinez

President-Director, Louvre Museum, Paris, France

Born in 1964, Jean-Luc Martinez is a French art historian and archeologist. He was appointed President-Director of Musée du Louvre by the French President on April 5, 2013 and reaffirmed in his position on April 4, 2018. An accomplished historian with a degree from École du Louvre, Jean-Luc Martinez came to the Louvre in 1997 and became head of the museum's Department of Greek, Etruscan, and Roman Antiquities. Martinez oversaw the renovations of the Greek art galleries, where the *Venus de Milo* holds pride of place. He also curated the Galerie du Temps at the Louvre-Lens.

With Martinez at the helm, Musée du Louvre has maintained its rank as the world's most popular and prominent museum, with visitors topping 8 million in 2017. Since 2013, 816 acquisitions have enriched Louvre's collections and more than 355.000 ft² of gallery or reception space have been renovated, to better to welcome the public. Since 2013 Martinez he has served as Chairman of the Scientific Board of Agence France-Muséums, in charge of the Louvre Abu Dhabi project.

In 2017, he was the impetus behind the creation of ALIPH, the International Alliance for the Protection of Heritage in Conflict Areas; he has to date served as Chairman of the Scientific Board. He is the Chairman of the Board of the French School at Athens, a member the High Council of the Museums of France, a member of the Scientific Board of the French Institute of Art History (INHA), the Board of Directors of the École du Louvre and the Artistic Council of National Museums. Jean-Luc Martinez has received a knighthood in the French National Order of Merit and the Legion of Honor.

Sophie Mouquin

Associate Professor, University of Lille and École du Louvre, Paris, France

Doctor in Art History of the University of Paris-Sorbonne (2003), Associate Professor in Art History of the universities of Bordeaux (2004-2007) and Lille (since 2007), and Academic Director of École du Louvre (2011-2016), Sophie Mouquin is specialised in decorative arts, architecture, history of collections and history of taste in 17th and 18th centuries. She has published numerous articles and several books (*Pierre IV Migeon*, 2001; Le style Louis XV, 2003; *Écrire la sculpture*, 2011; *Cuir de Russie, mémoire du Tan*, 2017; *Versailles en ses marbres, politique royale et marbriers du roi*, 2018). A member of diverse scientific committees and of the acquisition commission for French museums Service à compétence national, Mouquin has been awarded the Nicole Prize for her PhD in 2003 and by the SNA for her publication *Versailles en ses marbres* in 2018.

Souraya Noujaim

Director of the Scientific, Curatorial and Collections Management Department, Louvre Abu Dhabi, UAE

Souraya Noujaim was appointed Scientific, Curatorial and Collections Management Director at Louvre Abu Dhabi in February 2018. She oversees and leads the curatorial strategy of the museum, the new developments of its narrative, the acquisition and research strategy as well as the exhibition programming. Noujaim is closely involved in the transfer of knowledge which contributes to training new young curators. Prior to her assignment, she was the lead curator at the Agence-France Muséums responsible for the scientific and cultural programming of Medieval and Islamic art.

Noujaim began her career at Musée du Louvre and has since worked for major cultural institutions such as the Arab World Institute (IMA) and the British Museum. As part of the "Grand Louvre" project, she took part in the opening of the first Islamic Art Department rooms of Musée du Louvre and in landmark exhibitions at Musée du Louvre and Grand Palais. She taught at the École du Louvre for several years where in 2013 she held the Islamic Art History chair and is the author of a number of publications.

Souraya Noujaim holds a Ph.D. in Islamic Art History and Archaeology, with a degree in Museum studies and postgraduate research diplomas from École du Louvre and Paris- Sorbonne University. She also studied Arabic Islamic civilisation at the INALCO. She wrote her doctoral thesis on the poems of the Nasrid palaces of the Alhambra.

Martin Pitts
Associate Professor in Roman Archaeology, University of Exeter, UK

Martin Pitts is Associate Professor in Roman Archaeology at the University of Exeter (UK). His main area of research concerns the early Roman period in northwest Europe, as approached through quantitative studies of material culture, especially ceramics. He is particularly interested in the application of ideas of globalisation to reveal new insights into past societies through the study of circulating objects and their entanglements with people. This perspective has led to comparative research on the cultural impacts of Chinese porcelain around the world in the seventeenth and eighteenth centuries.

Major recent publications include *Globalisation and the Roman World: World history, connectivity and material culture* (edited with Miguel John Versluys, 2015, Cambridge University Press), and *Materialising Roman Histories* (edited with Astrid Van Oyen, 2017, Oxbow). He was also editor for the Europe section of *The Routledge Handbook of Archaeology and Globalization* (edited by Tamar Hodos, 2016). A monograph, implicitly exploring ideas of globalisation and materiality, *The Roman object revolution: Objectscapes and intra-cultural connectivity in Northwest Europe*, was published with Amsterdam University Press in 2019.

Manuel Rabaté
Director, Louvre Abu Dhabi, UAE

Manuel Rabaté is a graduate of the Institut d'Études Politiques de Paris (Sciences Po, 1998), and of HEC Business School (2001). He began his career as a Deputy Director of the auditorium of the Musée du Louvre from 2002 until 2005. He participated in the creation of new programmes on Islamic Arts in the context of the first performance contract between the French government and the museum for its modernisation. He joined the Musée du Quai Branly as Deputy Director of Cultural Development a year before its opening in 2006, then led the launching of the first exhibitions abroad.

Rabaté joined Agence France-Muséums in 2008, a year after the signing of the intergovernmental agreement between France and Abu Dhabi. He has followed the Louvre Abu Dhabi project from its conceptual phase until its operational implementation as a Secretary General and acting CEO since 2010. He was appointed CEO of Agence France- Museums in 2013 to set up in Abu Dhabi a multidisciplinary team of museum professionals and follow through the phases of the project realization in collaboration with the major French museums and their UAE partners. In September 2016, Manuel Rabaté was appointed Director of Louvre Abu Dhabi by the Department of Culture and Tourism – Abu Dhabi. Aside from his duties in the service of museums, Rabaté has also chaired the reflection group- Culture & Management, in which he had created the museum department. He has also taught Arts and Cultural Management at various universities in France and Abu Dhabi.

Sylvie Ramond
Director, Museums of Fine Arts and Contemporary Arts, Lyon, France
With the Musée des Beaux-Arts and the Musée d'Art Contemporain now united in a new group of art museums, Lyon is testing a new museological model, which has been under the direction of Sylvie Ramond since 2004.

A graduate of the Sorbonne and École du Louvre, a former pupil of the École nationale du patrimoine, a chief heritage officer and visiting professor at ENS Lyon, Sylvie Ramond has raised the Musée des Beaux-Arts de Lyon to the top rank of French museums of international stature.

A member of the management committee of the Bizot group, a guest researcher at the Terra Foundation (2013) and Getty Center in Los Angeles (2018), she has overseen the curation some thirty exhibitions (*Otto Dix, Fernand Léger, Braque/Laurens, Géricault, Repartir à zéro, Joseph Cornell et les surréalistes à New York, Henri Matisse. Le laboratoire intérieur*, among others).

At the request of the Minister of Culture Audrey Azoulay, Sylvie Ramond directed one of the study groups in the *Mission Musées du XXIᵉ siècle* (2017). The creation of this new entity, under her direction, gives the City of Lyon the largest art collection in France outside of Paris. It also offers France the unique opportunity to develop a new form of a universal/global art museum suited to the 21st century.

Kennie Ting
Director, Asian Civilisations Museum, Singapore
Kennie Ting is the Director of the Asian Civilisations Museum and the Peranakan Museum, and concurrently Group Director, Museums at the National Heritage Board (NHB) Singapore, overseeing national museums and festivals managed by the NHB. As Director of the Asian Civilisations Museum, he has overseen the shift in the museum's curatorial approach from a geographical focus to a thematic, cross-cultural focus, and has helmed recent exhibitions on the *Arts of Myanmar, Angkor and Korea*, on *Buddhist and Hindu Art across Asia*, and on the material culture of cosmopolitan *Asian Port Cities*. He is presently the Chairperson of the Asia – Europe Museum Network (ASEMUS), which aims to promote mutual understanding between the peoples of Asia and Europe through collaborative museum-based cultural activity.

Before NHB, he worked in the former Ministry of Information, Communications and the Arts, where he was involved in developing strategies for heritage and the arts, including the Renaissance City Plan III and the recent Arts and Culture Strategic Review. He is interested in the history of travel and the heritage of Asian port cities and is the author of the books, *The Romance of the Grand Tour – 100 Years of Travel in South East Asia and Singapore 1819 – A Living Legacy*.

About the Authors (Arabic)

معالي الشيخة مي بنت محمد آل خليفة

رئيسة هيئة البحرين للثقافة والتراث، مملكة البحرين

معالي الشيخة مي بنت محمد آل خليفة شخصيةٌ رائدة في المشهد الثقافي والفني العربي، حيث قادت الجهود الوطنية الرامية إلى تطوير البنية التحتية الثقافية في مملكة البحرين للحفاظ على التراث وتنمية السياحة المستدامة. تشغل الشيخة مي منصب رئيس هيئة البحرين للثقافة والآثار، وهي تعدّ الشخصية الأبرز في هذا المجال، إذ ترأست قبل منصبها الحالي حقيبتيّ وزارة الثقافة والإعلام ثم وزارة الثقافة.

وانطلاقاً من كونها مؤسس مركز الشيخ إبراهيم بن محمد آل خليفة للثقافة والبحوث ورئيس مجلس أمنائه منذ عام 2002، تعمل الشيخة مي دون كل لتعزيز الثقافة والحفاظ على التراث العمراني البحريني، وأطلقت في سبيل ذلك مبادرة "الاستثمار في الثقافة"، التي ساهمت في بناء شراكة غير مسبوقة بين القطاعين العام والخاص من أجل الحفاظ على التراث، وجاء ضمن أبرز ثمارها إنشاء متحف موقع قلعة البحرين وتشييد مسرح البحرين الوطني الذي يعدّ من أهمّ عوامل جذب السياحة الثقافية للمملكة.

من بين أهم إنجازاتها العديدة، إدراج موقعي قلعة البحرين وطريق اللؤلؤ ضمن لائحة مواقع التراث العالمي لليونسكو في عامي 2005و2012 على التوالي، بالإضافة إلى إنشاء المركز الإقليمي العربي للتراث العالمي، وهو مركز تابع لليونسكو من الفئة الثانية يسهر على التراث الطبيعي والثقافي لكافة الدول العربية. تعتبر الشيخة مي قدوة يُحتذى بها لدى مناصري الثقافة والتراث، وهي أول من حاز على جائزة كولبير للإبداع والتراث عام 2010. كما كرّمتها مؤسسة الفكر العربي بجائزة الإبداع الاجتماعي تقديرًا لقيادتها المتميزة للعديد من المبادرات الثقافية والسياحية السنوية مثل مهرجان ربيع الثقافة ومهرجان صيف البحرين. كما وساهمت ضمن عملها المتواصل لحفظ التراث البحريني وصونه في فوز جناح مملكة البحرين المشارك في إكسبو ميلانو 2015 «آثار خضراء» بالجائزة الفضية في فئة الهندسة المعمارية. ونُصّبت سفيرًا خاصاً للسنة الدولية للسياحة المستدامة من أجل التنمية بين عامي 2017 2019-. تعتبر الشيخة مي أيضاً مؤرخة مرموقة لها سبعة مؤلفات نُشرت في لندن وبيروت ووُزعت في مملكة البحرين وخارجها.

محمد خليفة المبارك

رئيس دائرة الثقافة والسياحة – أبوظبي، الإمارات العربية المتحدة

يشغل محمد خليفة المبارك منصب رئيس دائرة الثقافة والسياحة – أبوظبي التي تتولى مهمة الحفاظ على تراث وثقافة إمارة أبوظبي وصونها، والترويج لها والاستفادة منها في تطوير وجهة متميزة تثري تجربة الزوار والمواطنين والمقيمين على أرض الإمارة. في عام 2016، عُيّن محمد المبارك في منصب رئيس مجلس إدارة شركة التطوير والاستثمار السياحي، المطوّر الرئيسي لأبرز الوجهات السياحية والثقافية والسكنية في إمارة أبوظبي.

يشغل محمد المبارك أيضا منصب رئيس مجلس إدارة شركة مبرال لإدارة الأصول، المسؤولة عن إنشاء وإدارة الوجهات الترفيهية والسياحية في أبوظبي، ومنصب رئيس مجلس إدارة شركة الدار العقارية. وإلى جانب ذلك، يرأس مجلس إدارة أكاديميات الدار، ويشغل أيضاً منصب رئيس مجلس إدارة شركة إمج نيشن أبوظبي.

يحمل محمد خليفة المبارك شهادة البكالوريوس في تخصص مزدوج في الاقتصاد والعلوم السياسية من جامعة نورث إيسترن في الولايات المتحدة الأمريكية.

غيليم أندريه

رئيس أمناء قسم الفنون الآسيوية والعصر الوسيط، اللوفر أبوظبي، الإمارات العربية المتحدة

بدأ الدكتور غيليم أندريه مسيرته المهنية كعالم آثار ومؤرخ فني في متحف الفنون الآسيوية-غيميه، ثم التحق في عام 2001 بقسم الفن الصيني للمتحف خلال ترميمه، مساهما بذلك في المعرض الافتتاحي المخصص لسهوب آسيا. وفي أثناء عمله لدى متحف غيميه ثم لدى وكالة متاحف فرنسا، شارك في تنظيم العديد من الملتقيات الفنية في كل من أوروبا وآسيا وأمريكا الجنوبية والخليج العربي. وقد مكّنه منصبه كمسؤول علمي عن البعثة الأثرية الفرنسية في منغوليا من تنسيق عدد كبير من برامج البحث، وقادته أعماله إلى نشر العديد من المؤلفات والمقالات والدراسات العلمية.

حصل غيليم أندريه على شهادة الدكتوراه من جامعة السوربون بباريس، وتخرّج بعد ذلك من مدرسة اللوفر والمعهد الوطني للغات والحضارات الشرقية، ثم تلقى تدريبه في الصين في كليات جامعة بكين وجامعة سيشوان. وقد أسّس كرسي تاريخ فنون الشرق الأقصى بالمعهد الكاثوليكي لباريس، حيث درّس عدة سنوات وترأس كرسي فنون الشرق الأقصى بمدرسة اللوفر في عامي 2013 و2014. وبصفته رئيس أمناء متحف اللوفر أبوظبي، يعتبر حاليًا مسؤولاً عن قسم فنون العصور الوسطى في المتحف. أما فيما يخص فنون آسيا، فقد كانت خبرته بمثابة حجر الزاوية في التنسيق ما بين البرنامج العلمي والثقافي لإنشاء مجموعة المتحف الفنية منذ عام 2009.

كلير باربيون

مديرة مدرسة اللوفر، باريس، فرنسا

تدرّس الأستاذة كلير باربيون في عدة جامعات وتشغل منصب مديرة مدرسة اللوفر منذ ديسمبر 2017. وقبل ذلك، توزّعت مسيرتها المهنية بين المتاحف والجامعات. فقد عملت لمدة أربعة عشر سنة لدى متحف أورسيه، حيث ترأست أولاً القسم التعليمي ثم قسم إصدارات المتحف. بعد حصولها على شهادة الدكتوراه في موضوع نماذج الجسد في القرن التاسع عشر (صدرت سنة 2004 عن دار نشر أوديل جاكوب)، درست في المعهد الوطني لتاريخ الفن ثم عُيّنت أستاذة محاضرة بجامعتي بوردو وباريس نانتير. التحقت بعدها بمدرسة اللوفر لأوّل مرة، حيث عملت مديرة الدراسات بين عامي 2004 و2011.

بعد حصولها على شهادة التأهيل للإشراف على أبحاث حول "النقوش في ظل مختلف الفنون خلال القرن التاسع عشر" (صدر عن دار نشر بيكارد عام 2014)، عملت كلير باربيون أستاذة لتاريخ الفن المعاصر بجامعة بواتييه بين عامي 2014 و2017. وهي أيضا متخصصة في تاريخ الفن في القرن التاسع عشر وعلى وجه التحديد في النحت والتأريخ. نُشرت لها في السنوات الأخيرة ثلاثة مؤلفات هي على التوالي كتالوج معرض «بوردال والفن القديم» بعنوان "شغف معاصر" الذي أقيم بمعرض بوردال من 03 اكتوبر 2017 إلى غاية 04 فبراير 2018 والذي تولّت إعداده بالتعاون مع أ. سيمييه و ج. جودو (دار نشر باريس-موزيه)، وكتالوج منحوتات متحف الفنون الجميلة بليون ويتضمن عشرين دراسة وحوالي مائتي مذكرة مستفيضة فضلاً عن كتالوج تلخيصي أشرفت عليه بالاشتراك مع س. شوفيو و س. باكو (سوموجي، 2017) وكتابًا آخر عنوانه «كيف تنظر إلى النحت؟» صدر عن دار نشر هازان.

ناتالي بونديل

مديرة عامة ورئيسة أمناء متحف مونتريال للفنون الجميلة، مونتريال، كندا

ناتالي بونديل مؤرخة فنون وتشغل منصب مديرة عامة وأمينة متحف الفنون الجميلة لمدينة مونتريال منذ عام 2007. وقد لاقت معارضها الفنية المتعددة التخصصات والفريدة من نوعها نجاحا ملحوظا لدى إقامتها في 35 دولة على مدى عشر سنوات. تضاعف خلال فترة إدارتها إقبال الزوار على المتحف (1.3 مليون زائر عام 2017، ما يجعل المتحف يحتل المركز الثامن في أمريكا الشمالية والمركز التاسع والأربعون عالميا)، وتزايدت مساحته بثلاثين مع تدشين مبنيين هما جناح الفن الكيبيكي والكندي، كلير ومارك بورجي (2011) وجناح في سبيل السلام، ميشال وريناتا هورنشتاين (2016). وبوصفه مركزًا حضريا، يضم متحف مونتريال للفنون الجميلة قاعة حفلات تقدم مائة وخمسون حفلا في السنة، بالإضافة إلى قاعة سينمائية. أما جناح ثقافات العالم والعيش المشترك، ستيفان كريتييه وستيفاني مايري، فسوف يُفتتح عام 2019.

ناتالي بونديل هي كذلك مؤلفة «بيان من أجل متحف إنساني»، وقد قامت بزيادة الفضاءات التربوية ثلاثة أضعاف بالاشتراك مع الورشة الدولية للتربية وللعلاج النفسي عن طريق الفن ميشال دو لا شونلوير (2016)، إحدى كبرى الورش التي أقيمت في متحف للفنون في أمريكا الشمالية. يعد متحف مونتريال للفنون الجميلة من المتاحف الرائدة في تنظيم الأنشطة الاجتماعية والمجتمعية بحوالي 450 شريكاً (مدارس وجامعات وجمعيات ومشافي ومعاهد البحوث الطبية...). قام بإنشاء لجنة فن وصحة الذي يترأسها كبير العلماء في كيبيك، إلى جانب عدة مشروعات تجريبية أخرى وأولى الإرشادات الطبية المقدَّمة على الإطلاق عام 2017. تشغل ناتالي بونديل أيضًا منصب نائب رئيس مجلس الفنون بكندا، وقد حصلت على شهادة دكتوراه فخرية من جامعة ماكغيل وجامعة مونتريال، وهي عضوة في منظمات نيشن كيبيك وكندا، بالإضافة لنيلها وسام الجمهورية الفرنسية للفنون والآداب برتبة ضابط.

جيمس كونو

الرئيس والمدير التنفيذي، مؤسسة جي بول غيتي تراست، لوس أنجلوس، الولايات المتحدة

تحصل جامس كونو على شهادة البكالوريوس في التاريخ من جامعة ويلاميت عام 1973، ثم نال الماجستير في تاريخ الفن من جامعة أوريغون عام 1978 والماجستير والدكتوراه في الفنون الجميلة) تاريخ الفنون) من جامعة هارفارد بين عامي 1981و1985. وقد شغل مناصب تعليمية في جامعة فاسار وجامعة كاليفورنيا في لوس أنجلوس وجامعة دارتموث وهارفارد، وتقلد أيضًا منصب مدير مركز غرنولد بجامعة كاليفورنيا بلوس أنجلوس للفنون التشكيلية (1986-1989) ومتحف دارتموث هود للفنون (1989-1991)، ومتحف جامعة هارفارد للفنون (1991-2002)، ورئيس ومدير معهد كروتولد للفنون بجامعة لندن (2002-2004). وقد تولى منصبه الحالي كرئيس ومدير تنفيذي لمتحف غي بول غيتي في شهر أغسطس من عام 2011.

تولى جيمس بتقديم العديد من المحاضرات وكتب مؤلفات عدة في مجال المتاحف والثقافات والسياسة العامة، وقد نُشرت له منذ عام 2003 ثلاثة كتب بالتعاون مع مطبعة جامعة برينستون تراوحت بين التأليف والتحرير وهي على التوالي «من يملك الإلهام؟ متاحف الفنون وثقة الجمهور» و «لمن ترجع العصور القديمة؟» و «من يملك الثقافة؟» وعد المتاحف والجدل حول الآثار» بالإضافة إلى كتاب آخر أنجزه بالتعاون مع دار نشر جامعة شيكاغو عنوانه «أهمية المتاحف في الإشادة بالمتحف الموسوعي». يشغل جيمس حاليًا منصب زميل في الأكاديمية الأمريكية للفنون والعلوم وسكرتير أمانتها الدولية، وهو أيضًا عضو مجلس إدارتها وعضو مجلس إدارة معهد كورتولد للفنون، ومؤسسة بولتزر للفنون، وجامعة ويلاميت.

نويمي دوسيه

رئيسة أمناء قسم الآثار، اللوفر أبوظبي، الإمارات العربية المتحدة

أتمّت نويمي دوسيه دراستها الجامعية في معهد التراث الوطني في باريس، ثم تخرّجت في علم الآثار وتاريخ الفن من جامعة باريس 1 – بانتيون سوربون ومدرسة اللوفر. بعد تدريسها علم الآثار في الشرق الأدنى في مدرسة اللوفر، عُيّنت في عام 2010 أمينة للآثار في المتحف الفرني للفنون الجميلة وعلم الآثار في بيزنسون. تعمل نويمي بوجه وثيق مع اللوفر أبوظبي منذ عام 2014، وذلك بعد التحاقها بوكالة متاحف فرنسا في منصب أمينة متحف قسم الآثار. تكمن مهمتها حاليا في إدارة سياسة البحوث ومركز التوثيق في اللوفر أبوظبي، وقد عزّزت التعاون الدولي مع المؤسسات الأخرى في الإمارات العربية المتحدة والأردن وعُمان والمملكة العربية السعودية من خلال إدارتها للأعمال الفنية المُعارة من هذه المؤسسات. كما أشرفت نويمي على دراسة حول علم الآثار في الشرق الأدنى، وتاريخ علم الآثار وتاريخ المجموعات. وقد ركّزت أبحاثها في المقام الأول على الزخارف المعارية الأخمينية في شوشان، حيث سلطت الضوء على عملية الإبداع والجوانب الفنية للإنتاج التوفيقي الموروث عن أواخر العصرين البرونزي والحديدي في الشرق الأوسط. حصلت على جائزة جاك مورغان (أكاديمية العلوم والفنون والآداب في جامعة مارسيليا) تقديرًا لمساهمتها في تنسيق ونشر التقارير الأثرية لرولاند ميكوينم على الإنترنت. تجدر الإشارة إلى أنّ رولاند ميكوينم هو المدير السابق للبعثات الأثرية في شوشان من 1912 إلى 1939، وذلك بفضل منحة من برنامج مؤسسة ليون ليفي شيلبي وايت للنشر الأثري. تعمل نويمي حاليا في اللوفر أبوظبي على تطوير الدراسات المادية وعمليات التأسيس وتاريخ المجموعات الفنية.

هارتويغ فيشر

مدير المتحف البريطاني، لندن، المملكة المتحدة

تقلّد هارتويغ فيشر منصب مدير المتحف البريطاني في ربيع عام 2016، وهو متحصل على الدكتوراه في تاريخ الفن من جامعة بون عام 1993، بعد إنهاء دراسته في برلين وروما وباريس. بدأ مسيرته المهنية في المتاحف كمساعد باحث ثم أصبح أميناً للمتحف في قسم القرن التاسع عشر والفن الحديث بمتحف الفنون الجميلة ببازل في سويسرا، قبل أن يصبح مديراً لمتحف فولكوانج في إسن عام 2006. وقد قام خلال فترة إدارته لمتحف فولكوانج بالإشراف على تنفيذ مشروع بناء كبير مع المهندس المعماري الشهير ديفيد شيبرفيلد، بالإضافة إلى مشاركته في العديد من المعارض الناجحة وإسهامه في الحصول على الكثير من المقتنيات الأثرية المهمة.

عُيّن هارتوج فيشر مديراً عاماً للمجموعة الفنية للدولة في دريسدن خلال عام 2012. وقد كان مسؤولاً عن 14 متحفاً بالإضافة إلى المكتبات والسجلات ومراكز البحوث المرتبطة بها. وبصفته مديرا عاما لأحد أهم المتاحف في العالم، قام بالإشراف على إقامة معارض عالمية كبرى ومشروعات بحثية في مختلف دول العالم وأيضًا في ألمانيا، كما قام بالإشراف على مشروعات بناء وترميم المجموعة الفنية للدولة بدريدسن.

هيرفيه إنغلبيرت

أستاذ التاريخ الروماني، جامعة باريس نانتير، باريس، فرنسا

هيرفيه إنغلبيرت هو أستاذ التاريخ الروماني بجامعة باريس نانتير، وهو متخصص في دراسة التطورات الثقافية والدينية في العصور القديمة المتأخرة. وقد ألّف في هذا المجال ثلاثة أعمال وأطلساً، إلى جانب عدة مقالات في الاختصاص وتولى تنظيم عدة مؤتمرات والإشراف على نشر ما جاء فيها من محاضرات. كان من ضمن الأعضاء المبتدئين في المعهد الجامعي الفرنسي ثمّ أصبح بعد ذلك من بين كبار أعضاء المعهد.

شارك في عدة ندوات وألقى محاضرات في كل من أوروبا وأمريكا الشمالية وآسيا (الصين واليابان). وهو يقوم حاليا بالإشراف على إدارة المجلة الدولية المعنية بالعصور القديمة المتأخرة وكذلك مجموعة التاريخ الجديد «كليو» الصادرة عن المنشورات الجامعية الفرنسية. كما يهتم بابستمولوجيا العلوم الإنسانية والاجتماعية وكذلك بتأريخ التاريخ الكوني وهو الموضوع

الذي انجز فيه كتابين صدرا مؤخراً وهما «العالم والتاريخ دراسة عن التواريخ الكونية» (2014)، و«تاريخ كوني أم تاريخ شمولي؟» (2018).

شارك مؤخراً، من 2016 إلى 2018 في إدارة مشروع بحث حول موضوع: «تواريخ كونية ومتاحف عالمية» بالتعاون مع ساندرا كامب ومتحف فيكتوريا وألبرت وأندريه ديلبويش (متحف براناي)، وشارك في هذا الإطار، في تنظيم ثلاث ورشات عمل وهي «تطور المتاحف خلال القرن التاسع عشر وعلوم المتاحف المقارنة: الفنون الآسيوية نموذجا» و «بنية العالميات المتحفية الغربية المتنوعة في العواصم الثقافية في القرن التاسع عشر وبداية القرن العشرين». هذا بالإضافة إلى مؤتمر بعنوان «أيّ عالمية للمتاحف العالمية؟». ويعتزم تأليف كتاب جامع يهتم بالعلاقات الممكنة بين كتابة التاريخ العالمي وتصميم المتاحف العالمية.

روز ماري هيردا موسو

رئيسة أمناء قسم فنون الحقبة الحديثة الأولى، اللوفر أبوظبي، الإمارات العربية المتحدة

قبل التحاقها بمتحف اللوفر أبوظبي، عملت روز ماري موسو لدى متحف كارنافاليه، حيث شغلت منصب أمينة قسم الآثار الذي يضم المجموعات الفنية التي تعود إلى فترات ما قبل التاريخ وفجر التاريخ ومجموعات بلاد الغال الرومانية، إلى جانب المخازن الأثرية البلدية والسرداب الأثري لجزيرة المدينة في نهر السين وسراديب الموق في باريس. ساهمت روز ماري في تغيير العرض المتحفي في باريس بعد سلسلة من المعارض تناولت التأويلات المستوحاة من هذا الموقع الأثري (معرض «وأصبحت لوتيس باريس» عام 2010) ومعرض «باريس المفقودة وباريس المستعادة» عام 2011).

وبوصفها مديرة متحف كونيك جاي وأمينة قسم الفنون الزخرفية بين 2013 و2018، تولت مسؤولية الإشراف العلمي على معارض «الأضواء» و«بطاقة بيضاء» لكريستيان لاكروا عام 2014 و«شاي أم قهوة أم شوكولاتة؟» عام 2015 و«البندقية، صاحبة الجلالة تحتفي» لتيبولو غواردي عام 2017، وحاليا معرض «معمل الترف، الباعة المتجولون الباريسيون في القرن الثامن عشر». تتناول أعمالها الممارسات المتعلقة بالتبادل الثقافي والاستهلاك، وهو ما جعلها تتعاون مع فرق بحث دولية تهتم بدراسة توزيع المواد والأشكال الاجتماعية في القرن الثامن عشر.

سيسيليا هيرلي

مديرة المجموعات الفنية الخاصة في جامعة نيوشاتيل بسويسرا وعضوة فريق البحوث في مدرسة اللوفر بباريس، فرنسا

حصلت سيسيليا هيرلي على شهادة الماجستير في الآداب الإنسانية من جامعة أكسفورد والدكتوراه في التاريخ من جامعة نيوشاتيل وشهادة التأهيل للإشراف على البحوث في تاريخ الفن من جامعة ليون الثانية. شغلت سابقاً منصب مديرة المكتب الفرنسي في نوشاتيل (الذي تأسس عام 1540)، وهي الآن مديرة المجموعات الفنية الخاصة في جامعة نوشاتيل وعضوة في فريق البحوث وأستاذة محاضرة في مدرسة اللوفر.

كتبت سيسيليا العديد من المؤلفات في الكثير من الموضوعات بما في ذلك مقالات عن الفنانين السويسريين (ليوبولد روبرت وأورلي روبرت وماكسيميليان دي ميورون) وتاريخ المتاحف: الجمع والعرض، وكذلك تاريخ الفكر القديم، والتاريخ وتصنيف الأدب الفني ونشره وتاريخ الفن. ألّفت كتاب «معالم من أجل الناس» وحصلت عنه على ميدالية ذهبية عام 2013 من أكاديمية النقوش والرسائل الجميلة. شاركت في تحرير أعمال مؤتمرين (2007) حول المجموعات الفنية في القرن الثامن عشر و«الكتالوج في كل حالاته» بالاشتراك مع كلار باربيلو. كما أنّ لها العديد من المقالات الأخرى وسيحمل كتابها المنتظر عنوان «نماذج متنقلة»، وهو دراسة لتقاليد قاعات عرض التحف الفنية في متاحف الفنون الجميلة الأوروبية خلال القرن التاسع عشر.

هنري كيم
الرئيس التنفيذي لمتحف آغا خان، تورنتو، كندا

هنري كيم هو مدير متحف آغا خان في تورونتو ورئيسه التنفيذي. يتولى هذا المتحف مهمة تعزيز فهم مساهمة الحضارات الإسلامية في التراث العالمي وتقديرها. انضم هنري كيم إلى المتحف سنة 2012 وقاد جهودا حثيثة لتطوير الفريق المهني وافتتاح المتحف عام 2014. وقد كان قبل ذلك مؤرخا وعالم آثار، ثم التحق بمتحف آغا خان بعد عمله في جامعة أكسفورد، حيث درّس ونظم عروضا أثرية وأدار مشروعات على غاية من الأهمية في متحف أشموليان في الفترة ما بين 1994 و2012. تلقى تعليمه في جامعة هارفارد وأكسفورد، وعمل أمينًا للقطع النقدية اليونانية ومحاضرًا جامعيًا في علم المسكوكات اليونانية في الجامعة. ويشارك حاليا في مشروعات إنشاء الفن في باكستان وهو أحد المدافعين عن استخدام القطع الفنية في مجال التدريس.

آنماري مايلا عفيش
مديرة متحف بيروت الوطني، لبنان

تخرّجت آنماري مايلا عفيش من مدرسة اللوفر في باريس، ثم حصلت على شهادة الماجستير في تاريخ الفن وعلم الآثار من جامعة إيكس أون بروفانس في فرنسا بعد حصولها على إجازة من جامعة السوربون في باريس.

منذ سنة 1994، انضمت آنماري إلى فريق عمل وزارة الثقافة/ المديرية العامة للآثار- قسم المتاحف، حيث اهتمت بإدارة المجموعات الأثرية. كما عملت على إعادة تأهيل المتحف الوطني في بيروت الذي تضرّر بشدة خلال سنوات الحرب، وساهمت في الافتتاح الدائم للمتحف سنة 1999.

أصبحت أمينة المتحف الوطني في بيروت سنة 2009، ثم مسؤولة عن كل المتاحف الوطنية التابعة للمديرية العامة للآثار سنة 2011، مع الحفاظ على منصبها كمديرة لقسم الدراسات والمنشورات في المديرية العامة للآثار الذي شغلته منذ سنة 2001. تتولى آنماري رئاسة تحرير نشرة الآثار والعمارة اللبنانية التي تصدرها المديرية العامة للآثار في وزارة الثقافة، حيث تقوم بنشر النتائج السنوية للحفريات الأثرية والبحوث، بالإضافة الى كل الدراسات الأثرية والمعمارية التي تقام على الأراضي اللبنانية. أتاحت لها خبرتها الطويلة في مجال المتاحف تدريس علم المتاحف والتراث في جامعة القديس يوسف منذ سنة 2011. وفي أبريل من عام 2018، عُيّنت رئيسة مجلس إدارة الهيئة العامة للمتاحف ومديرة عامة لها.

فرانسوا رينيه مارتن
رئيس فريق البحوث في مدرسة اللوفر وأستاذ في مدرسة الفنون الجميلة، باريس، فرنسا

يشغل فرانسوا رينيه مارتن منصب مدير البحث العلمي بمدرسة اللوفر منذ عام 2018. حصل على دكتوراه في العلوم السياسية وتاريخ الفن، ونال أيضا درجة التأهيل في الإشراف على البحوث العلمية. وقد زوال دراسته كطالب في المعهد الوطنيّ لتاريخ الفن، كما شارك كمدير بحث مدعو في المركز الألمانيّ لتاريخ الفن بباريس بين عامي 2014-2015، وكباحث زائر لدى مركز غيتي عام 2018. بالإضافة إلى قيامه بنشر العديد من الدراسات عن الرسّامين غرونفالد وإينغرس وتاريخ مناهج تاريخ الفن.

جون لوك مارتينيز
رئيس ومدير متحف اللوفر، باريس، فرنسا

جون لوك مارتينيز مؤرخ فنون وعالم آثار فرنسي من مواليد سنة 1964، عيّنه رئيس الجمهورية الفرنسية رئيسًا ومديراً تنفيذياً لمتحف اللوفر في الخامس من نيسان/أبريل 2013، ثمّ أعيد تعيينه في الرابع من نيسان/أبريل 2018.

بدأ جون لوك مارتينيز مسيرته المهنية في متحف اللوفر عام 1997 بعد حصوله على شهادة التبريز في التاريخ وتخرجه من مدرسة اللوفر، حيث تولّى إدارة قسم الآثار الإغريقية والأتروسكانية والرومانية. كُلف بترميم قاعات عرض الفن الإغريقي المحيطة بتمثال

فينوس دي ميلو (عام 2010)، وقام كذلك بتصميم قاعة عرض رحلة عبر الزمن الموجودة في متحف اللوفر في مدينة لنس الفرنسية.

حافظ متحف اللوفر طوال فترة إدارته له على موقع الصدارة في تصنيف المتاحف العالمية، إذ بلغ عدد زواره ثمانية ملايين زائر عام 2017. اقتنى المتحف 816 قطعة فنية منذ عام 2013 ساهمت في إغناء مجموعاته الفنية، كما قام بترميم أكثر من 33 ألف متر مربع من قاعاته وتجديدها بغية تحسين تجربة الزوار. يترأس جون لوك مارتينيز منذ سنة 2013 المجلس العلمي لوكالة متاحف فرنسا، الجهة المسؤولة عن إنجاز مشروع اللوفر أبوظبي الذي افتتح في تشرين الثاني/ نوفمبر 2017. وقد كان جون لوك مارتينيز صاحب فكرة إنشاء التحالف الدولي لحماية التراث في مناطق النزاع (ALIPH) عام 2017، وهو يترأس مجلسه العلمي فضلا عن كونه رئيسا لمجلس إدارة المدرسة الفرنسية بأثينا وعضوا في المجلس الأعلى لمتاحف فرنسا وعضوا في المجلس العلمي للمعهد الوطني لتاريخ الفنّ وعضو في مجلس إدارة مدرسة اللوفر وفي المجلس الفنيّ للمتاحف الوطنية الفرنسية. وقد حاز على كل من وسام الاستحقاق الوطني ووسام جوقة الشرف برتبتي فارس.

صوفي موكان

أستاذة مشاركة في جامعة ليل ومدرسة اللوفر، باريس، فرنسا

حصلت صوفي موكين على الدكتوراه في تاريخ الفن من جامعة باريس سوربون عام 2003، وأصبحت أستاذة مشاركة في تاريخ الفن في جامعة بوردو (2004-2007) وجامعة ليل منذ عام 2007. عملت كذلك مديرة أكاديمية في مدرسة اللوفر خلال الفترة ما بين 2011-2016، وهي متخصصة في الفنون التصميمية والهندسة وتاريخ المجموعات الفنية وتاريخ الجمالية الفنية للقرنين السابع والثامن عشر. نُشرت لها مقالات وكتب عديدة منها كتاب حول الطراز الفني لبيير ميجون والطراز الفني للويس السابع عشر والكتابة حول المنحوتات وكتاب «الجلد الروسي، ذاكرة الصبغ» و«رخاميات فيرساي، السياسة الملكية وعمال رخام الملك»، وهي عضوة في لجان علمية عديدة منها لجنة جمع القطع الأثرية لخدمة المتاحف الفرنسية على الصعيد الوطني. وقد فازت بجائزة نيكول عن أطروحة الدكتوراه عام 2003 وجائزة النقابة الوطنية لتجار التحف القديمة عن منشوراتها في رخاميات فيرساي عام 2018.

ثريا نجيم

مديرة إدارة المقتنيات الفنية وأمناء المتحف والبحث العلمي، اللوفر أبوظبي، الإمارات العربية المتحدة

عُيّنت ثريا نجيم مديرة لإدارة المقتنيات الفنية وأمناء المتحف والبحث العلمي في اللوفر أبوظبي في شهر فبراير 2018، حيث تتولى منذ ذلك الوقت الإشراف على الاستراتيجية العلمية للمتحف وقيادتها، إلى جانب إشرافها على تطوير الرواية العلمية واستراتيجية مقتنياته وبحوثه، فضلاً عن برمجة معارضه الفنية. تشارك ثريا عن كثب في نقل المعارف التي تسهم في تدريب أمناء المتحف الجدد من الشباب. قبل تعيينها في منصبها الحالي، كانت تشغل منصب رئيسة أمناء المتاحف لدى وكالة متاحف فرنسا، حيث تولت مسؤولية تنسيق برمجة مجموعات الفن الإسلامي والعصور الوسطى.

بدأت ثريا مسيرتها المهنية في متحف اللوفر في باريس. وفي إطار مشاركتها في مشروع «متحف اللوفر الكبير»، ساهمت في افتتاح أول قاعات قسم الفن الإسلامي في متحف اللوفر، إلى جانب مشاركتها في تنظيم كبرى المعارض التاريخية في كل من متحف اللوفر والقصر الكبير. كما درّست في مدرسة اللوفر لعدة سنوات، لتترأس فيها عام 2013 قسم تاريخ الفن الإسلامي. وفي الأثناء، نُشرت لها العديد من المؤلفات العلمية.

تحمل ثريا نجيم شهادة الدكتوراه في تاريخ الفن والآثار الإسلامية، إلى جانب شهادة جامعية في دراسات المتاحف وشهادة دراسات عليا من مدرسة اللوفر وجامعة باريس السوربون. كما درست الحضارة العربية الإسلامية في معهد اللغات والحضارات الشرقية بباريس. وقد أعدت أطروحتها البحثية الخاصة بالدكتوراه حول قصائد قصر الحمراء في عهد بني نصر.

مارتن بيتس

أستاذ مشارك في علم الآثار الرومانية، جامعة إكزتر، المملكة المتحدة

يشغل مارتن بيتز منصب أستاذ مساعد في علوم الآثار الرومانية بجامعة إكزتر بالمملكة المتحدة. وتدور مجالات بحثه الرئيسية حول الفترة الرومانية القديمة في شمال غرب أوروبا كما تناولتها الدراسات الكمية حول الثقافة المادية وخاصة الخزفيات. وهو مهتم على وجه الخصوص بتطبيق أفكار العولمة للكشف عن رؤى جديدة في المجتمعات القديمة عبر دراسة تداول الممتلكات الثقافية وارتباطها بالبشر. وقد قاده هذا التوجه العلمي لإنجاز بحوثٍ مقارنة حول الأثر الثقافي للخزف الصيني عبر العالم في القرنين السابع عشر والثامن عشر.

ومن بين أهم منشوراته الحديثة نذكر كتاب «العولمة والعالم الروماني: تاريخ العالم، والتواصل والثقافة المادية» الذي تولى تحريره بالتعاون مع ميغيل جون فيرسليس عام 2015، دار نشر جامعة كامبريدج. و«تجسيد التاريخ الروماني» الذي حرّره بالتعاون مع أستريد فان إين عام 2017 (أوكسبو). عمل مارتن بيتس أيضًا محررا في القسم الأوروبي من دليل روتلدج لعلم الآثار والعولمة الذي حرّرته تامار هودوس عام 2016. أما بحثه التالي «ثورة الكائن الروماني: وجوه التواصل الثقافي في شمال غرب أوروبا» فقد تناول بالتحليل مفاهيم العولمة والمادية، وتولَّت نشره مطبعة جامعة أمستردام عام 2019.

مانويل راباتيه

مدير اللوفر أبوظبي، الإمارات العربية المتحدة

تخرج مانويل راباتيه من معهد الدراسات السياسية بباريس في العام 1998، ثم مدرسة الدراسات العليا التجارية في باريس عام 2001، واستهلّ مسيرته المهنية بمنصب نائب مدير مسرح متحف اللوفر في باريس خلال الفترة 2002-2005، حيث شارك في إعداد برامج جديدة حول الفنون الإسلامية بموجب أول عقد مبرم بين الحكومة الفرنسية والمتحف في إطار جهود تطويره وتحديثه. انضم مانويل إلى متحف براني في باريس في منصب نائب لمدير التطوير الثقافي قبل عام من افتتاحه عام 2001، وعقب افتتاح المتحف، قاد مانويل إطلاق سلسلة المعارض الأولى التابعة للمتحف التي أقيمت بالخارج. التحق مانويل بوكالة متاحف فرنسا في العام 2008، وذلك بعد عام واحد من توقيع اتفاقية التعاون المشترك بين الحكومة الفرنسية وأبوظبي. تمكَّن مانويل، بصفته السكرتير العام ونائب الرئيس التنفيذي في وكالة متاحف فرنسا منذ العام 2010، من متابعة مشروع اللوفر أبوظبي منذ مراحله الأولى، بداية من مرحلة الإعداد والتصوُّر وصولاً إلى مرحلة التنفيذ الفعلي. عُيّن مانويل رئيساً تنفيذياً لوكالة متاحف فرنسا عام 2013 لتشكيل فريق مخضرم من خبراء المتاحف في أبوظبي يتولى متابعة مراحل إنجاز متحف اللوفر أبوظبي بالتعاون مع أبرز المتاحف الفرنسية وغيرها من الشركاء المميّزين في دولة الإمارات العربية المتحدة. ثم عيّنته دائرة الثقافة والسياحة – أبوظبي مديراً لمتحف اللوفر أبوظبي في شهر سبتمبر من عام 2016. وإلى جانب مسؤولياته في خدمة المتاحف، ترأس مانويل مجموعة «كلتشر آند مانجمنت» لعدة سنوات وأنشأ فيها قسماً للمتاحف. كما عمل أستاذًا محاضراً في إدارة الفنون والثقافة في عدة جامعات بفرنسا وأبوظبي.

سيلفي راموند

مديرة متحف الفنون الجميلة والفن المعاصر، ليون، فرنسا

تتطلّع مدينة ليون إلى تجربة نموذج متحفي جديد بإدارة سيلفي راموند، مديرة متحف ليون للفنون الجميلة منذ سنة 2004، وذلك من خلال إنشاء قطب المتاحف الجديد الذي يجمع بين متحف الفنون الجميلة ومتحف الفن المعاصر. سيلفي راموند هي خريجة جامعة السوربون ومدرسة اللوفر وطالبة سابقة في المدرسة الوطنية للتراث ورئيسة أمناء التراث وأستاذة مشاركة في المدرسة العليا للأساتذة بليون، وقد نجحت في الارتقاء بمتحف الفنون الجميلة إلى مصاف المتاحف الفرنسية ذات المكانة الدولية المرموقة. تشغل سيلفي راموند عضوية اللجنة الإدارية لمجموعة بيوزو، وهي أيضًا باحثة زائرة لدى مؤسسة تيرا فاوندايشن (2013) ومركز غيتي في لوس أنجلوس (2018). وقد تولَّت تنظيم قرابة الثلاثين معرضًا فنيًا نذكر منها على سبيل المثال أوتو ديكس، فرناند ليجيه،

براك / لورينز، جيريكولت، الرجوع إلى البدء، جوزيف كورنيل والسرياليين في نيويورك، هنري ماتيس والمخبر الداخلي وغيرها من المعارض.

أشرفت سيلفي راموند بطلب من وزيرة الثقافة الفرنسية أودربه أزولاي على إحدى المراكز الفكرية ضمن ما يعرف باسم "رسالة المتاحف في القرن الحادي والعشرين". وقد مكّن إنشاء مثل هذا المركز الجديد بإدارتها من منح مدينة ليون أكبر مجموعة فنية في فرنسا خارج باريس. كما أتاح لفرنسا فرصة فريدة من نوعها لابتكار نموذج جديد من المتاحف الفنية والعالمية الكونية التي تتناسب مع القرن الحادي والعشرين.

كيني تينغ

مدير متحف الحضارات الآسيوية، سنغافورة

كيني تينغ هو مدير متحف الحضارات الآسيوية ومتحف البيراناكاني ومجموعة متاحف ولجنة التراث الوطني بسنغافورة. وهو مكلف بالإشراف على المتاحف الوطنية والمهرجانات التي تدار عبر هذه اللجنة. وقد عمل أثناء إدارته لمتحف الحضارات الآسيوية على تغيير المنهج التنظيمي للمتحف ليتحوّل من التركيز الجغرافي بين الثقافات إلى التركيز الموضوعي. ترأس مؤخراً معارض حول فنون ميانمار وأنغور وكوريا والفن البوذي والهندوسي عبر آسيا والثقافة المادية لمدن الموانئ الآسيوية العالمية. يشغل كيني حالياً منصب رئيس شبكة المتاحف الآسيوية الأوروبية التي تهدف إلى تعزيز التفاهم المشترك والتعاون المتبادل بين شعوب آسيا وأوروبا عبر المتاحف المبنية على النشاطات الثقافية.

وقبل انضمامه إلى لجنة التراث الوطني، عمل في الوزارة السابقة للمعلومات والاتصال والفنون، حيث شارك في تطوير استراتيجيات للتراث والفنون تتضمن خطة مدينة عصر النهضة الثالثة ونشر استراتيجيات الفنون والثقافة الحديثة. وهو مهتم بتاريخ الترحال ومدن الموانئ الآسيوية. ومن مؤلفاته كتاب «روح الجولة الكبرى 100 —سنة من السفر في جنوب شرق آسيا» وكتاب «سنغافورة عام — 1819 التراث الحي».

About the Authors (French)

S.E. Shaikha Mai bint Mohammed Al Khalifa
Présidente de l'Autorité de Bahreïn pour la Culture et les Antiquités, Royaume de Bahreïn
Figure emblématique des scènes de la culture et de l'art arabes, SE Shaikha Mai a été le fer de lance au niveau national du développement des infrastructures culturelles du Royaume de Bahreïn pour la conservation du patrimoine et la croissance d'un tourisme durable. SE Shaikha Mai, présidente de l'Autorité de la Culture et des Antiquités de Bahreïn, est la plus grande spécialiste du secteur public dans ce domaine, chargée des portefeuilles du ministère de la Culture et de l'Information et du ministère de la Culture.

En tant que fondatrice du Centre pour la Culture et la Recherche Shaikh Ebrahim bin Mohammed Al Khalifa, et présidente de son conseil d'administration depuis 2002, elle œuvre activement à la préservation de l'architecture traditionnelle de Bahreïn. A son actif, figurent les inscriptions au Patrimoine mondial de l'UNESCO du Fort de Bahreïn en 2005 et des Activité perlières, témoignage d'une économie insulaire en 2012; la création du Centre régional arabe du Patrimoine mondial; le Prix Colbert Création et Patrimoine (première lauréate) en 2010; le prix de la Social Creativity de l'Arab Thought Foundation; le prix des Femmes arabes de l'année (2015); le Watch award (2015) par le World Monuments Fund; la Légion d'Honneur, l'Ordre marocain de Ouissam Alaouite (Grand Officier) et l'Ordre de l'Étoile d'Italie et l'Ordre du Mérite de Première Classe de SM le Roi Hamad de Bahrein. Bahreïn a reçu la médaille d'argent d'architecture pour son pavillon à l'Expo Milan 2015 et SE Shaikha Mai est devenue ambassadrice spéciale de l'Année internationale du tourisme durable pour le développement 2017-2019 pour l'Organisation mondiale du tourisme. Elle est également une historienne locale de renom avec sept publications.

Mohamed Khalifa Al Mubarak
Président, Département de la Culture et du Tourisme – Abu Dhabi, Emirats arabes unis
Mohamed Khalifa Al Mubarak est Président du Département de la Culture et du Tourisme – Abu Dhabi, qui agit pour la conservation et la promotion du patrimoine et de la culture d'Abu

Dhabi, afin d'élever l'émirat au rang de destination unique et enrichissante, tant pour les visiteurs internationaux que pour les résidents.

En 2016, Al Mubarak a été nommé Président de Tourism Development and Investment Company (TDIC), leader dans la conception des destinations et sites touristiques, culturels et résidentiels à Abu Dhabi.

Al Mubarak est également Président de Miral Asset Management, une organisation en charge du développement et de la gestion de sites touristiques à Abu Dhabi. Il est aussi PDG d'Aldar Properties PJSC, et Président d'Aldar Academies. Il est également Président d'Image Nation Abu Dhabi.

Mohamed Khalifa Al Mubarak est diplômé de Northeastern University (États-Unis) en Économie et en Sciences Politiques.

Guilhem André
Conservateur en charge des Arts asiatiques et Temps médiévaux, Louvre Abu Dhabi, Émirats arabes unis

Archéologue et historien d'art, Dr. Guilhem André débute sa carrière au musée des Arts asiatiques-Guimet et rejoint en 2001 le département Chine du musée au moment de sa rénovation, contribuant à l'exposition inaugurale, consacrée au steppes d'Asie. Au musée puis à l'Agence France-Muséums, il participe à l'élaboration de nombreux événements en Europe, en Asie, en Amérique du Sud et dans le Golfe. Responsable scientifique de la Mission Archéologique Française en Mongolie, il coordonne un large programme de recherches et ses travaux l'amènent à éditer plusieurs ouvrages ainsi qu'à publier de nombreux articles et essais.

Docteur de l'Université Paris Sorbonne, Guilhem André est diplômé de l'École du Louvre et de l'Institut national des langues et civilisations orientales (INALCO) puis formé en Chine au sein des facultés de l'Université de Pékin et de l'Université du Sichuan. En France, il crée la chaire d'histoire des arts de l'Extrême Orient à l'Institut Catholique de Paris où il enseigne plusieurs années et préside la chaire des arts d'Extrême-Orient à l'École du Louvre en 2013 et 2014. Pour le Louvre Abu Dhabi, en tant que conservateur en chef, il est actuellement responsable de la partie médiévale du parcours. S'agissant des arts de l'Asie, depuis 2009, son expertise a été fondamentale pour coordonner le programme scientifique et culturel et pour constituer la collection du musée.

Claire Barbillon
Directrice, École du Louvre, Paris, France

Claire Barbillon, professeur des universités, est directrice de l'École du Louvre depuis décembre 2017. Sa carrière professionnelle s'est auparavant partagée entre les musées et l'université. Elle a travaillé pendant quatorze ans au musée d'Orsay, successivement responsable du secteur pédagogique puis des publications. Après avoir soutenu son doctorat sur la question des Canons du corps humain au XIXe siècle (publié en 2004 aux éditions Odile Jacob) elle a été pensionnaire à l'Institut national d'histoire de l'art, puis maître de conférences aux universités de Bordeaux, puis de Paris-Nanterre. Elle a ensuite rejoint l'École du Louvre une première fois comme directrice des études, entre 2004 et 2011.

Après avoir soutenu une habilitation à diriger des recherches sur le *Relief au croisement des arts au XIXᵉ siècle* (publié aux éditions Picard en 2014), Claire Barbillon a été professeur d'histoire de l'art contemporain à l'université de Poitiers entre 2014 et 2017. Elle est spécialiste d'histoire de l'art du XIXᵉ siècle, en particulier de sculpture et d'historiographie. Ses derniers ouvrages, publiés en 2017, sont le catalogue de l'exposition *Bourdelle et l'Antique, une passion moderne*, organisée au musée Bourdelle (3 octobre 2017-4 février 2018), qu'elle a co-dirigé avec A. Simier et J. Godeau, (éditions Paris-Musées), le catalogue des sculptures du musée des Beaux-Arts de Lyon, comprenant une vingtaine d'essais et environ 200 notices développées, ainsi qu'un catalogue sommaire, co-dirigé avec C. Chevillot et S. Paccoud, (Somogy, 2017) et un ouvrage personnel, *Comment regarder la sculpture ?* aux éditions Hazan.

Nathalie Bondil

Directrice générale et conservatrice en chef, Musée des Beaux-Arts de Montréal, Canada
Historienne de l'art, Nathalie Bondil est directrice générale et conservatrice en chef du MBAM depuis 2007. Ses expositions pluridisciplinaires originales s'exportent avec succès à l'international (35 étapes en dix ans). Sous sa direction, la fréquentation a doublé (1.3 million de visiteurs en 2017 soit le 8e en Amérique du Nord et 49e dans le monde) et la superficie a crû de 30 % avec l'inauguration de deux bâtiments : le Pavillon d'art québécois et canadien Claire et Marc Bourgie (2011) et le Pavillon pour la Paix Michel et Renata Hornstein (2016). Agora urbaine, le MBAM dispose d'une salle de concert professionnelle (2011) qui présente 150 concerts par an ainsi qu'une véritable salle de cinéma. L'Aile des cultures du monde et du vivre-ensemble Stéphan Crétier et Stéphany Maillery a ouvert en 2019.

Auteure d'un Manifeste pour un Musée humaniste, Nathalie Bondil a triplé les espaces éducatifs avec l'Atelier international d'Éducation et d'Art-thérapie Michel de la Chenelière (2016), l'un des plus grands dans un musée d'art nord-américain. Pionnier en action sociocommunautaire, le MBAM collabore avec quelque 450 partenaires (écoles, universitaires, associations, hôpitaux, et instituts de recherche médicale...). Il a lancé le *Comité Art et Santé* présidé par le Scientifique en Chef du Québec et plusieurs projets pilotes et les toutes premières prescriptions muséales en 2017. Vice-présidente du Conseil des arts du Canada, Nathalie Bondil est récipiendaire de deux doctorats *Honoris causa* de l'Université McGill et de l'Université de Montréal, membre des ordres du Québec et du Canada et officière des Arts et des Lettres de la République française.

James Cuno

Président et CEO, J. Paul Getty Trust, Los Angeles, États-Unis
Licencié d'histoire à la Willamette University en 1973, James Cuno a obtenu un Master en histoire de l'art à l'University of Oregon en 1978, puis un Master et un Doctorat d'histoire de l'art

à la Harvard University respectivement en 1981 et 1985. Il a occupé différents postes d'enseignant au Vassar College, à l'University of California à Los Angeles, à Dartmouth et à Harvard. Après avoir été Directeur du Grunwald Center of the Graphic Arts (UCLA) de 1986 à 1989, du Hood Museum of Art de Dartmouth (1989-1991), et des Harvard University Art Museums (1991-2002), il devient Directeur et Professeur au Courtauld Institute of Art, University of London (2002-2004) puis Président Directeur de l'Art Institute of Chicago (2004-11). Il a pris ses fonctions actuelles de Président Directeur Général du J. Paul Getty Trust en août 2011.

Il est connu pour ses nombreuses conférences et publications sur les musées et sur les politiques culturelles et publiques. Depuis 2003, il a publié trois ouvrages chez Princeton University Press – *Whose Muse? Art Museums and the Public's Trust* (auteur et directeur), *Who Owns Antiquity: Museums and the Battle Over Our Ancient Heritage* (auteur), et *Whose Culture? The Promise of Museums and the Debate Over Antiquities* (auteur et directeur); et un autre à l'University of Chicago Press, *Museums Matter: In Praise of the Encyclopedic Museum* (auteur). Jim est Membre et Secrétaire international de l'American Academy of Arts and Sciences. Il siège au Conseil de l'Academy et au Conseil d'Administration du Courtauld Institute of Art, de la Pulitzer Arts Foundation et de Willamette University.

Noëmi Daucé
Conservatrice en charge de l'archéologie, Louvre Abu Dhabi, Émirats arabes unis
Ancienne élève de l'Institut national du patrimoine à Paris (INP), Noëmi Daucé est diplômée d'archéologie et d'histoire de l'art de l'Université Panthéon-Sorbonne (Paris I) et de l'École du Louvre. Après avoir enseigné l'archéologie du Proche-Orient à l'École du Louvre, elle a été nommée en 2010 conservatrice du département archéologie au musée des beaux-arts et d'archéologie de Besançon. Noëmi Daucé a collaboré étroitement avec le Louvre Abu Dhabi depuis qu'elle a rejoint l'Agence France Muséums en 2014, en tant que conservatrice du département Archéologie. Elle est actuellement responsable de la politique de recherche et du centre de documentation du Louvre Abu Dhabi et, par sa gestion des prêts, a favorisé la coopération internationale avec d'autres institutions des Émirats arabes unis, de Jordanie, d'Oman et d'Arabie saoudite.

Ses recherches ont porté sur l'archéologie du Proche-Orient, l'histoire de l'archéologie et l'histoire des collections, avec une attention particulière à la décoration architecturale achéménide de Suse qui a mis en lumière le processus de création et les aspects techniques d'une production syncrétique héritée de la fin de l'âge du bronze et du fer au Moyen-Orient. Elle a reçu le prix Jacques Morgan (Académie des sciences, des arts et des lettres de Marseille) pour son travail de coordination de la publication en ligne des rapports archéologiques de Roland Mecquenem, directeur des missions archéologiques à Suse de 1912 à 1939, grâce à une bourse du Programme de publication archéologique de la Leon Levy Shelby White Foundation. Les domaines sur lesquels elle travaille actuellement au Louvre Abu Dhabi concernent l'étude des matériaux, les processus de création et l'histoire des collections.

Hartwig Fischer

Directeur, British Museum, Londres, Royaume-Uni

Hartwig Fischer a pris ses fonctions de Directeur du British Museum au printemps 2016. Il a obtenu son Doctorat en histoire de l'art à l'Université de Bonn en 1993 après des études à Berlin, Rome et Paris. Il débute sa carrière dans les musées en tant qu'assistant de recherches puis conservateur du Kunstmuseum Basel (Suisse) avant de devenir Directeur du Folkwang Museum à Essen en 2006. Pendant son mandat de directeur du Folkwang Museum, il supervise un grand projet de construction avec le célèbre architecte David Chipperfield, organise plusieurs expositions à grand succès et préside à de nombreuses acquisitions clés.

En 2012, Hartwig Fischer est nommé Directeur Général du Staatliche Kunstsammlungen, à Dresde (Collections nationales, Dresde), où il est responsable de 14 musées et bibliothèques associées, ainsi que de centres d'archives et de recherche. En tant que Directeur Général de l'un des plus importants musées du monde, il a dirigé l'organisation d'importantes expositions internationales et de projets de recherche à travers le monde ainsi qu'en Allemagne ; il a également supervisé plusieurs grands projets de construction et de rénovation du patrimoine des Collections Nationales à Dresde.

Hervé Inglebert

Professeur d'histoire romaine, Université de Paris-Nanterre, France

Hervé Inglebert est professeur d'histoire romaine à l'université Paris Nanterre, où il est spécialiste des évolutions culturelles et religieuses de l'Antiquité tardive. Sur ces thèmes, il a écrit trois ouvrages, un atlas, organisé et édité plusieurs colloques, et publié des dizaines d'articles. Il a été membre junior et membre senior de l'Institut universitaire de France. Il a participé à de nombreux colloques ou a donné des conférences en Europe, Amérique du nord ou Asie (Chine, Japon). Il dirige la revue internationale *Antiquité tardive*, ainsi que la collection d'histoire Nouvelle Clio aux PUF (Presses Universitaires de France). Il s'intéresse également à l'épistémologie des sciences humaines et sociales ainsi qu'à l'historiographie de l'histoire universelle sur laquelle il a écrit deux ouvrages récents : *Le Monde, l'Histoire. Essai sur les histoires universelles* (2014) et *Histoire universelle ou histoire globale ?* (2018).

Enfin, il a codirigé de 2016 à 2018 un projet de recherches sur le thème "*Histoires universelles et musées universels*", en collaboration avec Sandra Kemp (Victoria & Albert Museum) et André Delpuech (musée du quai Branly). Dans ce cadre, il a co-organisé trois ateliers ("L'évolution des musées au XIXᵉ siècle" ; "Muséographie comparée : l'exemple des arts asiatiques" ; "La constitution des diverses universalités muséales occidentales dans les grandes capitales culturelles au XIXᵉ siècle et au début du XXᵉ siècle") et un colloque ("Quelle universalité pour les musées universels ?"). Il prévoit d'écrire un ouvrage de synthèse sur les relations entre écriture de l'histoire universelle et conceptions des musées universels.

Rose-Marie Herda-Mousseaux

Conservatrice en charge des arts du 15e siècle au 18e siècle, Louvre Abu Dhabi, Émirats arabes unis

Rose-Marie Mousseaux a exercé au sein du musée Carnavalet la responsabilité scientifique des collections préhistoriques, protohistoriques et gallo-romaines, des réserves archéologiques municipales, de la crypte archéologique de l'Île de la Cité et des Catacombes de Paris, espace dont elle a contribué à modifier la présentation muséographique après une série d'expositions portant sur les interprétations de ce site archéologique (*Et Lutèce devint Paris* en 2010 ; *Paris disparu, Paris restitue* en 2011).

Directrice du musée Cognacq-Jay et responsable du fonds des arts décoratifs de 2013 à 2018, elle a assuré au sein de cette institution le commissariat scientifique des expositions *Lumières. Carte blanche à Christian Lacroix* en 2014, *Thé, café ou chocolat ?* en 2015, *Sérénissime ! Venise en fête, de Tiepolo à Guardi* en 2017 et actuellement *La fabrique du luxe – les marchands merciers parisiens au XVIIIe siècle*. Ses travaux portent sur les pratiques liées aux échanges culturels et aux phénomènes de consommation, ce qui l'a amenée à collaborer avec des groupes de recherche internationaux portant sur les transferts matériels et les sociabilités durant le long dix-huitième siècle.

Cecilia Hurley

Directrice, Collections Spéciales, Université de Neuchâtel, Suisse et École du Louvre, Paris, France

Cecilia Hurley a obtenu son Master de lettres à l'Université d'Oxford, son doctorat d'histoire à l'Université de Neuchâtel, et son Habilitation à diriger des recherches en histoire de l'art à l'Université de Lyon II. Elle a été conservatrice de la bibliothèque des Pasteurs à Neuchâtel (fondée en 1540) et est actuellement directrice des Collections Spéciales à l'Université de Neuchâtel. Elle est également membre de l'équipe de recherche et maître de conférence à l'École du Louvre.

Elle a beaucoup écrit, notamment sur les artistes suisses (Léopold Robert, Aurèle Robert et Maximilien de Meuron), l'histoire des musées, la muséologie, l'histoire de la pensée antique, ainsi que l'histoire, la classification et la diffusion des écrits sur l'art et l'histoire de l'art. Elle a publié *Monuments for the People* (2013, médaille d'or de l'Académie des inscriptions et des belles-lettres), et a co-édité deux colloques : *Sammeln und Sammlungen im 18. Jahrhundert in der Schweiz* (2007) et *Le Catalogue dans tous ses états* (avec Claire Barbillon, 2015) ainsi que divers articles. Son prochain livre, Canons mobiles, est une étude de la tradition des salles consacrées aux chefs-d'œuvre dans les musées européens des beaux-arts au cours du XIXe siècle.

Henry Kim

PDG, Musée Aga Khan, Toronto, Canada

Henry Kim est Président Directeur Général du Musée Aga Khan de Toronto. Sa mission est d'encourager une meilleure compréhension et une plus grande reconnaissance de la contribution des civilisations musulmanes au patrimoine mondial. Ayant rejoint le musée en 2012, il a dirigé la mise en place de l'équipe professionnelle en vue de l'ouverture du musée en 2014. Historien et archéologue classique de formation, M. Kim a rejoint le Musée Aga Khan après avoir enseigné à l'Université d'Oxford. Dans ce contexte, il était également conservateur des collections à l'Ashmolean Museum où il a dirigé d'importants projets de 1994 à 2012.

Formé à Harvard et à Oxford, il a été conservateur des monnaies grecques et maître de conférence en numismatique grecque à l'université. Il est actuellement impliqué dans des projets de création artistiques au Pakistan et est un défenseur de l'utilisation des objets d'art dans l'enseignement.

Anne-Marie Maïla Afeiche

Directrice, Musée National de Beyrouth, Liban

Diplômée de l'École du Louvre – Paris, Anne-Marie Maïla-Afeiche est titulaire d'une Maîtrise en Histoire de l'Art et Archéologie de l'Université d'Aix-en-Provence après l'obtention d'une licence dans la même discipline de l'Université Paris IV-Sorbonne.

Son implication auprès de la Direction Générale des Antiquités (Section des Musées) a débuté lors de son retour au Liban en 1993, après avoir passé quelques années à l'étranger. Elle œuvre alors, au sein d'une petite équipe à la réhabilitation du Musée National de Beyrouth, fortement endommagé durant les années de guerre et s'occupe plus particulièrement de la gestion des collections archéologiques. Elle participe à la remise en état du Musée et à son ouverture définitive en 1999.

En 2009, elle devient Conservatrice du Musée National de Beyrouth tout en poursuivant sa charge de Responsable des Etudes et des Publications qu'elle détient depuis 2001. Rédactrice en Chef de la Revue BAAL (Bulletin d'Archéologie et d'Architecture Libanaises), éditée par le Ministère de la Culture – Direction Générale des Antiquités, elle publie annuellement les résultats des fouilles et prospections archéologiques au Liban.

En charge de la documentation, de la recherche des objets archéologiques et de la réorganisation des réserves du Musée National, elle est également responsable des dossiers concernant le trafic illicite d'antiquités. Sa longue expérience dans le domaine muséal lui permet en outre d'assurer, depuis 2011, un cours de «Muséologie et Patrimoine» à l'Université Saint-Joseph de Beyrouth. Elle est nommée en avril 2018 Directeur Général et Présidente du Conseil d'Administration du Conseil National des Musées du Liban.

François-René Martin

Coordinateur de l'équipe de recherche, École du Louvre et professeur à l'École des Beaux-Arts, Paris, France

François-René Martin est professeur d'histoire de l'art à l'École nationale supérieure des Beaux-Arts de Paris. Il dirige la recherche à l'École du Louvre depuis 2018. Docteur en sciences politique et en histoire de l'art, habilité à diriger les recherches (HDR), il est ancien pensionnaire de l'Institut national d'histoire de l'art. Directeur de recherche invité au Deutsches Forum für Kunstgeschichte (centre allemand d'histoire de l'art) à Paris (2014-2015), chercheur invité au Getty Center (2018), il a publié de nombreuses études sur Grünewald, sur Ingres ou sur l'histoire des méthodes de l'histoire de l'art.

Jean-Luc Martinez
Président-directeur, musée du Louvre, Paris, France
Né en 1964, Jean-Luc Martinez est un historien de l'art et archéologue français, nommé président-directeur du musée du Louvre par le Président de la République le 5 avril 2013 et reconduit dans ses fonctions le 4 avril 2018. Agrégé d'histoire et diplômé de l'École du Louvre, Jean-Luc Martinez entre au Louvre en 1997 et prend en 2007 la direction du département des Antiquités grecques, étrusques et romaines. Il a été chargé de la rénovation des salles d'art grec autour de la *Vénus de Milo* (2010) et a conçu la Galerie du Temps du Louvre-Lens.

Sous sa direction, le Louvre a conservé son rang de premier musée au monde, avec plus de 8 millions de visiteurs en 2017. Depuis 2013, 816 acquisitions ont enrichi les collections du Louvre et 33.000 m² d'espaces ont été rénovés pour mieux accueillir les publics. Il préside depuis 2013 le conseil scientifique de l'Agence France-Museums en charge du projet du Louvre Abou Dhabi, ouvert en novembre 2017.

Jean-Luc Martinez est à l'origine de la création de l'ALIPH en 2017 (alliance internationale pour la protection du patrimoine dans les zones en conflit) dont il préside le Conseil Scientifique. Il est président du conseil d'administration de l'École Française d'Athènes et membre du Haut Conseil des Musées de France, du Conseil scientifique de l'Institut National d'Histoire de l'Art, du Conseil d'Administration de l'École du Louvre et du Conseil artistique des Musées Nationaux. Il est Chevalier de l'Ordre National du Mérite et Chevalier de la Légion d'Honneur.

Sophie Mouquin
Maître de conférences, Université de Lille et École du Louvre, Paris, France
Docteur en histoire de l'art de l'Université Paris-Sorbonne (2003), Maître de conférences (Histoire de l'art) des universités de Bordeaux (2004-2007) et de Lille (depuis 2007) et Directrice des études à l'École du Louvre (2011-2016), Sophie Mouquin est spécialisée dans les arts décoratifs, l'architecture, l'histoire des collections et l'histoire du goût aux XVIIᵉ et XVIIIᵉ siècles. Elle a publié de nombreux articles et plusieurs ouvrages (*Pierre IV Migeon*, 2001 ; *Le Style Louis XV*, 2003 ; *Écrire la sculpture*, 2011 ; *Cuir de Russie, mémoire du Tan*, 2017 ; *Versailles en ses marbres, politique royale et marbriers du roi*, 2018). Membre de divers comités scientifiques et de la Commission d'acquisitions (SNC) des musées français, elle a été récompensée par le prix Nicole pour son doctorat en 2003 et par le prix SNA pour sa publication *Versailles en ses marbres* en 2018.

Souraya Noujaim

Directrice scientifique en charge de la conservation et des collections, Louvre Abu Dhabi, Émirats arabes unis

Dr Souraya Noujaim a été nommée directrice scientifique en charge de la conservation et des collections du Louvre Abu Dhabi en février 2018. Elle dirige l'évolution du programme culturel et scientifique du musée, développe la stratégie d'acquisitions et le programme de recherche, ainsi que la programmation des expositions temporaires en partenariat avec les musées partenaires du projet. Elle encadre l'équipe scientifique du Louvre Abu Dhabi et contribue activement au transfert de compétences et d'expertise muséologique. Conservatrice en charge des Arts de l'Islam, Souraya Noujaim a coordonné au sein de l'Agence France Muséums, le programme scientifique et culturel consacré aux temps médiévaux.

Souraya Noujaim a débuté sa carrière au musée du Louvre et collaboré avec des institutions de renom telles que l'Institut du monde arabe (IMA) et le British Museum. Dans le cadre du projet du « Grand Louvre », elle a participé à l'ouverture des premières salles d'art islamique ainsi qu'à des expositions majeures au Louvre et au Grand Palais. Longtemps chargée de cours à l'École du Louvre, elle a présidé la chaire d'art islamique en 2013. Elle est aussi l'auteur de plusieurs publications.

Docteur en histoire et archéologie, spécialiste des arts de l'Islam, Souraya Noujaim est également titulaire du diplôme de recherche de l'École du Louvre. Ancienne élève de l'Institut national des langues orientales (INALCO) et de la Sorbonne, sa thèse a porté sur les poèmes nasrides de l'Alhambra.

Martin Pitts

Professeur Associé, Archéologie romaine, Université d'Exeter, Royaume-Uni

Martin Pitts est Professeur associé en Archéologie romaine à l'Université d'Exeter (Royaume-Uni). Son domaine de recherche principal concerne le début de la période romaine dans le Nord-Ouest de l'Europe, abordé par le biais d'études quantitatives sur la culture matérielle, en particulier la céramique. Il s'intéresse particulièrement à l'application des concepts de la mondialisation pour révéler de nouvelles perspectives sur les sociétés anciennes grâce à l'étude de la circulation des objets et leur histoire dans les sociétés. Cette perspective a mené à des recherches comparatives sur les impacts culturels de la porcelaine chinoise dans le monde aux XVIIe et XVIIIe siècles.

Parmi ses principaux ouvrages récents figurent Globalisation and the Roman World: *World history, connectivity and material culture* (co-dirigé avec Miguel John Versluys, 2015, Cambridge University Press) et *Materialising Roman Histories* (co-dirigé avec Astrid Van Oyen, 2017, Oxbow). Il a été également éditeur de la partie Europe du *Routledge Handbook of Archaeology and Globalization* (dir. Tamar Hodos, 2016). Une monographie explorant implicitement les idées de la mondialisation et de la matérialité *The Roman Object Revolution: Objectscapes and intra-cultural connectivity in Northwest Europe*, a été publiée par Amsterdam University Press en 2019.

Manuel Rabaté

Directeur, Louvre Abu Dhabi, Émirats arabes unis

Manuel Rabaté est diplômé de l'Institut d'études politiques de Paris (Sciences Po, 1998) et de L'École des hautes études commerciales de Paris (HEC, 2001). Il a débuté sa carrière en tant que Directeur Adjoint de l'Auditorium du musée du Louvre de 2002 à 2005. Il a notamment participé à la création de nouveaux programmes accompagnant la création du département des Arts Islamiques, dans le cadre du premier contrat de modernisation du Louvre conclu entre le gouvernement français et le musée. Il a ensuite rejoint le musée du quai Branly en tant que Directeur Adjoint du développement culturel, un an avant son inauguration, et a développé l'activité d'itinérance des expositions du musée à l'international.

Manuel Rabaté a rejoint l'Agence-France-Muséums en 2008, un an après la signature de l'accord intergouvernemental entre la France et Abu Dhabi. Il a suivi le projet depuis sa conceptualisation jusqu'aux étapes d'exécution opérationnelle, d'abord en tant que Secrétaire général de l'Agence-France-Muséums puis en tant que Directeur intérimaire à partir de 2010. Il a été nommé Directeur général en 2013 pour constituer, à Abu Dhabi, une équipe multidisciplinaire de professionnels de musées et coordonner chaque étape du projet, en étroite collaboration avec les musées français et les partenaires émiratis. En septembre 2016, Manuel Rabaté a été nommé Directeur du Louvre Abu Dhabi par le Department of Culture and Tourism – Abu Dhabi. Au-delà de ces activités, Manuel Rabaté a présidé le think tank Culture & Management, au sein duquel il a créé le département des musées. Il a également donné des cours sur l'art et la gestion culturelle à plusieurs universités en France et à Abu Dhabi.

Sylvie Ramond

Directrice, musées des Beaux-Arts et d'Art contemporain, Lyon, France

Avec le nouveau pôle des musées d'art qui réunit désormais le musée des Beaux-Arts et le musée d'Art contemporain, Lyon s'inscrit dans cette ambition d'expérimenter un nouveau modèle pour ses musées. Sa direction générale a été confiée à Sylvie Ramond, directeur du musée des Beaux-Arts de Lyon depuis 2004.

Diplômée de la Sorbonne et de l'École du Louvre, ancienne élève de l'École nationale du patrimoine, conservateur en chef du patrimoine et professeur associé à l'ENS Lyon, Sylvie Ramond a hissé le musée des Beaux-Arts au premier rang des musées français de stature internationale.

Membre du comité directeur du groupe Bizot, chercheuse invitée de la Terra Foundation (2013) et du Getty Center, à Los Angeles (2018), elle a assuré le commissariat d'une trentaine d'expositions (*Otto Dix, Fernand Léger, Braque/Laurens, Géricault, Repartir à zéro, Joseph Cornell et les surréalistes à New York, Henri Matisse. Le laboratoire intérieur...*).

A la demande de la Ministre de la culture Audrey Azoulay, Sylvie Ramond a dirigé un des groupes de réflexion de la « *Mission Musées du XXIᵉ siècle* » (2017). La création de cette nouvelle entité, placée sous sa direction, permet d'offrir à la Ville de Lyon la plus grande collection d'art en France, hors Paris. Elle lui donne aussi l'occasion unique de concevoir pour la France une nouvelle forme de musée d'art universel/global adapté au XXIᵉ siècle.

Kennie Ting

Directeur, Musée des Civilisations asiatiques, Singapour

Kennie Ting est Directeur l'Asian Civilisations Museum et du Peranakan Museum, et également Directeur du groupe Musées au National Heritage Board (NHB) de Singapour, dont la mission est de superviser les musées et festivals nationaux gérés par le NHB. En tant que Directeur du musée des Civilisations asiatiques, il a accompagné la transition d'une approche géographique de conservation du musée à une approche thématique et interculturelle, et a dirigé des expositions récentes : *Arts of Myanmar, Angkor and Korea* ; *Buddhist and Hindu Art across Asia*, et sur la culture matérielle des villes portuaires asiatiques cosmopolites (*Asian Port Cities*). Il est actuellement Président du réseau ASEMUS (Asia-Europe Museum Network), dont le but est de promouvoir la compréhension mutuelle entre les peuples d'Asie et d'Europe par le biais d'une activité culturelle collaborative axée sur les musées.

Avant d'intégrer le NHB, il travaillait à l'ancien ministère de l'Information, de la Communication et des Arts, où il a participé à l'élaboration de stratégies pour le patrimoine et les arts, notamment le Renaissance City Plan III et la récente Arts and Culture Strategic Review. Il s'intéresse à l'histoire des voyages et à l'héritage des villes portuaires asiatiques et est l'auteur des livres *The Romance of the Grand Tour – 100 Years of Travel in South East Asia* et *Singapore 1819 – A Living Legacy*.

GALLERY

WITH

COLOUR PLATES

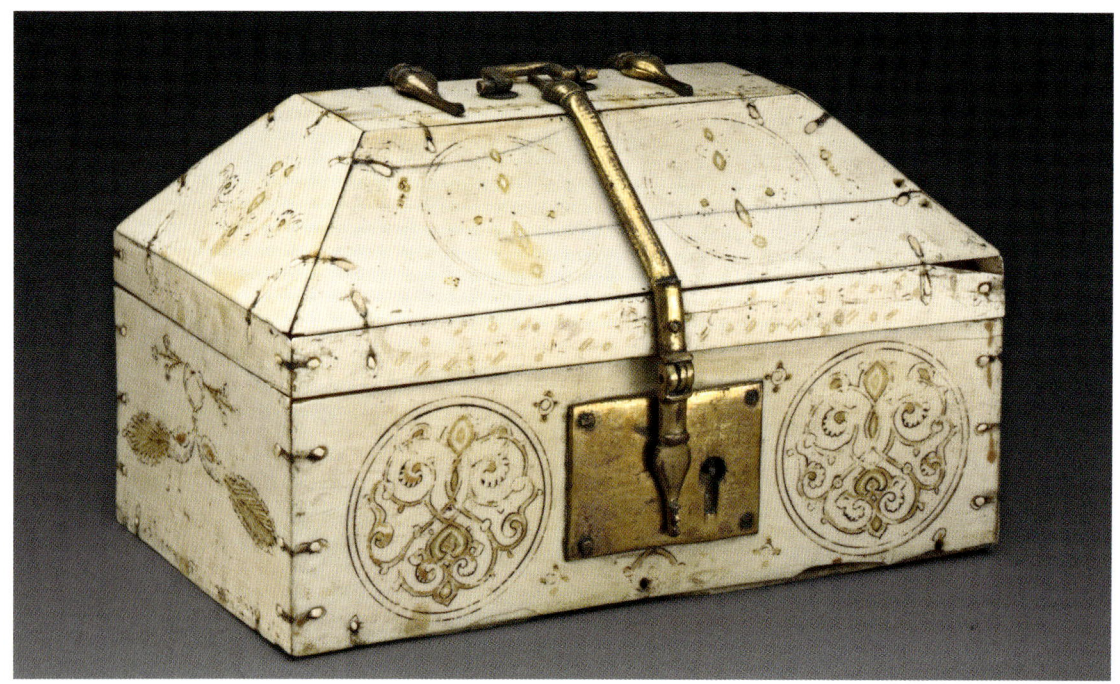

Plate 1. Casket, 1200/25. Sicily. Ivory, brass,
tempera, and gold leaf, 3 ⅞ × 6 ¼ × 3 ¼ in.
(Figure 1, p. 28).
The Art Institute of Chicago, Samuel P. Avery
Endowment, 1926.389. Photograph by Robert
Hashimoto.

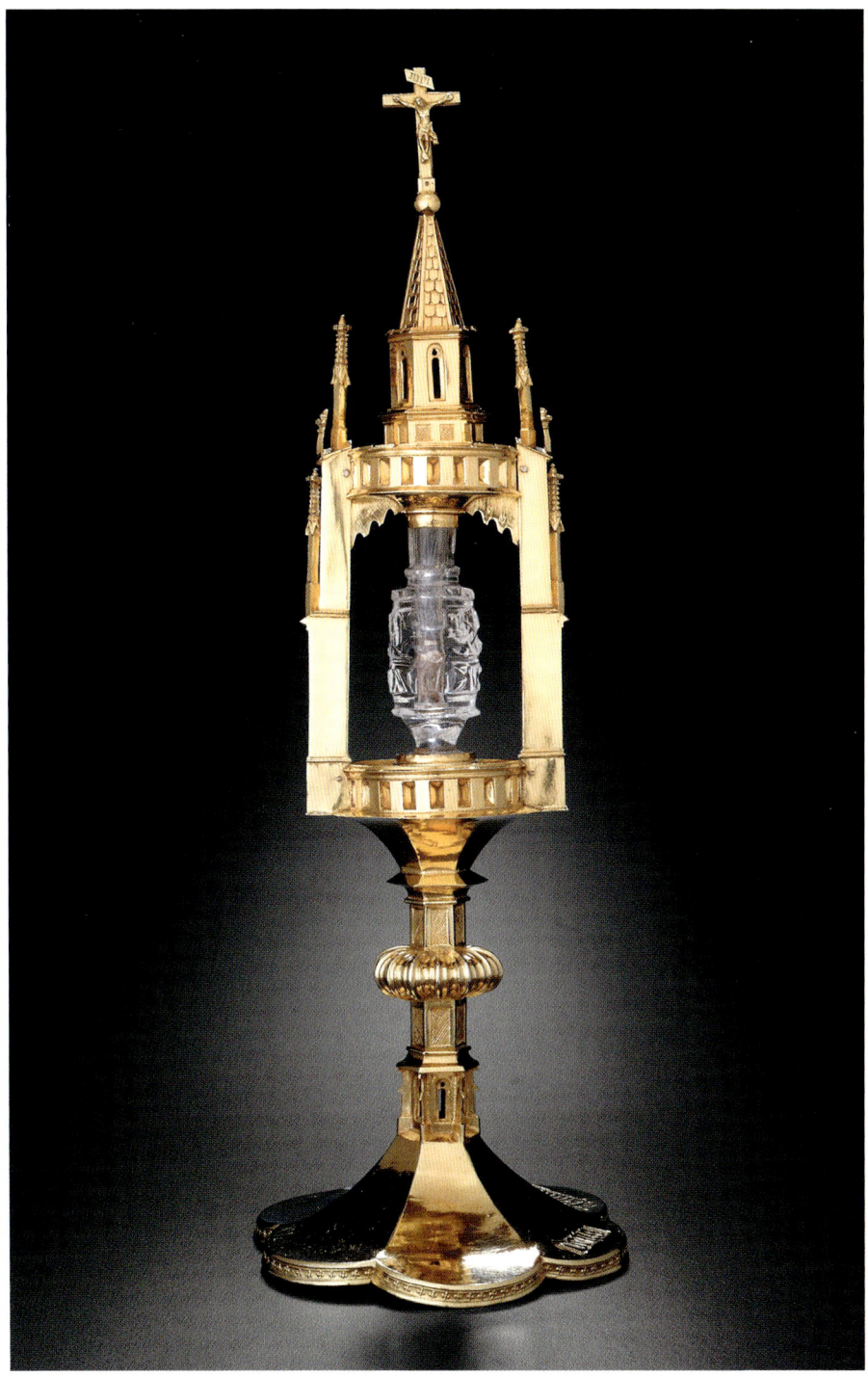

Plate 2. Monstrance with Tooth of St. John the Baptist, 1375/1400. Germany. Lower Saxony, Brunswick. Gilt silver (17 ⅞ × 5 ¼ in.). Rock crystal, 900/1000. Egypt, Fatimid Dynasty. (Figure 2, p. 28)

The Art Institute of Chicago, Gift of Mrs. Chauncey McCormick, 1962.91 side 1. Photograph by Robert Hashimoto.

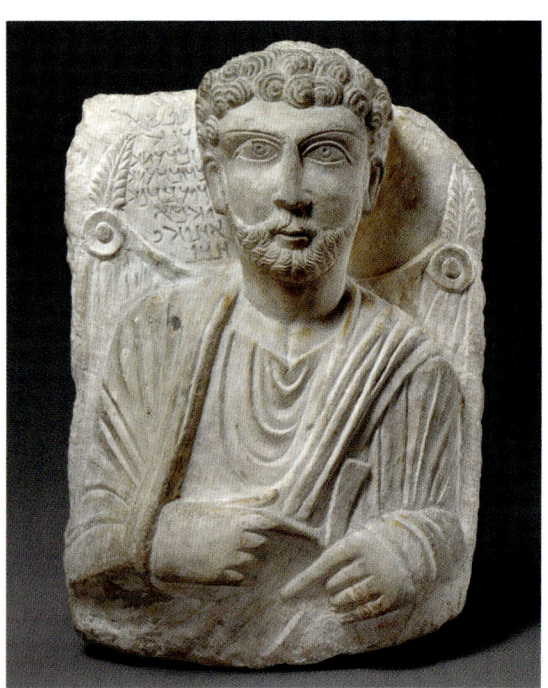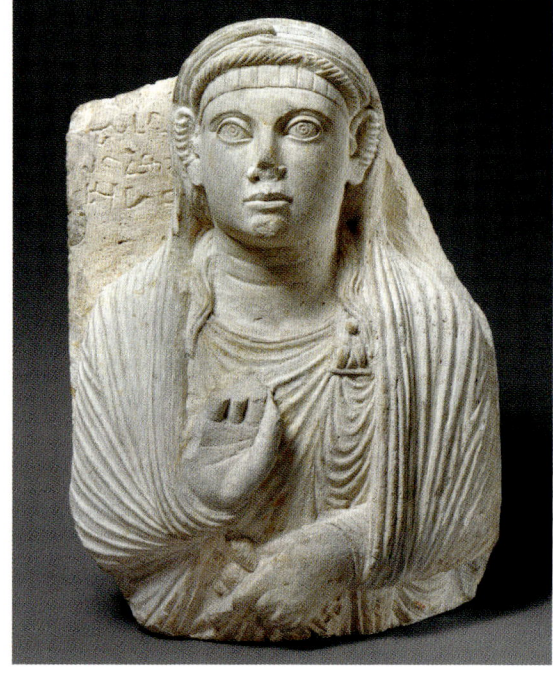

Plate 3. Left: Gravestone with Bust of a Man. Palmyra (Syria), 2nd century A.D. Limestone, H. 20 in. (50.8 cm). Right: Gravestone with Bust of a Woman. Palmyra (Syria), 2nd century A.D. Limestone, H. 20 in. (50.8 cm). (Figure 3, p. 29)

Both images from *The Year One, Art of the Ancient World East and West*, The Metropolitan Museum of Art, Yale University Press © 2000 by The Metropolitan Museum of Art.

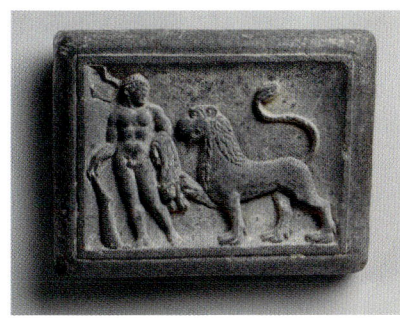
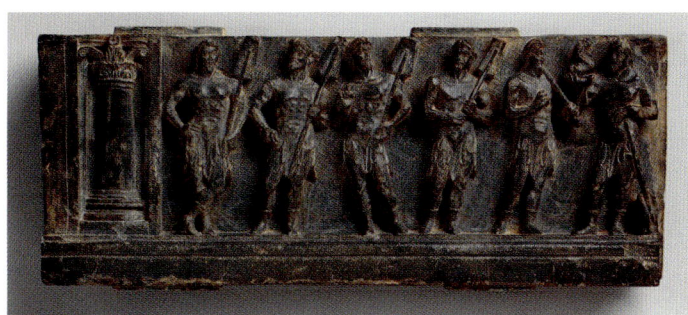

Plate 4. Left: Weight Depicting Herakles and the Memean Lion. Pakistan (ancient region of Gandharda), 1st century B.C. Schist, 10 ¼ × 13 ¾ in. (26 × 34.9 cm); Right: Stair Riser with Marine Deities. Pakistan (ancient region of Gandhara), 1st century A.D. Schist, 6 ⅝ × 17 in. (16.9 × 43.2 cm). (Figure 4, p. 30)

Both images from *The Year One, Art of the Ancient World East and West,* The Metropolitan Museum of Art, Yale University Press © 2000 by The Metropolitan Museum of Art.

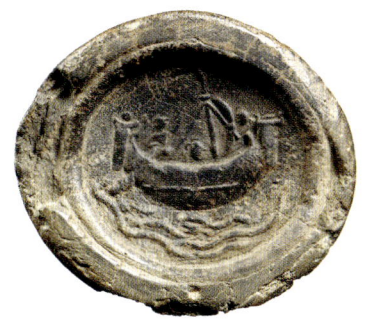

Plate 5. Impression from a Seal Depicting a Ship at Sea, 4th-5th century CE. India, probably Bengal or Andhra Pradesh. Clay. H. 1 ¾ in. (4.5 cm); W. 2 in. (5 cm). Lent by National Museum, Bangkok, Thailand (2309). (Figure 5, p. 30)

Art Resource, NY (ART586839) © The Metropolitan Museum of Art.

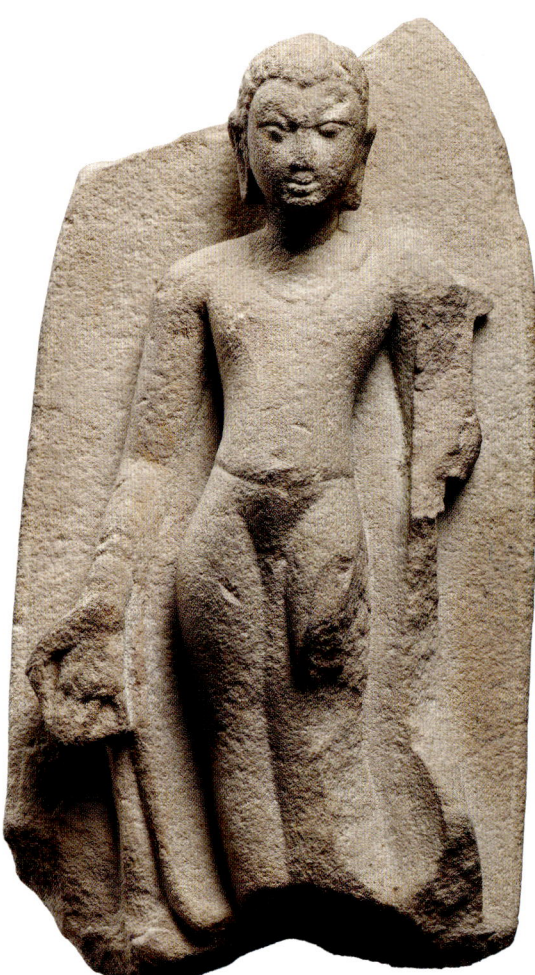

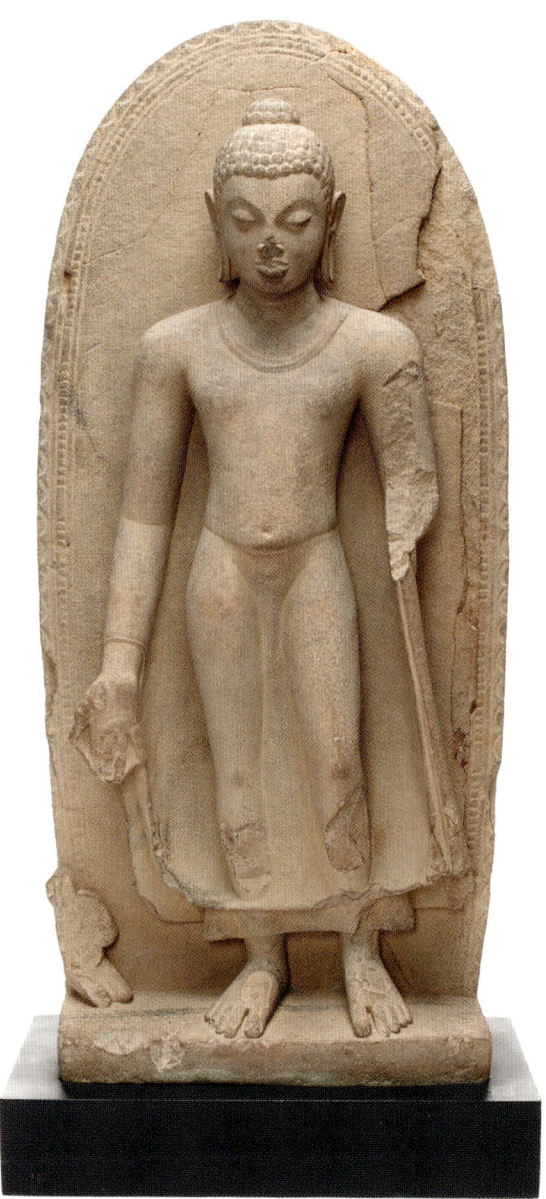

Plate 6. Buddha Granting Boons, first half of the 6th century CE. Northern India (Uttar Pradesh, Sarnath). Sandstone. H. 6 ½ in. (16.5 cm); W. 3 ¹⁵⁄₁₆ in. (10 cm); D. est. ¹³⁄₁₆ in. (2 cm); approx. Wt. 2.2. National Museum, Bangkok, Thailand. (Figure 6, p. 31)

Art Resource, NY (ART586838) © The Metropolitan Museum of Art.

Plate 7. Buddha Śākyamuni Granting Boons, Sarnath region, Uttar Pradesh, northern India, c. 475, Sandstone. H. 34 ⅛ in. (86.7 cm), w. 17 ⅝ in. (44.8 cm), Asia Society, New York, Mr. and Mrs. John D. Rockefeller 3rd Collection (1975.5). (Figure 7, p. 31)

From *Lost Kingdoms Hindu-Buddhist Sculpture of Early Southeast Asia,* The Metropolitan Museum of Art, Yale University Press, © 2014 by The Metropolitan Museum of Art.

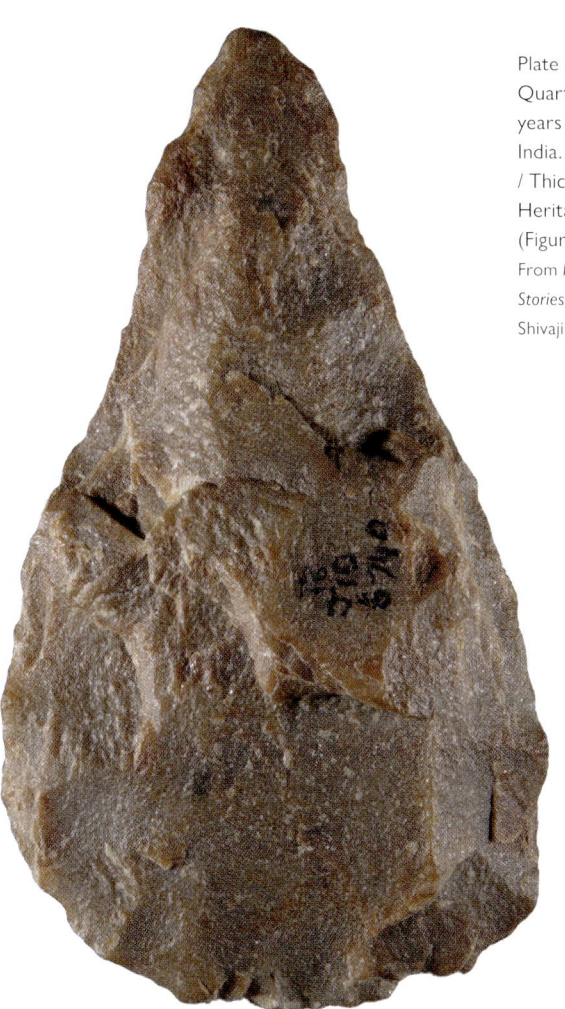

Plate 8. Lower Palaeolithic Hand-Axe, Quartzite, 1,700,000 – 1,070,000 years old, Attirampakkam, Tamil Nadu, India. Height: 13.5 cm / Width 7.6 cm / Thickness: 4 cm. Sharma Centre for Heritage Education, Chennai (T8 6740). (Figure 8, p. 32)

From *India and the World, A History in Nine Stories*, Penguin Books, © CSMVS (Chhatrapati Shivaji Maharaj Vastu Sangrahalaya, Mumbai).

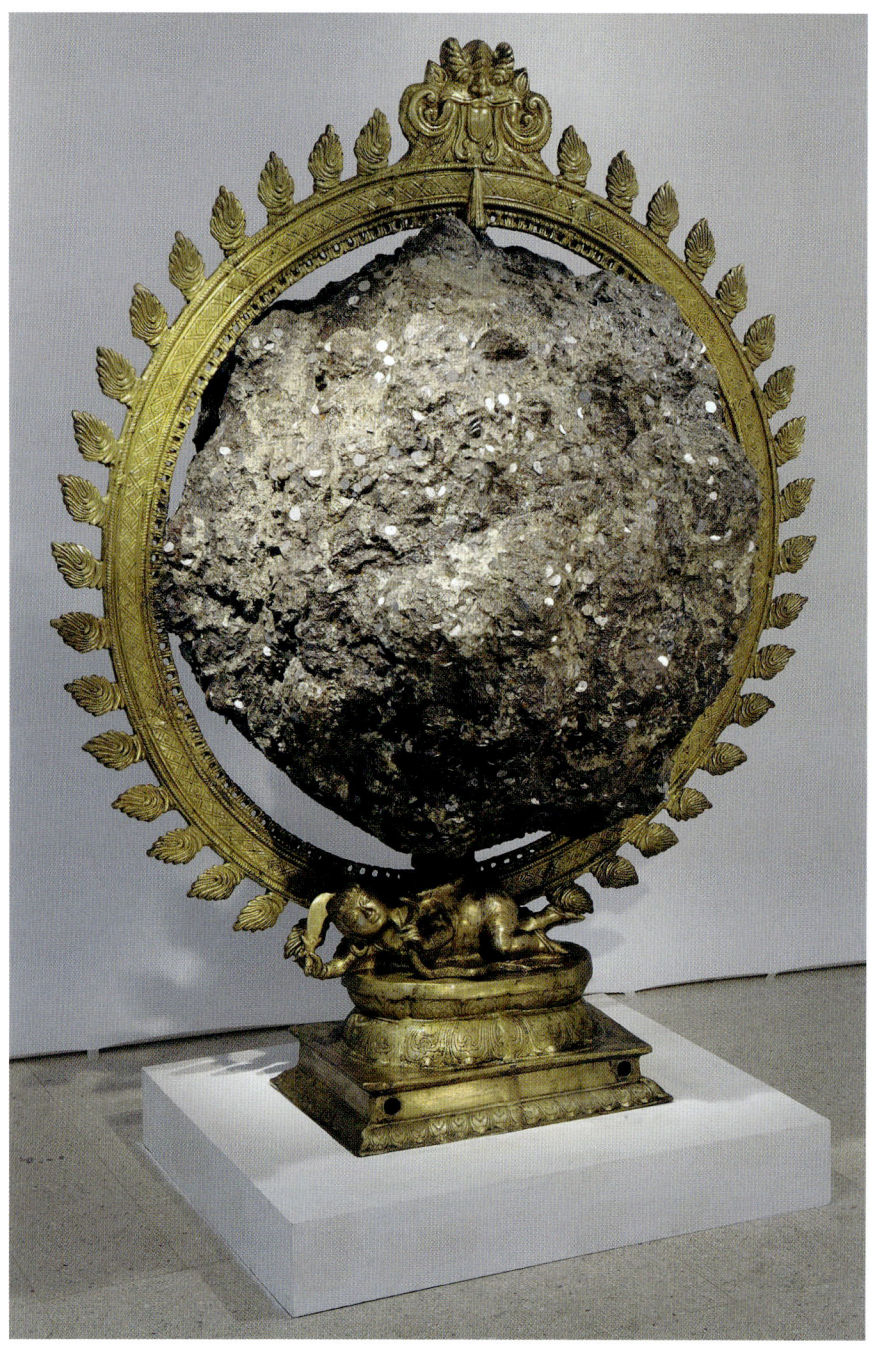

Plate 9. 'Unicode', by L.N. Tallur, AD 2011, Tallur Studio, Koteshwara, Karnataka, India, Bronze, coins and concrete. Height: 183 cm/ Width: 152 cm/ Depth: 117 cm. Kiran Nadar Museum of Art (33SCLNT001). (Figure 9, p. 33)

From *India and the World, A History in Nine Stories*, Penguin Books, © CSMVS (Chhatrapati Shivaji Maharaj Vastu Sangrahalaya, Mumbai).

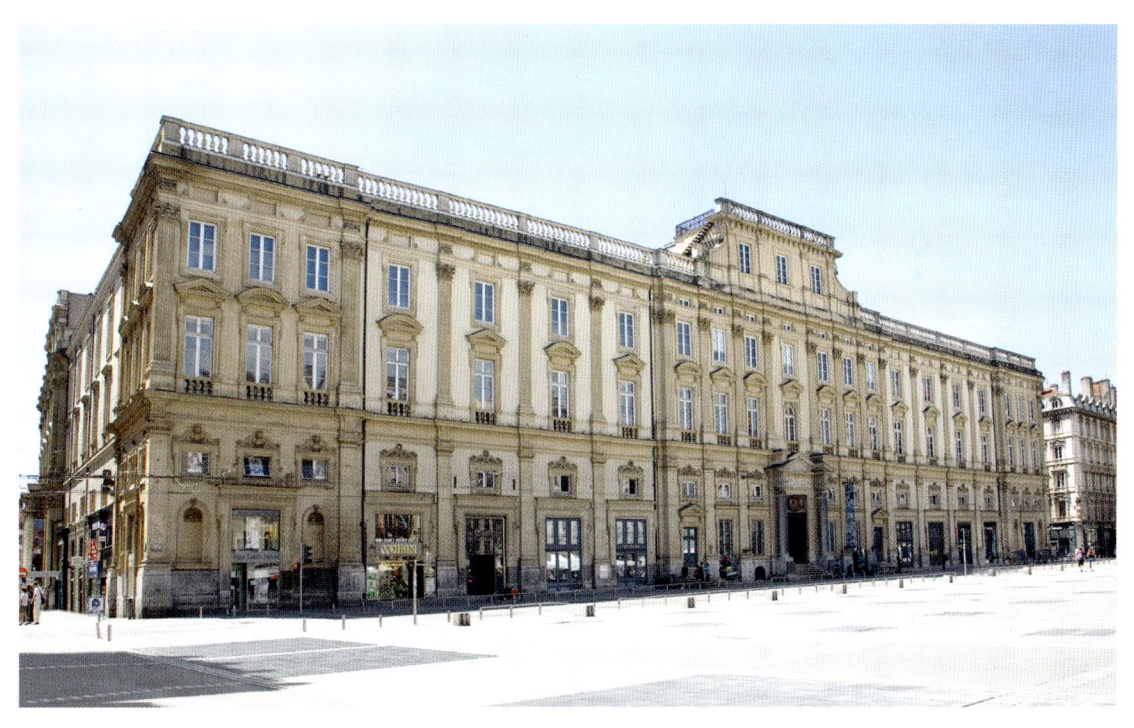

Plate 10. Lyon, view of the Musée des Beaux-Arts,
Place des Terreaux. (Figure 1, p. 108)
© Corentin Mossiere.

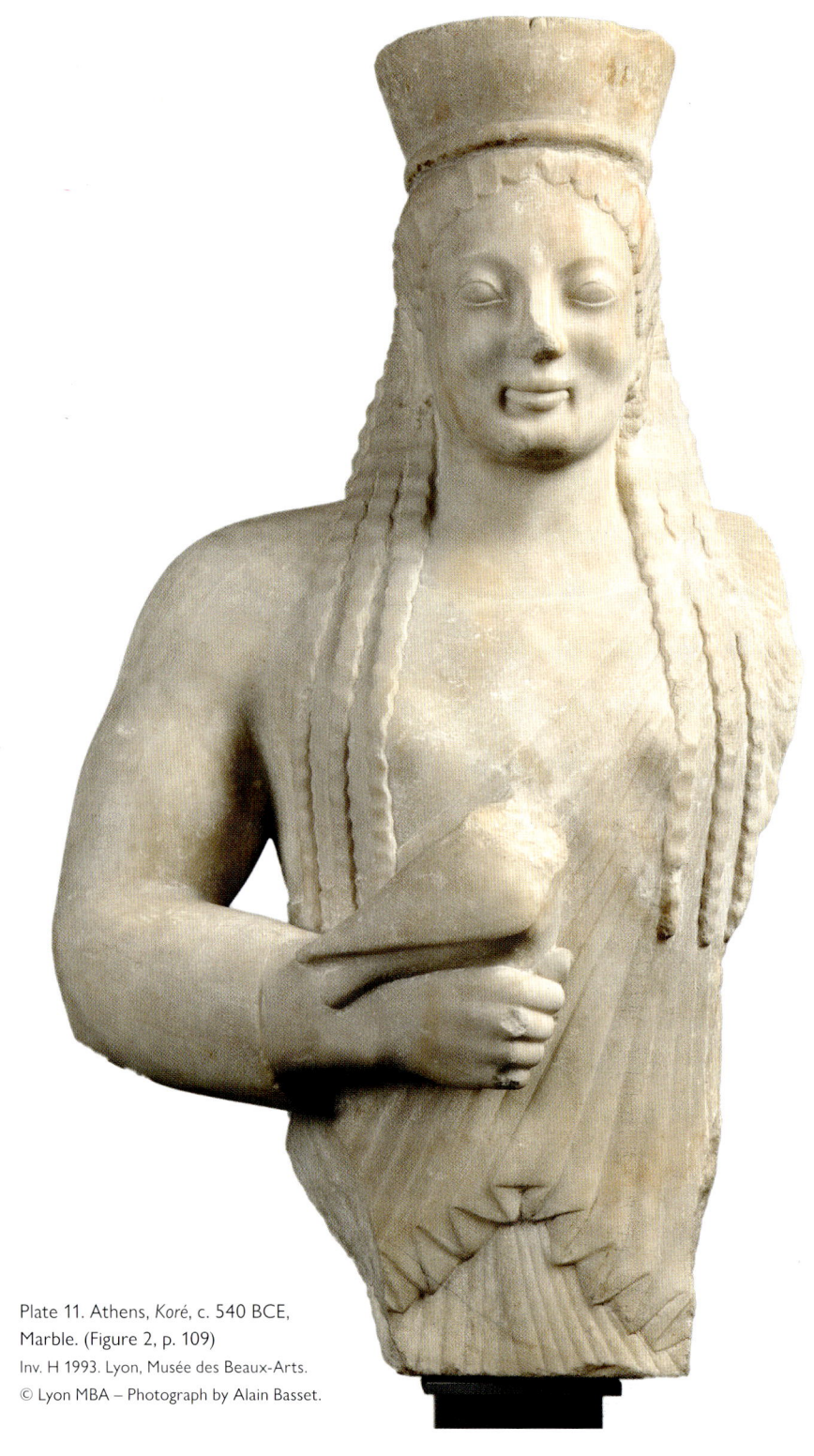

Plate 11. Athens, *Koré*, c. 540 BCE,
Marble. (Figure 2, p. 109)
Inv. H 1993. Lyon, Musée des Beaux-Arts.
© Lyon MBA – Photograph by Alain Basset.

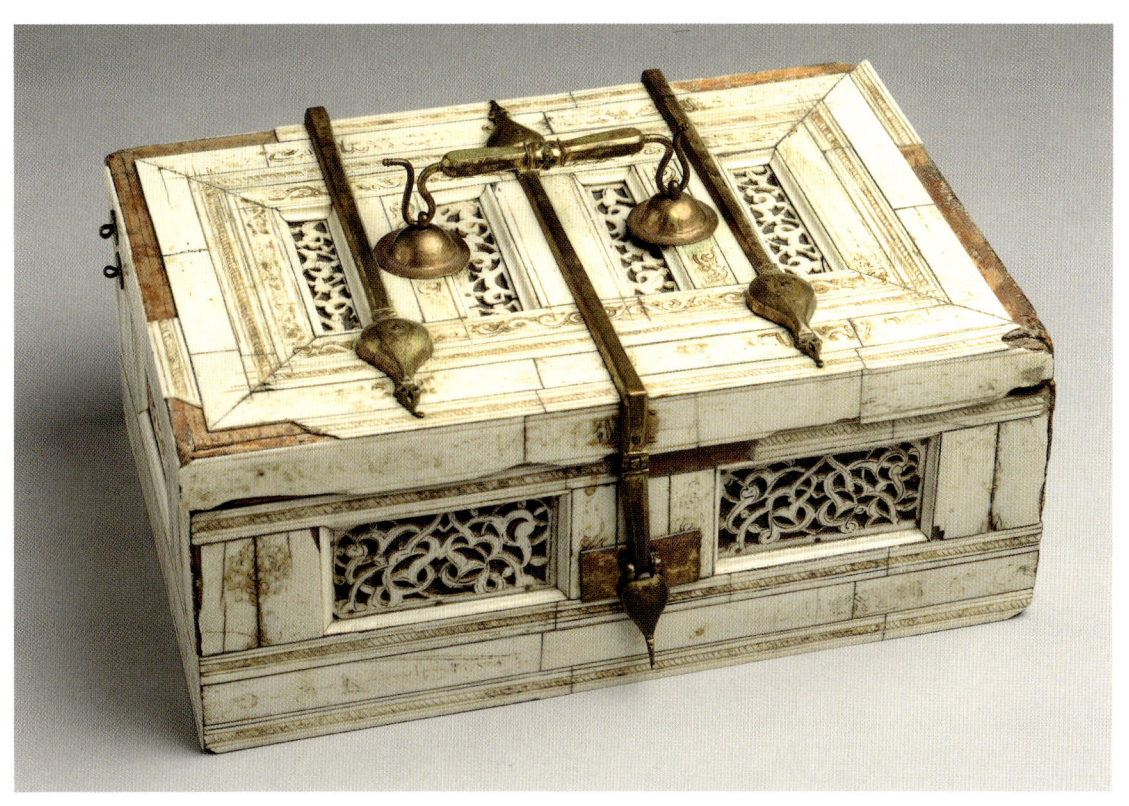

Plate 12. Islamic Art, Grenada, Casket,
14th century. Cedar wood from the Atlas,
sculpted bone, engraved and painted.
(Figure 3, p. 109)
Inv. D 378. Lyon, Musée des Beaux-Arts. © Lyon
MBA – Photograph by Alain Basset.

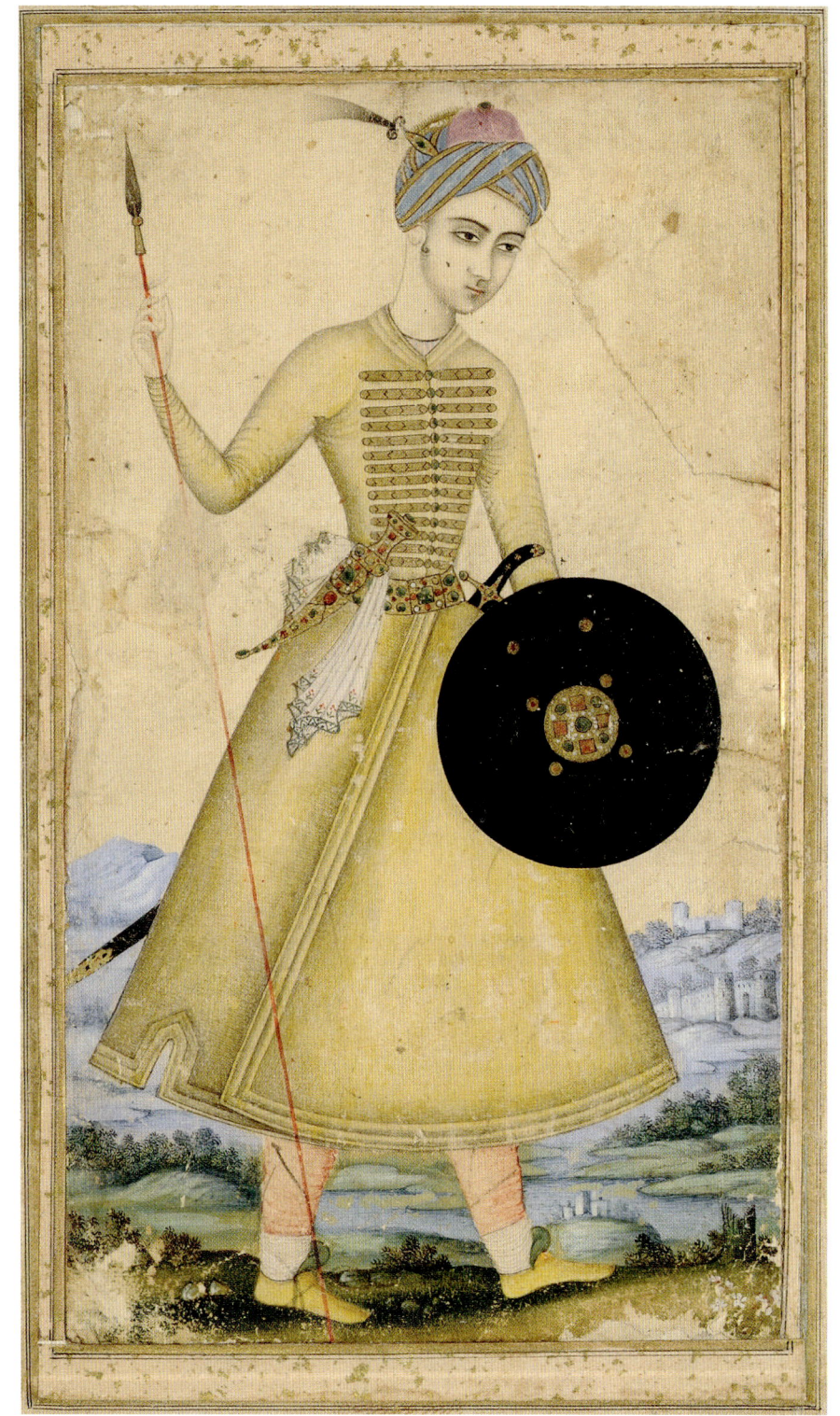

Plate 13. Ispahan, Ali Qoli (styled after), *An Indian Prince armed with a spear and shield*, c. 1660. Ink, gouache and watercolour on paper. (Figure 4, p. 110) Inv. E 585-a. Lyon, Musée des Beaux-Arts. © Lyon MBA – Photograph by Alain Basset.

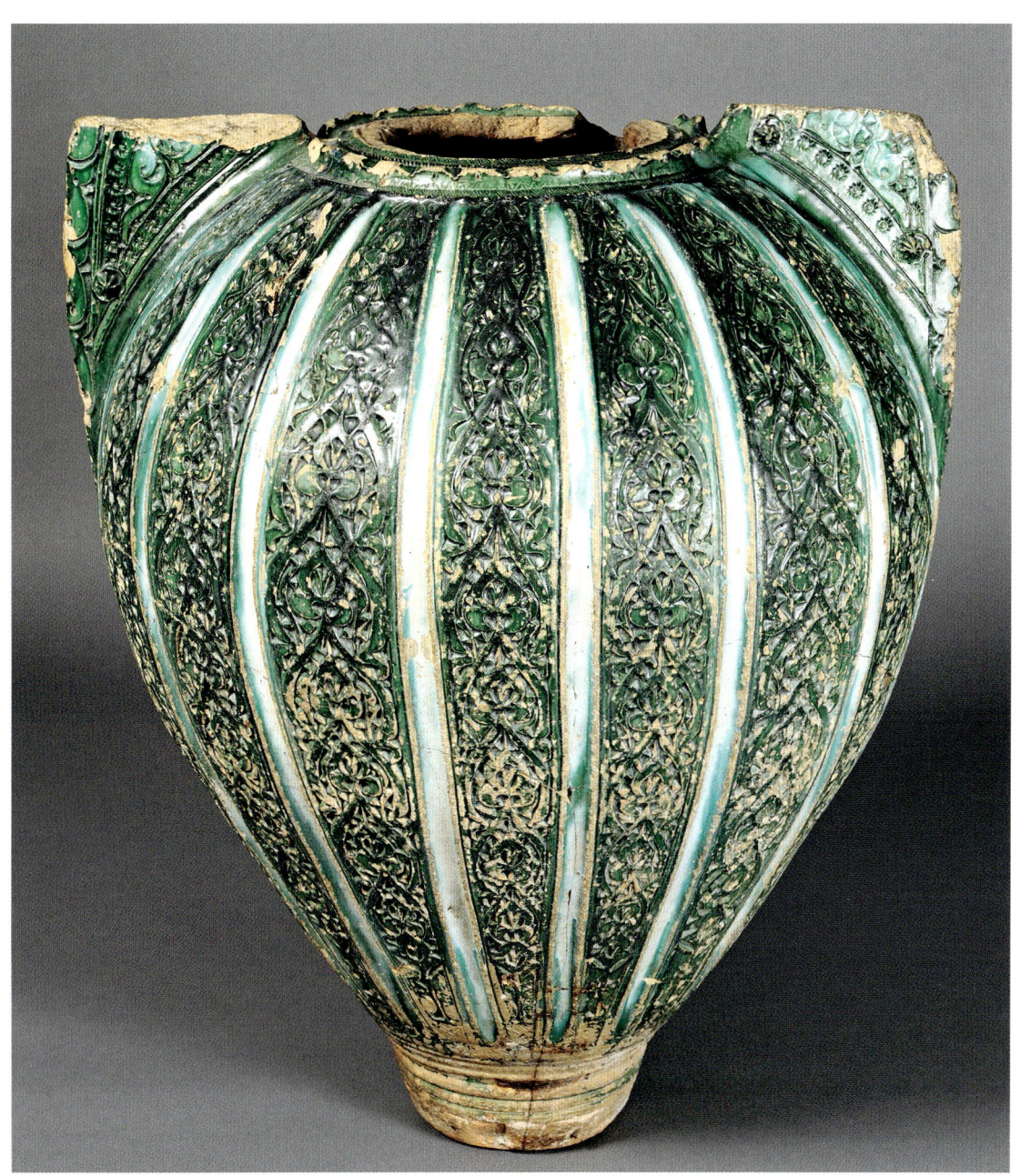

Plate 14. Islamic Art, Andalousia, Body of a
jar, 14th – 15th century. Ceramic with green
moulded glaze. (Figure 5, p. 110)
Inv. D 557. Lyon, Musée des Beaux-Arts.
© Lyon MBA – Photograph by Alain Basset.

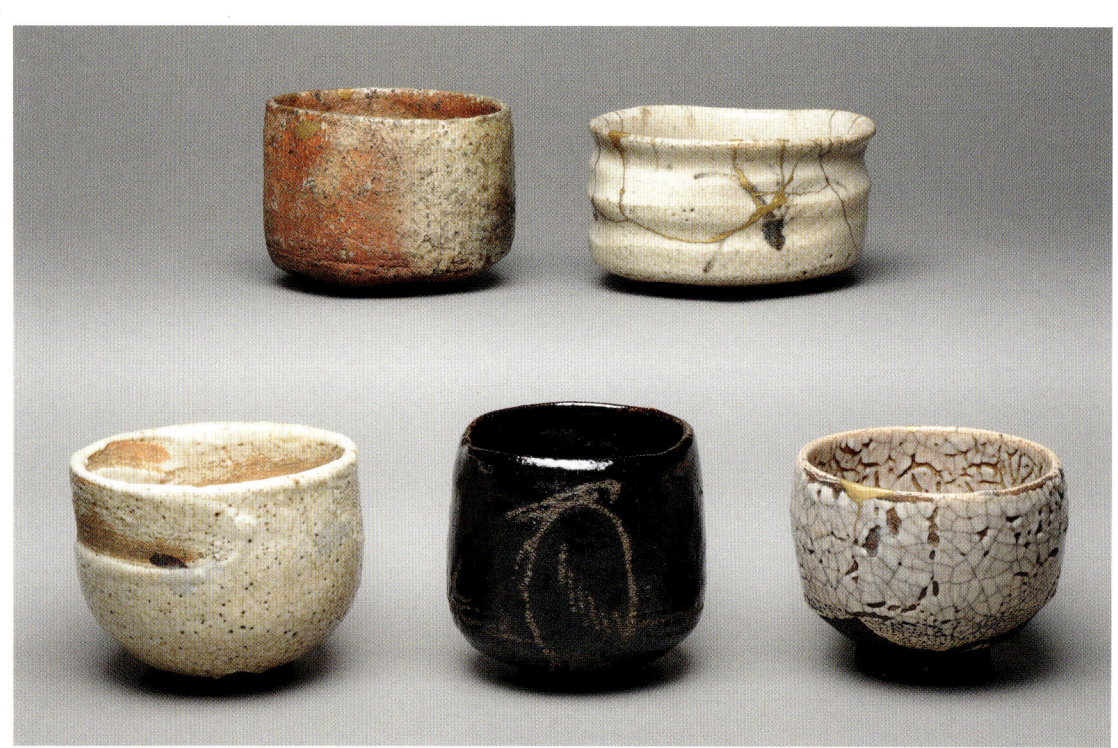

Plate 15. Japan, Bowls, 16th-18th century.
Stoneware. Collection Raphaël Collin.
(Figure 6, p. 111)
Inv. E 554-175, Inv. E 554-152, Inv. E 554-151,
Inv. E 554-438, Inv. E 554-345. Lyon, Musée des
Beaux-Arts. © Lyon MBA – Photograph by Alain
Basset.

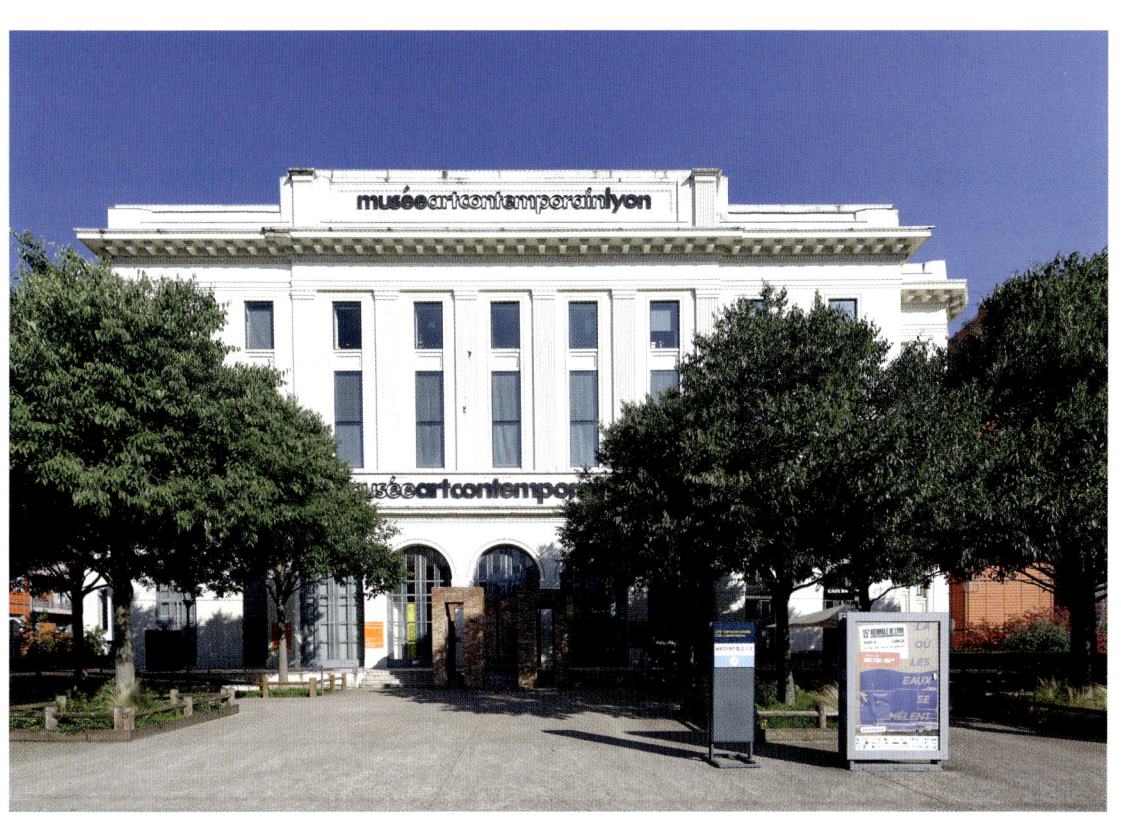

Plate 16. View of macLyon. (Figure 7, p. 112)

Photograph by Blaise Adilon.

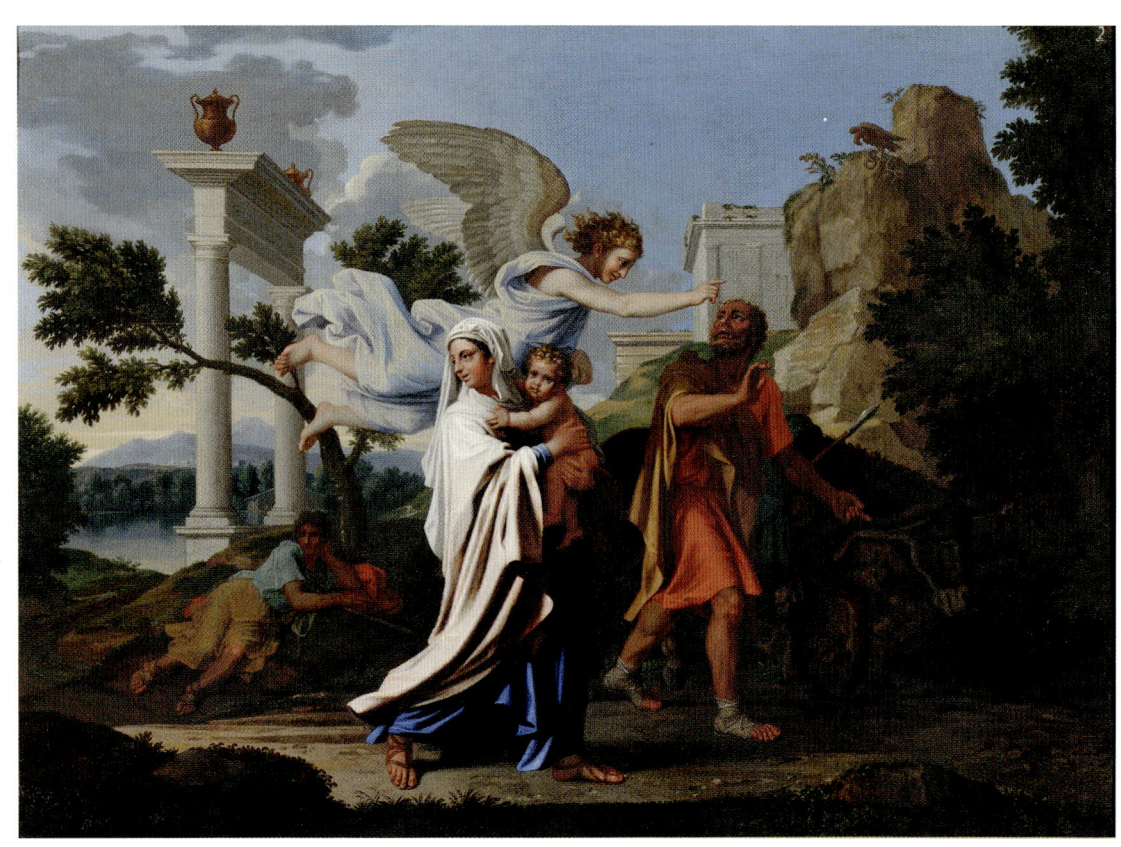

Plate 17. Nicolas Poussin, *Flight into Egypt*,
1657. Oil on canvas. (Figure 8, p. 113)
Inv. 2004.5.1. Lyon, Musée des Beaux-Arts. © Lyon
MBA – Photograph by Alain Basset.

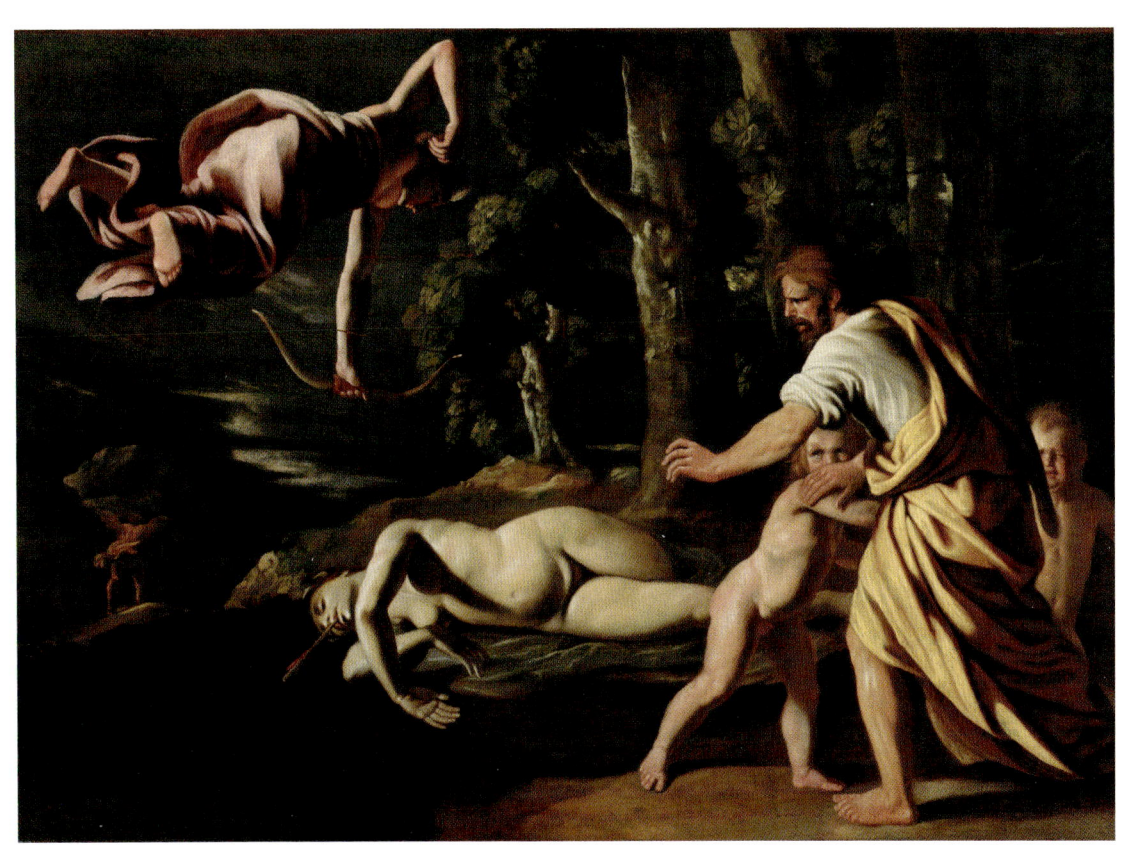

Plate 18. Nicolas Poussin, *Death of Chione*,
1619-1622. Oil on canvas. (Figure 9, p. 113)
Inv. 2016.1. Lyon, Musée des Beaux-Arts. © Lyon
MBA – Photograph by Alain Basset.

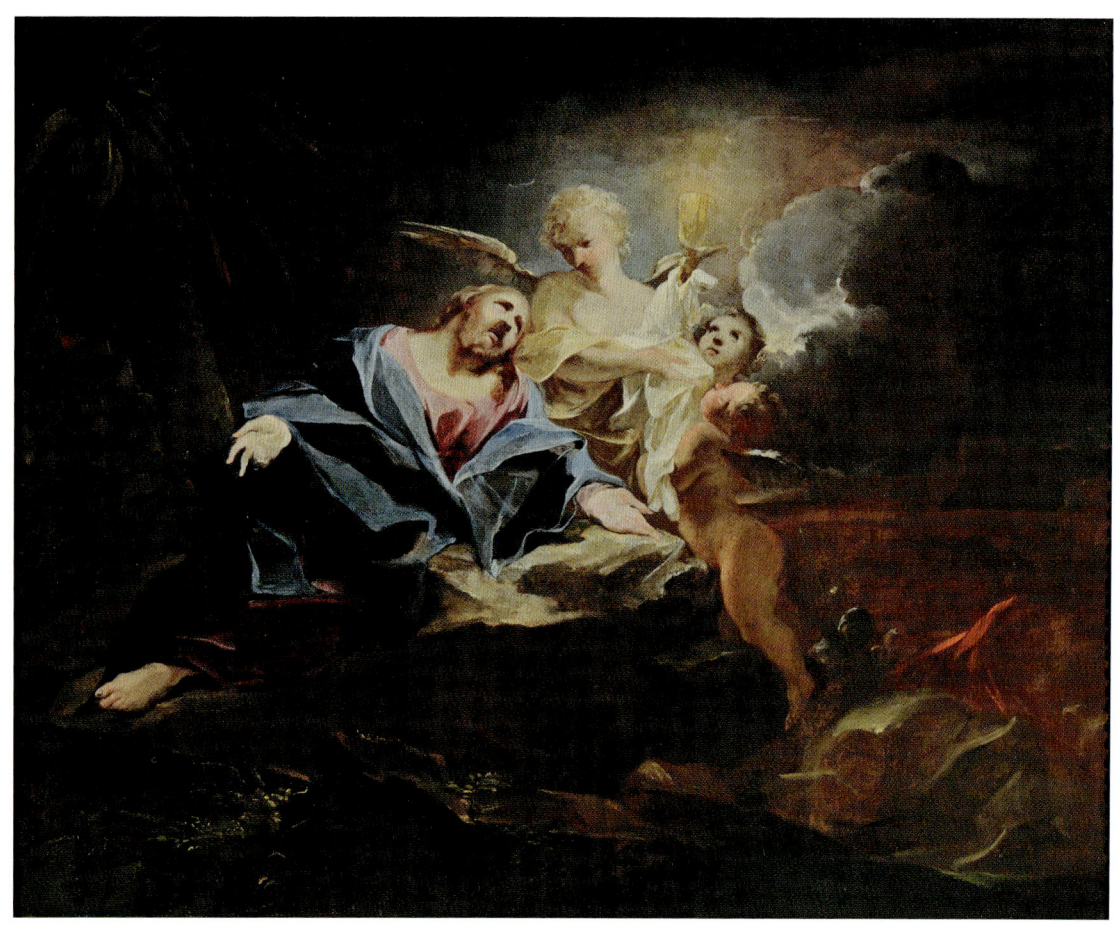

Plate 19. Louis Cretey, *Jesus in the Garden of Olives*, c. 1683. Oil on canvas. (Figure 10, p. 114)

Inv. 1976-1. Lyon, Musée des Beaux-Arts. © Lyon MBA – Photograph by Alain Basset.

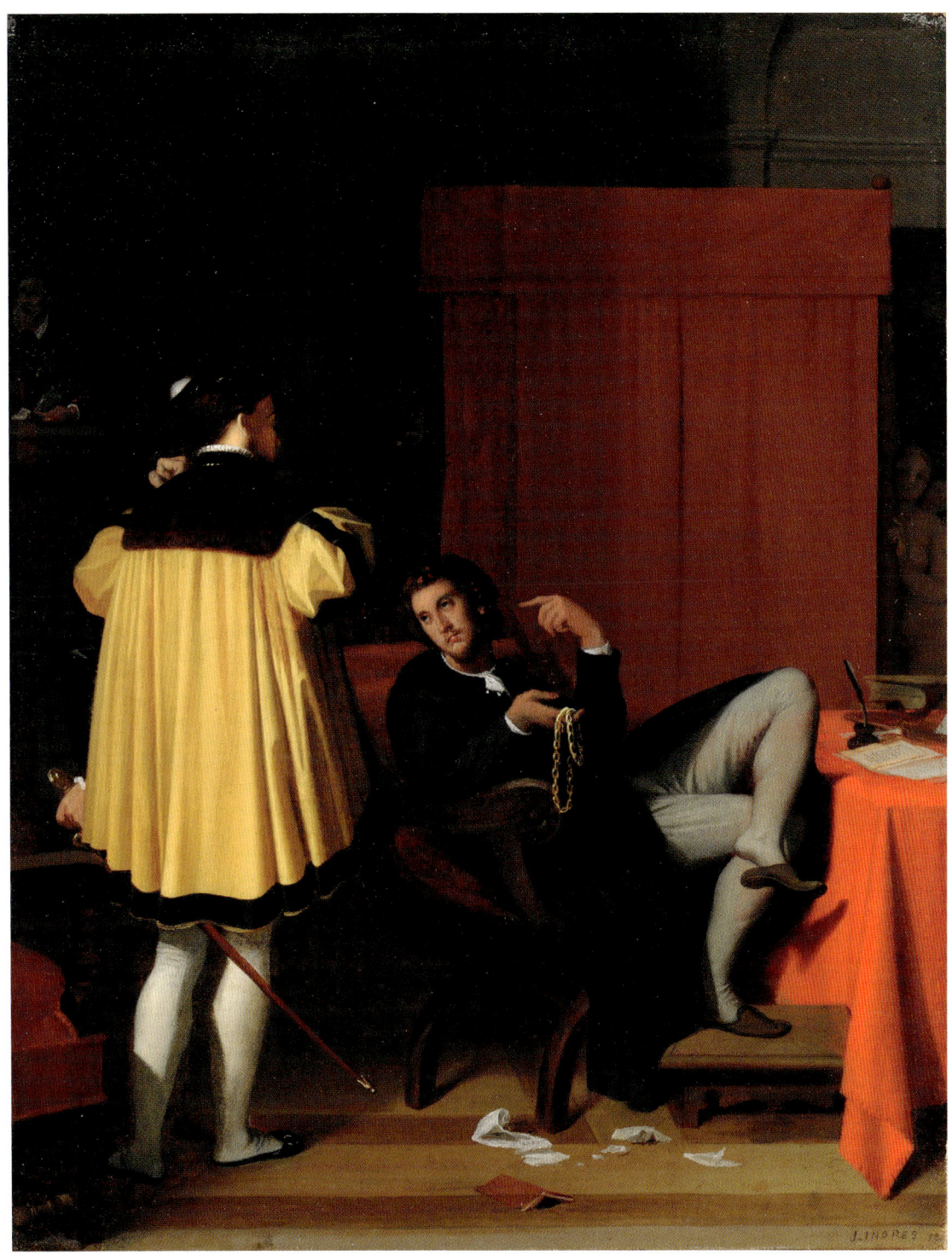

Plate 20. Jean-Auguste-Dominique Ingres, *Aretin and the Envoy of Charles V*, 1848. Oil on canvas. (Figure 11, p. 115)
Inv. 2013.1.1. Lyon, Musée des Beaux-Arts. © Lyon MBA – Photograph by Alain Basset.

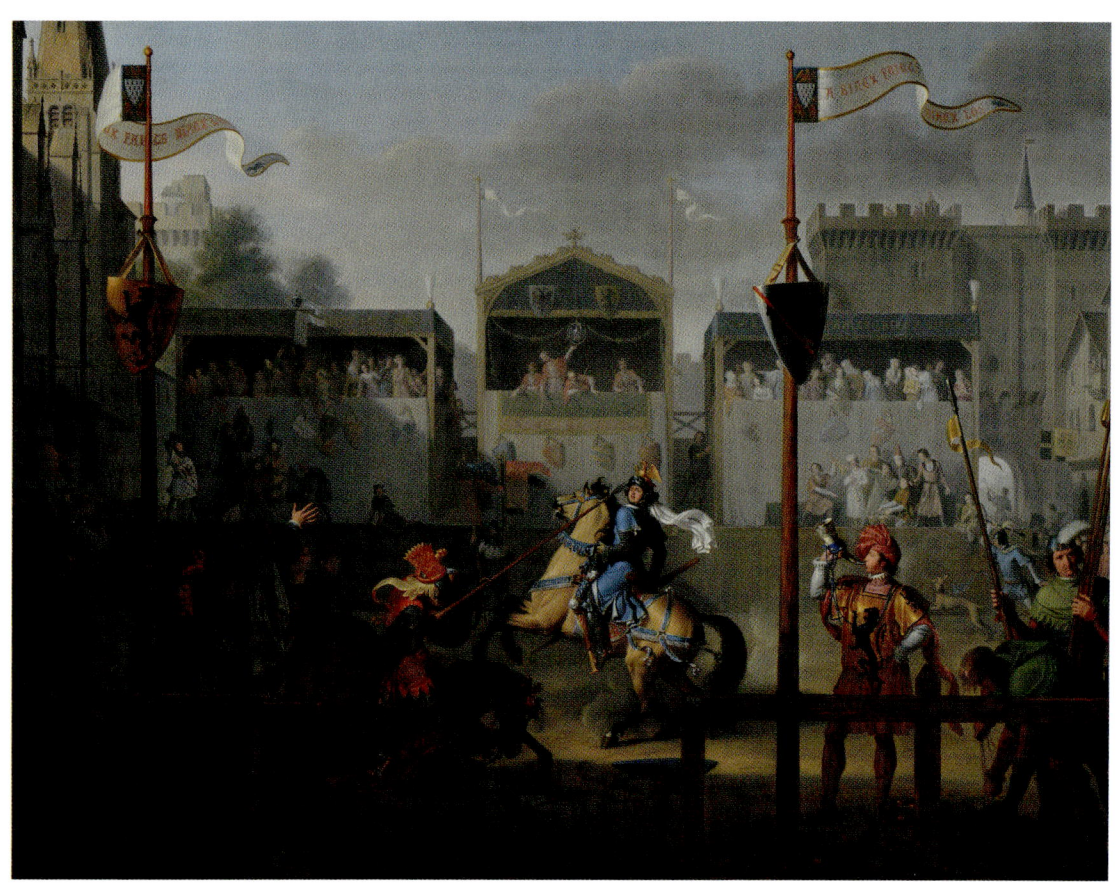

Plate 21. Pierre Révoil, *A Tournament*, 1812.
Oil on canvas. (Figure 12, p. 115)
Inv. A 164. Lyon, Musée des Beaux-Arts. © Lyon
MBA – Photograph by Alain Basset.

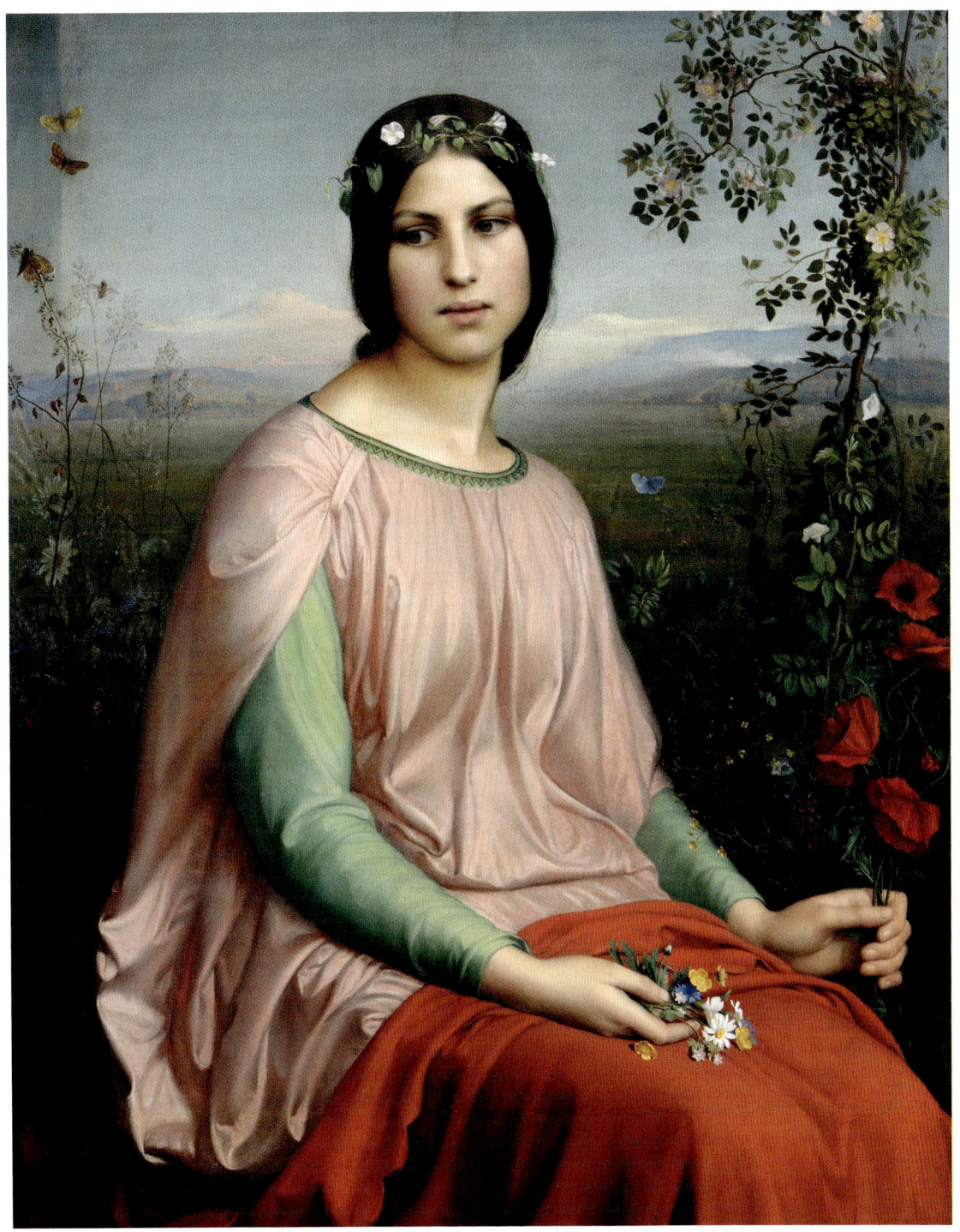

Plate 22. Louis Janmot, *Flower of the Fields*,. 1845. (Figure 13, p. 116)

Inv. B 502. Lyon, Musée des Beaux-Arts. Image © Lyon MBA – Photograph by Alain Basset.

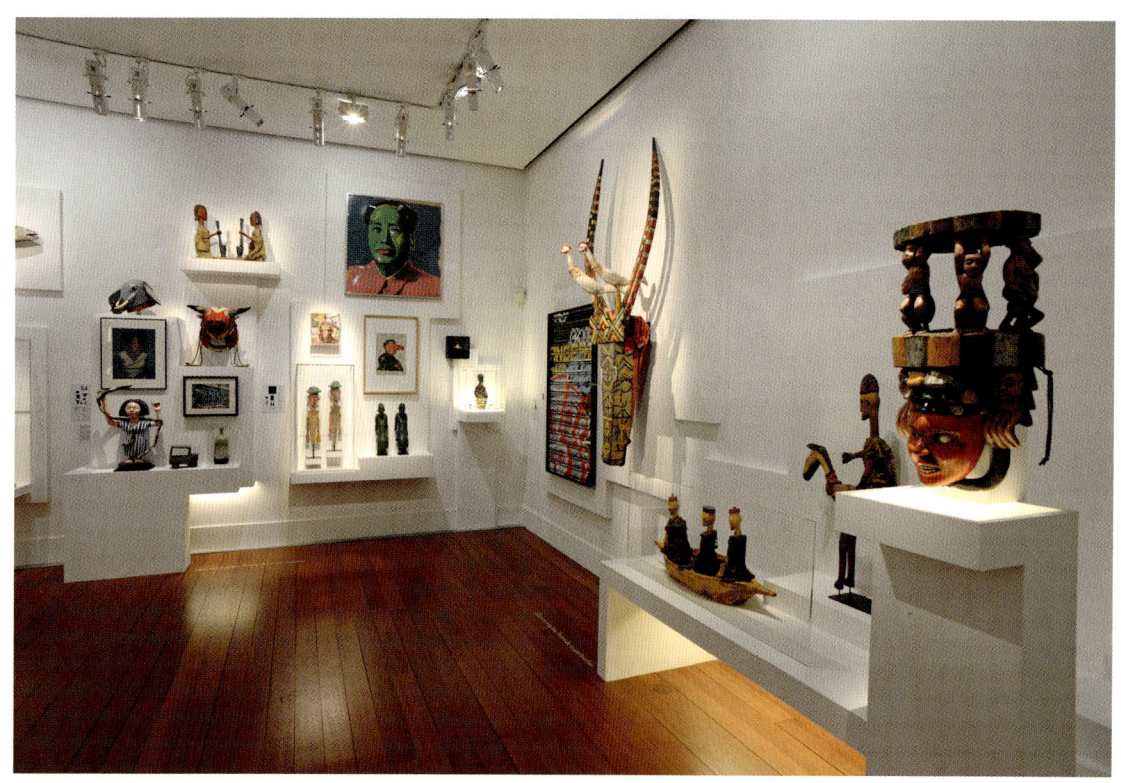

Plate 23. View of the exhibition *Métissages*
at the Musée des Beaux-Arts de Lyon, 2013.
(Figure 14, p. 119)
© Lyon MBA – Photograph by Alain Basset.

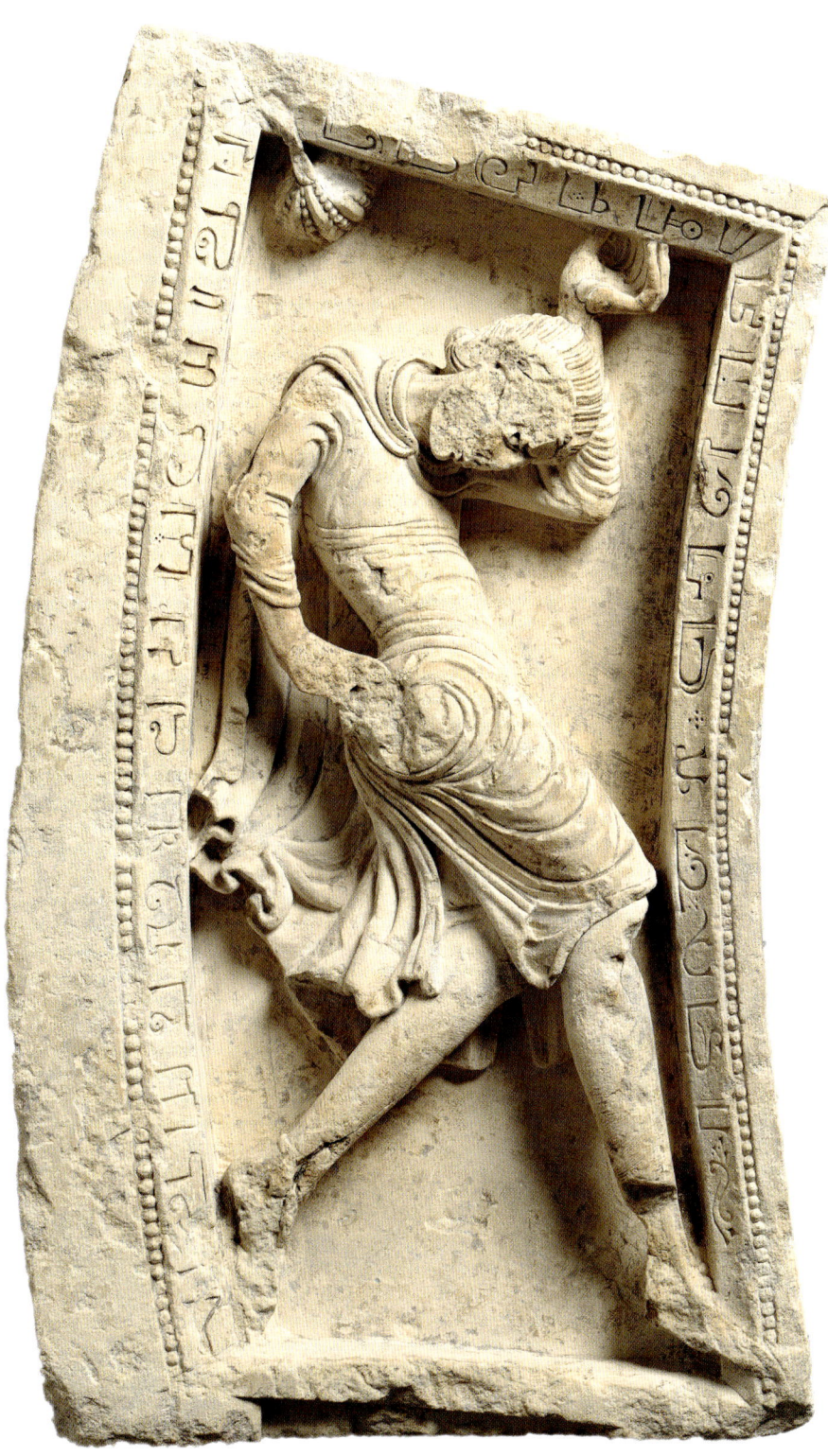

Plate 24. Unknown,
Juggler, France,
Last quarter of
the 12th century.
(Figure 15, p. 120)
Inv. D. 140. Lyon, Musée des
Beaux-Arts. © Lyon MBA –
Photograph by Alain Basset.

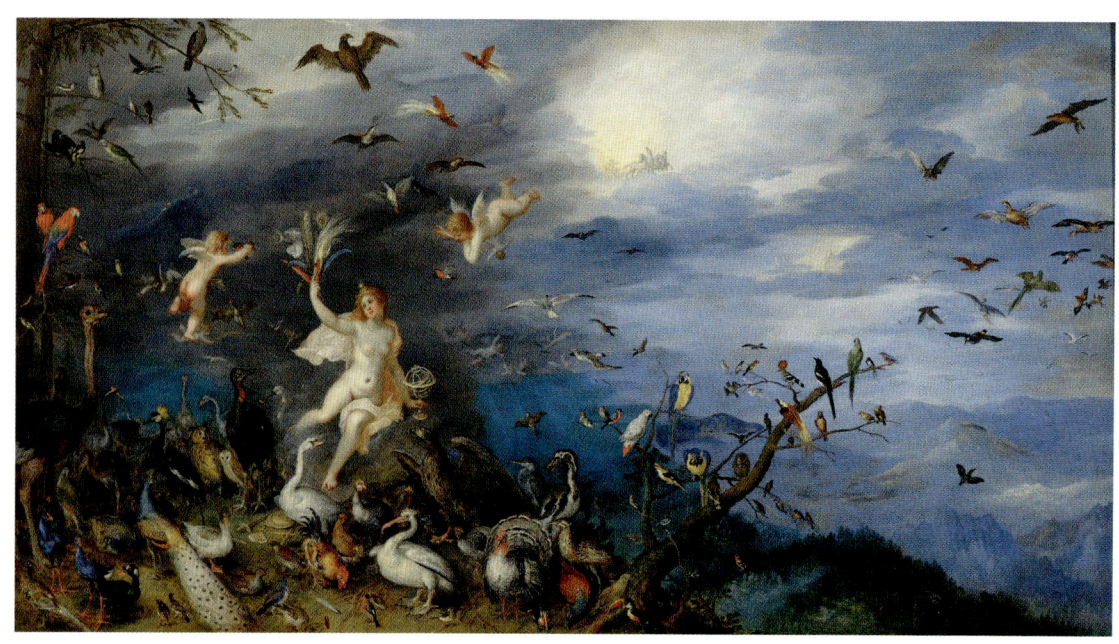

Plate 25. Jan Brueghel the Elder, *Air*, 16th-17th century.
Oil on wood. (Figure 16, p. 120)
Lyon, Musée des Beaux-Arts. © Lyon MBA –
Photograph by Alain Basset.

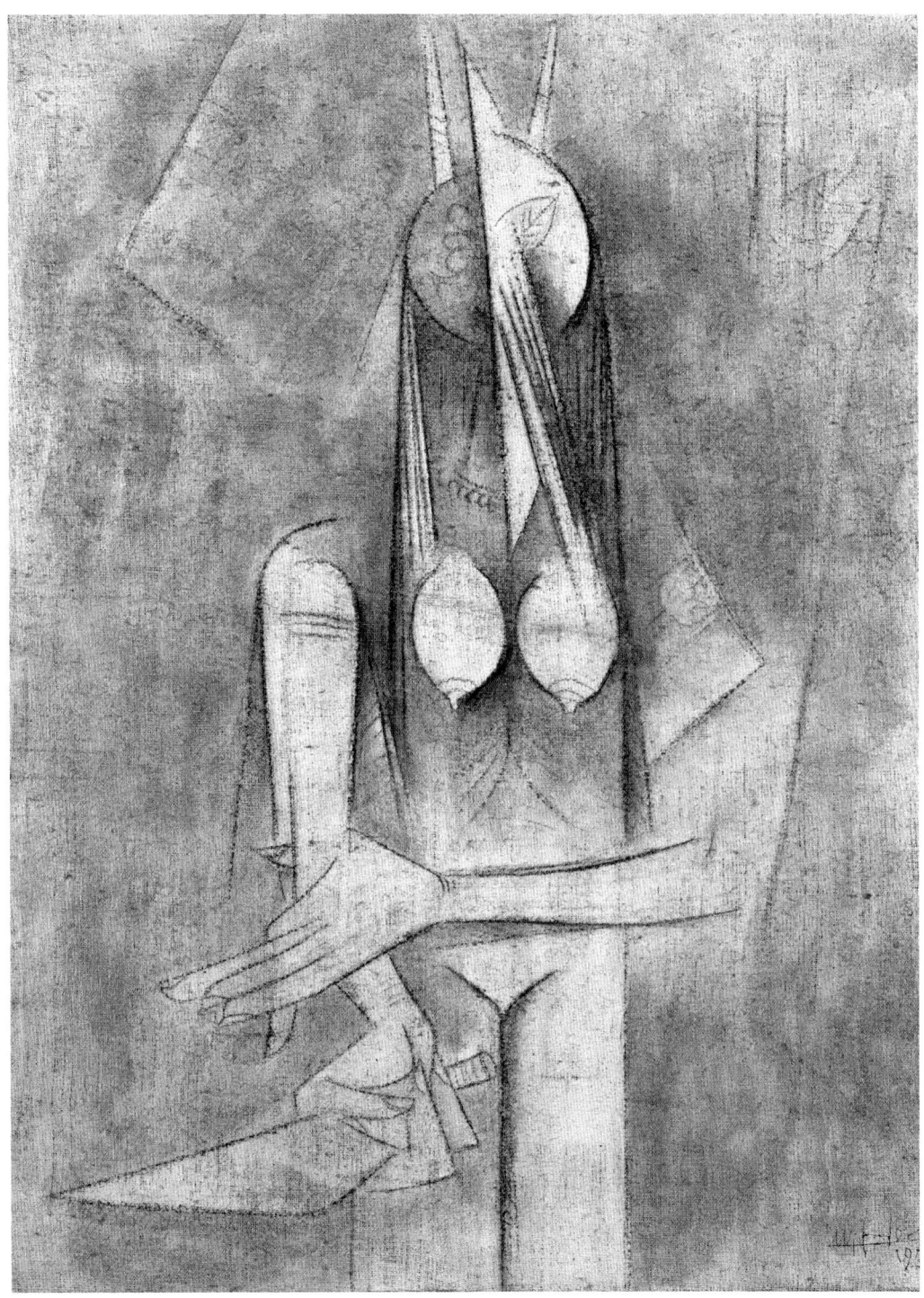

Plate 26. Wifredo Lam, *Woman with a Knife*, 1950. Oil on canvas. (Figure 17, p. 121)
Inv. 1997-37. Lyon, Musée des Beaux-Arts. © Lyon MBA – Photograph by RMN / Ojéda – Le Mage; © Adagp, Paris, 2019.

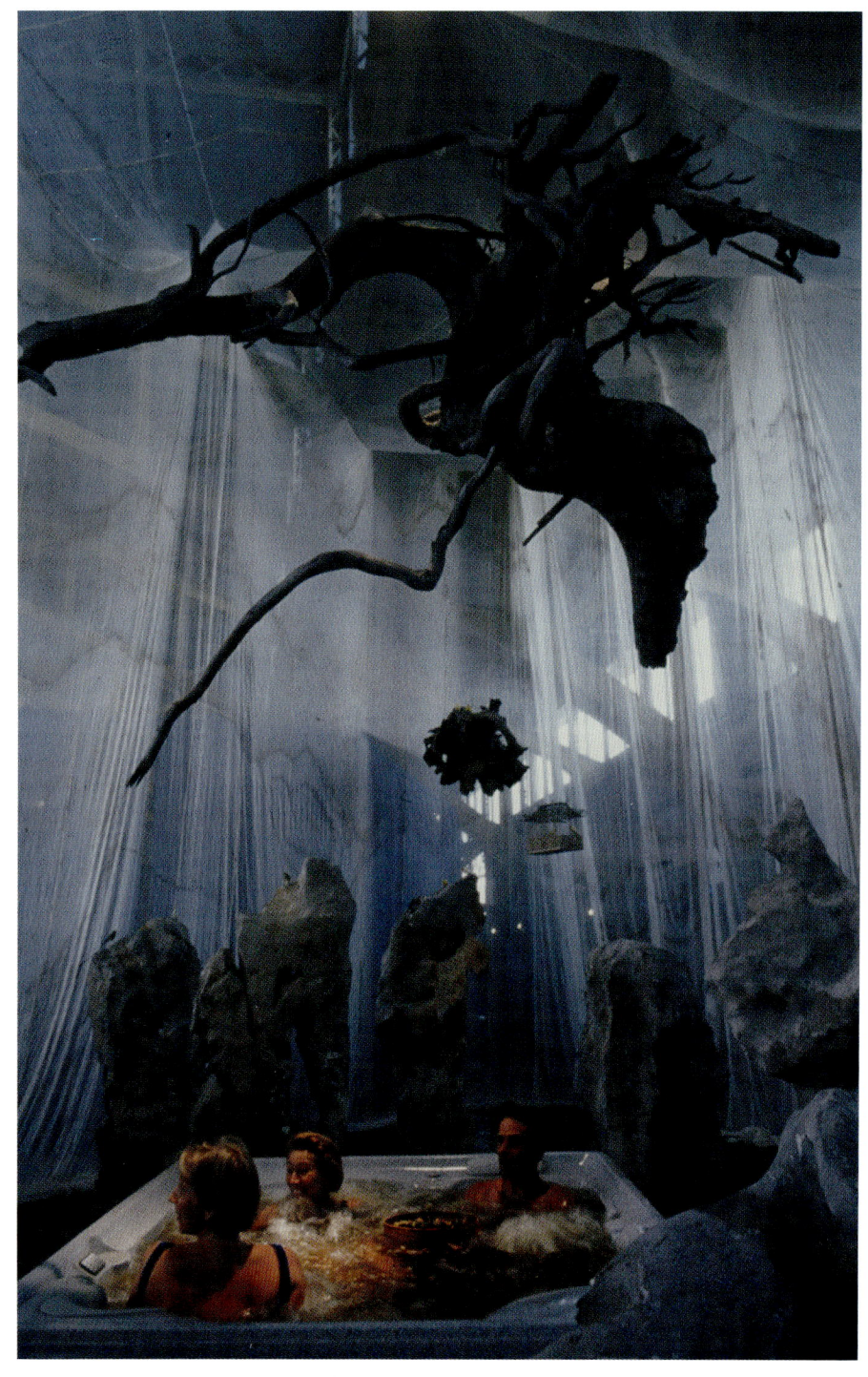

Plate 27. Cai Guo Qiang, *Cultural Melting Bath: Projects for the 20th Century, 1997*. View of the Lyon Contemporary Art Biennial, 2000. (Figure 18, p. 121)
©Cai Studio – Photograph by Blaise Adilon.

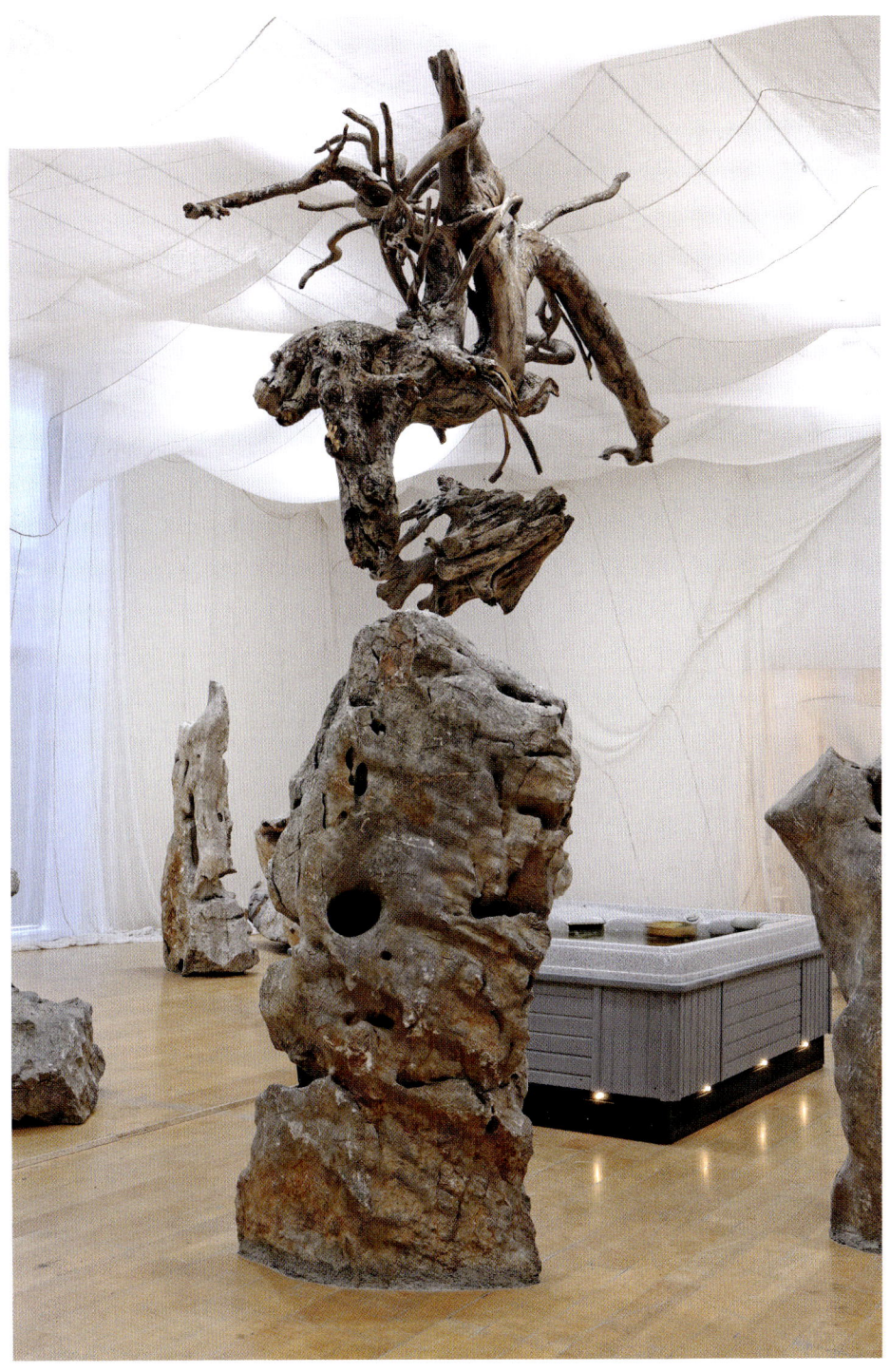

Plate 28. Cai Guo Qiang, *Cultural Melting Bath: Projects for the 20th Century, 1997.* View of the exhibition in 2016 in maclyon. (Figure 19, p. 122)

©Cai Studio – Photograph by Blaise Adilon.

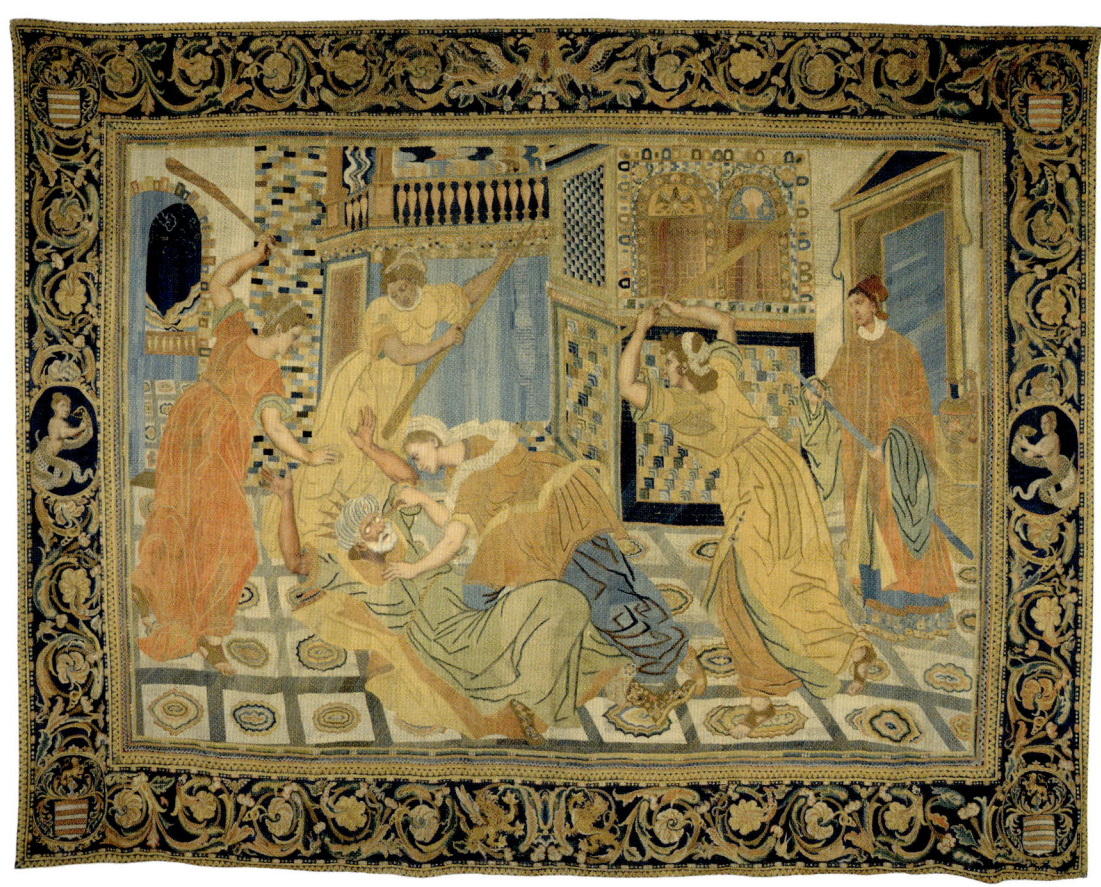

Plate 29. *The Vengence of Hecube*, Macao, 17th century.
Silk embroidery, gold thread and painted satin.
(Figure 20, p. 123)
Inv. 1970-537. Lyon, Musée des Beaux-Arts. © Lyon MBA –
Photograph by Alain Basset.

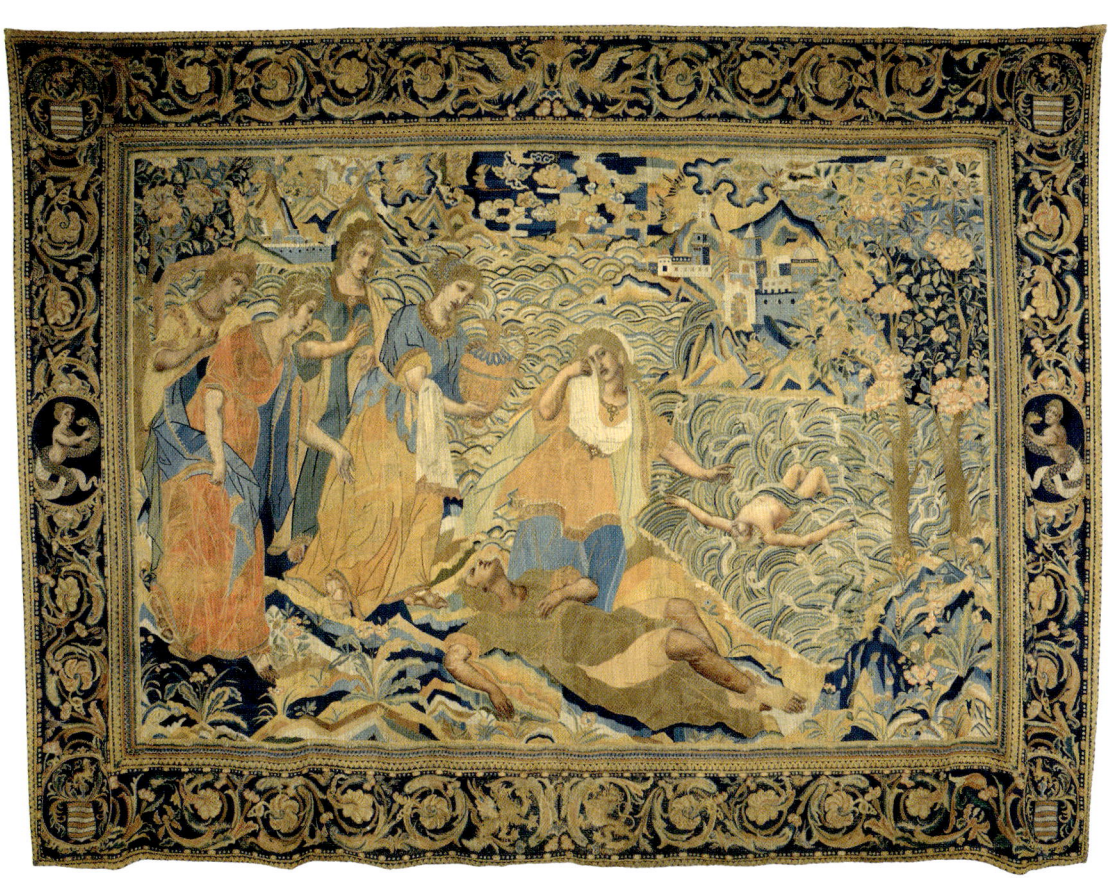

Plate 30. *The Death of Polydoros*, Macao, 17th century.
Silk embroidery, gold thread and painted satin.
(Figure 21, p. 123)
Inv. 1970-538. Lyon, Musée des Beaux-Arts. © Lyon MBA –
Photograph by Alain Basset.

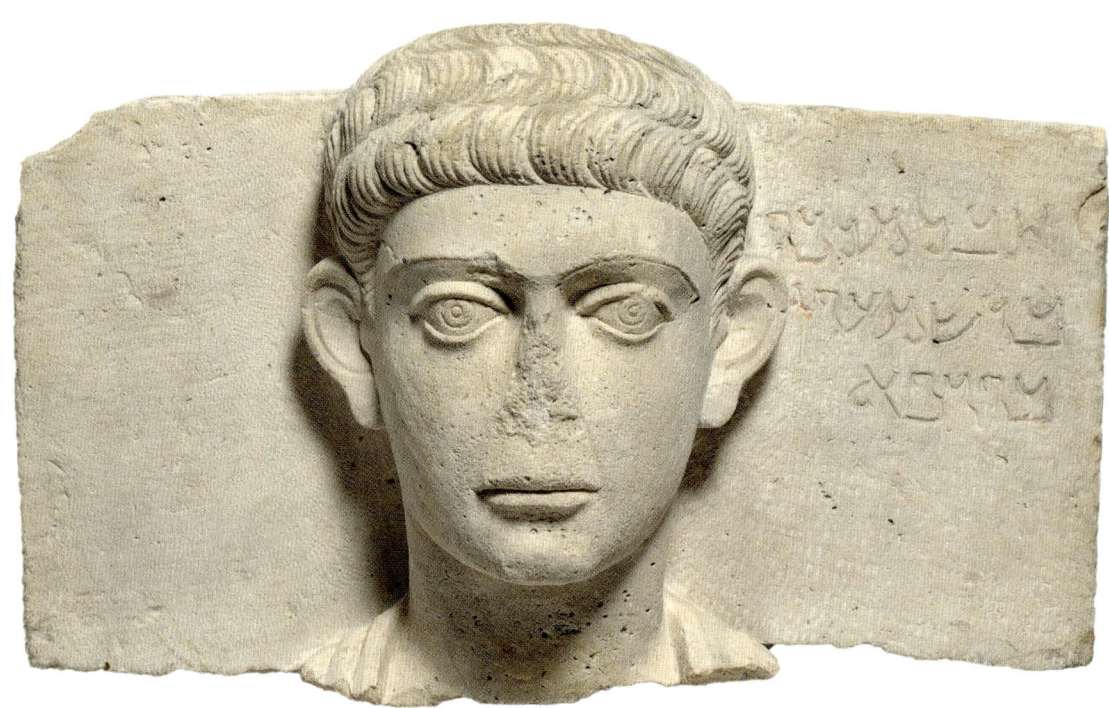

Plate 31. Bas-relief of Maliku, Palmyre, Roman period,
2nd century. Limestone. (Figure 22, p. 124)
Inv. 2011.11.2. Lyon, Musée des Beaux-Arts. © Lyon MBA –
Photograph by Alain Basset.

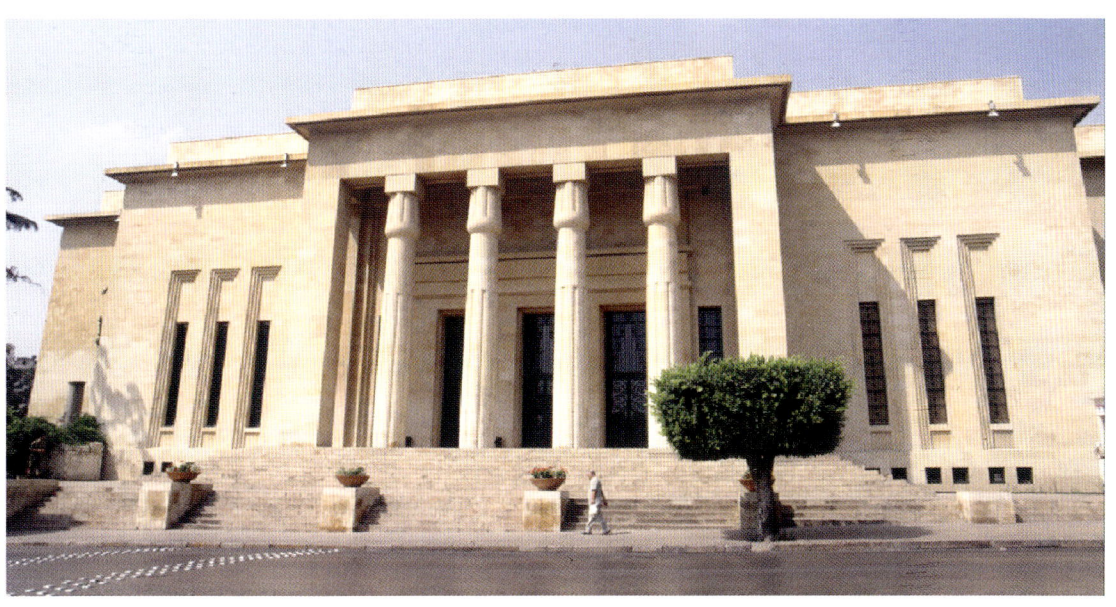

Plate 32. The National Museum of Beirut.
(Figure 1, p. 144)
©Ministry of Culture/Directorate General of
Antiquities of Lebanon/National Museum of Beirut.

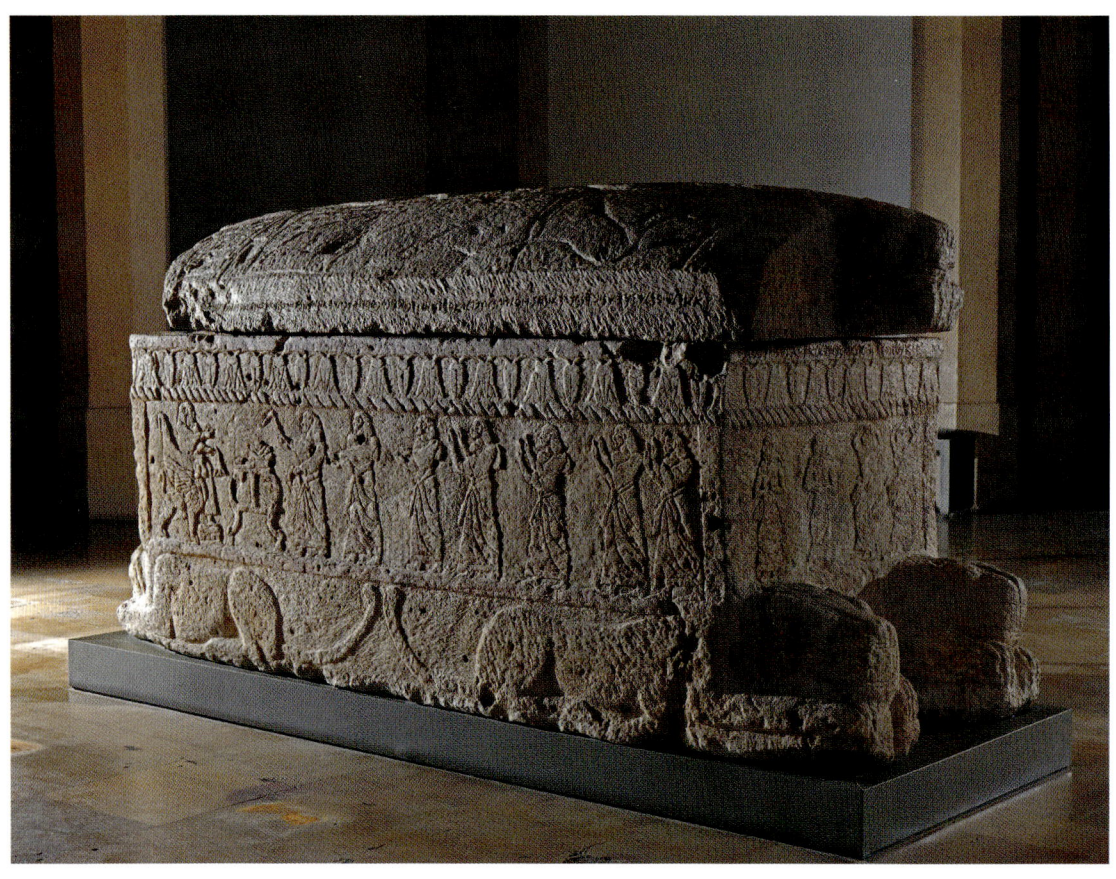

Plate 33. The sarcophagus of King Ahiram
10th century B.C. (Figure 2, p. 145)
©Ministry of Culture/Directorate General of
Antiquities of Lebanon/National Museum of Beirut.

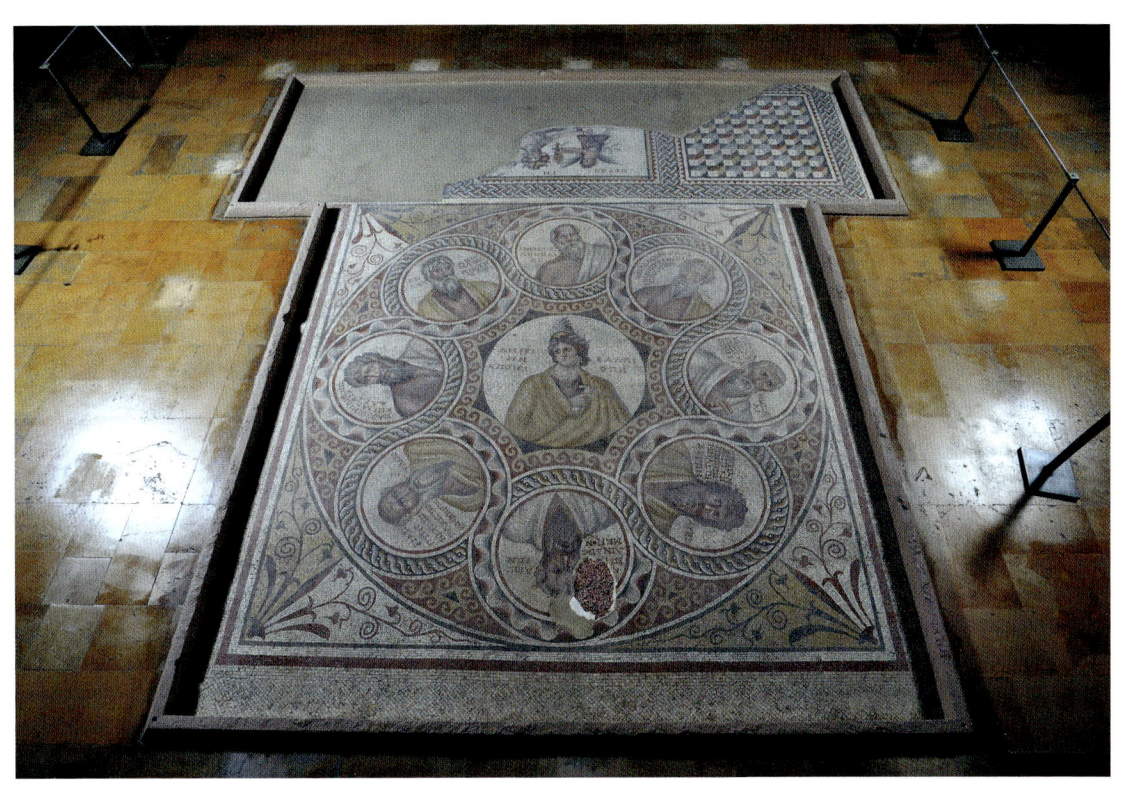

Plate 34. Roman mosaic of the Seven Wise Men,
Baalbeck. (Figure 3, p. 145)
©Ministry of Culture/Directorate General of
Antiquities of Lebanon/National Museum of Beirut.

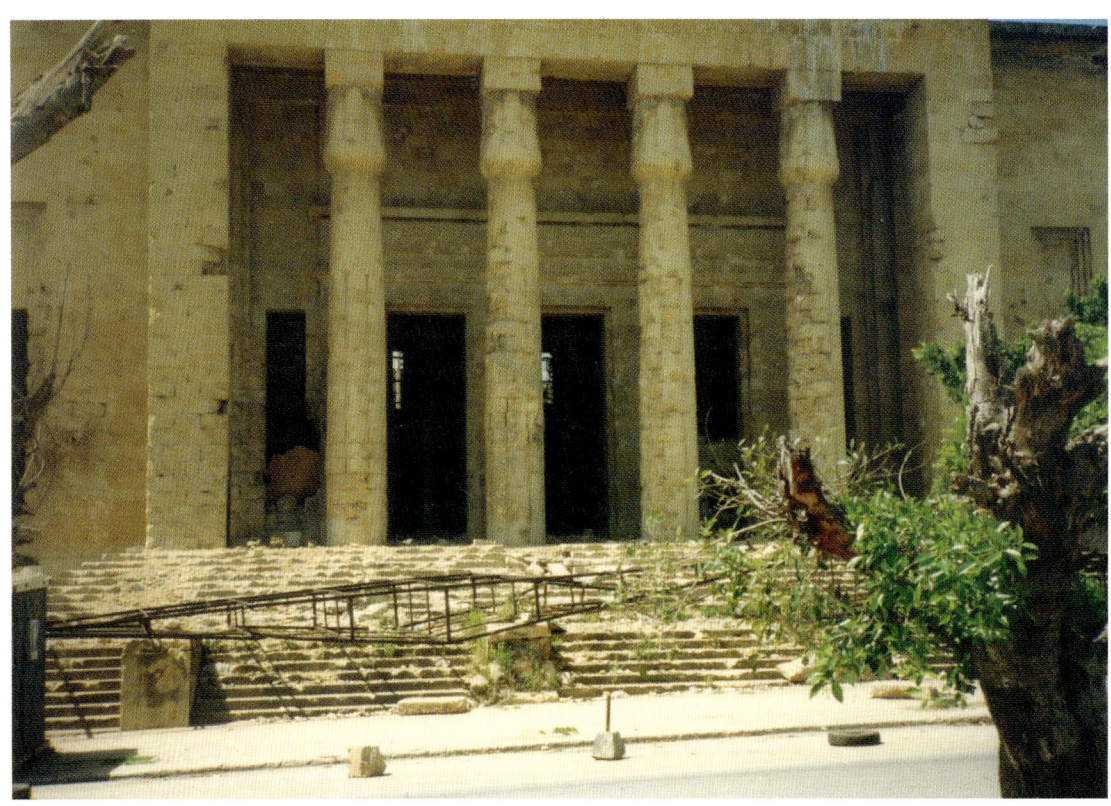

Plate 35. The National Museum of Beirut at
the end of the war (1993). (Figure 4, p. 146)
©Ministry of Culture/Directorate General of
Antiquities of Lebanon/National Museum of Beirut.

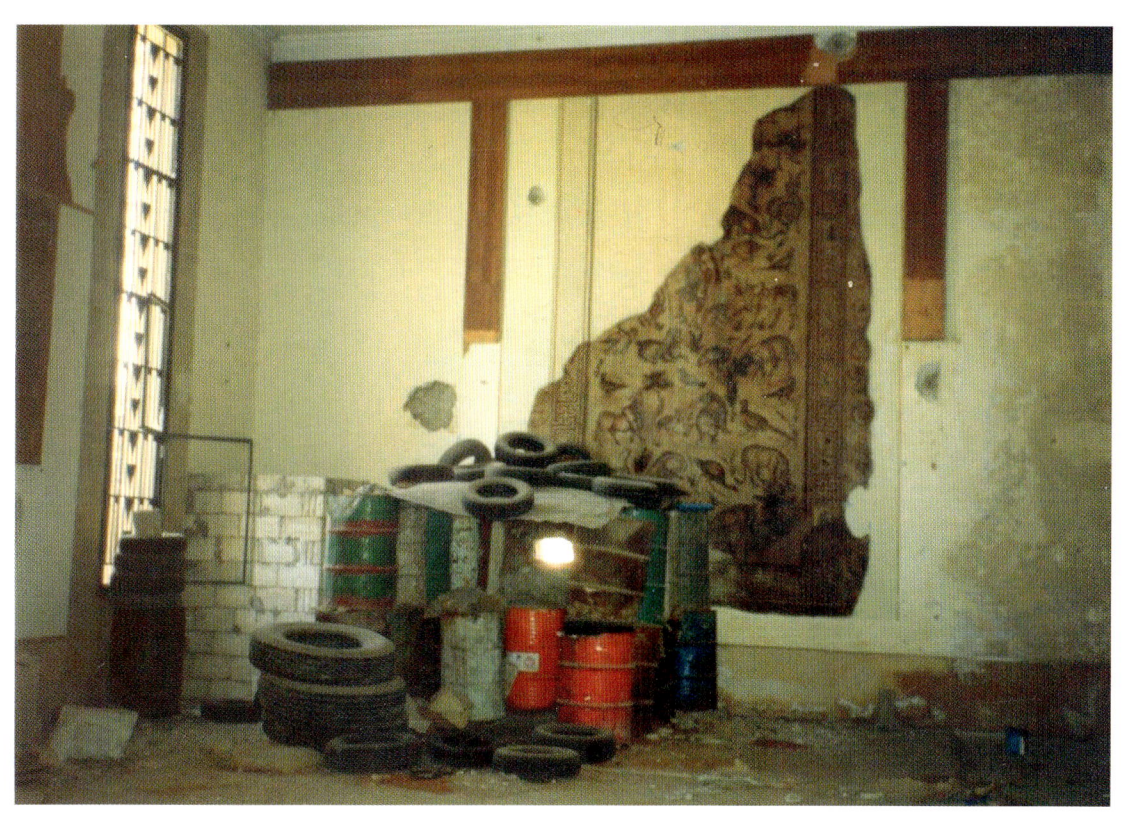

Plate 36. The Byzantine "mosaic of the
Good Shepherd" showing the sniper hole.
(Figure 5, p. 146)
©Ministry of Culture/Directorate General of
Antiquities of Lebanon/National Museum of Beirut.

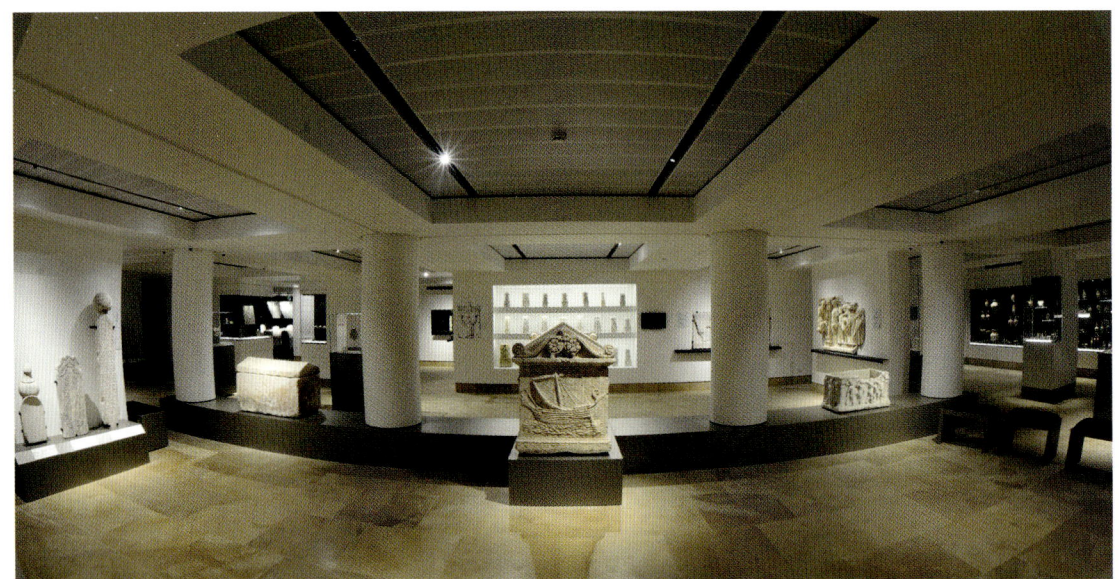

Plate 37. The National Museum basement floor.
(Figure 6, p. 146)
©Ministry of Culture/Directorate General of
Antiquities of Lebanon/National Museum of Beirut.

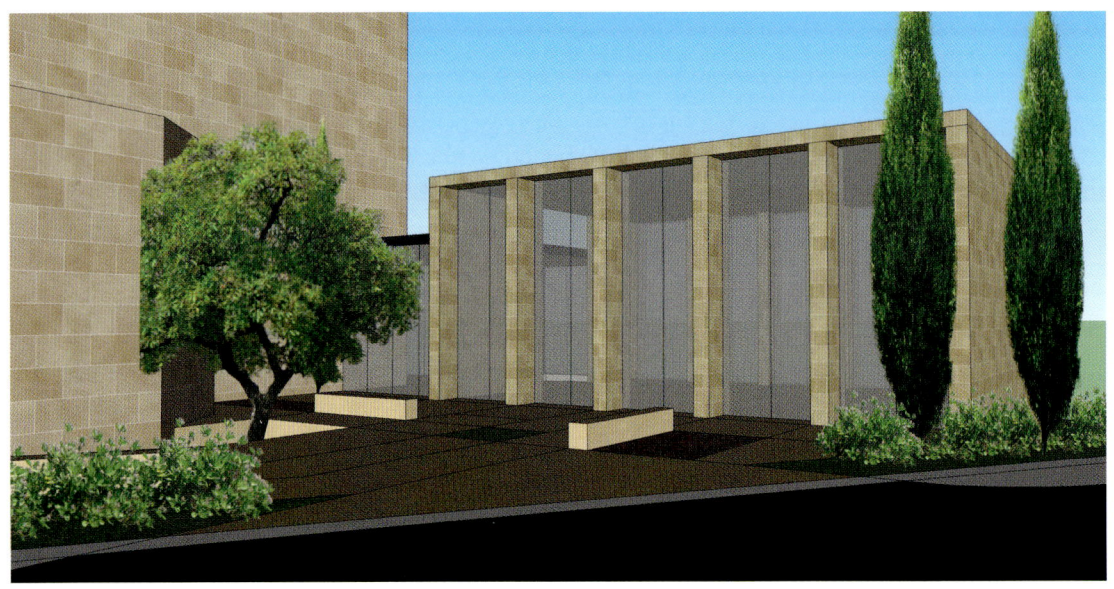

Plate 38. The new annex project.
(Figure 7, p. 147)
©Raed Abillama architect.

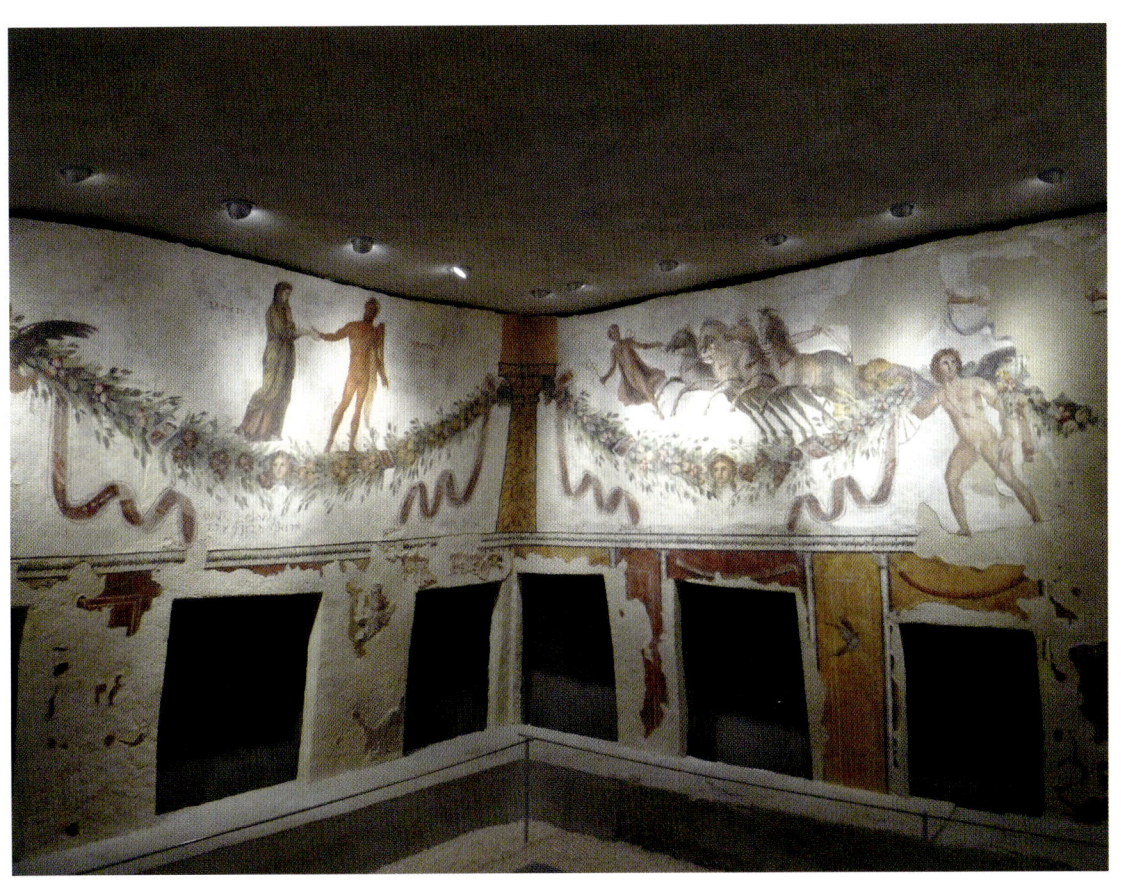

Plate 39. The Tomb of Tyre. (Figure 8, p. 148)
©Ministry of Culture/Directorate General of
Antiquities of Lebanon/National Museum of Beirut.

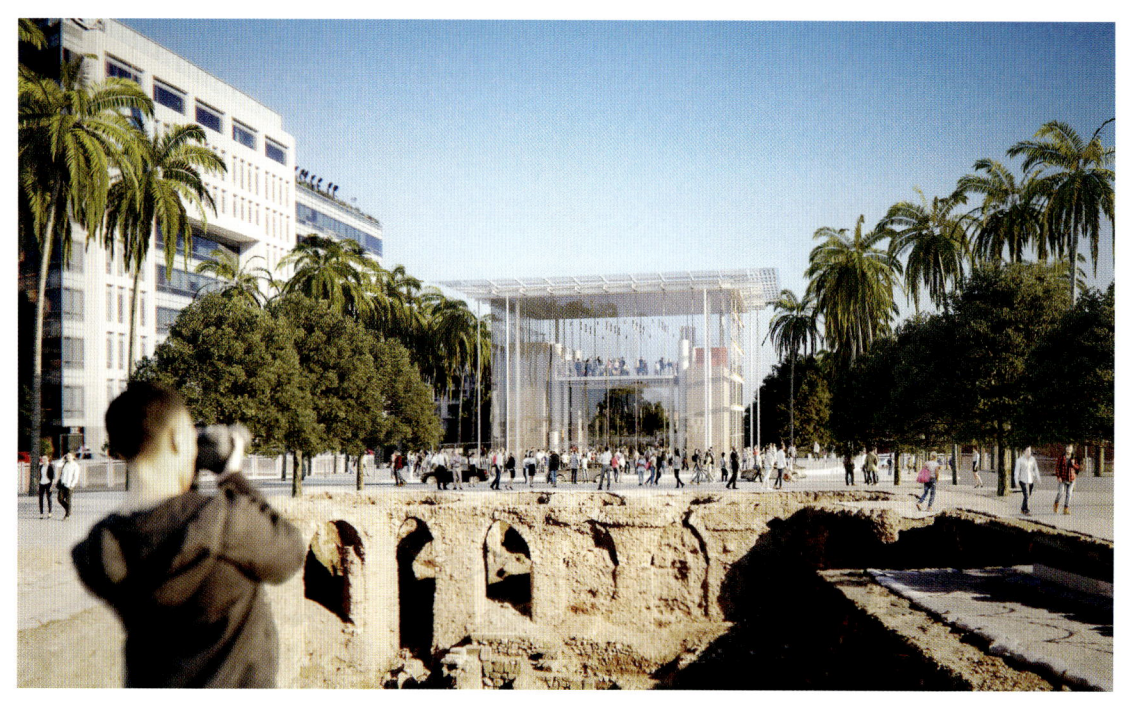

Plate 40. Beirut History Museum.
(Figure 9, p. 150)
©RPBW-architects.

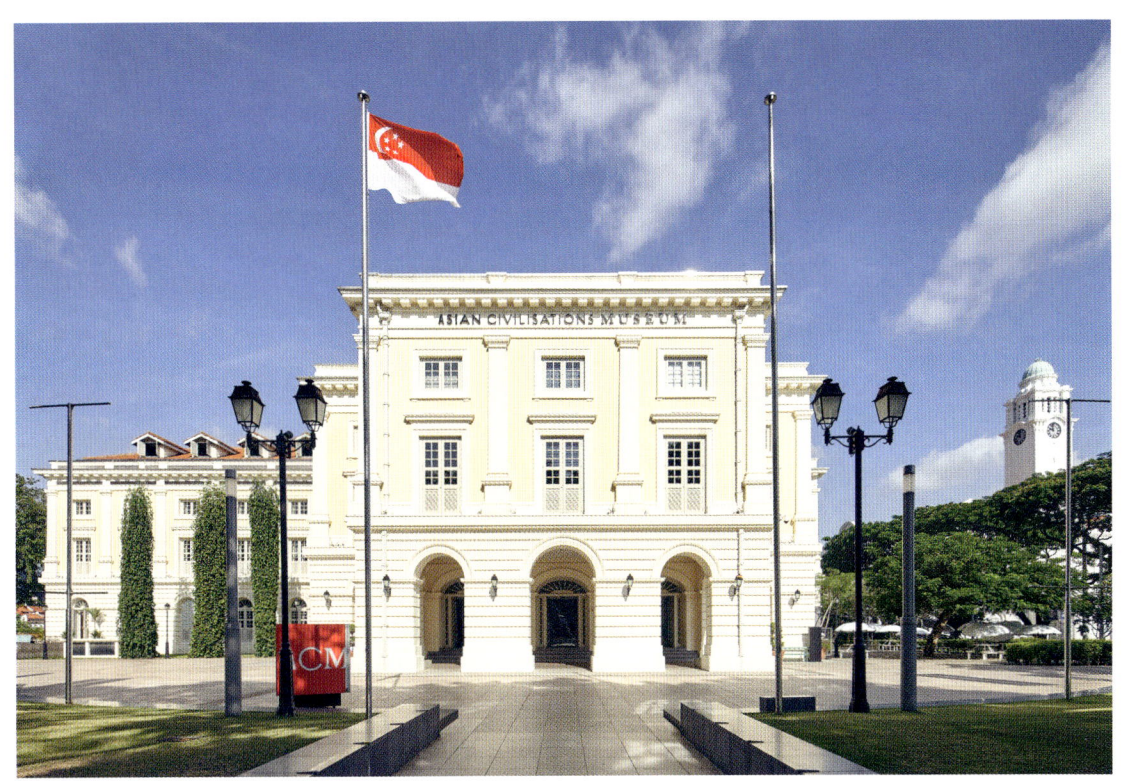

Plate 41. Asian Civilisations Museum,
Singapore. (Figure 1, p. 152)

Image courtesy of Asian Civilisations Museum.

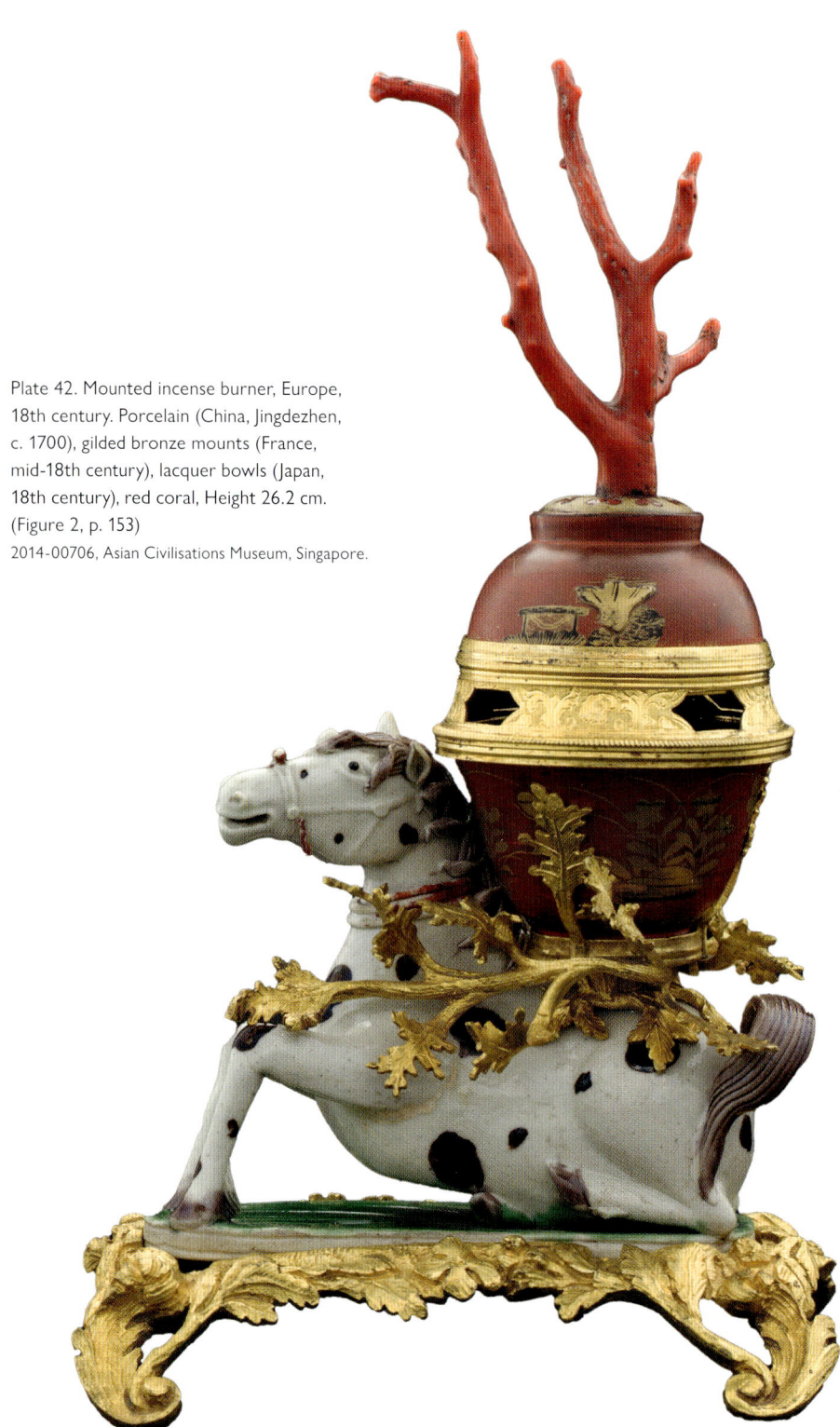

Plate 42. Mounted incense burner, Europe, 18th century. Porcelain (China, Jingdezhen, c. 1700), gilded bronze mounts (France, mid-18th century), lacquer bowls (Japan, 18th century), red coral, Height 26.2 cm. (Figure 2, p. 153)

2014-00706, Asian Civilisations Museum, Singapore.

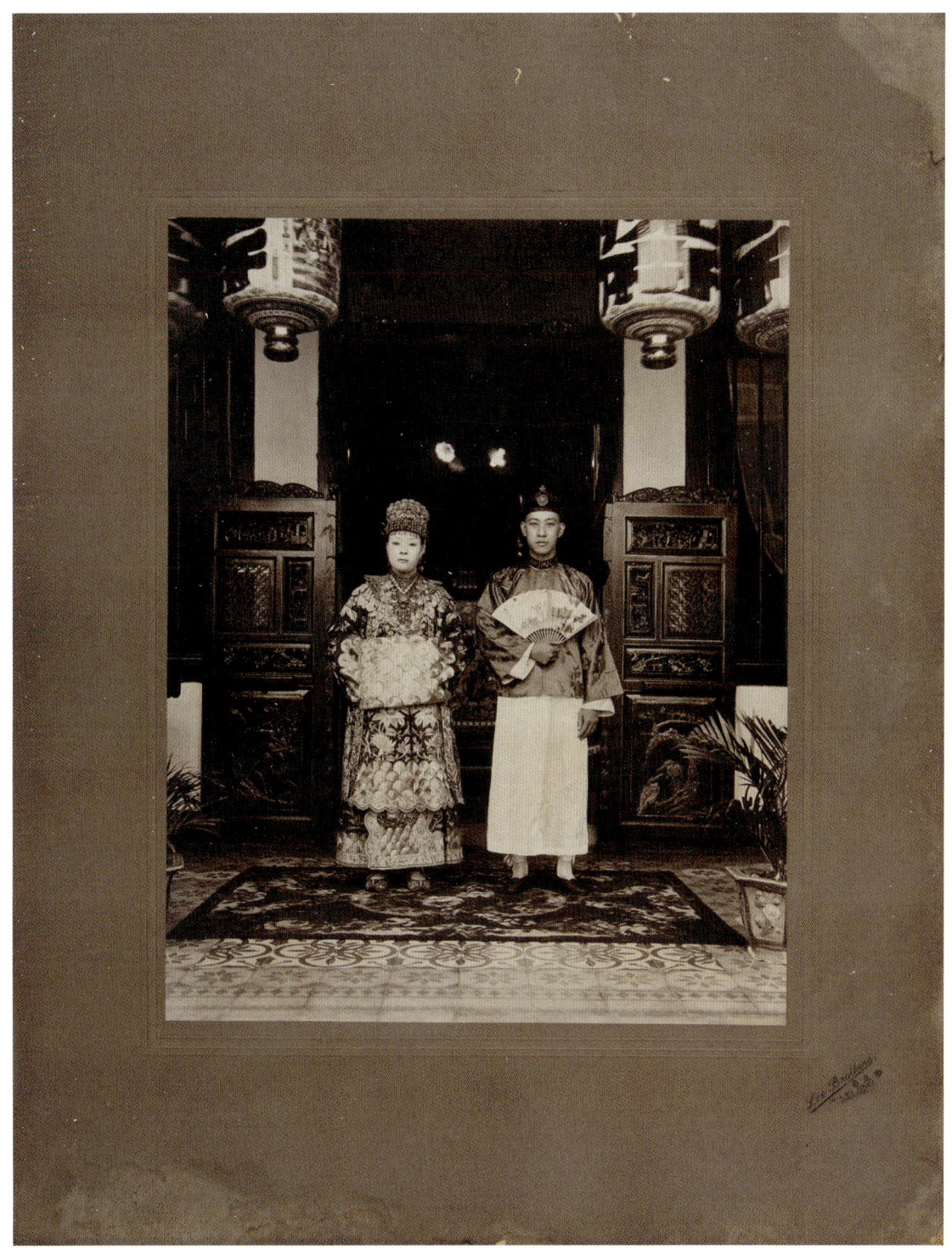

Plate 43. Untitled. Lee Brothers (李昆昌), Singapore, around 1920s. Gelatin silver print, 45.6 × 35.2 × 0.2 cm. (Figure 3, p. 154)
2015-00886, Peranakan Museum, Singapore. Gift of Mr and Mrs Lee Kip Lee.

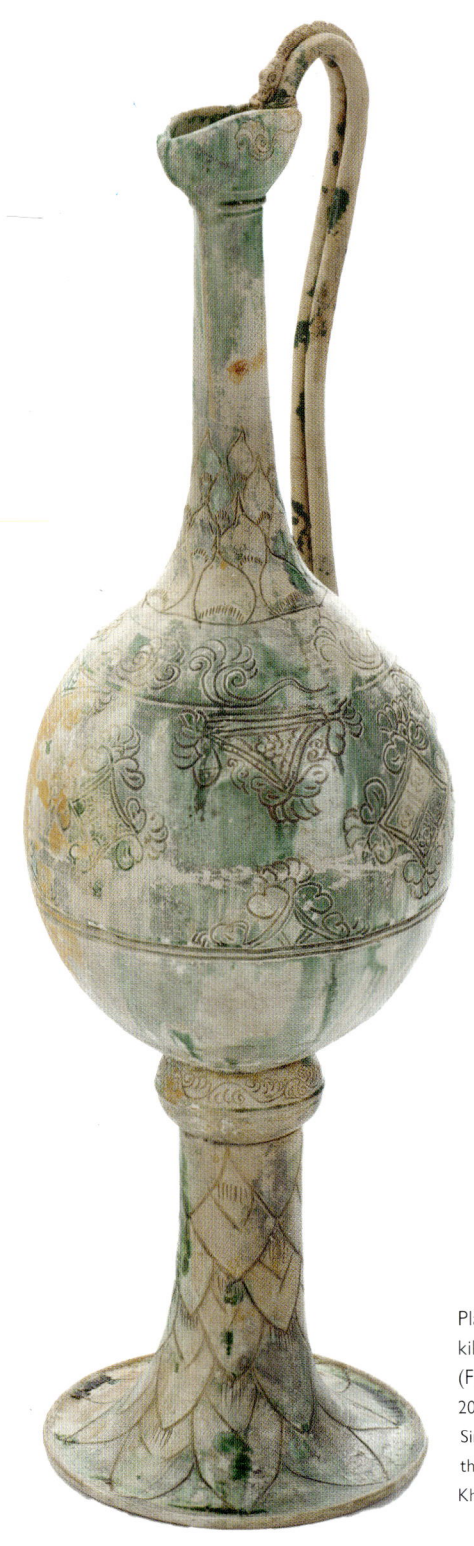

Plate 44. Ewer, China, probably Gongxian kilns, c. 830s. Stoneware, height 104 cm. (Figure 4, p. 154)
2005.1.00900, Asian Civilisations Museum, Singapore. The Tang Shipwreck was acquired through the generous donation of the Estate of Khoo Teck Puat.

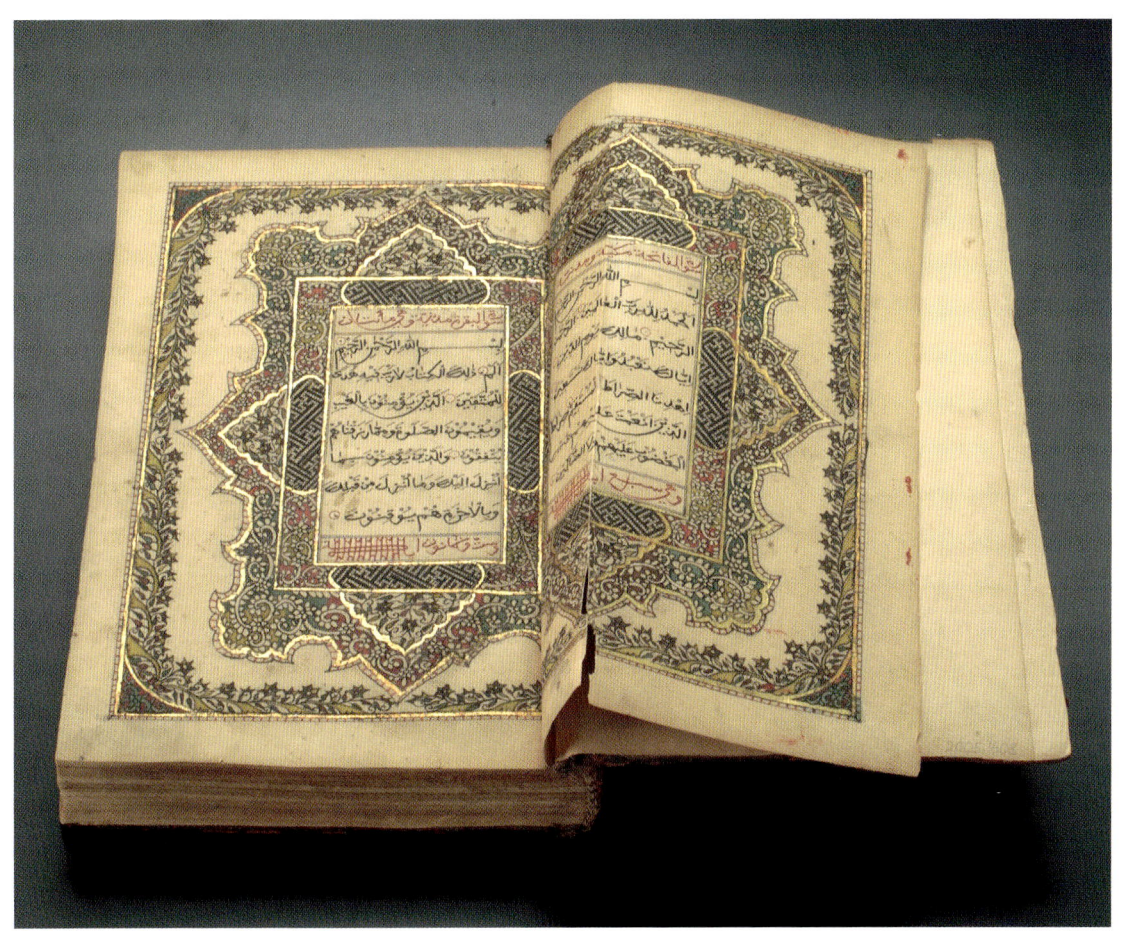

Plate 45. Quran, Central Java, late 19th or
early 20th century. Paper, ink, coloured
pigments, leather binding. Inscription: Quran
1: 1–7 (Surah al-Fatihah, The Opener),
2: 1–4 (Surah al-Baqarah, The Heifer).
(Figure 5, p. 155)
2005-01608-001, Asian Civilisations Museum,
Singapore.

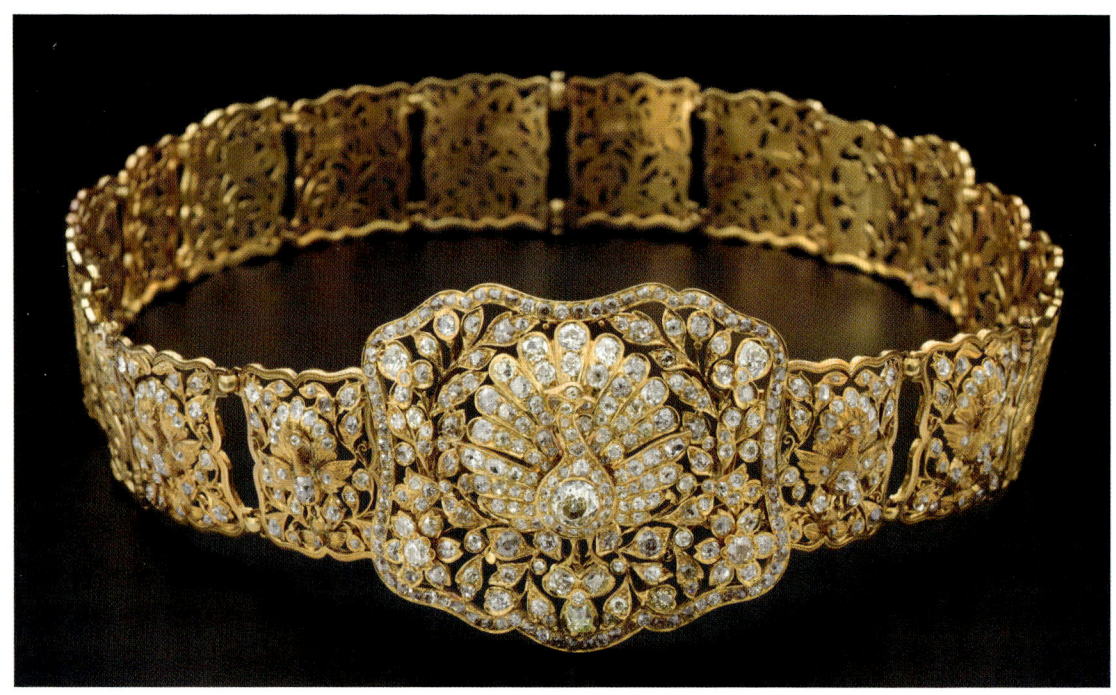

Plate 46. Peacock belt, Singapore, c. 1900.
Gold, diamonds, Buckle: 7 × 8.3 × 2.8 cm;
Belt: 68.5 × 4 × 0.7 cm. (Figure 6, p. 156)
2015-01994, Peranakan Museum, Singapore,
Gift of Mr Edmond Chin.

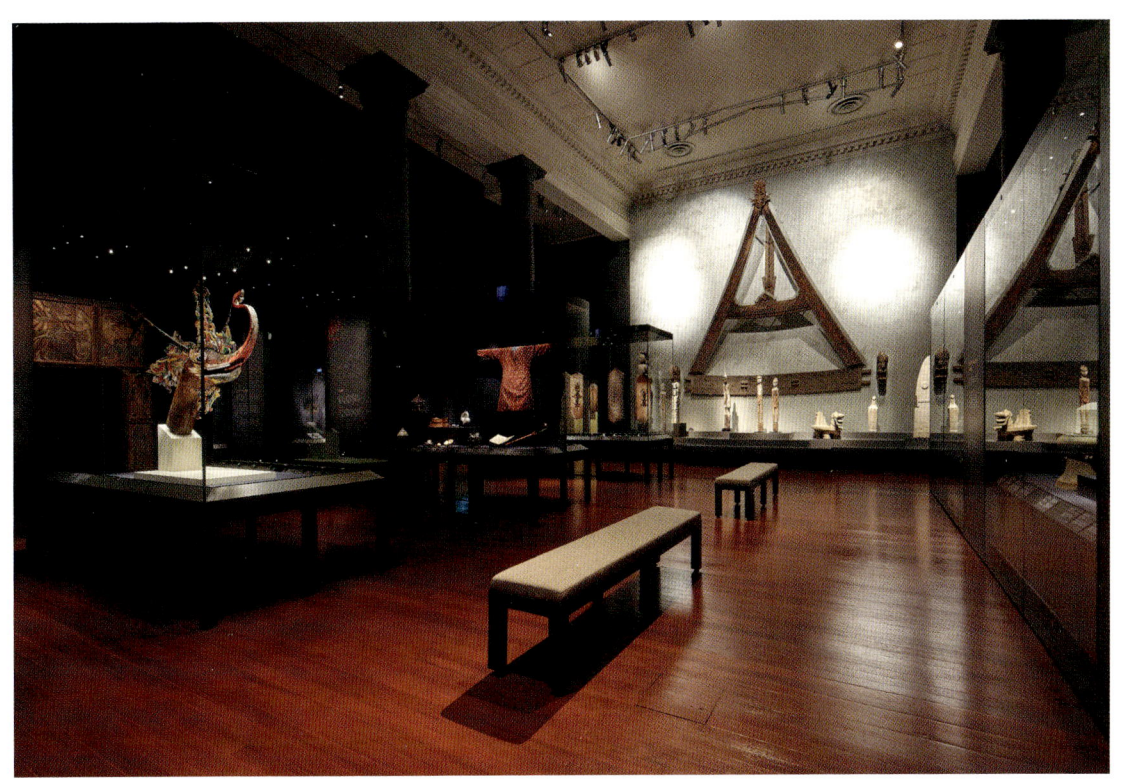

Plate 47. Ancestors & Rituals gallery at
the Asian Civilisations Museum, Singapore.
(Figure 7, p. 157)
Image courtesy of Asian Civilisations Museum.

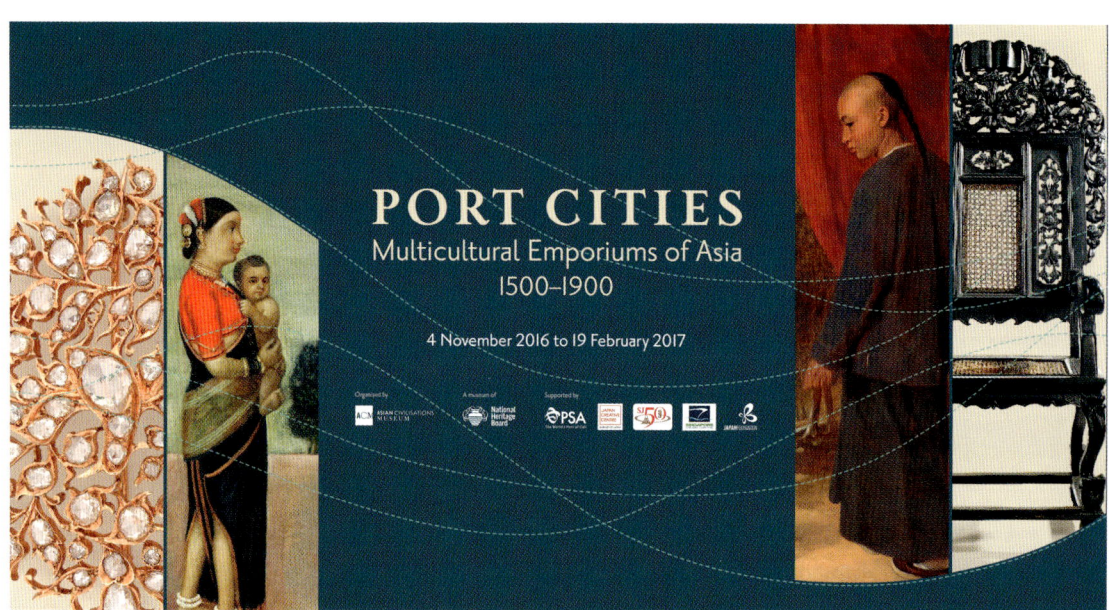

Plate 48. *Port Cities: Multicultural Emporiums
of Asia 1500-1900* exhibition banner
(Figure 8, p. 158)
Image courtesy of Asian Civilisations Museum.

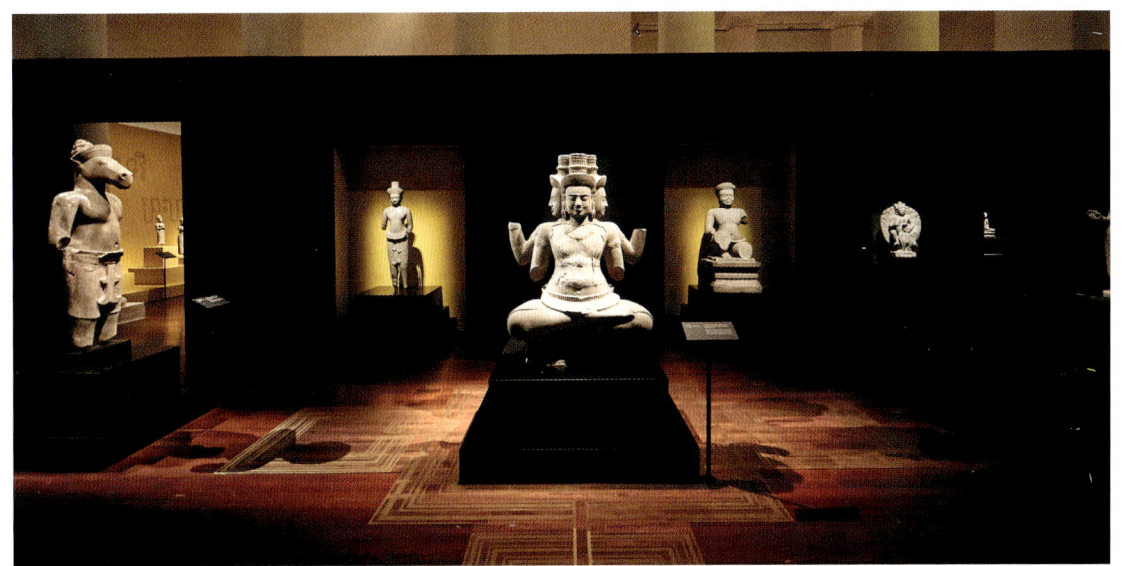

Plate 49. *Angkor: Exploring Cambodia's Sacred City* exhibition at the Asian Civilisations Museum, Singapore. (Figure 9, p. 159)
Image courtesy of Asian Civilisations Museum.

RAFFLES
IN
SOUTHEAST
ASIA

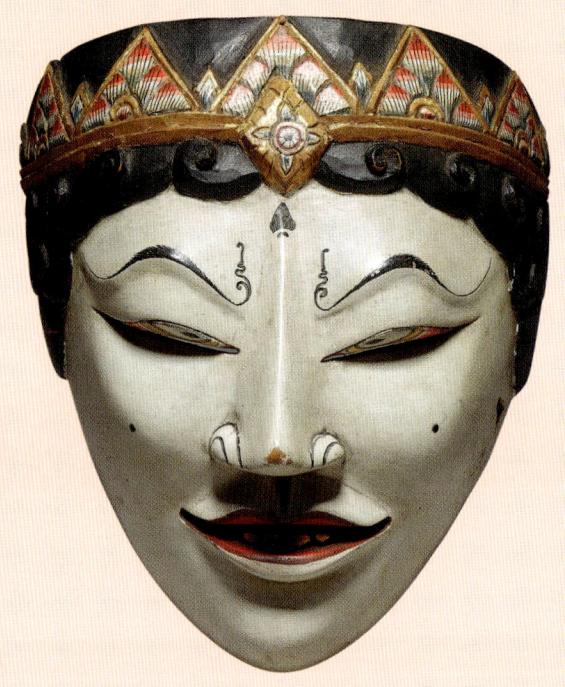

REVISITING
THE SCHOLAR
AND
STATESMAN

Plate 50. *Raffles in Southeast Asia* exhibition
catalogue cover (Figure 10, p. 160)
Image courtesy of Asian Civilisations Museum.